Advances in Computer Science Applications and Research 13

Series Editors

Juan E. Gilbert, *Department of Computer and Information Science and Engineering, University of Florida, Gainesville, FL, USA*
Pablo Rivas, *School of Computer Science and Mathematics, Marist College, Poughkeepsie, NY, USA*

This outstanding new series publishes state-of-the-art research spanning the entire spectrum of informatics ranging from foundational topics in the theory of computing to information and communications science and technology. A broad variety of multidisciplinary and interdisciplinary topics are welcome, as well.

While the focus is on publication of peer-reviewed full papers presenting mature work, inclusion of reviewed short papers reporting on work in progress are welcome, too. Besides globally relevant meetings with internationally representative program committees guaranteeing a strict peer-reviewing and paper selection process, conferences run by societies or of high regional or national relevance are also considered for publication.

Publication in ACSAR is free of charge. No royalties are paid, however, we offer registered conference participants temporary free access to the online version of the conference proceedings on SpringerLink (http://link.springer.com) by means of an http referrer from the conference website and/or a number of complimentary printed copies, as specified in the official acceptance email of the event.

ACSAR proceedings can be published in time for distribution at conferences or as post-proceedings, and delivered in the form of printed books and/or electronically as USBs and/or e-content licenses for accessing proceedings at SpringerLink. Furthermore, ACSAR proceedings are included in the ACSAR electronic book series hosted in the SpringerLink digital library at https://link.springer.com/bookseries/7899. Conferences publishing in ACSAR are allowed to use our online conference service (Meteor) for managing the whole proceedings lifecycle (from submission and reviewing to preparing for publication) free of charge.

Publication process

The language of publication is exclusively English. Authors publishing in ACSAR have to sign the Springer ACSAR copyright transfer form, however, they are free to use their material published in ACSAR for substantially changed, more elaborate subsequent publications elsewhere. For the preparation of the camera-ready papers/files, authors have to strictly adhere to the Springer ACSAR Authors' Instructions and are strongly encouraged to use the ACSAR LaTeX style files or templates.

How to start

To start the evaluation of your proposal for inclusion in the ACSAR series, please send an e-mail to acsar@springer.com, or directly to the editor responsible for your region. For more information about the responsible editor for your region please check the **Editors** section.

Paulo C. Rodrigues · Rohmatul Fajriyah ·
Kartick C. Mondal · Somnath Mukhopadhyay
Editors

Business and Industrial Statistics

First International Conference, ISBIS 2024, Yogyakarta, Indonesia, July 11–13, 2024, Revised Selected Papers

Springer

Editors
Paulo C. Rodrigues
Bahia University
Bahia, Brazil

Rohmatul Fajriyah
Universitas Islam Indonesia
Yogyakarta, Indonesia

Kartick C. Mondal
Jadavpur University
Kolkata, West Bengal, India

Somnath Mukhopadhyay
Assam University
Silchar, Assam, India

ISSN 3091-2954 ISSN 3091-2962 (electronic)
Advances in Computer Science Applications and Research
ISBN 978-3-032-32457-3 ISBN 978-3-032-32458-0 (eBook)
https://doi.org/10.1007/978-3-032-32458-0

This Springer imprint is published by the registered company Springer Nature Switzerland AG
The registered company address is: Gewerbestrasse 11, 6330 Cham, Switzerland

Preface

It is our great pleasure to present the proceedings of the International Symposium on Business and Industrial Statistics (ISBIS 2024), organized by the International Society for Business and Industrial Statistics (ISBIS) and the Department of Statistics, Universitas Islam Indonesia, Yogyakarta, held from July 11 to 13, 2024. ISBIS has established itself as a leading forum for promoting business and industrial statistics around the world. ISBIS promotes the application, research, and best practices of statistics in business and industry, facilitating technology transfer and bridging communication between members and practitioners in the world.

ISBIS 2024 had the honor of hosting distinguished keynote speakers, each an expert in their respective fields. We were privileged to welcome Prof. Fathul Wahid, S.T., M.Sc., Ph.D., the Rector of Universitas Islam Indonesia, Yogyakarta, Indonesia, Emma Jingfei Zhang, B.S., Ph.D., Goizueta Business School, Emory University, USA, Debasis Kundu, B.Stat., M.Stat., M.A., Ph.D., Department of Mathematics and Statistics, IIT Kanpur, India.

We are pleased to have partnered with Springer ACSAR Series for the publication of ISBIS proceedings, ensuring both high quality and broad dissemination of the conference contributions. The review process for ISBIS 2024 was rigorous, beginning with an initial assessment by the Program Committee (PC) Board. Papers that passed the initial scrutiny received desk acceptance notifications, followed by a double-blind review process. Each paper was evaluated based on originality, technical content, correctness, relevance, contributions, and clarity. Of the 68 submissions, 18 papers were accepted, registered, and presented at the conference venue, resulting in an acceptance rate of 26.5%.

The proceeding features 18 papers under the track "Statistics, AI and Machine Learning," and these papers showcase cutting-edge research in the fields of Statistics, AI, and Machine Learning in Business and Industry, covering a broad range of topics.

These papers highlight theories and applications of Statistics, AI, and Machine Learning in Business and Industry. Key topics include the use of AI-ML for business, industry, social media, plant, and healthcare applications such as early detection of plant disease, lung cancer, skin cancer, AI for mental health prediction through social media analysis, and forgery. Several works focus on actuarial science such as insurance claims and pensions. Some papers also explore reliability models through Bayesian and stochastic process approaches and the biodiversity concept for self-citation. There are papers on data analytics and machine learning that address predictive and robust models for diarrhea, forecasting earthquakes, temperature, flight activities, air quality, traffic accidents, and population prediction.

Since its inception in 2005, ISBIS has grown significantly, attracting high-quality research from across the globe. We are deeply grateful to our keynote speakers, the organizing committees, reviewers, and all the authors and participants who contributed to making ISBIS 2024 an outstanding platform for the exchange of ideas and innovations.

We hope the proceeding will inspire and inform the research and practice of Statistics, AI, and Machine Learning in the fields of Business and Industry. As we look forward to future editions of ISBIS, we remain committed to delivering an enriching and dynamic experience for all participants.

Bahia, Brazil — Paulo C. Rodrigues
Yogyakarta, Indonesia — Rohmatul Fajriyah
Kolkata, India — Kartick C. Mondal
Silchar, India — Somnath Mukhopadhyay

Organization

Chief Patron

Prof. Fathul Wahid	S.T., M.Sc., Ph.D., Universitas Islam Indonesia, Indonesia

Program Chairs

Paulo Canas Rodrigues	Federal University of Bahia, Salvador, Brazil
Rohmatul Fajriyah	Universitas Islam Indonesia, Indonesia
Kartick Chandra Mondal	Jadavpur University, India
Somnath Mukhopadhyay	Assam University Silchar, India

International Advisory Board

Nathaniel Stevens	ISBIS Vice-President Scientific Program, Canada
Chunh-Houh	IASC President, Taiwan
Daniel Jeske	Past ISBIS President, USA
Eman Khorsheed	ISBIS Council Member, Bahrain
Fabrizio Ruggeri	ISI President-Elect, Italy
Hizir Sofyan	Chair, ISI South-East Asia Outreach Committee, Indonesia
Lizanne Raubenheimer	ISBIS Council Member, South Africa
Matilde Bini	ISBIS President-Elect, Italy
Mike K. P. So	Chair of the East Asian Outreach Committee, Hong Kong
Nalini Ravishanker	ASMBI Editor-in-Chief, USA
Nick Fisher	Past ISBIS President, Australia
Rahim Mahmoudvand	ISBIS Vice-President Membership, Iran
Xuming He	ISI President, USA

Organising Chairs

Paulo Canas Rodrigues	Federal University of Bahia, Salvador, Brazil
Rohmatul Fajriyah	Universitas Islam Indonesia, Indonesia

Finance Chairs

Arum Handini Primandari	Universitas Islam Indonesia, Indonesia
Sekti Kartika Dini	Universitas Islam Indonesia, Indonesia

Publicity Chairs

Abdullah Ahmad Dzikrullah	Universitas Islam Indonesia, Indonesia
Achmad Fauzan	Universitas Islam Indonesia, Indonesia
Asyharul Muala	Universitas Islam Indonesia, Indonesia

Hospitality cum Registration Chair

Sri Devi Maheswari	Universitas Islam Indonesia, Indonesia
Ridhani Anggit Safitri	Universitas Islam Indonesia, Indonesia
Muhammad Achnaf	Universitas Islam Indonesia, Indonesia
Bagus Supriyanto	Universitas Islam Indonesia, Indonesia
Teguh Dwi Prayogo	Universitas Islam Indonesia, Indonesia
Sigit Mujiarto	Universitas Islam Indonesia, Indonesia
Rizal Pratama Putra	Universitas Islam Indonesia, Indonesia

PC Board

Akhmad Fauzy	Universitas Islam Indonesia, Indonesia
Jaka Nugraha	Universitas Islam Indonesia, Indonesia
Edy Widodo	Universitas Islam Indonesia, Indonesia
Raden Bagus Fajriya Hakim	Universitas Islam Indonesia, Indonesia
Atina Ahdika	Universitas Islam Indonesia, Indonesia
Kariyam	Universitas Islam Indonesia, Indonesia
Isnandar Slamet	Universitas Sebelas Maret, Indonesia
Hasih Pratiwi	Universitas Sebelas Maret, Indonesia
Nanang Susyanto	Universitas Gadjah Mada, Indonesia
Made Tantrawan	Universitas Gadjah Mada, Indonesia
Atina Husnaqilati	Universitas Gadjah Mada, Indonesia
Muhammad Muhajir	Universitas Islam Indonesia, Indonesia
Winita Sulandari	Universitas Sebelas Maret, Indonesia
Dina Tri Utari	Universitas Islam Indonesia, Indonesia
Rahmadi Yotenka	Universitas Islam Indonesia, Indonesia
Ayundyah Kesumawati	Universitas Islam Indonesia, Indonesia

Tuti Purwaningsih	Universitas Islam Indonesia, Indonesia
M. Hasan Sidiq Kurniawan	Universitas Islam Indonesia, Indonesia
Made Tantrawan	Universitas Gadjah Mada, Indonesia
Mahmoud Barhamgi	Qatar University, Qatar
Mario Guarracino	University of Cassino, Italy
Md. Zakirul Alam Bhuiyan	Fordham University NY, USA
Megha Quamara	CEA-LIST, Paris
Mohammed Hasanuzzaman	Cork Institute of Technology, Ireland
Mohan Pratap Pradhan	Sikkim University Gangtok, India
Mohsin Kamal	National University of Computer and Emerging Sciences, Pakistan
Moirangthem Marjit Singh	NERIST, India
Monjed H. Samuh	Palestine Polytechnique University, Palestine
Moumita Ghosh	Narula Institute of Technology, India
Muhammad Iqbal Al-Banna bin Ismail	Sunway University, Malaysia
Muhammad Naveed Aman	National University of Singapore, Singapore
Nanang Susyanto	Universitas Gadjah Mada, Indonesia
Nguyen Ha Huy Cuong	University of Danang, Vietnam
Noodchanath Kongchouy	Prince Songkla University, Thailand
Pawan K. Singh	Jadavpur University, India
R. B. Fajriya Hakim	Universitas Islam Indonesia, Indonesia
S. B. Goyal	City University of Malaysia, Malaysia
Sandeep Kautish	Lord Buddha Education Foundation, Nepal
Santi Wulan Purnami	Institut Teknologi Sepuluh November, Indonesia
Soumya Shankar Basu	Sheffield Hellam University, UK
Stefano Berretti	University of Florence (UNIFI), Italy
Sugiyarto Surono	Universitas Ahmad Dahlan, Indonesia
Sunita Sarkar	Assam University Silchar, India
Tien Anh Tran	Vietnam Maritime University, Vietnam
Tutut Herawan	University of Malaya, Malaysia
Weizhi Meng	Technical University of Denmark, Denmark
Yekti Widyaningsih	Universitas Indonesia, Indonesia
Arindam Sarkar	Belur Vidyamandir, India
Atina Ahdika	Universitas Islam Indonesia, Indonesia
Atina Husnaqilati	Universitas Gadjah Mada, Indonesia
Bernard Fong	Providence University, Taiwan
Bok-Min Goi	Universiti Tunku Abdul Rahman, Malaysia
Dewi Anggraini	Universitas Lambung Mangkurat, Indonesia
Edy Widodo	Universitas Islam Indonesia, Indonesia
Gautam Srivastava	Brandon University, Canada
Georg K. F. Heiler	Complexity Science Hub, Austria

Girijasankar Mallik	University of Western Sydney, Australia
Hannan Elsaied	Taibah University, Saudi Arabia
Hizir Sofyan	Universitas Syiah Kuala, Indonesia
Houbing Herbert Song	University of Maryland, USA
Hrishav Bakul Barua	Monash University, Australia
Husna Nugrahapraja	Institut Teknologi Bandung, Indonesia
Irwan Susanto	Universitas Sebelas Maret, Indonesia
Isnandar Slamet	Universitas Sebelas Maret, Indonesia
Istvan Berkes	Renyi Institute, Hungary
Jabar H. Yousif	Sohar University, Saudi Arabia
Jaka Nugraha	Universitas Islam Indonesia, Indonesia
Jerry Chun-Wei Lin	Western Norway University of Applied Sciences, Bergen, Norway
Joshua Thomas	Penang University Malaysia
Khalid Yahya	Istanbul Gelisim University Istanbul, Turkey
Khang Tsung Fei	University of Malaya, Malaysia
Kouichi Sakurai	Kyushu University, Japan

Contents

Bayesian Analysis of the Availability of Systems in the Presence of Common Cause and Human Error Subject to Variant Hardware Repair Models 1
Paul J. Mostert

The Application of Wavelet Neural Networks for Individual Claims Forecasting 17
Devi Nurtiyasari, Adhitya Ronnie Effendie, Dedi Rosadi, and Abdurakhman

Estimating System Reliability When Components Follow the Littlewood Model with Imperfect Debugging–Large Sample Properties Using the Counting Process Framework 28
Marcus A. Agustin, Ma. Zenia N. Agustin, and Atwood J. Huff

Climate Change Adaptation Insurance for Farmers Based on the Index Harvest Area (IHA) 39
Silvina Rosita Yulianti, Adhitya Ronnie Effendie, and Nanang Susyanto

Model Selection of Poisson Point Processes on a Linear Network: A Case Study of Traffic Accident Modeling in Nganjuk 55
Vanda Fitriyanah, Nabila Isna Nurazizah, Achmad Choiruddin, and Sutikno

SETAR and SETAR-Tree Methods for $PM_{2.5}$ Air Quality Forecasting 70
Dinda Ayu Safira, Heri Kuswanto, and Muhammad Ahsan

Robust Regression Model on Toddler Diarrhea Case in East Java Province: Maximum Likelihood and Generalized Maximum Likelihood Estimations 86
Yuliana Susanti, Hasih Pratiwi, Andreas Rony Wijaya, Respatiwulan, Sri Sulistijowati Handajani, and Muhammad Bayu Nirwana

Classification Analysis on Social Media Cyberbullying in Indonesia 100
Arum Handini Primandari, Rini Aprilianty Riadi, Ayundyah Kesumawati, and Dedi Rosadi

Hybrid Approach for Signature Forgery Detection Using Convolutional Neural Network and Support Vector Machine 117
Yaumil Afwan and Sri Mulyana

Utilizing YOLOv7 Algorithm for Gossypium sp. Detection: An Implementation Study 134
Bianda Shafira Kartika Anggraini, Dina Tri Utari, and R. B. Fajriya Hakim

Classification of Lung Cancer Disease in CT-Scan Images Using CNN with SMOTE and SMOTE-ENN Resampling Techniques 152
Regita Diah Pramesti, Sri S. Handajani, Winita Sulandari, Hasih Pratiwi, Hilman F. Pardede, and Vicky Zilvan

When Self-Citations Bother You: A Case Study on Google Scholar 163
Kartick Chandra Mondal, Ari Kusumastuti, Ananya Pal, Isika Samanta, and Ansh Kumar

Comparative Forecasting of Domestic Flight Activity Patterns in Indonesia During and Post-COVID-19 with XGBoost and ARIMA 175
Zahra Maharani Putri Sumarna, Rohmatul Fajriyah, Yoel Christopher Tjen, and Fandy A. Ariady

Skin Disease Classification Using Hybrid Convolutional Neural Network 191
Alfito Putra Fajar Pratama, Hasih Pratiwi, and Isnandar Slamet

Comparison of `ETAS` and `etasFLP` for Fitting Space-Time ETAS Model to Large Earthquake Data 205
Annisa Auliya Rahman, Achmad Choiruddin, and Hidayatul Khusna

Forecasting Temperature Variations in Surakarta Using Semiparametric Penalized Fourier Series Estimator Based on Cosinus Function 219
Ihsan Fathoni Amri, Nur Chamidah, and Toha Saifudin

Self-exciting Threshold Autoregressive Model with Application to Data Inflow and Outflow for NTT Province and National Level 232
Veronika Kolo, Muhammad Sjahid Akbar, and Setiawan

Implementation of Vasicek and Cox-Ingersoll-Ross Models in Calculating Civil Servants' Pension Using the Accrued Benefit Cost Method 254
Mukhlisah and Novriana Sumarti

Author Index 269

Bayesian Analysis of the Availability of Systems in the Presence of Common Cause and Human Error Subject to Variant Hardware Repair Models

Paul J. Mostert(✉)

Department of Statistics and Actuarial Science, Stellenbosch University, Stellenbosch, South Africa
pjmos@sun.ac.za

Abstract. In this paper the availability analysis of a two-unit system of two different configurations (series and parallel) subject to unit failures, common cause failures and human error is studied when the repair time of hardware failure is either constant hypo-exponential, 2-stage hypo-exponential or Erlang distributed. A Bayesian approach is adopted with different types of priors assumed for the unknown parameters to evaluate the availability of the system. Monte Carlo Markov chain methods are used to derive realizations of the posterior distribution for the steady-state availability. The performance of the estimators is evaluated in terms of bias, mean squared error and frequentist coverage by means of a simulation study to highlight the importance of the study.

Keywords: Availability · Bayesian estimation · Common cause failures · Frequentist coverage · Human error · Metropolis-Hastings algorithm

1 Introduction

Through technological advancements, industrial systems become smoother, more efficient and more reliable, but with an increase in complexity. Such systems need to be available in a working condition for maximum duration, however, it may fail due to a variety of reasons. The problems related to availability analysis have been addressed by several authors, using different mathematical techniques under various conditions. Furthermore, the steady-state availability is an important measure in determining the long-term performance of a system that is to be operated continuously.

The analysis of modern complex systems entails an integrated approach in which the hardware, common cause errors and human elements are considered in a combined frame, which also accounts for their dynamic interdependences within the system. A common cause shock (CCS) failure [3] is defined as any instance where multiple units or elements fail due to a single cause. Common cause could occur owing to environmental hazards, design errors, manufacturing errors and assembly errors. The concept of human error (HE) according to [5], is a failure to perform a prescribed task (or the performance

P. C. Rodrigues et al. (Eds.): ISBIS 2024, 13, pp. 1–16, 2027.
https://doi.org/10.1007/978-3-032-32458-0_1

of a prohibited action), which could result in damage to equipment and property or disruption of scheduled operations. Some examples of human errors are wrong actions, maintenance errors, misinterpretation of instruments, inspection error, etc. In 2010, [9] studied a two-unit cold standby system considering the human and hardware failures (HF) with an introduction of preventive maintenance. Various authors have investigated the repairable system under different assumptions, amongst others [2, 4, 6] and [10]. Most of the studies on two-unit systems are confined to obtaining expressions for various measures of system performance and do not consider the associated inference problems, nor considered it from a Bayesian perspective.

In this paper the focus is on the Bayesian approach that incorporates prior knowledge for the system parameters based on prior experience and that this prior knowledge can be mathematically translated into suitable prior densities (see also [7, 8]). Interval estimates can be obtained without relying on asymptotic results, and hence, are accurate even for small and moderate samples. With little or no prior information about a parameter, a noninformative prior distribution can be used to represent the knowledge of the parameter, see [1] for further explanation of noninformative priors. In [11], the paper discussed the use of a Bayesian approach to study a two-unit system with common-cause shock failures by considering different prior distributions on the parameters of the exponential failure and repair patterns. This paper is an extension of [11] for statistical inference of system availability for a two-unit system in the presence of CCS failures and HE in which the failure rates and repair rates are constant, while the repair time of HF follows different distributions. The contribution of this research includes also the modeling of HF in a two-stage repair process, each of the stages incorporating a Bayesian approach.

The detailed model description, the assumptions and the steady-state availability behavior of the repairable system are presented in Sect. 2. The Bayesian approach with different prior distributions of the system parameters is developed in Sect. 3. Coping with the complexity of the systems from a quantifiable point-of-view, requires computational methodologies to provide a basis for simulating the environment to reproduce the stochastic occurrence of failures and repairs to study the system characteristics. Therefore, in Sect. 4 the posterior analysis is performed using the Gibbs sampler and the Metropolis Hastings algorithm to obtain numerical results for comparative purposes. All simulations were carried out using FORTRAN®.

2 System Description and Steady-State Availability

The model description and assumptions under which the steady-state availability are studied, are discussed below:

- The system consists of two identical units.
- There is only one repair facility. If repair occur simultaneously due to CCS or HE or HF, the units will be taken for repair on the first-come-first- served basis.
- The HF is constant with rate parameter λ. Three different repair time distributions due to HF for a two-unit system are considered:

  I The first repair distribution to be considered is the constant 2-stage hypo-exponential distribution. Let random variables Y_1 and Y_2 be independent exponentially distributed, i.e. $Y_1 \sim exp(\mu_1)$ and $Y_2 \sim exp(\mu_2)$ for each of the two repair stages. The total repair time, $Z = Y_1 + Y_2$, has a constant 2-stage hypo-exponential distribution, for $\mu_1 \neq \mu_2$:

$$h(z) = \frac{\mu_1\mu_2}{(\mu_2 - \mu_1)}\left(e^{-\mu_2 z} - e^{-\mu_1 z}\right), z > 0,$$

with expected value $\frac{1}{\mu_1} + \frac{1}{\mu_2}$ and variance $\frac{1}{\mu_1^2} + \frac{1}{\mu_2^2}$.

II The second repair distribution is the 2-stage hypo-exponential distribution. This is derived from $Y_1 \sim exp(\mu)$ and $Y_2 \sim exp(\frac{\mu}{k})$ be independent random variables for each of the two repair stages. The total repair time, Z, has a 2-stage hypo-exponential distribution, with $k > 1$:

$h(z) = \frac{\mu}{(k-1)}\left(e^{-\frac{\mu}{k}z} - e^{-\mu z}\right), z > 0,$ # with expected value $\frac{k+1}{\mu}$ and variance $\frac{k^2+1}{\mu^2}$.
The rate parameter for the first stage of repair is defined as $\mu_1 = \mu$ and for the second stage $\mu_2 = \frac{\mu}{k}$.

III The third repair distribution to be considered is the Erlang distribution. This is derived from $Y_1 \sim exp(\mu)$ and $Y_2 \sim exp(\mu)$ be identical independent random variables for each of the two repair stages. The total repair time, Z, has an Erlang distribution:

$h(z) = \mu^2 z e^{-\mu z}, z > 0$. This repair distribution (in III) will not explicitly be used in further discussions, due to the equivalence to (in I), with $\mu_1 = \mu_2 = \mu$.

- The system consists of CCS failures which are *s-independent*. The failure rate and repair rate of CCS failures are constant with rate parameters λ_c and μ_c, respectively.
- If the system fails due to HE, the failure rate is in that case assumed to be exponentially distributed with rate parameter λ_h, while the repair rate is μ_h.
- The unit failure, CCS failure and HE are assumed to be independent.
- Each unit is new after repair. If repair of unit is completed, to come to an operable state, switch is perfect and switch-over is instantaneous.

Table 1 gives a summary of the state space at any time *t*, while Fig. 2 displays the transition diagram of the state space.

From the transition diagram (in Fig. 1), the following set of the differential equations are constructed by using the defined transition rates as follows:

$$P_0'(t) = -(2\lambda + 2\lambda_h + \lambda_c)P_0(t) + \mu_c P_{10}(t) + \mu_h P_2(t) + \mu_2 P_4(t)$$

$$P_1'(t) = -(\lambda + \lambda_h + \mu_1)P_1(t) + 2\lambda P_0(t) + \mu_h P_6(t) + \mu_2 P_8(t)$$

$$P_2'(t) = -(\mu_h + \lambda + \lambda_h)P_2(t) + 2\lambda_h P_0(t) + \mu_h P_7(t) + \mu_2 P_9(t)$$

$$P_3'(t) = -\mu_1 P_3(t) + \lambda P_1(t)$$

$$P_4'(t) = -(\lambda + \lambda_h + \mu_2)P_4(t) + \mu_1 P_1(t)$$

$$P_5'(t) = -\mu_1 P_5(t) + \lambda_h P_1(t)$$

Table 1. State space of the two-unit system.

	One unit	Second unit
S_0	Operable	Operable
S_1	Operable	HF occurred, in 1st stage of repair
S_2	HE occurred and under repair	Operable
S_3	HF occurred and awaiting repair	HF occurred, in 1st stage of repair
S_4	Operable	HF occurred, in 2nd stage of repair
S_5	HF occurred, in 1st stage of repair	HE occurred and awaiting repair
S_6	HE occurred and under repair	HF occurred and awaiting repair
S_7	HE occurred and under repair	HE occurred and awaiting repair
S_8	HF occurred and awaiting repair	HF occurred, in 2nd stage of repair
S_9	HE occurred and awaiting repair	HF occurred, in 2nd stage of repair
S_{10}	System failed due to CCS	System failed due to CCS

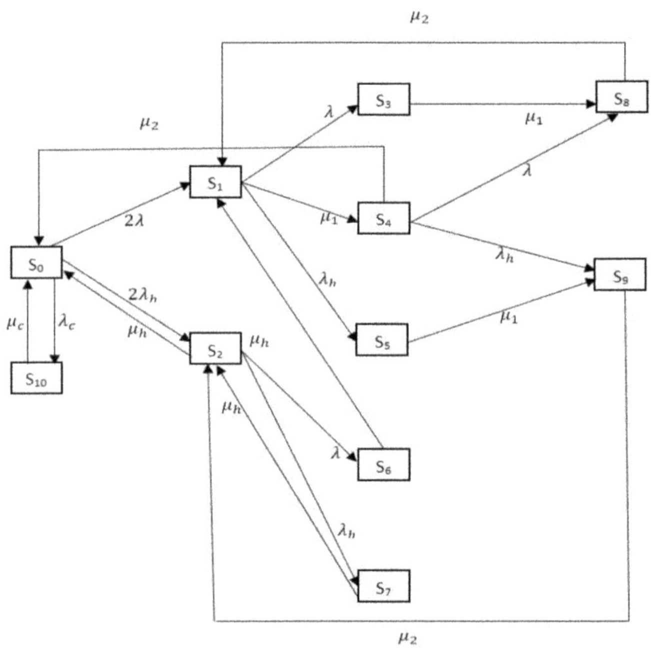

Fig. 1. The generalized transition diagram.

$$P_6{\prime}(t) = -\mu_h P_6(t) + \lambda P_2(t)$$

$$P_7{\prime}(t) = -\mu_h P_7(t) + \lambda_h P_2(t)$$

$$P_{8}\prime(t) = -\mu_2 P_8(t) + \mu_1 P_3(t) + \lambda P_4(t)$$

$$P_{9}\prime(t) = -\mu_2 P_9(t) + \mu_1 P_5(t) + \lambda_h P_4(t)$$

$$P_{10}\prime(t) = -\mu_c P_{10}(t) + \lambda_c P_0(t)$$

At time $t = 0$, $P_0(0) = 1$ and $P_{\text{i}}(0) = 0$ for $i = 1,\ldots,10$ and $P_i(t)$ is defined as the probability that the system is in state S_i ($i = 0, 1, \ldots, 10$) at time t. By setting these derivatives equal to zero and solving the resulting system of equations, using the normalizing condition $\sum_{i=0}^{10} P_i = 1$, the expressions for steady-state availability for the two configurations (series and parallel) can be obtained. Configuration in series requires that both units should be operable (see Table 1) and hence, steady-state availability in this case is obtained as the limiting probability of state $j = 0$. The steady-state availabilities for a series configuration ($A_{S_I}(\infty)$ and $A_{S_{II}}(\infty)$) are now obtained for the two types of models used (in I and II) for hardware repair:

$$A_{S_I}(\infty) = \mu_1\mu_h\mu_2\mu_c(\lambda(\lambda_h\mu_h + \mu_1\mu_2) + \mu_h(\lambda_h + \mu_1)(\lambda_h + \mu_2))$$
$$/(\lambda\Big(\mu_h\Big(2\Big(\lambda^3\mu_c(\mu_1 + \mu_2)\Big) + \lambda_c\mu_1\mu_2(\lambda_h\mu_h + \mu_1\mu_2)\Big)$$
$$+ \mu_c(\lambda(2\,(\lambda(\lambda_h(3(\mu_h\mu_2) + \mu_1(3\mu_h + \mu_2)) + \mu_h(\mu_1 + \mu_h + \mu_2)(\mu_1 + \mu_2)))$$
$$+ 2(\lambda_h((2(\mu_h\mu_2) + \mu_1(2\mu_h + \mu_2))(\mu_1 + \mu_h + \mu_2) + 3(\lambda_h(\mu_1\mu_h + \mu_2(\mu_1 + \mu_h))))$$
$$+\mu_h(\mu_1\mu_h + \mu_2(\mu_1 + \mu_h))(\mu_1 + \mu_2))\lambda_h\Big(2\Big(\mu_2^2\Big(\mu_1 + \mu_h)^2\Big)$$
$$+ \lambda_h(2((\mu_1(2\mu_2 + \mu_h) + \mu_h\mu_2)(\mu_1 + \mu_h + \mu_2)) + 2(\lambda_h(\mu_1(3\mu_2 + \mu_h) + \mu_h\mu_2)))$$
$$+\mu_1\mu_h(2(\mu_1\mu_h) + \mu_2(4\mu_1 + 5\mu_h))) + \mu_1\mu_h\mu_2(2(\mu_h\mu_2) + \mu_1(2\mu_h + \mu_2))))$$
$$+\mu_1\mu_2\Big(2\Big(\lambda_h^2\mu_c\Big) + \mu_h(2(\lambda_h\mu_c) + \mu_h(\lambda_c + \mu_c))\Big)(\lambda_h + \mu_1)(\lambda_h + \mu_2)\Big),$$

$$A_{S_{II}}(\infty) = \mu\mu_h\mu_c\Big(\lambda\Big(\lambda_h\mu_h k + \mu^2\Big) + \mu_h(\lambda_h k + \mu)(\lambda_h + \mu)\Big)/(\lambda\Big(\lambda_c\mu\mu_h\Big(\lambda_h\mu_h k + \mu^2\Big)$$
$$+ \mu_c\Big(\lambda\Big(2\Big(\Big(3(\lambda_h^2 k\Big) + \mu\mu_h(1 + k)\Big)(\mu + \mu_h(1 + k))$$
$$+\lambda_h(2(\mu_h(1 + k)) + \mu)(\mu + k(\mu + \mu_h)))$$
$$+ \lambda\Big(2(\lambda\mu_h k(1 + k)) + 2\Big(\mu\Big(\lambda_h k + \mu_h\Big(1 + k)^2\Big) + \mu_h k(1 + k)(3\lambda_h + \mu_h)\Big)\Big)\Big)$$
$$+ \lambda_h(\lambda_h(2((2\mu + \mu_h(1 + k))(\mu + k(\mu + \mu_h)))$$
$$+2(\lambda_h k(3\mu + \mu_h(1 + k)))) + \mu(\mu(2\mu + 4(\mu_h(1 + k))))$$
$$+\mu_h^2(1 + 2k)(2 + k)\Big) + \mu^2\mu_h(2(\mu_h(1 + k)) + \mu)))$$
$$+ \mu\Big(2\Big(\lambda_h^2\mu_c\Big) + \mu_h(2(\lambda_h\mu_c) + \mu_h(\lambda_c + \mu_c))\Big)(\lambda_h k + \mu)(\lambda_h + \mu)\Big),$$

Configuration in parallel requires that at least one unit should be operable (see Table 1) and hence, steady-state availability in this case is obtained as the joint limiting probabilities of state $j = 0$, 1, 2 or 4. The steady-state availabilities for a parallel configuration ($A_{P_I}(\infty)$ and $A_{P_{II}}(\infty)$) are now obtained for the two types of models used (in I and II, and III) for hardware repair:

$$A_{P_I}(\infty) = \mu_1\mu_h\mu_2\mu_c((2\lambda_h + \mu_h)(\lambda_h + \mu_1)(\lambda_h + \mu_2)$$

$$
\begin{aligned}
&+ \lambda((2\lambda_h + \mu_h)(2\mu_1 + 3\lambda_h) + \lambda(2(3\lambda_h + \mu_1 + \mu_h + \mu_2) + 2\lambda)\\
&+\mu_2(2\mu_h + 4\lambda_h + \mu_1)))/(\lambda(\mu_h\left(2\left(\lambda^3\mu_c(\mu_1 + \mu_2)\right)\right.\\
&+\lambda_c\mu_1\mu_2(\lambda_h\mu_h + \mu_1\mu_2)) + \mu_c(\lambda(2(\lambda(\lambda_h(3(\mu_h\mu_2)\\
&+\mu_1(3\mu_h + \mu_2)) + \mu_h(\mu_1 + \mu_h + \mu_2)(\mu_1 + \mu_2)))\\
&+ 2(\lambda_h((2(\mu_h\mu_2) + \mu_1(2\mu_h + \mu_2))(\mu_1 + \mu_h + \mu_2)\\
&+3(\lambda_h(\mu_1\mu_h + \mu_2(\mu_1 + \mu_h))))\\
&+\mu_h(\mu_1\mu_h + \mu_2(\mu_1 + \mu_h))(\mu_1 + \mu_2))) + \lambda_h\left(2\left(\mu_2^2\left(\mu_1 + \mu_h\right)^2\right)\right.\\
&+ \lambda_h(2((\mu_1(2\mu_2 + \mu_h) + \mu_h\mu_2)(\mu_1 + \mu_h + \mu_2))\\
&+2(\lambda_h(\mu_1(3\mu_2 + \mu_h) + \mu_h\mu_2)))\\
&+\mu_1\mu_h(2(\mu_1\mu_h) + \mu_2(4\mu_1 + 5\mu_h)))\\
&+\mu_1\mu_h\mu_2(2(\mu_h\mu_2) + \mu_1(2\mu_h + \mu_2))) + \mu_1\mu_2\left(2\left(\lambda_h^2\mu_c\right)\right.\\
&+\mu_h(2(\lambda_h\mu_c) + \mu_h(\lambda_c + \mu_c)))(\lambda_h + \mu_1)(\lambda_h + \mu_2)),
\end{aligned}
$$

$$
\begin{aligned}
A_{P_{II}}(\infty) = {}& \mu\mu_h\mu_c(\mu((2\lambda_h + \mu_h)(\lambda_h + \mu)\\
&+\lambda(2\lambda + 2\mu_h + 4\lambda_h + \mu))\\
&+ k\left(2\left(\lambda + \lambda_h\right)^2 + \mu_h(2\lambda + \lambda_h)\right)(\lambda + \lambda_h + \mu)\Big)\\
&/(\lambda\left(\left(\lambda_c\mu\mu_h\left(\lambda_h\mu_h k + \mu^2\right)\right.\right.\\
&+ \mu_c\lambda\left(2\left(3\left(\lambda_h^2 k\right) + \mu\mu_h(1 + k)(\mu + \mu_h(1 + k))\right.\right.\\
&+\lambda_h(2(\mu_h(1 + k)) + \mu)(\mu + k(\mu + \mu_h)))\\
&+ \lambda\left(2(\lambda\mu_h k(1 + k)) + 2\left(\mu\left(\lambda_h k + \mu_h\left(1 + k\right)^2\right)\right)\right.\\
&+\mu_h k(1 + k)(3\lambda_h + \mu_h))))\\
&+ \lambda_h(\lambda_h(2((2\mu + \mu_h(1 + k))(\mu + k(\mu + \mu_h)))\\
&+2(\lambda_h k(3\mu + \mu_h(1 + k))))\\
&+\mu\left(\mu(2\mu + 4(\mu_h(1 + k))) + \mu_h^2(1 + 2k)(2 + k)\right)\Big)\\
&+\mu^2\mu_h(2(\mu_h(1 + k)) + \mu)\Big)\Big)\\
&+ \mu\left(2\left(\lambda_h^2\mu_c\right) + \mu_h(2(\lambda_h\mu_c)\right.\\
&+\mu_h(\lambda_c + \mu_c)))(\lambda_h k + \mu)(\lambda_h + \mu))
\end{aligned}
$$

It can be noted with $k > 1$, the second stage repair resulted in a lower rate and is relevant if more extensive repairs are needed resulted in the repair rate being slower in the second stage, leading to longer down-times and reducing availability. The case where both HF repair rates are equal ($\mu_1 = \mu_2 = \mu$) arises when the repair actions at each stage are effectively similar in terms of time, complexity, and resource requirement. Careful consideration should be given to the model choice applicable for HF repair.

3 Bayesian Approach of Steady-State Availability

Consider random samples of size n for each failure and repair due to HF, CCS and HE. Let U_i $(i = 1, 2, 3)$ denote the exponentially distributed random variables representing the failure times due to HF, CCS and HE, respectively. Furthermore, let U_i $(i = 4, 5)$ denote the exponentially distributed random variables representing the repair times due to CCS and HE, respectively. Let U_6 denote the random variable representing the repair times due to HF when considering model I or II. Note that different samples sizes of n_i, $i = 1, \ldots, 6$ can be observed with minimal impact on the definition of the likelihood functions. The joint partial likelihood function, excluding hardware repair, is

$$L(\underline{T}) \propto (\lambda\lambda_c\lambda_h\mu_c\mu_h)^n e^{-(\lambda T_1+\lambda_c T_2+\lambda_h T_3+\mu_c T_4+\mu_h T_5)}, \tag{1}$$

where

$$\underline{T} = (T_1, T_2, T_3, T_4, T_5) \text{ and } T_i = \sum_{j=1}^{n} u_{ij}, i = 1, \ldots, 5$$

are sufficient for λ, λ_c, λ_h, μ_c and μ_h, respectively.

Conjugate priors have similar tails to the likelihood and in the case of a random sample observed from an exponentially distributed variable, the conjugate prior is a gamma distribution, gamma(α,β). The hyperparameters of the gamma prior distribution, α and β, allow the analyst to select the model that best represent the parameter of interest. The posterior distribution of λ given T_1 is

$$h(T_1) \propto \lambda^{n+\alpha_1} e^{-(T_1+\beta_1)\lambda},$$

denoted by $\lambda| \, T_1 \sim$ gamma($n + \alpha_1$,$T_1 + \beta_1$).

Similarly, for λ_c, λ_h, μ_c and μ_h, the posterior distributions are derived as

$$\lambda_c|T_2 \sim gamma(n + \alpha_2, T_2 + \beta_2);$$

$$\lambda_h|T_3 \sim gamma(n + \alpha_3, T_3 + \beta_3);$$

$$\mu_c|T_4 \sim gamma(n + \alpha_4, T_4 + \beta_4);$$

$$\mu_h|T_5 \sim gamma(n + \alpha_5, T_5 + \beta_5).$$

In the case of non-informative priors or vague priors, let $\alpha_i \to 0$ and $\beta_i \to 0$ in the gamma priors to obtain the corresponding posterior distributions for λ, λ_c, λ_h, μ_c and μ_h. The following subsections discuss the format of the remainder term in the likelihood (1) under the two different model assumptions for hardware repair.

3.1 Model I: Constant 2-stage Hypo-Exponentially Distributed Repair Time

The complete likelihood function adding model I hardware repair component is

$$L(data) \propto (\lambda\lambda_c\lambda_h\mu_c\mu_h)^n e^{-(\lambda T_1+\lambda_c T_2+\lambda_h T_3+\mu_c T_4+\mu_h T_5)} \times$$

$$\left(\frac{\mu_1\mu_2}{(\mu_1-\mu_2)}\right)^n \prod_{j=1}^{n}\left(e^{-\mu_2 u_{6j}} - e^{-\mu_1 u_{6j}}\right),$$

The conjugate prior distributions for the repair rates, μ_1 and μ_2, due to hardware failure are

$$\mu_1|\mu_2 \sim gamma(\alpha_{61}, \beta_{61});$$

$$\mu_2|\mu_1 \sim gamma(\alpha_{62}, \beta_{62}).$$

Therefore, the posterior distributions for the repair rates, μ_1 and μ_2, due to hardware failure are

$$h(\mu_1|data, \mu_2) \propto \left(\frac{\mu_1\mu_2}{(\mu_1-\mu_2)}\right)^n \mu_1^{\alpha_{61}-1} e^{-\beta_{61}\mu_1} \prod_{j=1}^{n}\left(e^{-\mu_2 u_{6j}} - e^{-\mu_1 u_{6j}}\right)$$

$$h(\mu_2|data, \mu_1) \propto \left(\frac{\mu_1\mu_2}{(\mu_1-\mu_2)}\right)^n \mu_2^{\alpha_{62}-1} e^{-\beta_{62}\mu_2} \prod_{j=1}^{n}\left(e^{-\mu_2 u_{6j}} - e^{-\mu_1 u_{6j}}\right)$$

Again, in the case of non-informative priors the corresponding posterior distributions for μ_1 and μ_2 are obtained by setting the hyperparameters in the posterior distributions equal to zero.

3.2 Model II: 2-stage Hypo-Exponentially Distributed Repair Time

The complete posterior distribution adding model II hardware repair component is

$$L(data, k) \propto (\lambda\lambda_c\lambda_h\mu_c\mu_h\mu)^n e^{-(\lambda T_1+\lambda_c T_2+\lambda_h T_3+\mu_c T_4+\mu_h T_5)} \times \prod_{j=1}^{n}\left(e^{-\frac{\mu}{k}u_{6j}} - e^{-\mu u_{6j}}\right).$$

Hence, the posterior distributions for the repair rate, μ, using the conjugate prior is derived as

$$h(data) \propto \mu^{(n+\alpha_6)-1} e^{-\beta_6\mu} \prod_{j=1}^{n}\left(e^{-\frac{\mu}{k}u_{6j}} - e^{-\mu u_{6j}}\right).$$

It can be noted that for repair model III where $\mu_1 = \mu_2 = \mu$, the conjugate posterior distribution for the Erlang repair model, is a gamma pdf with parameters $2n + \alpha_6$ and $T_6 + \beta_6$. Realizations for the above posteriors are generated using the Gibbs sampling method for the parameters λ, λ_c, λ_h, μ_c and μ_h. On the other hand, realizations for the posteriors of the repair rates due to hardware failure, the Metropolis-Hastings algorithm is used in the simulation process, due to the complex nature of these obtained posteriors. FORTRAN® was used for all simulations.

4 Simulation Study and Comparisons

The simulation process starts off by selecting a set of true rate parameter values. Random samples are then drawn from the underlying distributions for these given parameter choices. Simulated variates from the posteriors are obtained using specific priors on the parameters of interest. Performance measures are subsequently obtained from a sufficient large number of posteriors to evaluate the different results of the inferential process. Table 2 gives a summary of the true parameter values for the various repair rates under models I and II, while the other rate parameters were kept fixed at $\lambda = 1.1$, $\lambda_c = 1.1$, $\lambda_h = 3$, $\mu_c = 3$ and $\mu_h = 3$.

Table 2. True values of the repair rate parameters.

Rate parameter	Value assigned
Model I: μ_1	1.1
Model I: μ_2	0.55
Model II: $\mu_1 = \mu$	1.1 (for $k = 2$ and $k = 1.2$)
Model II: $\mu_2 = \mu/k$	$1.1/2.0 = 0.55$ and $1.1/1.2 \approx 0.9167$

The posterior distributions are therefore simulated by either direct Gibbs-sampling or by using the Metropolis-Hastings algorithm. The hyperparameters associated with the conjugate gamma prior distributions are chosen such that the expected value of the prior distribution is approximately equal to the true parameter value of the different rates, as given in Table 2. The method of determining the hyperparameter values is discussed in the next paragraph.

Determining the hyperparameters of the conjugate gamma distribution. A method to obtain values for the hyperparameters of shape, α_0 and scale, β_0 is as follows:

1. Generate a sample of size n from $X \sim exp(\theta_0)$, where $\theta = \theta_0$ represents anyone of the rates λ, λ_c, λ_h, μ_c and μ_h corresponding to the known values in Table 2.
2. Determine the mean, $\underline{X}$, of X.
3. Initialize $\alpha = k\underline{X}$, where k $(k < n)$ is a random number of observations observed from the data generated in step 1.
4. Choose β such that $\frac{\alpha}{\beta} \approx \theta_0$.

Note that the hyperparameters associated with each of the two models concerning the repair rate due to hardware failure is determined using the same method described above, but instead of generating data from the exponential distribution in step 1, a data set is generated from the constant 2-stage hypo-exponential distribution (in I) and the 2-stage hypo-exponential distribution (in II).

Simulated samples from the standard posterior distributions. The algorithm provides the steps in the process to simulate directly from the gamma posteriors for the rate parameters λ, λ_c, λ_h, μ_c and μ_h. These parameters are indicated as θ in the algorithm and the known values of these rate parameters as θ_0, as in Table 2. The data is represented by a random sample of size n. The simulated posterior variates are indexed by $m = 10$ 000 and the number of posteriors obtained in the simulation study is indexed by $N = 1$ 000. The algorithm is as follows for each of λ, λ_c, λ_h, μ_c and μ_h:

1. Determine the hyperparameter values as described in the paragraph above.
2. Generate a random sample of size n from $U \sim exp(\theta_0)$.
3. Determine $T = \sum_{i=1}^{n} U_i$.
4. Simulate m actual posterior variates, while discarding the first 1 000 as burn-in variates, from the $gamma(n + \alpha, T + \beta)$ distribution, indicated as $\tilde{\theta}_i$, $i = 1, \ldots, m$.
5. Calculate posterior characteristics needed for evaluating performance (see last paragraph).
6. Repeat steps 1—5 N times.
7. Repeat steps 1—6 for different n, ($n = 25$, 40 and 100).

Sampling from a posterior for hardware repair. The simulation process is similar to steps 1—7 in previous paragraph, except steps 2, 3 and 4 are replaced according to the underlying repair model and subsequent posteriors. Steps 2 and 3 involves generating a sample of size n from the 2-stage hardware repair models (models I and II), according to a set of known values for μ_1 and μ_2, as given in Table 2. Generating samples from the 2-stage hardware repair models proceed as follows: generate Y_{11}, ..., Y_{1n}, where Y_1 ~ $exp(\mu_1)$ and then Y_{21}, ..., Y_{2n}, where Y_2 ~ $exp(\mu_2)$. Define $U_6 = Y_1 + Y_2$, then U_{61}, ..., U_{6n} will be a random sample of hardware repair times. Step 4 will involve simulating from the appropriate posterior for model I and II using the Metropolis-Hastings algorithm. The posterior realizations are indicated with $\tilde{\theta}_i$, $i = 1, \ldots, m$ (for corresponding and relevant rate parameters).

Posterior steady-state availabilities and performance measures. The posterior steady-state availabilities of the three models are obtained by substituting the posterior realizations $\tilde{\theta}_i$, $i = 1, \ldots, m$ (for relevant rate parameters θ: λ, λ_c, λ_h, μ_c, μ_h, μ_1 and μ_2) into the limiting steady-state probabilities. Obtaining posteriors using non-informative priors are obtained without performing step 1 and setting all hyperparameters in the posteriors equal to zero.

The posterior means are

$$E(\theta_j)_{post} = \frac{1}{m} \sum_{i=1}^{m} (\tilde{\theta}_i), \; (m = 10000, j = 1, \ldots, N),$$

while the (1-γ) credible intervals are obtained using the appropriate percentiles of simulated values and indicated by

$$\left(\tilde{\theta}_{(\frac{\gamma}{2})}, \tilde{\theta}_{(1-\frac{\gamma}{2})}\right)_j, j = 1, \ldots, N,$$

with a width indicated as $\tilde{\Delta}_{(1-\gamma),j} = \tilde{\theta}_{(1-\frac{\gamma}{2})} - \tilde{\theta}_{(\frac{\gamma}{2})}, j = 1, \ldots, N$. The expected value of $\Delta_{1-\gamma}$ is

$$E(\Delta_{1-\gamma}) = \frac{1}{N} \sum_{j=1}^{N} \tilde{\Delta}_{(1-\gamma),j}.$$

The coverage is calculated to assess frequentist properties and is defined as the relative number of times θ_0 under H_0: $\theta = \theta_0$ is contained in the obtained (1-γ) credible intervals.

$$Cover(\%) = \frac{100}{N}\sum_{j=1}^{N} I\left(\theta_0 \in \left(\tilde{\theta}_{\frac{\gamma}{2}}, \tilde{\theta}_{1-\frac{\gamma}{2}}\right)_j\right)$$

where $I(.)$ is the indicator function.

The MSE and bias are calculated as follows

$$MSE = \frac{1}{N}\sum_{j=1}^{N}\left(E(\theta_j)_{post} - \theta_0\right)^2,$$

$$bias = \sqrt{MSE - var(E(\theta_j)_{post})}.$$

An extensive simulation study was done to evaluate the performance of the various estimators by comparing them to their true underlying values as given in Table 2. Samples of different sizes were generated in the simulation study where the different performance measures were calculated under the different prior dispensation. It is necessary to mention that all performance measures stabilized when sample sizes were chosen larger than $n = 100$.

Tables 3 and 4 give a summary of the simulation results based on the posterior variates using the non-informative or improper priors for the different parameters in the two repair models. Table 3 gives a summary of the performance measures of all the rate parameters using simulated data and true parameters as defined in Table 2. It can be noted that for model III, performances were also investigated for equal two-stage repair rate parameters and simulation results were no different in trend as what were generally observed in Tables 3 and 4. Table 5 gives a summary of the availability performance measures in the simulation study. The true values of the parameters are displayed in brackets. The performance measures were well within the acceptable limits as far as coverages are concerned even in the presence of vague information about the parameters, as well as minimal regarding bias and MSE.

Tables 5 and 6 give a summary of the simulation results based on the posterior variates using conjugate priors for the different parameters in the two repair models.

Table 5 gives a summary of the performance measures of all the rate parameters using simulated data and true parameters as defined in Table 2. Table 6 gives a summary of the availability performance measures in the simulation study under conjugacy. Using appropriate conjugate priors on all parameters resulted superior coverages and a significant reduction in bias and MSE.

Table 3. Performance measures using non-informative priors for parameters in repair models.

	n	$bias$	MSE	$Cover(\%)$	$E[\Delta_{0.95}]$	$Var(\Delta_{0.95})$
	25	0.05281	0.05774	96.0	0.90025	0.03354
λ	40	0.03386	0.03424	95.6	0.70100	0.01277
(1.1)	100	0.01218	0.01236	95.6	0.43529	0.00190
	25	0.04181	0.05410	95.9	0.89150	0.03204
λ_c	40	0.02709	0.03421	94.9	0.69695	0.01290
(1.1)	100	0.00899	0.01104	96.4	0.43392	0.00170
	25	0.13765	0.42550	95.8	2.45059	0.24899
λ_h	40	0.06221	0.24638	94.6	1.89222	0.09272
(3)	100	0.01817	0.08834	95.7	1.18222	0.01364
	25	0.10730	0.43134	95.4	2.42634	0.25601
μ_c	40	0.06553	0.25932	95.1	1.89556	0.09807
(3)	100	0.00885	0.09584	94.8	1.17727	0.01482
	25	0.11650	0.40646	95.9	2.43351	0.23960
μ_h	40	0.08763	0.24930	95.0	1.90846	0.09297
(3)	100	0.01987	0.09968	94.6	1.18214	0.01563
Model I	25	0.04479	0.02275	99.9	0.91906	0.00570
μ_1	40	0.03284	0.01907	98.8	0.92657	0.00720
(1.1)	100	0.07335	0.02211	99.8	1.23912	0.02872
Model I	25	0.03068	0.01378	96.7	0.47961	0.00636
μ_2	40	0.03856	0.01208	96.0	0.42525	0.00338
(0.55)	100	0.00530	0.00546	98.6	0.35233	0.00155
Model II	25	0.08756	0.07167	88.2	0.76174	0.02539
μ $(k = 2)$	40	0.05833	0.04171	88.4	0.59233	0.00985
(1.1)	100	0.03919	0.01522	87.8	0.37237	0.00147
Model II	25	0.05680	0.06185	87.4	0.70815	0.02131
μ $(k = 1.2)$	40	0.03376	0.03344	88.4	0.55348	0.00770
(1.1)	100	0.01347	0.01341	87.7	0.34692	0.00131

From all the tables it is evident that as n increases, the bias and the MSE decreased over all inference scenarios. For $n > 100$ it can be noted that performance stabilize over all models and for all choices of the true parameters—evidence that large samples resulted in a dominant likelihood as what is expected with the Bayesian approach. Over the 1 000 simulated posteriors it is evident that the expected length of the credible intervals decrease as the larger sample sizes are utilized in obtaining the posteriors. The variance of these 1 000 intervals also decreased for the larger sample sizes in the

Table 4. Non-informative performance measures for the availability under two configurations.

	n	*bias*	*MSE*	*Cover*(%)	$E[\Delta_{0.95}]$	$Var(\Delta_{0.95})$
Model I	25	0.00222	0.00012	93.7	0.04313	0.00012
$A_{SI}(\infty)$	40	0.00137	0.00008	93.5	0.03473	0.00005
(0.037464)	100	0.00021	0.00003	94.4	0.02266	0.00001
Model I	25	0.01473	0.00128	90.8	0.12892	0.00027
$A_{PI}(\infty)$	40	0.00970	0.00089	90.8	0.10437	0.00012
(0.199736)	100	0.00246	0.00034	94.6	0.06897	0.00002
Model II ($k =$ 1.2)	25	0.00120	0.00021	95.2	0.05657	0.00019
$A_{SII}(\infty)$	40	0.00085	0.00014	93.7	0.04435	0.00008
(0.046739)	100	0.00053	0.00001	93.7	0.02785	0.00010
Model II ($k =$ 1.2)	25	0.00038	0.00165	93.7	0.15120	0.00026
$A_{PII}(\infty)$	40	0.00032	0.00113	92.6	0.12026	0.00012
(0.245799)	100	0.00068	0.00048	92.8	0.07674	0.00002

posterior analyses as expected. The coverages in all inference scenarios seem to be acceptable around the desired levels. The system steady-state availability for the parallel configuration is higher than the system availability for the series configuration. It is also evident that inference of the availability measures is more robust and not so sensitive to the resulting posteriors from the CCS and HE parameters. As expected with the value added of conjugate priors relative to noninformative or vague prior knowledge, smaller coverages as well as smaller expected credible intervals and variances thereof were obtained. However, the use of noninformative priors resulted in higher bias and MSE if compared to the use of conjugate priors.

Table 5. Performance measures using conjugate priors for parameters in repair models.

	n	*bias*	*MSE*	*Cover*(%)	$E[\Delta_{0.95}]$	$Var(\Delta_{0.95})$
	25	0.03476	0.03856	97.8	0.80938	0.01898
λ	40	0.01193	0.02373	96.3	0.64852	0.00807
(1.1)	100	0.01839	0.01233	95.3	0.42733	0.00176
	25	0.01762	0.03483	97.1	0.79704	0.01780
λ_c	40	0.02260	0.02557	96.5	0.65426	0.00851
(1.1)	100	0.00634	0.01107	95.9	0.42289	0.00163
	25	0.10690	0.30669	96.8	2.21640	0.15087
λ_h	40	0.07423	0.18447	97.1	1.79341	0.06176
(3)	100	0.03818	0.08575	96.6	1.16030	0.01246
	25	0.06705	0.27291	96.6	2.18935	0.13790
μ_c	40	0.06110	0.20599	96.1	1.78377	0.06898
(3)	100	0.02923	0.07798	96.2	1.15742	0.01136
	25	0.06340	0.26711	97.1	2.18382	0.13326
μ_h	40	0.06068	0.19299	95.5	1.78409	0.06392
(3)	100	0.02501	0.08701	85.6	1.15564	0.01285
Model I	25	0.04301	0.02163	99.7	0.92211	0.00784
μ_1	40	0.10137	0.02602	98.6	0.96474	0.01600
(1.1)	100	0.04003	0.02754	99.9	1.06456	0.03340
Model I	25	0.03263	0.01041	97.8	0.43866	0.00363
μ_2	40	0.04355	0.01033	96.3	0.39641	0.00233
(0.55)	100	0.00853	0.00553	97.4	0.33024	0.00146
Model II	25	0.06777	0.05068	91.0	0.71198	0.01645
μ $(k = 2)$	40	0.06087	0.03462	89.9	0.57470	0.00743
(1.1)	100	0.03931	0.01351	89.9	0.36732	0.00124
Model II	25	0.05984	0.05102	88.9	0.67772	0.01583
μ $(k = 1.2)$	40	0.03668	0.02912	89.5	0.53891	0.00615
(1.1)	100	0.01614	0.01259	89.6	0.34329	0.00118

Table 6. Conjugate performance measures for the availability under two configurations.

	n	*bias*	*MSE*	*Cover* (%)	$E[\Delta_{0.95}]$	$Var(\Delta_{0.95})$
Model I	25	0.00260	0.00009	85.0	0.03895	0.00007
$A_{SI}(\infty)$	40	0.00084	0.00007	95.8	0.03311	0.00004
(0.037464)	100	0.00042	0.00003	95.6	0.02199	0.00001
Model I	25	0.01478	0.00094	93.3	0.11776	0.00002
$A_{PI}(\infty)$	40	0.00746	0.00067	93.8	0.09899	0.00008
(0.199736)	100	0.00335	0.00031	93.8	0.06686	0.00002
Model II ($k =$ 1.2)	25	0.00100	0.00016	95.9	0.05179	0.00012
$A_{SII}(\infty)$	40	0.00165	0.00011	95.7	0.04259	0.00006
(0.046739)	100	0.00044	0.00005	94.2	0.02721	0.00001
Model II ($k =$ 1.2)	25	0.00105	0.00138	94.5	0.14112	0.00019
$A_{PII}(\infty)$	40	0.00296	0.00094	94.5	0.11572	0.00009
(0.245799)	100	0.00047	0.00043	93.5	0.07525	0.00002

5 Conclusion

The Bayesian approach presented in this paper, using different and appropriate prior distributions, provides an alternative way to deal with repairable systems, specifically for small samples. Reliable estimations for the steady-state availability are obtained even when samples are small using vague or noninformative prior information. The major advantage of using informative conjugate priors in these models is that whenever vague information exists about the parameters of interest, a subsequent sequential posterior analysis will adequately update the information about the parameters, which is the one of the strengths of conjugacy. Incorporating that the hardware failure may have variant hypo-exponential distributions, it is always worthy to investigate since this is a real assumption in practice. This approach can be utilized in industrial situations to study the effect of various operational parameters.

Disclosure of Interests.

The author has no competing interests to declare that are relevant to the content of this article.

References

1. Berger, J.O.: Statistical Decision Theory and Bayesian Analysis. Springer, New York (1985)
2. Chung, W.K.: Reliability analysis of a repairable parallel system with standby involving human error and common-cause failures. Microelectron. Reliab. **27**(2), 269–271 (1987)
3. Dhillon, B.S., Yang, N.: Stochastic analysis of standby systems with common-cause failures and human errors. Microelectron. Reliab. **32**(12), 1699–1712 (1992)
4. EL-Sherbeny, M.S.: Stochastic analysis of a two non-identical unit parallel system with different types of failures subject to preventive maintenance and repairs. J. Qual. Maint. Eng. **16**(3), 319–334 (2010)
5. EL-Sherbeny, M.S.: Stochastic Analysis of a two non-identical unit parallel system with different types of failures subject to preventive maintenance and repairs. Hindawi Publishing Corporation: Mathematical Problems in Engineering, 1–10 (2013)
6. Jain, M., Rani, S.: Availability analysis for repairable system with warm standby, switching failure and reboot delay. Int. J. Math. Oper. Res. **5**(1), 19–39 (2013)
7. Ke, J., Chang, C., Lee, W.: An availability-based system with general repair via Bayesian aspect. Math. Comput. Simul **144**, 247–265 (2018)
8. Khan, M.A., Islam, H.M.: Bayesian analysis of system availability with half-normal life time quality. Technol. & Quant. Manag. **9**(2), 203–209 (2012)
9. Mahmoud, M.A.W., Moshref, M.E.: On a two-unit cold standby system considering hardware, human error failures and preventive maintenance. Math. Comput. Model. **51**, 736–774 (2010)
10. Ram, M., Singh, S.B.: Analysis of a complex system with common cause failure and two types of repair facilities with different distributions in failure. Int. J. Reliab. Saf. **4**(4), 381–392 (2010)
11. Yadavalli, V.S.S., Bekker, A., Pauw, J.: Bayesian study of a two-component system with common-cause shock failures. Asia-Pacific J. Oper. Res. **22**(1), 105–119 (2005)

The Application of Wavelet Neural Networks for Individual Claims Forecasting

Devi Nurtiyasari[1,2(✉)], Adhitya Ronnie Effendie[1], Dedi Rosadi[1], and Abdurakhman[1]

[1] Department of Mathematics, Gadjah Mada University, Yogyakarta, Indonesia
rachmanstat@ugm.ac.id

[2] Mathematics Education, Sunan Kalijaga State Islamic University, Yogyakarta, Indonesia

Abstract. We applied the combinations of wavelet and neural networks (NN) for predicting individual claims. This method employs a wavelet in the preprocessing phase for data denoising technique and a NN in the forecasting phase. We use publicly available information to develop and evaluate the modeling framework, and then compare prediction performance using NN and Wavelet NN.

Keywords: Wavelet · Neural network · Forecasting · Individual claims

1 Introduction

The claims reserving procedure is the foundation of general insurance companies financial management [11]. It influences the insurance costs that are charged, the capital that is maintained to sustain the organization's stability. The operational integrity and financial stability of an insurance company depend on the selection of suitable reserving strategies and underlying assumptions, as well as their successful application to actual situations. For loss reserving purposes, insurance claim data is aggregated and structured into development triangles, thereby omitting details related to individual claims. Each individual claim is characterized by two variables, an occurrence time, a reporting delay, and a procedure outlining partial payments and claim settlement [9].

The field of claims level reserving research is getting a rapid advancements as the insurance industry continuously improves its methods to managing claims reserves. For decades, the industry has been focused on optimizing claim management procedures to ensure accurate estimation of future liabilities and to maintain financial stability. One of the earliest studies on non-life insurance claims reserving was conducted by Reid [15], that examined many popular claim reserving strategies. Recently, micro level loss reserving techniques have been used to extract important details from the individual claim characteristics for

P. C. Rodrigues et al. (Eds.): ISBIS 2024, 13, pp. 17–27, 2027.
https://doi.org/10.1007/978-3-032-32458-0_2

forecasting future liabilities. A Markov based method for loss reserving is presented in Hesselager's fundamental contribution to the field of actuarial science [10], with a focus on its use in estimating reserves for recorded but unresolved claims. The practical application of Markov models to depict the evolution of claims over time is examined in this study. Another important study by Charpentier et al. [4] compares the two main strategies for reserving non life insurance claims: macro methods and micro methods. Using an econometric methodology, the study examines how each method can be used to forecast future liabilities for unresolved claims in the non life insurance industry. Later, by employing a deep triangle model, Kuo [13] presented a novel approach to claims reserving that signified an essential difference from traditional methods. Although the deep triangle model presents a promising path in the field of claims reserving, its functioning is inherently linked to the scope and structure of the dataset.

Even though the field of claims reserving is continually changing due to new methods and technological advancements, the chain ladder approach is a fundamental and widely used tool in the insurance sector. The claim reserve is estimated using the chain ladder method using individual information and a statistician has to take into account additional collective information if the individual information is insufficient [12]. As an alternative to conventional methods such as the chain ladder, a study on the use of dynamic factor models (DFMs) for the reserving of non-life insurance claims was conducted by Nomura [14]. This method offers a new way to predict the evolution of insurance claims over time. However, it is important to constantly evaluate its limitations and applicability, particularly as emerging data analytics techniques provides new approaches to improving the precision and dependability of claims reserving procedures.

Gabrielli [7] and Wuhtrich [16] introduce the use of neural networks and individual claim specific information to enhance conventional claims reserving strategies. The study states that the inclusion of individual claims specific information in the improved model allows for the examination of reserves on a per claim basis, providing an advanced view of the claims data. The study shows how neural networks, by providing claims data with accurate and advanced insights, might enhance conventional claims reserving procedures. The neural network approach produces precise reserves for many business lines. Later, the conventional claims reserving methods are enhanced by the development of neural network models using ensemble and hybrid approaches, as demonstrated by the work of Chaoubi et al. [3] and Al Mudafer, et al. [1]. A discrete time individual reserving framework incorporating spesific information is introduced by Chaoubi et al. [3] using a deep learning technique called the Long Short Term Memory (LSTM) neural network. This study enhances loss reserving in the insurance sector by obtaining the specific characteristics of individual claims to improve forecasting accuracy. By applying the LSTM neural network and building on a large claim forecasting framework, the proposed individual loss reserving model achieves more accuracy than the conventional chain ladder approach. In the meantime, the application of mixture density neural networks (MDN) in loss reserving by Al Mudafer, et al. [1] provides a versatile and precise method for forecasting the variability of individual claims. The study shows the ability of neural network techniques to enhance both the precision and flexibility of loss reserving practices.

Neural networks are advanced machine learning models that are being used increasingly in the insurance sector to forecast individual claims. Neural networks use advanced algorithms and multi layered architectures to identify complex patterns and relationships within large datasets. The neural network model can be improved considerably by comprise wavelets, which are used in the data denoising stage. Errors in datasets, known as noise, can result from both human mistake and imprecise data collection equipment. Machine learning problems might arise when an algorithm starts to generalize after misinterpreting noise in the input as a pattern. Thus, the properties of data that may contain noise are our focus in this research, and we used wavelet and neural network combinations to forecast individual claims. Wavelets are employed in the pre-processing stage to reduce data noise, whereas NN is utilized in the forecasting stage. For this reason, we believe that this research will expand our understanding of individual claims reserving, NN, and wavelets.

Overall, the contributions of this paper can be summarized as follows:

1. a proposal for an improved neural network model utilizing wavelet for individual claims forecasting
2. integration of neural networks and wavelet for individual claims forecasting to enable reducing data noise

This is how the rest of the paper is organized. The data are described in Sect. 2. After that, we explain the topics discussed and then provides a brief explanation of model in Sect. 3 and the algorithm in Sect. 4. The study's findings are covered in Sect. 5, and the conclusion which includes some suggestions for further research is presented in Sect. 6.

2 Data

We generate sample data for our study using the individual claims history simulator developed by Gabrielli and Wüthrich [8], which they describe in their research as the framework for simulating individual claims histories. This simulator operates through eight modeling steps: (1) simulation of the reporting delay T; (2) simulation of the payment indicator Z; (3) simulation of the number of payments K; (4) simulation of the total claim size Y; (5) simulation of the number of recoveries; (6) simulation of the recovery size Y; (7) simulation of the cash flow; and (8) simulation of the claim status [8]. They also state that throughout the simulation technique, not all of the following stages (1)-(8) may be required. The main variables employed in this investigation are thoroughly discussed and summarized in Table 1.

We run the first phase modeling using a data set of 1000 individual claim histories, each with the following static information:

Table 1. Variables

Variables	Type	Preprocessing
Line of Business (LoB)	Categorical	Indexed in $\{1, 2, 3, 4\}$
Claim code (cc)	Categorical	Indexed in $\{1, 2, ..., 52, 53\}$
Accident Year (AY)	$in\{1994, 1995, ..., 2004, 2005\}$	
Age of the injured part (age)	in $\{15, 20, ..., 70\}$	
Injured part (inj)	Categorical	Indexed in $\{10, ..., 99\}$

1. line of business (LoB) refers to the specific type or category of insurance coverage that the claim falls within. LoB is categorical type and has been preprocessed to be indexed in $\{1, 2, 3, 4\}$
2. claims code (cc) refers to a special identification number or classification code that the insurance provider uses to categorize the particular claim. It is the injured's labor sector in categorical type and has been preprocessed to be indexed in $\{1, 2, ..., 52, 53\}$
3. accident year (AY) refers to the year in which the incident or accident occurred that triggered the claim, which is in $\{1994, 1995, ..., 2004, 2005\}$
4. the age of the injured (age) is the age of the individual who suffered the injury, which is in $\{15, 20, ..., 70\}$
5. injured part (inj) refers to the specific body part or area of the body that was injured in the accident. Its is a categorical type with indexes in $\{10, ..., 99\}$ and identifies the injured body part

3 Wavelet Neural Networks

The dataset was divided into a train set of up to 848 data points and a test set of up to 212 data points. Figure 1 demonstrates the procedure's direction map. After separating the dataset, we apply the model Neural Network, whose architecture is shown in Fig. 2, and Wavelet Neural Networks, whose architecture is shown in Fig. 1. The model will be used to evaluate and compare performance.

NN is a network architecture constructed out of several neurons that collaborate to respond to input [5]. Generally, NN is a structure made up of three layers: the input layer, the hidden layer, and the output layer. The input layer receives information from the outside world in the form of a problem description. The output layer returns NN solutions to issues received by the input layer. An activation function is used to change the input layer, which is connected to one or more output layers via hidden layers. The activation function will determine a unit's output (converting an input signal into an output signal) and send it to another unit [6]. The activation function is employed as a NN activator, which means it is used to activate every neuron in the network.

In this research, the input variables for the Neural Network model are LoB, cc, AQ, age, and inj, while the output is the reporting delay T, which represents

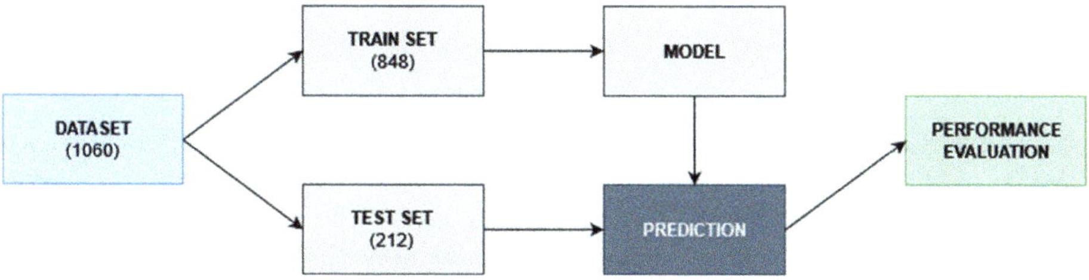

Fig. 1. Procedure's direction map

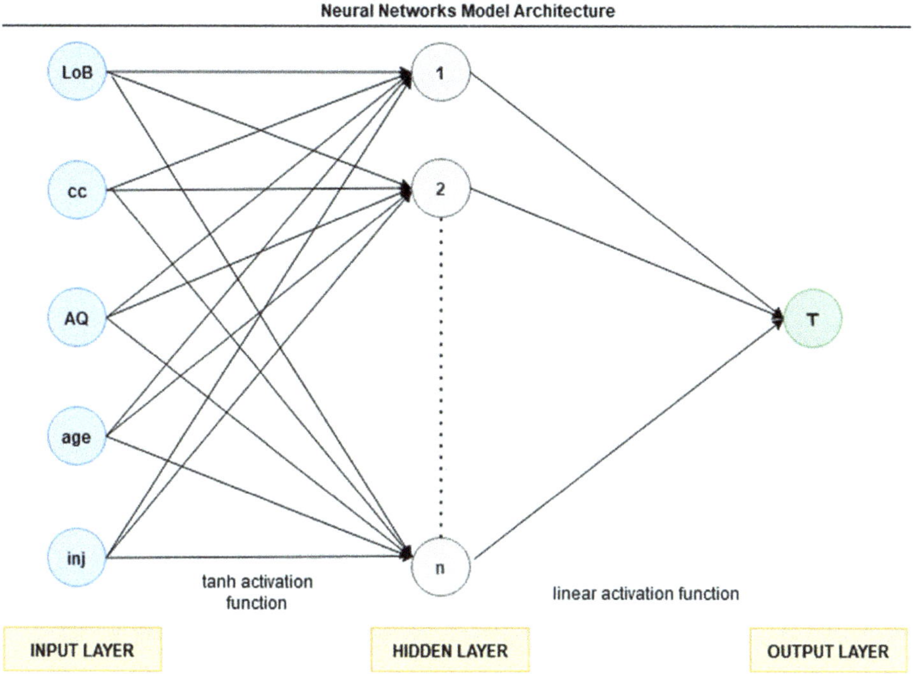

Fig. 2. Neural networks architecture

the annualized difference between the reporting year and the accident year, as illustrated in Fig. 2. Consider the (annualized) reporting delays T_i, provided by

$$T_i = RY_i - AY_i \in= \{0, 1, 2, ..., 11\},$$

where AY_i is the accident year and RY_i is the reporting year of claim i, $i = 0, 1, ..., n$, and $n = 1000$. Tanh and linear activation functions were utilized in this study, with the following formula:

$$f(x) = x \tag{1}$$

and

$$f(x) = \frac{e^x - e^{-x}}{e^x + e^{-x}} \tag{2}$$

As shown in Fig. 3, for the Wavelet Neural Network, the input variables are LoB, cc, AQ, age, and inj, while the output is the reporting delay T. Before transmitting the input signal to the hidden layer, the WNN model denoises the data using wavelets. This is done to reduce noise in the data and improve data quality. Wavelets are little waves that can aggregate and concentrate visual energy in a limited group of coefficients [2]. Other groupings of coefficients contain only minor quantities of energy that can be deleted without lowering the data's information value. This energy and coefficient group is then utilized as a reference for data denoising. Mathematically, a wavelet function is defined as $psi(j,k)$ if it meets the following two conditions:

$$\int_{-\infty}^{\infty} \psi(j,k)dx = 0 \tag{3}$$

and

$$\int_{-\infty}^{\infty} \psi^2(j,k)dx = 0 \tag{4}$$

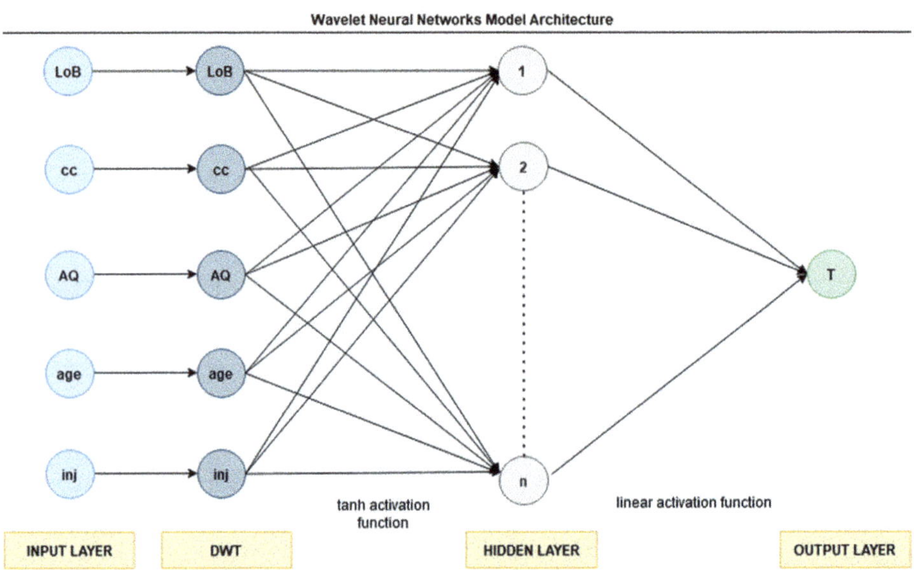

Fig. 3. Wavelet neural networks architecture

The fundamental idea of splitting signals based on frequency differences (the decomposition process) can then be applied to perform wavelet processing. According to Burrus [2], wavelets are defined as a family of translation and dilation functions known as mother wavelets (basic wavelets) $\psi_{j,k}(t)$.

$$\psi_{j,k}(t) = 2^{j/2}\psi(2^j t - k) \quad , j, k \in Z, j \neq 0 \tag{5}$$

where k is a translation parameter that establishes the wavelet's time position and j is a frequency or scaling parameter that expresses the degree of compression. The frequency is higher if $|j| < 1$ since $\psi_{j,k}(x)$ is a compressed form of the basic wavelet with a smaller temporal domain. Conversely, if $|j| > 1$, the frequency of $\psi_{j,k}(x)$ is smaller since it has a broader temporal domain. The time-width (or span of a wavelet) varies with frequency. Both the frequency and the temporal domains are used for wavelet transformation. In addition, the wavelet-based data denoising process involves the following steps: (1) computing the data's wavelet transform; (2) thresholding the wavelet coefficients; and (3) computing the wavelet transform's inverse to obtain a denoised estimate.

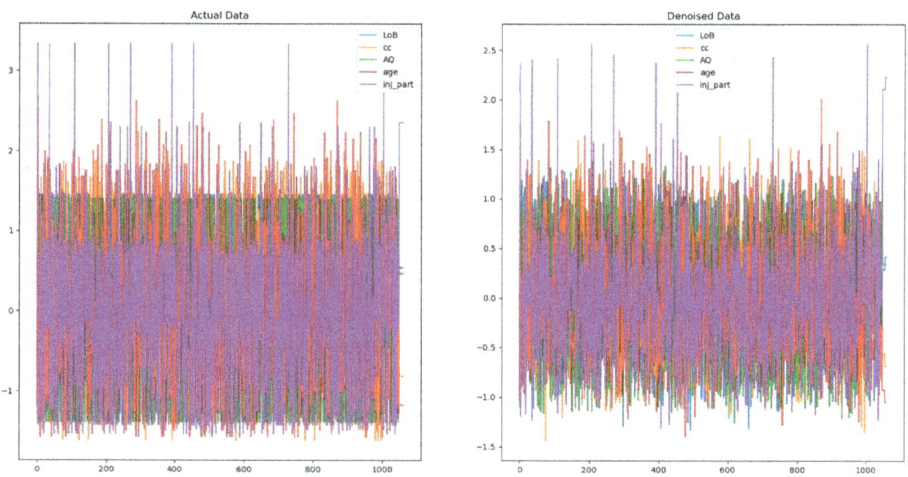

Fig. 4. Actual data and denoised data

Figure 4 show the data plot before and after denoising process using wavelet. After denoising the data with wavelets, the WNN modeling stages are identical to the NN technique described above. Furthermore, in this work, the NN and Wavelet NN architectures used 20 hidden layers rather than 30, 40, or 50 hidden layers.

Finally, the prediction model is assessed using the Mean Square Error (MSE) and Root Mean Square Error (RMSE). MSE is the average sum of the squares of the differences between the target and the network output results. The accuracy of the resulting forecast increases with a model's MSE score. MSE is formulated as follows.

$$MSE = \frac{1}{n}\sum_{t=1}^{n}(g_t - z_t)^2 \tag{6}$$

where $t = 1, 2, ..n$, n = number of observation data, and g_t = t-th target, z_t = t-th network output. Meanwhile, the formula for RMSE, which is derived from MSE by calculating the square root of MSE, is as follows.

$$RMSE = \sqrt{\frac{1}{n}\sum_{t=1}^{n}(g_t - z_t)^2} \tag{7}$$

4 Algorithm

This section provides algorithmic details. The proposed technique integrates the advantages of neural network and wavelet transform models to increase the forecasting accuracy of individual claims. The procedure is divided into a number of components. Each algorithmic phase is provided below:

Phase 1: Data Preprocessing Using Wavelet Transform The algorithm's initial phase, data preprocessing, is transforming the claims data using a wavelet transform. Wavelet transforms are powerful mathematical tools that decompose the data into components at different frequencies and time scales. During this phase, the data is prepared for neural network training, which can improve the forecasting model's overall performance.

Phase 2: Neural Network Model In the second phase, a neural network model is constructed. The neural network acts as a nonlinear model that learns complex relationships between the input features (preprocessed claims data) and the target variable.

Phase 3: Training the Model Training the model using the preprocessed claims data is the third stage after configuring the neural network.

Phase 4: Prediction The next phase is to utilize the model to make predictions.

Phase 5: Evaluation Lastly, the algorithm involves a phase to evaluate the model's performance. It involves comparing the actual observed claims data with the predictions generated by the neural network.

5 Results and Discussion

The prediction results using Neural Networks with 20, 30, 40, and 50 hidden layers and Wavelet Neural Networks with 20, 30, 40, and 50 hidden layers are presented in Table 2. Based on the data provided in Table 2, it can be observed that the smallest for both MSE and RMSE are obtained by Neural Networks and Wavelet Neural Networks with 20 hidden layers. The selection of 20 hidden layers achieves the best compromise between over fitting and model complexity, enabling the neural networks to discover complicated relationships in the data. The integration of wavelet transforms with neural networks, enhance the model's capacity to capture both low frequency trends and high frequency details, yielding results that are comparable to traditional neural networks. The effectiveness of deep learning architectures, especially those with several hidden layers, in

Algorithm - Wavelet Neural Networks for Individual Claims Forecasting

Phase 1: Data preprocessing using wavelet

DWT_i = cA, cD

Set threshold

Reconstruct = IWT_i = denoised data

Phase 2: Neural Network Model

```
def create_cl_model(input_shape):
model = tf.keras.Sequential()
model.add(tf.keras.layers.Dense(50, activation='sigmoid',
            input_shape=(input_shape,))) # Hidden layer
model.add(tf.keras.layers.Dense(2, activation='sigmoid')) # Output layer
return model
```

Phase 3: Training Model

Set maximum epoch

```
for epoch in max_epoch
for the batch in the dataset
inputs,labels = batch
out = model(inputs.float())
loss = criterion(out,labels.float())
loss.backward()
optimizer.step()
```

Phase 4: Prediction

```
predicted_values = cl_model.predict(inputs,verbose=False)
return cl_model,predicted_values
```

Phase 5: Evaluation

$MSE = \frac{1}{n}\sum_{t=1}^{n}(g_t - z_t)^2$ and

$RMSE = \sqrt{\frac{1}{n}\sum_{t=1}^{n}(g_t - z_t)^2}$

improving performance in individual claims prediction is demonstrated by the success of these models. The practicality of both approaches in predicting outcomes is shown by this study.

Furthermore, a comparative analysis of the performance outcomes produced by both models shows remarkable competitiveness. Since NN can identify nonlinear data patterns, it ensures precise and accurate predictions. On the other hand, the outcomes of employing NN and adding wavelets to denoise data are essentially comparable. Wavelets have significance for denoising data in the preprocessing phase, as wavelet transforms decompose the data into distinct frequency components, efficiently removes noise and keeps the important information. The input data is improved by this preprocessing phase using wavelet transform, making it more suitable for training the neural network.

As a result, both models demonstrate robust competitive performance, with the neural network utilizing its nonlinear learning capabilities, while the wavelet neural network achieves comparable performance with the added advantage of noise reduction in the preprocessing phase. Consequently, both approaches represent valuable tools for predictive modeling tasks.

Table 2. Performance Analysis

Model	Hidden Layers	MSE	RMSE
Neural Networks	20	92.906	9.639
	30	97.535	9.876
	40	95.316	9.763
	50	102.774	10.138
Wavelet Neural Networks	20	94.673	9.729
	30	99.349	9.967
	40	102.098	10.104
	50	110.936	10.533

6 Conclusions

Neural networks are known to be capable of making well informed decisions, primarily because of their inherent ability to learn from data and model complex, nonlinear relationships between input and output variables. Unlike traditional models, which rely on predefined rules or linear assumptions, neural networks are adaptive and flexible, capable of identifying complex patterns in data without requiring prior knowledge of these patterns.

In an attempt to eliminate noise from the data, wavelet transforms are integrated with neural networks to improve the quality of the data and increase prediction accuracy. The objective of this integration is to remove data noise, which is prevalent in many real world datasets. By combining wavelet transforms with neural networks, the hybrid model enhances data quality and optimizes the performance of the neural network, resulting in competitive performance outcomes.

The subsequent model developed by Gabrielli and Wüthrich, known as the individual claims history simulator, provides a robust framework that can be utilized to construct various architectures of Neural Networks and Wavelet Neural Networks for further study. As a fundamental tool for investigating and evaluating various predictive models in claims reserving, this simulator is especially made to replicate the historical development of individual claims over time.

References

1. Muhammed Taher Al-Mudafer, B., Avanzi, G., Taylor, B., Wong: Stochastic loss reserving with mixture density neural networks. Insurance Math. Econom. **105**, 144–174 (2022)
2. Burrus, C.S.: Introduction to Wavelets and Wavelet Transforms. Prentice Hall (1988)
3. Chaoubi, I., Besse, C., Cossette, H., Côté, M.-P.: Micro-level reserving for general insurance claims using a long short-term memory network. Appl. Stoch. Model. Bus. Ind. **39**(3), 382–407 (2023). February

4. Charpentier, A., Pigeon, M.: Macro versus micro methods in non-life claims reserving (an econometric perspective). Risks **4**(2), 12 (2016)
5. Daming Shi Wing, W.Y., Ng Daniel, S., Yeung, I., Cloete: Sensitivity Analysis for Neural Networks. Springer (2010)
6. Fausett, L.V.: Fundamentals of Neural Networks: Architectures, Algorithms, and Applications. Prentice Hall (1994)
7. Gabrielli, A.: A neural network boosted double overdispersed poisson claims reserving model. ASTIN Bull. **50**(1), 25–60 (2019). December
8. Gabrielli, A., Wüthrich, M.V.: An individual claims history simulation machine. Risks **6**(2), 29 (2018). March
9. Haastrup, S., Arjas, E., Claims reserving in continuous time; a nonparametric bayesian approach. ASTIN Bull. **26**(2), 139–164: Cited by: 40. All Open Access, Bronze Open Access, Green Open Access (1996)
10. Ole Hesselager, A., markov model for loss reserving. ASTIN Bull. **24**(2), 183–193: Cited by: 11. All Open Access, Bronze Open Access, Green Open Access (1994)
11. Hindley, D.: Introduction, International Series on Actuarial Science, pp. 1–15. Cambridge University Press (2017)
12. Karmila, S., Nurrohmah, S., Sari, S.F.: Claim reserve prediction using the credibility theory for the chain ladder method. J. Phys: Conf. Ser. **1442**(1), 012038 (2020). January
13. Kuo, K.: Deeptriangle: A deep learning approach to loss reserving. Risks **7**(3), 97 (2019). September
14. Nomura, S., Matsumori, Y.: Dynamic factor models for claim reserving. Jpn. J. Stat. Data Sci. **7**(2), 895–919 (2024). June
15. Reid, D.H.: Discussion of methods of claim reserving in non-life insurance. Insurance Math. Econom. **5**(1), 45–56 (1986)
16. Wüthrich, M.V.: Neural networks applied to chain–ladder reserving. Eur. Actuar. J. **8**(2), 407–436 (2018). October

Estimating System Reliability When Components Follow the Littlewood Model with Imperfect Debugging–Large Sample Properties Using the Counting Process Framework

Marcus A. Agustin[1(✉)], Ma. Zenia N. Agustin[1], and Atwood J. Huff[2]

[1] Southern Illinois University Edwardsville, Edwardsville, IL 62026, USA
{magusti,zagusti}@siue.edu
[2] Accenture, St. Louis, MO, USA
jackson.huff01@gmail.com

Abstract. This paper considers a series system of m software where the failure of each software follows the Littlewood model with imperfect debugging. Upon system failure, the bug responsible for the failure is completely removed with a probability equal to p_j. At the conclusion of a fixed observation and debugging phase, tasks with random completion times are assigned to the system in order to assess system reliability. Estimators of relevant parameters associated with the failure process of each software as well as the system reliability are derived. At the end of a finite testing period, the asymptotic properties of the estimators are established.

Keywords: Competing risks · Maximum likelihood estimation · Software reliability

1 Introduction

Software reliability focuses on quantifying the performance of a software over time through the use of probabilistic or statistical models. Recognizing that software inherently contains errors or bugs, it is subject to failure. Software reliability models are used to analyze failure data in order to facilitate decision making during the testing and debugging stage as well as to predict the software's reliability once it is released for operational use.

One of the earlier models in software reliability is that by [10]. An example of an error counting model in software reliability (see [11]), the failure rate of a software depends on the remaining number of bugs. Given a fixed number of bugs in the software, each of which causes a failure independent of one another, and inter-arrival times of software failures assumed to be exponentially distributed

P. C. Rodrigues et al. (Eds.): ISBIS 2024, 13, pp. 28–38, 2027.
https://doi.org/10.1007/978-3-032-32458-0_3

with a rate that follows a gamma distribution, the resulting density function of the ith inter-arrival time is

$$f(t_i; B, \gamma, \phi) = \frac{(B-(i-1))\phi(\gamma + \sum_{j=1}^{i-1} t_j)^{(B-(i-1))\phi}}{(\gamma + \sum_{j=1}^{i} t_j)^{(B-(i-1))\phi+1}}.$$

The quantity B represents the initial number of bugs while ϕ and γ are the respective scale and shape parameters of the gamma distribution. Estimation of the parameters and resulting reliability have been studied, among others, by [1,5,12,16]. In all these papers, perfect debugging is assumed since the number of bugs decrease by 1 whenever a software failure is observed.

The nature of how a software is improved considers the possibility of not removing a defect during the debugging phase. Hence, it is necessary to look at models that incorporate imperfect debugging in software development. The imperfect debugging of a software with exponential failure times was proposed by [7]. Whenever the software failed, there is a probability p that the bug that caused failure is removed perfectly. [9] extended [7] by considering a probability r of introducing a new bug, with $p > r$. [2] extended the imperfect debugging proposed by [7] by considering a series system of components while [3] considered the probability of bug removal to be a function of time. [13] considered an imperfect debugging scenario for the Littlewood model where the bug that caused failure is removed, but introduced a probability α of adding a bug. Thus, at each observed failure time, the number of remaining bugs decreases by 1 with probability $1 - \alpha$. An imperfect debugging software reliability growth model based on a Non-Homogeneous Poisson Process have been considered by [8,15]. Other papers that dealt with imperfect debugging of a software include [6,14,17], among others.

This paper considers a series system of m components and assumes that component failure times follow the Littlewood model with imperfect debugging. Whenever a component fails, the probability of successfully removing the bug that caused the failure is given by p. When $p = 1$, the series system set-up assuming perfect debugging presented in [1] is obtained. Model description and the process used for obtaining the resulting estimators will be presented in Sect. 2. The large sample properties of the resulting estimators will be examined in Sect. 3. Finally, concluding remarks and possible future directions will be presented in Sect. 4.

2 Model Description

We consider a series system with m components. Let $N_j(t)$ denote the number of observed component j failures by time t and p_j is the fixed probability associated with the successful removal of a defect, for $j = 1, \ldots, m$. The resulting failure time of component j will have a hazard function given by

$$\lambda_j(t; \gamma_j, B_j, \phi_j) = \frac{\phi_j(B_j - p_j N_j(t-))}{\gamma_j + t}, \quad \text{for } j = 1, \ldots, m.$$

Following [12], we set $\phi_j = 1$ resulting in B_j and γ_j to be fixed but unknown parameters. In addition, the system is assigned tasks to be completed with each task completion time having a hazard function $\lambda_0(t;\beta) = \beta$. Thus, if we consider the parameter vector $\boldsymbol{\theta} = (\beta, \gamma_1, \ldots, \gamma_m, B_1, \ldots, B_m)$, and let $N_0(t)$ denote the number of task completions observed by time t, we have the counting process vector $\boldsymbol{N}(t) = (N_0(t), N_1(t), \ldots, N_m(t))$. A univariate counting process $N_j(t)$ depends on observed data up to time t, has a value equal to 0 at $t = 0$, is nondecreasing and piecewise constant with jumps of size 1 at the time of an event of type j. For a counting process vector $\boldsymbol{N}(t) = (N_0(t), N_1(t), \ldots, N_m(t))$, only a single $N_j(t)$ can jump at any time t. The resulting hazard function vector associated with $\boldsymbol{N}(t)$ is given by $\boldsymbol{\lambda}(t;\boldsymbol{\theta}) = (\lambda_0(t;\boldsymbol{\theta}), \lambda_1(t;\boldsymbol{\theta}), \ldots, \lambda_m(t;\boldsymbol{\theta}))$ such that

$$\lambda_j(t;\boldsymbol{\theta}) = \begin{cases} \beta & \text{for } j = 0 \\ \dfrac{B_j - p_j N_j(t-)}{\gamma_j + t} & \text{for } j = 1, \ldots, m \end{cases}. \tag{1}$$

If $\boldsymbol{\theta}^0 = (\beta^0, \gamma_1^0, \ldots, \gamma_m^0, B_1^0, \ldots, B_m^0)$ is the true but unknown value of $\boldsymbol{\theta}$, the process $\boldsymbol{M}(t;\boldsymbol{\theta}^0) = \boldsymbol{N}(t) - \int_0^t \boldsymbol{\lambda}(u;\boldsymbol{\theta}^0)\,\mathrm{d}u$ is a vector of square-integrable martingales. For an extensive discussion on counting processes, the reader is referred to [4].

The log-likelihood function based on data observed on a fixed interval $[0, \tau]$ is

$$\begin{aligned} l_\tau(\boldsymbol{\theta}) = & \int_0^\tau \log\beta\,\mathrm{d}N_0(t) - \int_0^\tau \beta\,\mathrm{dt} \\ & + \sum_{j=1}^m \left[\int_0^\tau \log\left(\frac{B_j - p_j N_j(t-)}{\gamma_j + t}\right) \mathrm{d}N_j(t) - \int_0^\tau \frac{B_j - p_j N_j(t-)}{\gamma_j + t}\,\mathrm{dt} \right], \end{aligned}$$

and the resulting partial derivatives of $l_\tau(\boldsymbol{\theta})$ is the score process $\boldsymbol{U}_\tau(\boldsymbol{\theta}) = \frac{\partial}{\partial\boldsymbol{\theta}} l_\tau(\boldsymbol{\theta})$. By defining the $(1 + 2m) \times (1 + 2m)$ matrix

$$\boldsymbol{H}(u;\boldsymbol{\theta}) = \begin{bmatrix} \frac{1}{\beta} & \mathbf{0} \\ \mathbf{0} & \mathrm{Diag}(\frac{-1}{\gamma_j + u}) \\ \mathbf{0} & \mathrm{Diag}(\frac{1}{B_j - p_j N_j(u-)}) \end{bmatrix} \tag{2}$$

where $\mathrm{Diag}(x_j)$ is a diagonal matrix and x_j is the $(j,j)^{\mathrm{th}}$ diagonal entry, the stochastic integral representation of $\boldsymbol{U}_\tau(\boldsymbol{\theta})$ is

$$\boldsymbol{U}_\tau(\boldsymbol{\theta}) = \int_0^\tau \boldsymbol{H}(u;\boldsymbol{\theta})\,\mathrm{d}\boldsymbol{M}(u;\boldsymbol{\theta}). \tag{3}$$

When (3) is evaluated at $\boldsymbol{\theta} = \boldsymbol{\theta}^0$, we have a vector of square-integrable martingales with predictable covariation process

$$\begin{aligned} <\boldsymbol{U}_{\cdot}(\boldsymbol{\theta}^0), \boldsymbol{U}_{\cdot}(\boldsymbol{\theta}^0)>(\tau) = & \int_0^\tau \boldsymbol{H}(u;\boldsymbol{\theta}^0)\,\mathrm{d} <\boldsymbol{M}(\cdot;\boldsymbol{\theta}^0), \boldsymbol{M}(\cdot;\boldsymbol{\theta}^0)>(u) \\ & \left(\boldsymbol{H}(u;\boldsymbol{\theta}^0)\right)^{\mathrm{t}}, \end{aligned} \tag{4}$$

with $\boldsymbol{x}^{t}$ denoting the transpose of a matrix and

$$< M_j(\cdot;\boldsymbol{\theta}^0), M_k(\cdot;\boldsymbol{\theta}^0) > (t) = \begin{cases} \lambda_j(t;\boldsymbol{\theta}^0) \text{ if } j=k \text{ and } j,k=0,\dots,m \\ 0 \qquad\qquad\qquad \text{otherwise} \end{cases}.$$

Following [1], the system reliability depends on system data observed up to a fixed time τ. At the end of the observation period $[0,\tau]$, the reliability of the system is assessed by randomly selecting a task for the system to complete since in practice, a software is developed to perform specified tasks. The objective is to observe the event that the task is completed prior to the failure of the system. We assume that the task completion time is denoted by the random variable C with hazard function $\lambda_0(t;\beta)=\beta$ and $T=\min(T_1,T_2,\dots,T_m)$ is the time to failure of the system, with T_j is the jth component failure time with hazard function given in (1). The resulting system reliability will be defined as

$$\rho_\tau(\boldsymbol{\theta}) = \mathbf{P}\{C<\min(T_1,\dots,T_m)\} = \int_0^\infty \mathbf{P}\{T>t\}\beta \mathrm{e}^{-\beta t}\mathrm{d}t.$$

After straightforward simplifications, the system reliability as a function of $\boldsymbol{\theta}^0$ is

$$\rho_\tau(\boldsymbol{\theta}^0) = \int_0^\infty \prod_{j=1}^m \left(\frac{\gamma_j^0+\tau+t}{\gamma_j^0+\tau}\right)^{-(B_j^0-p_jN_j(\tau))} \beta^0\mathrm{e}^{-\beta^0 t}\,\mathrm{d}t = g(\boldsymbol{\theta}^0,\boldsymbol{N}_*(\tau)) \quad (5)$$

where $\boldsymbol{N}_*(\tau)=(N_1(\tau),\dots,N_m(\tau))$.

3 Large Sample Properties of the System Reliability Estimator

We examine the large sample properties of the relevant estimators using the framework presented in [1] with the addition of the imperfect debugging scheme that was used in [2]. We consider the nth model hazard function

$$\lambda_j^{(n)}\left(t;\frac{N_j^{(n)}(t-)}{s^{(n)}},\boldsymbol{\theta}\right) = \begin{cases} s^{(n)}\beta & \text{for } j=0 \\ s^{(n)}\left(\dfrac{\alpha_j - p_j\frac{N_j^{(n)}(t-)}{s^{(n)}}}{\gamma_j+t}\right) & \text{for } j=1,\dots,m \end{cases}, \quad (6)$$

where $s^{(n)}$ represents the size of the nth model, with $\gamma_j^{(n)}=\gamma_j$, $B_j^{(n)}=s^{(n)}\alpha_j$, and $\beta^{(n)}=s^{(n)}\beta$. The parameter α_j represents the initial number of bugs per unit size present in component j. The resulting parameter vector is $\boldsymbol{\theta}=(\beta,\gamma_1,\dots,\gamma_m,\alpha_1,\dots,\alpha_m)$. We let $\boldsymbol{\theta}^0=(\beta^0,\gamma_1^0,\dots,\gamma_m^0,\alpha_1^0,\dots,\alpha_m^0)$ be the true value of $\boldsymbol{\theta}$ and the nth process

$$\boldsymbol{M}^{(n)}(t;\boldsymbol{\theta}^0) = \boldsymbol{N}^{(n)}(t) - \int_0^t \boldsymbol{\lambda}^{(n)}\left(u;\frac{\boldsymbol{N}^{(n)}(u-)}{s^{(n)}},\boldsymbol{\theta}^0\right)\mathrm{d}u$$

is a vector of square-integrable martingales.

We will now establish the convergence in probability and large sample distribution of a solution to the equation $\boldsymbol{U}_\tau(\boldsymbol{\theta}) = \mathbf{0}$. The maximum likelihood estimator (MLE) of the parameter vector $\boldsymbol{\theta}$ is denoted by $\hat{\boldsymbol{\theta}}$. Let $U_\tau^k(\boldsymbol{\theta}) = \frac{\partial}{\partial \theta_k} l_\tau(\boldsymbol{\theta})$, $\mathcal{I}_\tau^{ki}(\boldsymbol{\theta}) = \frac{\partial}{\partial \theta_i} U_\tau^k(\boldsymbol{\theta})$, $\mathcal{R}_\tau^{kil}(\boldsymbol{\theta}) = \frac{\partial}{\partial \theta_l} \mathcal{I}_\tau^{ki}(\boldsymbol{\theta})$, and

$$\boldsymbol{\Sigma}^0(\tau) = \begin{bmatrix} \Sigma_1^0(\tau) & \mathbf{0} & \mathbf{0} \\ \mathbf{0} & \boldsymbol{\Sigma}_2^0(\tau) & \boldsymbol{\Sigma}_3^0(\tau) \\ \mathbf{0} & \boldsymbol{\Sigma}_3^0(\tau) & \boldsymbol{\Sigma}_4^0(\tau) \end{bmatrix}, \tag{7}$$

where $\Sigma_1^0(\tau) = \frac{\tau}{\beta^0}$ and $\boldsymbol{\Sigma}_2^0(\tau)$, $\boldsymbol{\Sigma}_3^0(\tau)$, and $\boldsymbol{\Sigma}_4^0(\tau)$ are $m \times m$ diagonal matrices with respective i^{th} diagonal entries

$$\sigma_{2,i}^0(\tau) = \frac{\alpha_i^0(\gamma_i^0)^{p_i}}{p_i+2}\left[\left(\frac{1}{\gamma_i^0}\right)^{p_i+2} - \left(\frac{1}{\gamma_i^0+\tau}\right)^{p_i+2}\right],$$
$$\sigma_{3,i}^0(\tau) = \frac{\tau}{\gamma_i^0(\gamma_i^0+\tau)},$$
$$\sigma_{4,i}^0(\tau) = \frac{1}{\alpha_i^0 p_i}\left[\left(\frac{\gamma_i^0+\tau}{\gamma_i^0}\right)^{p_i+2} - 1\right].$$

The existence of an MLE $\hat{\boldsymbol{\theta}}$ that converges in probability to $\boldsymbol{\theta}^0$ will follow if the following convergence in probability holds:

$$\frac{1}{s^{(n)}} U_\tau^k(\boldsymbol{\theta}^0) \xrightarrow{\text{pr}} 0, \tag{8}$$

$$\frac{1}{s^{(n)}} \mathcal{I}_\tau^{ki}(\boldsymbol{\theta}^0) \xrightarrow{\text{pr}} -\sigma_{ki}(\boldsymbol{\theta}^0), \tag{9}$$

$$\mathcal{R}_\tau^{kil}(\boldsymbol{\theta}^0) \xrightarrow{\text{pr}} \text{finite quantity}. \tag{10}$$

To show (8), we establish

$$\frac{1}{s^{(n)}} < U_\cdot^k(\boldsymbol{\theta}^0), U_\cdot^k(\boldsymbol{\theta}^0) > (\tau) \xrightarrow{\text{pr}} \sigma_{k,k}^0(\tau)$$

by using the result

$$\frac{N_j^{(n)}(t)}{s^{(n)}} \xrightarrow{\text{pr}} X_j(t;\boldsymbol{\theta}^0) = \begin{cases} \beta^0 t & \text{if } j = 0 \\ \left(\frac{\alpha_j^0}{p_j}\right)\left(1 - \left(\frac{\gamma_j^0}{\gamma_j^0+t}\right)^{p_j}\right) & \text{if } j = 1,\ldots,m \end{cases} \tag{11}$$

and then applying Lenglart's Inequality (see [4]). Since

$$\frac{1}{s^{(n)}}\mathcal{I}_\tau^{ki}(\boldsymbol{\theta}^0) = \frac{1}{s^{(n)}}\left[\int_0^\tau \sum_{j=0}^m \frac{\partial^2}{\partial\theta_i\partial\theta_k}\log\lambda_j^{(n)}\left(t;\frac{N_j^{(n)}(t-)}{s^{(n)}},\boldsymbol{\theta}^0\right)\mathrm{d}M_j^{(n)}(t;\boldsymbol{\theta}^0)\right.$$
$$-\int_0^\tau \sum_{j=0}^m \left(\frac{\partial}{\partial\theta_k}\log\lambda_j^{(n)}\left(t;\frac{N_j^{(n)}(t-)}{s^{(n)}}\boldsymbol{\theta}^0\right)\right)$$
$$\left.\left(\frac{\partial}{\partial\theta_i}\log\lambda_j^{(n)}\left(t;\frac{N_j^{(n)}(t-)}{s^{(n)}},\boldsymbol{\theta}^0\right)\right)\lambda_j^{(n)}\left(t;\frac{N_j^{(n)}(t-)}{s^{(n)}},\boldsymbol{\theta}^0\right)\mathrm{d}t\right],$$

another application of (11) and Lenglart's Inequality establishes (9). Furthermore, evaluating the third partial derivative of $\log\lambda_j^{(n)}(t;\boldsymbol{\theta})$ and $\lambda_j^{(n)}(t;\boldsymbol{\theta})$, it can be shown that $\left|\frac{1}{s^{(n)}}\mathcal{R}_\tau^{kil}(\boldsymbol{\theta}^0)\right|$ is bounded by a finite quantity by using (11) and the Martingale Central Limit Theorem (see [4]).

In order to examine the asymptotic distribution of the consistent estimator of $\boldsymbol{\theta}^0$, we establish the following:

$$\frac{1}{\sqrt{s^{(n)}}}\boldsymbol{U}_\tau(\boldsymbol{\theta}^0) \xrightarrow{\mathrm{d}} \boldsymbol{N}_{2m+1}(\boldsymbol{0},\boldsymbol{\Sigma}^0(\tau)), \tag{12}$$

$$\frac{1}{s^{(n)}}\mathcal{I}_\tau^{ki}(\boldsymbol{\theta}^*) \xrightarrow{\mathrm{pr}} -\sigma_{ki}(\boldsymbol{\theta}^0) \tag{13}$$

for a vector $\boldsymbol{\theta}^* \xrightarrow{\mathrm{pr}} \boldsymbol{\theta}^0$. Since $\frac{1}{\sqrt{s^{(n)}}}U_\tau^k(\boldsymbol{\theta}^0)$ is a local square-integrable martingale with predictable variation process given in (4), the proof of (9) will be extended to establish the convergence in probability of $< \frac{1}{\sqrt{s^{(n)}}}U_\cdot^k(\boldsymbol{\theta}^0), \frac{1}{\sqrt{s^{(n)}}}U_\cdot^k(\boldsymbol{\theta}^0) > (\tau)$ to $-\sigma_{ki}(\boldsymbol{\theta}^0)$. In addition, we can show, for $\epsilon > 0$, the convergence in probability to 0 of $< U_\cdot^{k\epsilon}(\boldsymbol{\theta}^0), U_\cdot^{k\epsilon}(\boldsymbol{\theta}^0) > (\tau)$ where

$$U_\tau^{k\epsilon}(\boldsymbol{\theta}^0) = \frac{1}{\sqrt{s^{(n)}}}\left(\int_0^\tau \sum_{j=0}^m \left(\frac{\partial}{\partial\theta_k}\log\lambda_j^{(n)}\left(t;\frac{N_j^{(n)}(t-)}{s^{(n)}},\boldsymbol{\theta}\right)\right)\right.$$
$$I\left\{\left|\frac{1}{\sqrt{s^{(n)}}}\left(\frac{\partial}{\partial\theta_k}\log\lambda_j^{(n)}\left(t;\frac{N_j^{(n)}(t-)}{s^{(n)}},\boldsymbol{\theta}\right)\right)\right| > \epsilon\right\}$$
$$\left.\mathrm{d}M_j^{(n)}(t;\boldsymbol{\theta})\right)\Big|_{\boldsymbol{\theta}=\boldsymbol{\theta}^0}$$

by using (11). Hence, (12) is established after applying the Martingale Central Limit Theorem. Finally, taking a Taylor series expansion of $\mathcal{I}_\tau^{ki}(\boldsymbol{\theta}^*)$ at $\boldsymbol{\theta}^0$ and using similar arguments to establish (9) and (10), we obtain (13). We have established the following theorem.

Theorem 1. *Consider m components with n^{th} hazard function $\lambda_j^{(n)}(t;\boldsymbol{\theta})$ for $j=1,\ldots,m$ and n^{th} hazard function of the task completion times given in (6). Consider the $(2m+1)\times(2m+1)$ matrix $\boldsymbol{\Sigma}^0(\tau)$ given in (7). Then as $s^{(n)}\rightarrow\infty$, there exists $\hat{\boldsymbol{\theta}}$ that is a solution to $\boldsymbol{U}_\tau(\boldsymbol{\theta})=\boldsymbol{0}$ such that $\hat{\boldsymbol{\theta}}\xrightarrow{\text{pr}}\boldsymbol{\theta}^0$. Furthermore, $\sqrt{s^{(n)}}(\hat{\boldsymbol{\theta}}-\boldsymbol{\theta}^0)\xrightarrow{\text{d}}\boldsymbol{N}_{2m+1}(\boldsymbol{0},(\boldsymbol{\Sigma}^0(\tau))^{-1})$.*

It is of interest to examine the asymptotic properties of the system reliability estimator. Replacing $\boldsymbol{\theta}^0$ in (5) by $\hat{\boldsymbol{\theta}}$, an estimator of $\rho_\tau(\boldsymbol{\theta}^0)$ is

$$\hat{\rho}_\tau=\int_0^\infty\prod_{j=1}^m\left(\frac{\hat{\gamma}_j+\tau+t}{\hat{\gamma}_j+\tau}\right)^{-s^{(n)}\left(\hat{\alpha}_j-p_j\frac{N_j^{(n)}(\tau)}{s^{(n)}}\right)}\hat{\beta}\mathrm{e}^{-\hat{\beta}t}\,\mathrm{d}t=g(\hat{\boldsymbol{Q}}_\tau^{(n)})\tag{14}$$

where $\hat{\boldsymbol{Q}}_\tau^{(n)}=\left(\hat{\boldsymbol{\theta}},\frac{\boldsymbol{N}_*^{(n)}(\tau)}{s^{(n)}}\right)$. Let $\boldsymbol{Q}_\tau^0=(\boldsymbol{\theta}^0,\boldsymbol{X}_*^0(\tau))=(\boldsymbol{\theta}^0,X_1^0(\tau),\ldots,X_m^0(\tau))$ where $X_j^0(\tau)=\left(\frac{\alpha_j^0}{p_j}\right)\left(1-\left(\frac{\gamma_j^0}{\gamma_j^0+\tau}\right)^{p_j}\right)$ for $j=1,\ldots,m$. Extending (3) and (11), we get the following stochastic integral representation of $\boldsymbol{W}_\tau(\boldsymbol{\theta}^0)=\sqrt{s^{(n)}}(\hat{\boldsymbol{Q}}_\tau^{(n)}-\boldsymbol{Q}_\tau^0)$ given by

$$\sqrt{s^{(n)}}(\hat{\boldsymbol{Q}}_\tau^{(n)}-\boldsymbol{Q}_\tau^0)=\begin{bmatrix}(\boldsymbol{\Sigma}^0(\tau))^{-1} & \boldsymbol{0}\\ \boldsymbol{0} & \mathrm{Diag}(b_j^0(\tau)^{-1})\end{bmatrix}$$
$$\frac{1}{s^{(n)}}\int_0^\tau\begin{bmatrix}\boldsymbol{H}^{(n)}(u;\boldsymbol{\theta}^0)\\ \boldsymbol{H}_*^{(n)}(u;\boldsymbol{\theta}^0)\end{bmatrix}\mathrm{d}\boldsymbol{M}^{(n)}(u;\boldsymbol{\theta}^0),$$

where $b_j^0(\tau)=(\gamma_j^0+\tau)^{p_j}$, for $j=1,\ldots m$, $\boldsymbol{H}_*^{(n)}(u;\boldsymbol{\theta}^0)=\left[\boldsymbol{0}\ \mathrm{Diag}(b_j^0(\tau))\right]$, and $\boldsymbol{H}^{(n)}(u;\boldsymbol{\theta}^0)$ is given in (2). The convergence of the predictable covariation process $<\boldsymbol{W}_\cdot(\boldsymbol{\theta}^0),\boldsymbol{W}_\cdot(\boldsymbol{\theta}^0)>(\tau)$ is established by using (11), Lenglart's Inequality, and extending the result on the convergence in probability of $\hat{\boldsymbol{\theta}}$ to $\boldsymbol{\theta}^0$ (see Theorem 1). Extending the proof of the convergence in probability of $\hat{\boldsymbol{\theta}}$, we establish $\hat{\boldsymbol{Q}}_\tau^{(n)}\xrightarrow{\text{pr}}\boldsymbol{Q}_\tau^0$, and by the Martingale Central Limit Theorem,

$$\boldsymbol{W}_\tau(\boldsymbol{\theta}^0)=\sqrt{s^{(n)}}(\hat{\boldsymbol{Q}}_\tau^{(n)}-\boldsymbol{Q}_\tau^0)\xrightarrow{\text{d}}\boldsymbol{N}_{3m+1}(\boldsymbol{0},\boldsymbol{\Psi}^0(\tau))\tag{15}$$

where $\boldsymbol{\Psi}^0(\tau)=\begin{bmatrix}\boldsymbol{\Psi}_1^0(\tau) & (\boldsymbol{\Psi}_2^0(\tau))^{\mathrm{t}}\\ \boldsymbol{\Psi}_2^0(\tau) & \boldsymbol{\Psi}_3^0(\tau)\end{bmatrix}$ is a $(1+3m)\times(1+3m)$ matrix with entries

$$\boldsymbol{\Psi}_1^0(\tau)=(\boldsymbol{\Sigma}^0(\tau))^{-1},$$
$$\boldsymbol{\Psi}_2^0(\tau)=\left[\boldsymbol{0}\ \ \Psi_{22}^0(\tau)\ \ \Psi_{23}^0(\tau)\right](\boldsymbol{\Sigma}^0(\tau))^{-1},$$
$$\boldsymbol{\Psi}_3^0(\tau)=\mathrm{Diag}\left(\frac{\alpha_j^0}{p_j}\left(\frac{\gamma_j^0}{\gamma_j^0+\tau}\right)^{p_j}\left(1-\left(\frac{\gamma_j^0}{\gamma_j^0+\tau}\right)\right)\right).$$

The quantities $\Psi_{22}^0(\tau)$ and $\Psi_{23}^0(\tau)$ are given by

$$\Psi_{22}^0(\tau) = \mathrm{Diag}\left(\left(\frac{-\alpha_j^0\tau}{\gamma_j^0(\gamma_j^0+\tau)}\right)\left(\frac{\gamma_j^0}{\gamma_j^0+\tau}\right)^{p_j}\right)$$
$$\Psi_{23}^0(\tau) = \mathrm{Diag}\left(\frac{1}{p_j}\left(1-\left(\frac{\gamma_j^0}{\gamma_j^0+\tau}\right)^{p_j}\right)\right).$$

From (14), we obtain the $(3m+1)\times 1$ matrix of partial derivatives of $g(\boldsymbol{x})$ with respect to $\boldsymbol{x}$ and evaluated at $\boldsymbol{x} = \boldsymbol{Q}_\tau^0$. In addition, let $\rho_\tau^0 = g(\boldsymbol{Q}_\tau^0)$. Thus, using (15) and the multivariate δ-method (see [4]). the following theorem is established.

Theorem 2. *Suppose $\hat{\boldsymbol{\theta}}_\tau$ is the consistent estimator of $\boldsymbol{\theta}^0$ obtained from Theorem 1. Let $\boldsymbol{D}_g^0 = \left(\left.\frac{\partial g}{\partial \boldsymbol{x}}\right|_{\boldsymbol{x}=\boldsymbol{Q}_\tau^0}\right)$ be the $(3m+1)\times 1$ matrix of partial derivatives of g evaluated at $\boldsymbol{Q}_\tau^0$. Then, as $n\to\infty$, $\hat{\rho}_\tau \xrightarrow{\text{pr}} \rho_\tau^0$, and*

$$\sqrt{s^{(n)}}(\hat{\rho}_\tau - \rho_\tau^0) \xrightarrow{\text{d}} N(0, \sigma_\tau^2(\boldsymbol{\theta}^0)), \tag{16}$$

where $\sigma_\tau^2(\boldsymbol{\theta}^0) = (\boldsymbol{D}_g^0)^{\text{t}}\boldsymbol{\Psi}^0(\tau)\boldsymbol{D}_g^0$.

To provide an illustration of the behavior of the system reliability estimator as indicated in Theorem 2, a simulation study was conducted. We arbitrarily considered a system with $m = 3$ components, a fixed testing time of $\tau = 50$, and a probability of perfect repair $p_j = 0.95, j = 1,2,3$. Furthermore, we examine arbitrary values of the parameter vector $\boldsymbol{\theta}^0 = (\beta^0, \gamma_1^0, \gamma_2^0, \gamma_3^0, B_1^0, B_2^0, B_3^0)$ and system size $s^{(n)}$. Recall that the effect of the size on the initial number of bugs for component j and the completion time parameter are $B_j = s^{(n)}\alpha_j^0$ and $\beta = s^{(n)}\beta^0$, respectively.

For the case $\boldsymbol{\theta}^0 = (1, 10, 10, 10, 25, 25, 25)$, we present simulation results for system sizes $s^{(n)} = 10, 15$. For $s^{(n)} = 10$, the histogram and normal probability plots are presented in Figs. 1 and 2, respectively. Note that the distribution of the estimated system reliability seems close to a normal distribution except possibly at the tails. The mean of the estimated system reliabilities came out to be 0.81456.

Figures 3 and 4 correspond to the histogram and normal probability plot, respectively, when $s^{(n)} = 15$. The histogram shows a roughly symmetric distribution similar to the case when $s^{(n)} = 10$. The quantiles of the estimated system reliability agree with the theoretical quantiles of a normal distribution. The mean of the estimated system reliabilities is 0.81432. The results for system sizes bigger than 15 were not much different from those at $s^{(n)} = 15$, suggesting that the normal approximation is acceptable at system size as small as 15.

4 Concluding Remarks and Future Directions

In this paper, we considered the estimation of the system reliability of a series system of m components at the end of a fixed testing period. Each

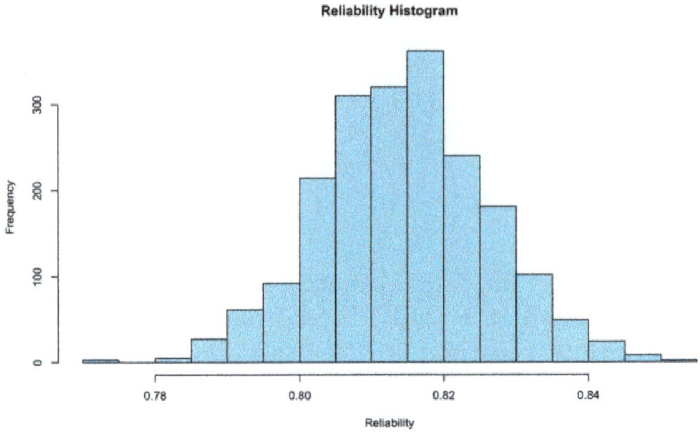

Fig. 1. Histogram of system reliability estimator, $\hat{\rho}_T$, for $\boldsymbol{\theta}^0 = (1, 10, 10, 10, 25, 25, 25)$ and $s^{(n)} = 10$

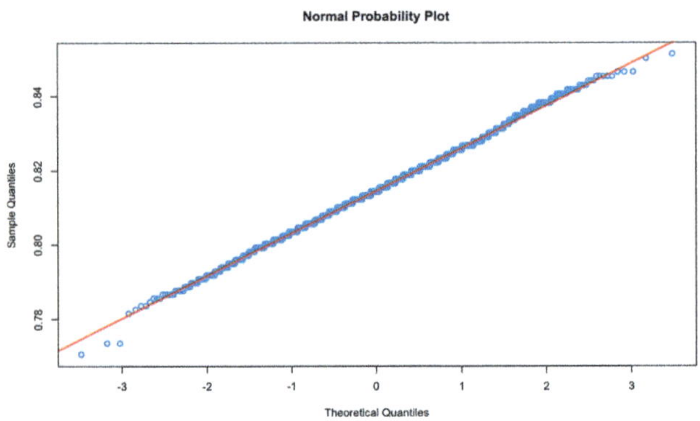

Fig. 2. Normal probability plot of system reliability estimator, $\hat{\rho}_T$, for $\boldsymbol{\theta}^0 = (1, 10, 10, 10, 25, 25, 25)$ and $s^{(n)} = 10$

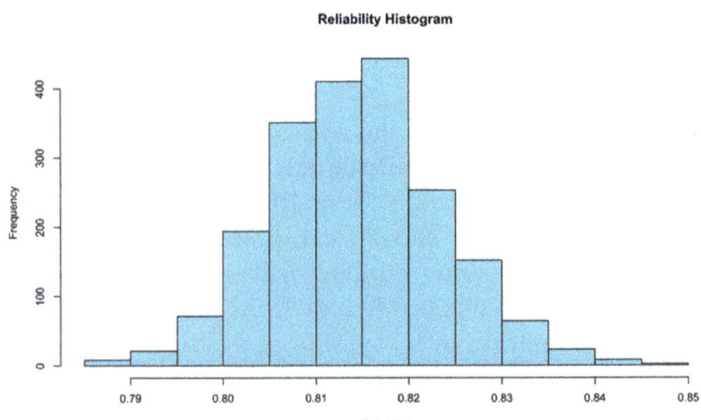

Fig. 3. Histogram of system reliability estimator, $\hat{\rho}_T$, for $\boldsymbol{\theta}^0 = (1, 10, 10, 10, 25, 25, 25)$ and $s^{(n)} = 15$

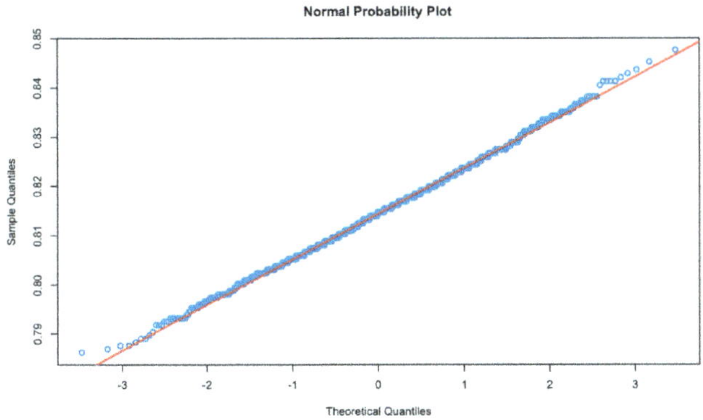

Fig. 4. Normal probability plot of system reliability estimator, $\hat{\rho}_{\mathcal{T}}$, for $\boldsymbol{\theta}^0 = (1, 10, 10, 10, 25, 25, 25)$ and $s^{(n)} = 15$

component failure time is assumed to follow the Littlewood model and at each failure, the defect that caused the failure is successfully removed with probability $p, 0 < p \leq 1$. At the end of a fixed testing period, a randomly selected task is assigned to the system and system reliability is defined to be the probability that task completion occurs before system failure is observed. Asymptotic properties of the system reliability estimator were derived using the counting process framework, and a simulation example was presented to illustrate the behavior of the system reliability estimator for even a small value of the system size.

A natural extension to the model considered in this paper involves a more general imperfect debugging scenario where it is possible to introduce a new defect with some fixed probability. Taking the probabilities of successful defect removal and new defect introduction to be functions of time will also be plausible. Building on the results presented in this paper, there is ongoing work that addresses the choice of an optimal stopping time for the testing or debugging phase. Another extension to the paper is to examine the finite sample properties of the system reliability estimator, both for the fixed testing period scenario and that which considers a stopping time to the testing.

References

1. Agustin, M.: Statistical properties of a system reliability estimator using the Littlewood software reliability model. J. Appl. Probab. **40**, 766–778 (2003)
2. Agustin, M., Agustin, Z.: Asymptotic properties of a system reliability estimator under an imperfect debugging model. J. Probab. Stat. Sci. **12**, 1–14 (2014)
3. Agustin, M., Agustin, Z., Thompson, N.: A system reliability estimator for imperfect debugging models and its large-sample properties. J. Appl. Probab. Stat. **16**, 19–36 (2021)
4. Andersen, P., Borgan, Ø., Gill, R., Keiding, N.: Statistical Models Based on Counting Processes. Springer-Verlag, New York (1993)

5. Barendregt, L.G., van Pul, M.C.: On the estimation of the parameters for the Littlewood model in software reliability. Stat. Neerl. **49**, 165–184 (1995)
6. Chatterjee, S., Shukla, A.: Software reliability modeling with different type of faults incorporating both imperfect debugging and change point. In: 4th International Conference on Reliability, Infocom Technologies and Optimization (ICRITO 2014) (Trends and Future Directions (2015)
7. Goel, A.: Software reliability models: assumption, limitations, and applicability. IEEE Trans. Software Eng. **11**, 1411–1423 (1985)
8. Huang, Y, Chiu, K., and Chen, W.: A software reliability growth model for imperfect debugging. J. Syst. Softw. **188**, 111267 (2022)
9. Kaswan, K.S., Choudhary, S., Singh, S.P., Pise, A.A., and Hinga, S.K.: A new variant of JM software reliability model. Sci. Program. 7257564 (2022)
10. Littlewood, B.: Theories of software reliability: how good are they and how can they be improved? IEEE Trans. Software Eng. **6**, 489–500 (1980)
11. Mazzuchi, T., Singpurwalla, N.: Software Reliability Models. In: Krishnaia, P.R., Rao, C.R. (eds.) Handbook of Statistics, vol. 7, pp. 73–98. Elsevier Science Publishers B.V, New York (1988)
12. Moek, G.: Comparison of some software reliability models for simulated and real failure data. Int. J. Model. Simul. **4**, 29–41 (1984)
13. Ohba, M., Chou, X.M.: Does imperfect debugging affect software reliability growth?. In: ICSE '89: Proceeding of the 11th International Conference on Software Engineering, pp. 237-244 (1989)
14. Rani, P., Mahapatra, G.S.: A single change point hazard rate software reliability model with imperfect debugging. In: 13th Annual IEEE International Systems Conference (2019)
15. Saraf, I., Iqbal, J.: Generalized multi-release modelling of software reliability growth models from the perspective of two types of imperfect debugging and change point. Qual. Reliab. Eng. Int. **35**, 2358–2370 (2019)
16. Tantri, B.P., Murulidhar, N.N.: Estimation of software reliability for Littlewood pareto failure time model. Int. J. Softw. Eng. Its Appl. **11**, 25–34 (2017)
17. Wang, J.: An imperfect software debugging model considering irregular fluctuation of fault introduction rate. Qual. Eng. **29**, 377–394 (2017)

Climate Change Adaptation Insurance for Farmers Based on the Index Harvest Area (IHA)

Silvina Rosita Yulianti, Adhitya Ronnie Effendie(✉), and Nanang Susyanto

Department of Mathematics, Universitas Gadjah Mada, Sekip Utara Bulaksumur, Yogyakarta 55598, Indonesia
adhityaronnie@ugm.ac.id

Abstract. The current uncertain climate changes significantly impact various sectors of life, particularly agriculture, creating uncertainty for multiple stakeholders in predicting agricultural productivity and maintaining economic stability in the agricultural sector. One crucial metric influencing agricultural productivity is the agricultural harvested area. This study proposes agricultural insurance based on the Index Harvest Area (IHA), which divides the agricultural harvest area by the agricultural land area, to mitigate the risk of loss. Generally, IHA determines the indemnity, which determines the present value, which is used to calculate the premium by dividing the PV by the deductible and multiplying by one index price. The objective of this study is to reduce the likelihood of disastrous crop failures that are experienced by farmers. Geographically Weighted Regression (GWR), forecasting, and pricing are some of the strategies that are used in this particular piece of scholarship. The use of GWR is intended to analyze the condition of each area based on its geographical characteristics so that the model obtained can reflect the actual conditions based on each region. In addition, ARIMAX is used for forecasting, taking into account geographical factors. Then the forecast results are used to calculate the premium. This method also aims to align the analysis of future IHA value forecasts in premium calculations with the IHA model with GWR, which is used to determine the amount of compensation received. This study uses secondary data, especially agricultural harvest area and agricultural land area, obtained from the Central Statistics Agency of Central Java Province.

Keywords: Agricultural · Climate change · Risk · Insurance · Index Harvest Area (IHA)

P. C. Rodrigues et al. (Eds.): ISBIS 2024, 13, pp. 39–54, 2027.
https://doi.org/10.1007/978-3-032-32458-0_4

1 Introduction

Agricultural insurance helps policyholders reduce the risk of loss due to suboptimal agricultural yields. Various countries, especially those where agriculture is a crucial sector, have widely implemented this type of insurance. Agricultural insurance is very popular and is undergoing a lot of development. In each country that implements agricultural insurance, there are different regulations according to the circumstances of each country, and the management system is also in accordance with the policies of the country concerned. Some of the countries that have implemented agricultural insurance are Malaysia [1], Brazil [4], Nigeria [6], Nepal [7], Ghana [13], Rwanda [16], and India [17]. The study in Malaysia involved conducting a primary survey with 320 farmers at IADA, Selangor, and conducting a literature review. Variables included participation in crop insurance and risk management strategies, with socio-demographic factors, perceptions of insurance, and economic motivation as independent variables[1]. In Brazil, a primary survey approach and logit regression model were used to analyze insurance adoption, with variables such as education, experience, risk propensity, and farm size as determinants of adoption [4]. In Nigeria, a secondary data-based study using the Ordinary Least Squares (OLS) method measured the effect of insurance claims and insurance reserves on credit volume in the food and livestock sector [6]. Meanwhile, in Nepal, data were obtained through questionnaires from farmers in Kaski and Chitwan districts, focusing on farmers' awareness and perceptions of insurance, with demographics and claims as the main variables [7]. In Ghana, a farmer survey and regression analysis were used to assess factors influencing willingness to pay for insurance, with variables such as farmer demographics, type of insurance product, and insurance awareness being the focus [13]. In Rwanda, a descriptive and correlational study using multiple linear regression examined the relationship between agricultural insurance and farmer performance, measured by production, income, and savings [16]. Additionally, in India, the study used content analysis of secondary literature, focusing on the evolution of insurance schemes, performance indicators, and accessibility challenges to agricultural insurance [17]. Currently, Indonesia only offers rice farming insurance. Since its inception in 2015, the government has directly managed this type of insurance in collaboration with PT. Jasa Asuransi Indonesia (Jasindo). Like agricultural insurance that applies in other countries, AUTP in Indonesia also has several rules in its insurance policy, including:

1. AUTP participants may only insure their land for a maximum of 2 hectares.
2. The AUTP premium is set at an insurance premium rate of 3% of the insured value; the insured value is IDR. 6,000,000.00/hectare/planting season, and the insurance premium is worth IDR 180,000.00/hectare/planting season, as well as premium assistance sourced from the Anggaran Pendapatan dan Belanja Negara (APBN) amounting to 80%, or IDR 144,000.00/hectare/planting season, and farmers only need to pay a premium of 20%, or IDR 36,000.00/hectare/planting season.

3. Types of risks that can be insured or claims made include drought, floods, and attacks by Plant Destruction Organisms, which are organisms that can disturb, harm, and ultimately kill plants.
4. The insurance coverage period is valid for a single planting season.
5. Farmers will receive compensation of IDR 6,000,000.00 if and only if they can harvest a maximum of 25% of the planted area.

The exact formula for calculating the set premium in AUTP remains unknown. Numerous studies have explored the mechanism, evaluation, and calculation of premiums, including their formulation, for example: [2,8,11,12,15, 19]. In its research, no study has taken weather factors, geographical location, harvest area, and rice field area into account simultaneously. In fact, weather factors also influence agriculture's success, as in[3,10,14,20]. The weather factors referred to include rainfall, air humidity, wind speed, duration of sunlight, air pressure, and others. Good and favorable weather will produce agricultural results, and vice versa. Likewise, geographical location will also affect agricultural results because a strategic geographic location will, of course, have stable and good weather for the growth of agricultural plants.

Furthermore, one indicator of the success of the agricultural sector is the Index Harvest Area (IHA), which is the result of dividing the harvested area by the planted area. On this study, we will conduct this premium calculation analysis using IHA, examining weather factors and an area's geographical location. We chose IHA as a consideration variable to determine the premium because it accurately displays the harvest and rice field areas, making it a good indicator of the agricultural sector's success. The methods used in the analysis include Geographically Weighted Regression (GWR), Autoregressive Integrated Moving Average with Exogenous Variable (ARIMAX), and Forecasting. We used secondary data from the Meteorology, Climatology, and Geophysical Agency (BMKG) and the Central Statistics Agency (BPS). The aim of this research is to obtain new results in calculating agricultural insurance premiums. The obtained results serve as recommendations for customizing premium setting policies to meet specific needs.

This study organizes the remaining sections as follows: Sect. 2 will elaborate on several topics. The first is the GWR Model, which includes the model specifications and methods used for data analysis when incorporating new information into an existing model using a fixed Gaussian kernel. Next, what will be discussed is the ARIMAX model, which includes assumptions, models, methods, and selecting the best model for forecasting. Next, Sect. 3 will thereafter provide a more thorough description of the data used, the application of the model, and an overall analysis of the outcomes. The conclusion and policy recommendations for the government to administer better agricultural insurance, in this case, AUTP in Indonesia are finally provided in Sect. 4.

2 Material and Method

This study will analyze secondary time series data from 35 districts/cities in Central Java between 2018 and 2022, including the harvest area, rice field area, rainfall, air humidity, duration of sunlight, area height, longitude, and latitude. The geographic information data taken is daily data, which is then aggregated into monthly data to adjust agricultural data. This data was taken from open source data from the Central Java Province Central Statistics Agency (BPS) (https://jateng.bps.go.id) and the Meteorology, Climatology, and Geophysics Agency (BMKG) (https://dataonline.bmkg.go.id). Furthermore, we will use statistical methods such as GWR, ARIMAX for forecasting, and premium calculations in our analysis of the obtained data.

2.1 Geographically Weighted Regression (GWR)

GWR is one of the methods used to explore nonstationary spatial space. This method refers to the nature and significant relationships between variables that vary from one location to another. The parameters for the regression model at each location will produce different values. Eq. (1) expresses the GWR model [9] as follows:

$$y_i = \beta_0 (u_i, v_i) + \sum_{k=1}^{p} \beta_k (u_i, v_i) x_{ik} + \varepsilon_i, i = 1, 2, \ldots, n \tag{1}$$

where y_i explains the observed value of the ith dependent variable, x_{ik} explains the observation value of the ith independent variable k at the ith observation location, and the variables i and k indicate the number of observation locations and independent variables, respectively. Next $\beta_0 (u_i, v_i)$ represents the intercept at the ith observation, (u_i, v_i) denotes the longitude and latitude of the ith observation location, $\beta_k (u_i, v_i)$ indicate the observed value of the kth independent variable at the ith observation location i, and ε_i represent the error in the ith observation.

When putting the GWR model to the test, data that are seen close to point i has a greater impact on the predicted parameters than data that is further away. The close association between the model and the point i may be quantified using Eq. (1), allowing for the estimation of the parameters of the GWR model by assigning weights to each observation based on how near the point i is. This estimating technique is known as the Weighted Least Square (WLS) approach, and it works by assigning a different weight to each observation based on its position. Suppose the weighting for each i-th location is $w_j(u_i, v_i), j = 1, 2, \cdots, n$, then the parameters at location (u_i, v_i) are estimated by adding the weighting element $w_j(u_i, v_i)$ and then minimize the number of squared errors presented in Eq. (2):

$$\sum_{j=1}^{n} w_j(u_i, v_i)\varepsilon_j^2 = \sum_{j=1}^{n} w_j(u_i, v_i)[y_j - \beta_0(u_i, v_i) - \beta_1(u_i, v_i)x_{j1} - \cdots - \beta_p(u_i, v_i)x_{jp}]^2 \tag{2}$$

Let

$$X_{n\times(p+1)} = \begin{pmatrix} 1 & x_{11} & x_{12} & \cdots & x_{1p} \\ 1 & x_{21} & x_{22} & \cdots & x_{2p} \\ \vdots & \vdots & \vdots & \ddots & \vdots \\ 1 & x_{n1} & x_{n2} & \cdots & x_{np} \end{pmatrix}, \quad Y_{n\times 1} = \begin{pmatrix} y_1 \\ y_2 \\ \vdots \\ y_n \end{pmatrix}$$

$$\beta(u_i, v_i)_{(p+1)\times 1} = \begin{pmatrix} \beta_0(u_i, v_i) \\ \beta_1(u_i, v_i) \\ \vdots \\ \beta_p(u_i, v_i) \end{pmatrix}$$

And it has the GWR equation in matrix form which can be written as in Eqs. (3) (4), and (5).

$$Y = X\beta \tag{3}$$

$$W(u_i, v_i) = diag[w_1(u_i, v_i), w_2(u_i, v_i), \cdots, w_n(u_i, v_i)] \tag{4}$$

$$\varepsilon = (\varepsilon_1, \varepsilon_2, \cdots, \varepsilon_n)^T \tag{5}$$

and the estimated parameters of the GWR model for each location can be written as in Eq. (6).

$$\hat{\beta}(u_i, v_i) = (X^T W(u_i, v_i)X)^{-1} X^T W(u_i, v_i)Y. \tag{6}$$

Because there are n sample locations, this estimate is an estimate for each row of the local matrix of parameters for all research locations, given in Eq. (7).

$$\beta = \begin{pmatrix} \beta_0(u_1, v_1) & \beta_1(u_1, v_1) & \beta_2(u_1, v_1) & \cdots & \beta_p(u_1, v_1) \\ \beta_0(u_2, v_2) & \beta_1(u_2, v_2) & \beta_2(u_2, v_2) & \cdots & \beta_p(u_2, v_2) \\ \vdots & \vdots & \vdots & \ddots & \cdots \\ \beta_0(u_n, v_n) & \beta_1(u_n, v_n) & \beta_2(u_n, v_n) & \cdots & \beta_p(u_n, v_n) \end{pmatrix} \tag{7}$$

If the distance function in GWR is continuous and monotonically decreasing, we can use the kernel function to estimate the model's parameters. The weighting formed using this kernel function is a Gaussian distance function, which can be expressed as in the Eq. (8).

$$w_j(u_i, v_j) = \phi(d_{ij}/\sigma h) \tag{8}$$

where ϕ is the standard normal density and σ shows the standard deviation of the distance vector d_{ij}, which can be written as in Eq. (9).

$$d_i j = \sqrt{(u_i - u_j)^2 + (v_i - v_j)^2} \tag{9}$$

Furthermore, the variable h is a known smoothing parameter (bandwidth) and has a non-negative value. There are several methods used to select the optimum bandwidth, one of which is the Cross Validation (CV) method, which can be written mathematically as in the Eq. (10).

$$CV = \sum_{i=1}^{n} \left(y_i - \hat{y}_{\neq i}(h)\right)^2 \tag{10}$$

where $\hat{y}_{\neq i}(h)$ is the estimator value y_i, observations at location (u_i, v_i) are removed in the estimation process. Next, to get the optimal bandwidth value, the minimum CV is selected.

2.2 Moving Average with Exogenous Variable (ARIMAX)

One of the methods used in time series data analysis is the ARIMA model. This model can be used to predict future values using historical data. However, during forecasting, several other variables may influence the model, leading to suboptimal future accuracy values. The existence of variables that influence the model can cause some observation values to experience a drastic increase or decrease, which can occur repeatedly over different and specific time spans [18]. To overcome this, an extension of the ARIMA model was developed, namely the ARIMAX model, which was built with consideration of additional variables or exogenous variables that were considered to have a significant influence on the data. In general, the ARIMAX model (p,d,q) can be written as in the Eq. (11) with variable B representing the forward operator [5].

$$Z_t = \alpha_0 + \alpha_1 X_{1,t} + \alpha_2 X_{2,t} + \cdots + \alpha_t X_{k,t} + \frac{(1 - \zeta_1 B - \zeta_2 B^2 - \cdots - \zeta_q B^q}{1 - \iota_1 B - \iota_2 B^2 - \cdots - \iota_p B^q} \tag{11}$$

where the variable Z_t represents the t-th observation of the dependent variables, whereas t represents the corresponding observation for the factors that explain the data. In addition, the variables α_0, α_1, α_2, $\cdots$, and α_k denote the parameters of the regression component. Similarly, the variables ι_1, ι_2, $\cdots$, and ι_p, as well as ζ_1, ζ_2, $\cdots$, and ζ_q, represent the weights for the nonseasonal and seasonal autoregressive terms and moving average terms, respectively.

One way to select the best model is to consider the value of *Root Mean Square Error* (RMSE), which is the result of the square root of *Mean Square Error* (MSE). This metric measures the difference between the predicted or estimated results of a model and the actual or observed results. People widely use RMSE as a good error metric for numerical predictions. The accuracy of the measurement error is indicated by obtaining the smallest RMSE value in the estimation method. Furthermore, RMSE can be written mathematically as in Eq. (12).

$$\text{RMSE} = \sqrt{\frac{1}{n} \sum_{i=n}^{n} (S_i - O_i)^2} \tag{12}$$

where O_i is the actual data value, S_i is the forecasted value, and n is the number of observations available for analysis. Apart from that, we can also use the Akaike

Information Criterion (AIC), which can be expressed as in Eq. (13).

$$AIC = n \ln(\hat{\sigma}_{\varepsilon}^{2}) + 2(p + q + 1) \tag{13}$$

where $\hat{\sigma}_{\varepsilon}^{2} = \frac{SSE}{n}$ and $SSE = Sum\ of\ Square\ Error$ which is estimated from the sum of the squares of all residual values. However, in the autoregressive model, the AIC criterion does not provide a consistent p value, so other information criteria are used, such as the Schwarzt Bayesian Information Criteria (SBC), which can be expressed with the Eq. (14).

$$SBC = n \ln(\hat{\sigma}_{\varepsilon}^{2}) + (p + q + 1) \ln n \tag{14}$$

or other forms of criteria.

2.3 Premium Calculation

IHA-based insurance premium calculation is carried out by considering relevant geographical factors in each region. In this approach, IHA serves as the primary indicator for assessing the risk that insurance participants, specifically farmers, face. The ARIMAX model predicts the IHA value, which serves as the foundation for calculating the indemnity or compensation amount. Furthermore, the premium calculation is carried out carefully using various parameters, including interest rates and deductibles. Here are the steps for calculating the premium:

1. Determining the IHA Model with GWR from each region in the district or city will be used to determine the specific conditions of each region, the amount of compensation received.
2. Predicting the IHA value with ARIMAX by considering geographical factors.
3. Determining indemnity by using the model's IHA prediction results.
4. Calculating the present value using the Bank Indonesia interest rate of 0.0575 to obtain the present value of the indemnity to be paid.
5. Calculating the premium by dividing the present value obtained by the deductible (the amount not covered by insurance), then multiplying it by the price per unit index adopted from AUTP, which is IDR 6,000,000.00.

3 Result and Discussion

The study used 35 districts and cities in Central Java Province, including 29 districts and 6 cities, as the spatial units. The dependent variable in this research is IHA (Y), which can be expressed mathematically as the Eq. (15)

$$IHA = \frac{HarvestArea}{RiceFieldArea}. \tag{15}$$

Meanwhile, the predictor variables used include rainfall (x_1), air humidity (x_2), duration of sunlight (x_3), and area height (x_4). The data above is statistically described in Table 1.

Table 1. Data description

Variable	Minimum	Maximum	Mean	Standard deviation
IHA (Y)	0.1035	0.4779	0.3285	0.05365834
Rainfall (x_1)	130	96279	8449	18036.87
Air humidity (x_2)	778.0	1178.0	962.4	62.94154
Duration of sunlight (x_3)	43.2	976.0	595.5	276.3204
Height area (x_4)	5.188	794.004	140.432	195.1309

This study will not use all available X variables in its analysis. This decision was made after going through a series of calculations that showed that the ARIMAX model built using all variables did not provide satisfactory results. This is indicated by the emergence of NaN (Not a Number) values in the coefficients of the X variables in the ARIMAX model, which indicates a problem in the estimation of model parameters. After conducting several identifications, it was found that only two variables, namely rainfall (x_1) and duration of sunlight (x_3), produced a more optimal ARIMAX model. The use of these two variables allows the model to better capture data patterns and provide more accurate estimates. Henceforth, the next study will just take into account these two factors. Furthermore, we must first determine the latitude-longitude coordinates of each district or city in Central Java in order to build the GWR model, as shown in Table 2.

Table 2. Latitude and longitude coordinates in central java

District/City	**Longitude**	**Latitude**
Cilacap	109	-7.733333
Banyumas	109.140438	-7.4832133
Purbalingga	109.3638	-7.390747
⋮	⋮	⋮
Tegal city	109.1333333	-6.8666667

According to Table 2, the Euclidean distance obtained for each district or city in Central Java Province is presented in Table 3.

Further analysis continued using the R Studio program, it was obtained that the optimum bandwidth for the Gaussian kernel was 0.9999573 with a minimum CV of 0.1140642. In addition, the parameter estimates for the Gaussian kernel weighting function in the GWR model are included in Table 4.

From the output presented in Table 4, the estimated value of the rainfall parameter is in the range of 0.00000011472 to 0.00000039782. When the rainfall period is considered in the analysis, this value indicates that the estimated effect of the predictor variable on the response variable falls within that range. The

Table 3. Euclidean distance

Euclidean Distance					
	Cilacap	Banyumas	Purbalingga	⋯	Tegal city
Cilacap	0.0000000	0.5469159	0.51033075	⋯	0.2217508
Banyumas	0.5469159	0.0000000	0.82882242	⋯	0.7685623
Purbalingga	0.5103307	0.8288224	0.00000000	⋯	0.4999794
⋮	⋮	⋮	⋮	⋮	⋮
Tegal city	0.2217508	0.7685623	0.4999794	⋯	0.0000000

Table 4. GWR estimation model parameter output

Variable	Parameter coefficient	
	Min	Max
Intercept	0.32345	0.33187
Rainfall	0.00000011472	0.00000039782
Duration of sunlight	−0.000011103	0.0000043148
AIC	−102.7564	
Quasi-global R2	0.02754883	

same thing also has similar interpretations for other parameter values in each predictor variable. Estimation of GWR model parameters with Kernel Gaussian weighting produces global $R^2 = 0.02754883$ and $AIC = -102.7564$. This means that the GWR model obtained can explain the variables of rainfall and duration of solar radiation, which influence the IHA variable by 2%, while the rest is influenced by other factors. Additionally, the results of the GWR model testing employing Gaussian kernel evaluation functions are shown in Table 5.

Table 5. ANOVA test

Variable	Degree of fredom (DF)	Sum of square	Mean square	F-count	P-value
OLS Residuals	3.0000	0.097501			
GWR Improvement	2.5872	0.002304	0.0008907		
GWR Residuals	29.4128	0.095197	0.0032366	0.2752	0.9962

The acquired findings may be deemed significant if the value of $F_{count} > F_{table}$ or $p - value < \alpha$. According to the Table 5, the analysis findings indicate that the p-value is 0.9962, which is more than the significance threshold of 0.05. Therefore, it can be concluded that there is no significant difference between the OLS model and the GWR model with weights fixed Gaussian kernel at the 0.05 significance level. Put simply, both models exhibit comparable performance in observing the correlation between the examined variables. Then, the estimated values for each predictor coefficient are shown in Table 6.

Table 6. GWR model parameter estimation.

District/city	Intercept	Rainfall	Durofsunlight
Cilacap	0.3273524	0.0000002004830	-0.000004507075
Banyumas	0.3273723	0.0000001307953	0.000001087156
Purbalingga	0.3306024	0.0000002223732	-0.000009297622
⋮	⋮	⋮	⋮
Tegal city	0.3272373	0.0000002223732	-0.000005974638

The GWR estimate models for Cilacap Regency, Banyumas Regency, and Purbalingga Regency were created using a fixed Gaussian kernel weighting, as demonstrated in Eqs. (16) (17), and (18), respectively, as shown in Table 6. Moreover, other regions may be created using a similar method.

$$\hat{Y}_{Cilacap.Gauss} = 0.3273524 + 0.0000002004830x_1 - 0.000004507075x_3 \quad (16)$$

$$\hat{Y}_{Banyumas.Gauss} = 0.3273723 + 0.0000001307953x_1 + 0.000001087156x_3 \quad (17)$$

$$\hat{Y}_{Purbalingga.Gauss} = 0.3306024 + 0.0000002223732x_1 - 0.000009297622x_3 \quad (18)$$

Furthermore, Fig. 1 illustrates the distribution pattern of the coefficients of factors that have an impact on IHA in Central Java.

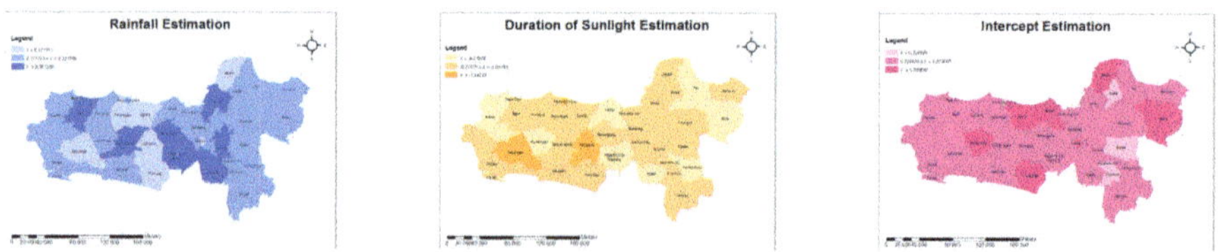

Fig. 1. Illustration of GWR model parameter estimation

Based on Fig. 1, it can be seen that the distribution of each variable is divided into 3 groups, and on average, adjacent locations have relatively the same coefficient values, so grouping occurs. Globally, it can be seen that the influence of rainfall and the duration of sunlight in each region in Central Java have different characteristics. For example, in the Klaten area, the estimated rainfall parameter has a high value, but the duration of sunlight has a low value. This shows how weather and geographic location affect IHA in each district or city in Central Java.

Next, we will discuss the formation of the ARIMAX model. However, first a linear regression model is formed, whose estimated parameters are presented in Table 7, and the prediction model can be written as in Eq. (19)

Table 7. Data description

Variable	Estimation
Intercept (Z)	0.0997016
Rainfall (X_1)	–0.0003366
Duration of sunlight (X_3)	0.0048297

$$\hat{Z} = 0.0997016 - 0.0003366X_1 + 0.0048297X_3 \tag{19}$$

According to the model expressed in Eq. (19) above, when all explanatory variables have a value of 0, the Y variable or IHA data is 0.0997016. Furthermore, for each addition of one rainfall variable, the IHA data will decrease by 0.0003366 on average, provided that all variables are constant, and for each addition of one variable for the duration of sunlight, the IHA data will increase by 0.0048297 on average. This is based on the assumption that all variables remain constant.

Next, modeling will be carried out using ARIMA, which can be determined based on the results of the ACF and PACF plots, as illustrated in Fig. 2.

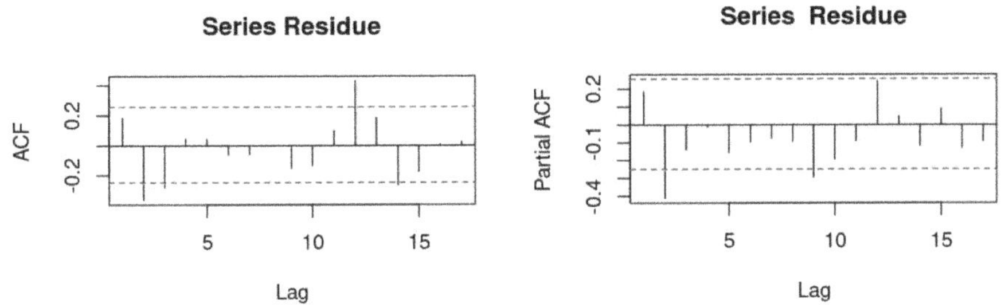

Fig. 2. ACF and PACF plots

Based on Fig. 2, it can be seen that the correlation value between data and lag does not decrease slowly, where in the ACF plot a significant cutoff is obtained at the 3rd lag and in the PACF plot it is found to be significant at lag 2. Based

Table 8. AIC value for different ARIMAX models

Model	AIC
ARIMAX(2,0,0)	–13.73
ARIMAX(0,0,3)	–22.38
ARIMAX(2,0,3)	–20.47
ARIMAX(2,0,2)	–20.31
ARIMAX(2,0,1)	–20.78
ARIMAX(1,0,3)	–21.11
ARIMAX(3,0,0)	–12.42

on the exploration results above, a summary of the models that can be formed is obtained in Table 8.

Based on the summary of the models presented in Table 8, information was obtained that the ARIMAX (0,0,3) model had the lowest AIC value, so the ARIMAX (0,0,3) model was chosen for the next analysis. After that, as shown in Fig. 3, we will compare the Original Data with Forecast Results using the ARIMAX (0,0,3) Model.

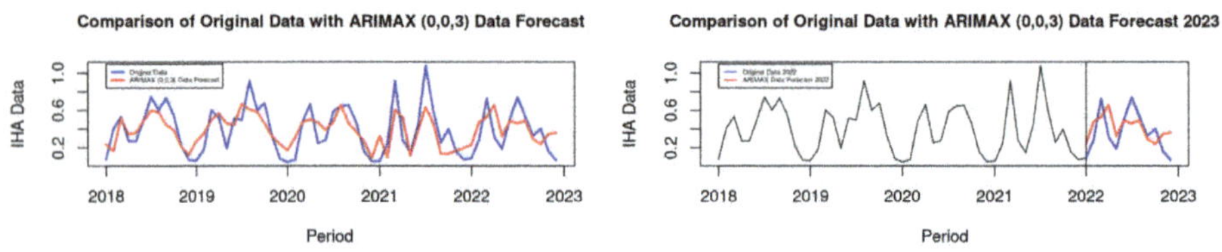

Fig. 3. The Original data versus forecast results using the ARIMAX (0,0,3) model

From Fig. 3, it can be seen that the ARIMAX (0,0,3) model gives quite good results, as seen from the model prediction line, which tends to run in harmony with the original data. Furthermore, forecasting is carried out from the model for the three future periods given in Table 9.

Table 9. forecasting results

Month	IHA predictive value
January 2023	0.2288194
February 2023	0.3846143
March 2023	0.4560692

According to Table 9, the IHA value always increases from January to March. In general, March is one of the biggest harvest times for farmers in Indonesia in a year, which has a significant influence on the IHA value obtained. Furthermore, the results obtained will be used to calculate agricultural insurance premiums.

Actually, there are many methods for calculating premiums. We certainly adapt the selection of assumptions, methods, and formulations to the specific circumstances of each object of observation whose risks we intend to protect. However, among the several formulations used in calculating premiums, there are two concepts that are often taken into consideration, namely Indemnity (IDM) and Present Value (PV).

IDM is a form of comprehensive insurance compensation for damage or loss. Generally, two parties refer to IDM as a contractual agreement. In this arrangement, one party agrees to pay for potential losses or damage caused by the other party. For example, the insurer or recipient of compensation agrees to provide compensation to another party for any damage or loss as an imbalance in the premium guaranteed by the insured to the insurance company. With IDM, the value of the coverage provided must match the claim value without any reduction or addition. In other words, the insured or customer only receives compensation equal to the amount of the loss they experienced.

Furthermore, the concept of Present Value (PV) describes the idea that the value of money in the current time period can exceed its value in the next time period, even though the nominal amount has not changed. Evaluation of this idea is carried out by calculating the rate of return that has been calculated or stated previously using a discount rate. Determining PV requires a comprehensive understanding of future value or discount rate. Alternative interpretations of PV involve the nominal value of money or cash flows, or a comprehensive breakdown of cash flows, depending on a predetermined rate of return. A predetermined discount rate will determine the discounting of the cash flows received. There is an inverse relationship between the discount rate and the PV of future cash flows, where an increase in the discount rate causes a decrease in the PV. An important factor in the proper evaluation of future cash flows is obtaining an appropriate discount rate.

In the case discussed in the study, the IDM formula is given as in the Eq. (20).

$$IDM(IHA,\omega) = \begin{cases} 0, & IHA \geq \omega \\ \omega - IHA, & IHA < \omega \end{cases} \tag{20}$$

The ω value is the amount of the *deductible* or the amount that must be paid by the insured before the company provides compensation for the claim submitted. Furthermore, to determine the amount of premium paid by the policy holder so that it is relevant to future value, the PV rule is used which can be presented as in Eq. (21).

$$PV = \frac{IDM}{(1 + 0.0575)^{\frac{4}{12}}} \tag{21}$$

with 0.0575 being the rate following the reference interest rate set by Bank Indonesia (BI) in controlling monetary policy.

In calculating agricultural insurance premiums in this discussion, a formula is used, as in the Eq. 22

$$Premium = \frac{PV}{\omega} \times IDR6,000,000.00 \tag{22}$$

The value of IDR 6,000,000.00 was chosen as the value per index adopted from the calculation of compensation costs that already apply to AUTP in Indonesia.The following are the premium amounts derived from the calculations:

1. For $\omega = 0.5$
   Obtained
   $$IDM(IHA, 0.5) = \begin{cases} 0, IHA \geq 0.5 \\ 0.5 - IHA, IHA < 0.5 \end{cases}$$
   with Premium (P_1) = $IDR288,207.1$, which has a percentage of 0.04803452 or 5% of the amount of compensation that will be obtained.
2. For $\omega = 0.75$
   Obtained
   $$IDM(IHA, 0.6) = \begin{cases} 0, IHA \geq 0.6 \\ 0.6 - IHA, IHA < 0.6 \end{cases}$$
   with Premium (P_2) = $IDR786,879.3$, which has a percentage of 0.1311465 or 13% of the amount of compensation that will be obtained.
3. For $\omega = 0.75$
   Obtained
   $$IDM(IHA, 0.75) = \begin{cases} 0, IHA \geq 0.75 \\ 0.75 - IHA, IHA < 0.75 \end{cases}$$
   with Premium (P_3) = $IDR1,285,551$, which has a percentage of 0.2142586 or 21% of the amount of compensation that will be obtained.

From the results obtained, the determination of the premium amount in each district or city in the Central Java Province region can be different based on the mapping that has been carried out by including climate factors so that there is no bias because they have looked at geographical factors, which indirectly also take into account the risk of possible losses. Scenarios can be adjusted to the policies that apply in each region. For example, because the Banyumas region has low rainfall and a long duration of sunlight, based on the regression model expressed in Eq. (19) created in this research, this region is predicted to have a large IHA. Therefore, a scenario for determining the premium can be chosen by taking a small ω and so on.

4 Conclusion

From the results obtained above, it can be seen that the comparison of premiums and compensation amounts for Rice Farming Business Insurance (AUTP), which is managed by the government, is not much different from the results of the calculations carried out in this research. In general, the agricultural insurance proposed in this research can be adjusted to the geographical conditions of each region, and the premiums obtained can be cheaper or more expensive, so that prospective policyholders can choose the amount of risk they will cover according to their individual circumstances. In running this type of insurance, we can also follow the rules set by the government. Some policy recommendations that are adjustments to the AUTP insurance scheme that already applies in Indonesia include, farmers as insurance participants do not have limitations on the area of land that can be insured, farmers are free to choose the type of insurance they will participate in such as AUTP insurance premium of 5% of the insured value and can only file a claim if the IHA value is at least 0.5, AUTP insurance premium of 13% of the insured value and can only file a claim if the IHA value is at least 0.6, AUTP insurance premium is 21% of the insured value and can only file a claim if the IHA value is at least 0.75, and also the insurance coverage period is valid for one planting season.

Disclosure of Interests. No potential conflict of interest was reported by the authors.

References

1. Alam, A.S.A.F., Begum, H., Masud, M.M., Al-Amin, A.Q., Filho, W.L.: Agriculture insurance for disaster risk reduction: a case study of Malaysia. Int. J. Disaster Risk Reduct. **47**, 101626 (2020)
2. Algazali, M., Jamil, M.H., Lanuhu, N.: Persepsi petani terhadap asuransi usaha tani padi (autp) di kecamatan paleteang, kabupaten pinrang. Hasanuddin J. Sustain. Agric. **1**(1), 39–45 (2019)
3. Boamah, P.O., Onumah, J., Apam, B., Salifu, T., Abunkudugu, A.A., Alabil, S.A.: Climate variability impact on crop evapotranspiration in the upper east region of ghana. Environ. Chall. **14**, 100828 (2024)
4. Carrer, M.J., Silveira, R.L.F.D., Vinholis, M.D.M.B., De Souza Filho, H.M.: Determinants of agricultural insurance adoption: evidence from farmers in the state of são paulo, brazil. RAUSP Manag. J. **55**(4), 547–566 (2020)
5. Cools, M., Moons, E., Wets, G.: Investigating the variability in daily traffic counts through use of arimax and sarimax models. Transp. Res. Rec. **2163**, 57–66 (2009)
6. Ehiogu, C.P., Joseph, A.: Investigating the variability in daily traffic counts through use of arimax and sarimax models. J. Agric. Food Sci. **17**(1), 123–135 (2019)
7. Ghimire, R., Chapagain, R.K., Jagari, D.B., Shahi, L.B.: Farmers' perception and awareness towards agriculture insurance as a tool of risk management in kaski and chitwan districts of nepal. Lumbini J. Bus. Econ. **11**(1), 191–212 (2023)
8. Hakim, L., Wardhana, M.Y., Mulia, S.: Sofyan: Analisis willingness to pay petani terhadap pelaksanaan program asuransi usaha tani padi (autp) di kabupaten aceh besar. MAHATANI: J. Agribisnis. Agribus. Agric. Econ. J. **4**(1), 281–298 (2021)

9. Kemp, K.: Encyclopedia of Geographic Information Science. Geographically Weighted Regression (GWR) (2014)
10. Leelavinodhan, P.B., Vecchio, M., Antonelli, F., Maestrini, A., Brunelli, D.: Design and implementation of an energy-efficient weather station for wind data collection†. Sensors **21**(11), 1–18 (2021)
11. Marphy, T., Priminingtyas, D.: Analisis faktor-faktor yang mempengaruhi tingkat partisipasi petani dalam program asuransi usahatani padi (autp) di desa watugede, kecamatan singosari, kabupaten malang. Habitat **30**(2), 62–70 (2019)
12. Nisa, S.L., Nurhadi, E.K.O., Hendrarini, H.: Measuring the seriousness of farmers in participating in the rice farming insurance program based on the arnstein participation ladder. Jurnal Ilmiah Mahasiswa AGROINFO GALUH **9**(1), 351–361 (2022)
13. Nunoo, J., Acheampong, B.N.: Protecting financial investment: agriculture insurance in Ghana. Agric. Financ Rev. **74**(2), 236–247 (2014)
14. Plastina, A., Lence, S.H., Ortiz-Bobea, A.: How weather affects the decomposition of total factor productivity in U. S. agriculture. Agric. Econ. (U. K.)**52**(2), 215–234 (2021)
15. Prasetyo, K., Fariyanti, A.: Socio-economic factors affecting farmers' decisions to join the rice farm insurance (autp) program. Jurnal AgribiSains **5**(1), 1–12 (2019)
16. Robinah, B., Njenga, G.: Agriculture insurance and farmers performance in rwanda, a case of national agriculture insurance project. J. Entrep. Proj. Manag. **7**(1), 104–125 (2023)
17. Singh, P., Agrawal, G.: Development, present status and performance analysis of agriculture insurance schemes in India: review of evidence. Int. J. Soc. Econ. **47**(4), 461–481 (2020)
18. Tasya, E.S., Yanti, T.S.: Pemodelan arimax (autoregressive integrated moving average with exogenous variable). Prosiding Statistika **6**(2), 113–118 (2020)
19. Wahyuningsih, T.A., Hasan, F.: Perception and participation of farmers on usahatani padi insurance in pilangkenceng district, madiun regency. Jsep **12**(3), 11–21 (2019)
20. Yadav, S.A., Sahoo, B.M., Sharma, S., Das, L.: An analysis of data mining techniques to analyze the effect of weather on agriculture. In: Proceedings of International Conference on Intelligent Engineering and Management ICIEM, vol. 2020, pp. 29–32 (2020)

Model Selection of Poisson Point Processes on a Linear Network: A Case Study of Traffic Accident Modeling in Nganjuk

Vanda Fitriyanah, Nabila Isna Nurazizah, Achmad Choiruddin(✉), and Sutikno

Department of Statistics, Faculty of Science and Data Analytics, Institut Teknologi Sepuluh Nopember, Surabaya 60111, Indonesia
choiruddin@its.ac.id

Abstract. The utilization of point coordinates of traffic accidents is able to provide more detailed spatial analysis and identify high-risk locations. The point process on a linear network is an appropriate model for analyzing road crash risk, as it can map and analyze the distribution of crashes along the road network. This study focuses on modeling the risk of road accidents in Nganjuk Regency using a Poisson point process on a linear network. The estimation technique combines the Berman-Turner device with an Iteratively Reweighted Least Squares approach. In modeling the distribution of road accidents in Nganjuk, we involve spatial covariates representing environmental factors that influence road accidents (distance to the closest traffic light) and road geometry factors (road type, number of paths and line roads, presence of road marking, presence of curb on the left and right side of the road). We also perform a backward method for model selection. The results indicate that covariates distance of a point to the nearest traffic light location, road types, number of lines, and presence of road markings significantly impact the risk of traffic accidents in Nganjuk Regency. The presence of road markings and number of lines on a road have a substantial effect, increasing the risk of road accidents by 42 and 21%, respectively. These results can serve as a basis for developing a road accidents risk map for Nganjuk Regency.

Keywords: Linear network · Nganjuk regency · Poisson point process · Road traffic accidents risk · Road safety

1 Introduction

Rapid population growth in many countries is one of the main factors contributing to the high use of motorized vehicles. This condition can potentially increase road congestion and violations of road rules, which can result in road accidents. According to WHO [1], an estimated 1.19 million people die each year due to road accidents. With this number, WHO predicts that vehicle accidents will become the seventh leading cause of death worldwide by 2030. In Indonesia, the number of road accidents in Indonesia consistently exceeds 100 thousand accidents yearly [2], and most victims are of productive age (26–55 years). Thus, the high frequency of accidents will impact the reduction of productive labor due to disability or death.

P. C. Rodrigues et al. (Eds.): ISBIS 2024, 13, pp. 55–69, 2027.
https://doi.org/10.1007/978-3-032-32458-0_5

In order to minimize the frequency of road accidents, it is important to be proactive and take preventive action to avoid road accidents. One popular statistical method is to consider crash frequency modeling by implementing the Poisson regression of the number of road accidents with respect to some covariates. This approach has been employed [3–6]. However, other studies show that such a technique is often inappropriate to conduct a detailed analysis because of the bias caused by aggregation, the division of areas into sub-areas of observation can be modified according to the preferences of the researcher [7].

In addition, this approach results in the loss of spatial information necessary to prove the existence of clustering. The point process method is used to account for the coordinate of road accident events [8]. The approach employed in this study preserves the spatial coordinates of each event, allowing the intensity or risk of accidents to vary across different sections of the network. This adaptation is advantageous for analyzing events on linear networks, such as road accidents within a city [7]. Spatial point process models on linear networks consider various factors [9]. A spatio-temporal approach on linear networks with road accident cases is also conducted to estimate the frequency of road accidents on a specific road section and to generate risk maps over the entire road network [10].

In Indonesia, only a few studies have considered the point process method for road accidents. The point process method used on a linear network [11]. However, only one covariate considered for modeling at a time for modeling. In contrast, several factors contributing to car accidents have been identified [9]. In this study, we apply the Poisson point processes within a linear network to analyze the road accidents in Nganjuk with seven covariates, incorporating seven covariates consisting of road geometry and environmental factors [9]. If all variables are included, the model may be too complex. In this study, a model selection with variables is performed with the aim of building a parsimonious model using the backward method. This means that limited but relevant variables avoid overfitting and speed up the computation without compromising the quality of the analysis results obtained. The rest of the paper is organized as follows. Section 2 describes the methodology, while Sect. 3 details the data description. Results are presented in Sect. 4. The conclusion given in Sect. 5.

2 Methods

We detail in this section the dataset and the statistical methodology. We in general employ R software for the computation with stepAIC() function from the MASS library and lppm function from the spatstat.linnet library as the main tool for modeling [12].

2.1 Inhomogeneous Poisson Point Processes on a Linear Network

A linear network L consists of the set of m line sections $\ell_1, \ell_2, \ldots, \ell_j, \ldots \ell_m$, so that $L = \bigcup_{j=1}^{m} \ell_j$, with $m \leq \infty$ (See Fig. 1). Every line section ℓ_j is represented by a point $\boldsymbol{y}_j$, $z_j \in \mathbb{R}^2$ as its endpoints denoted as $\ell_j = [y_j, z_j] = \{w : w = ty_j + (1-t)z_j, 0 \leq t \leq 1\}$. The sum of all sections of line L is given by $|L| = \sum_{j=1}^{M} |\ell_j|$ [8].

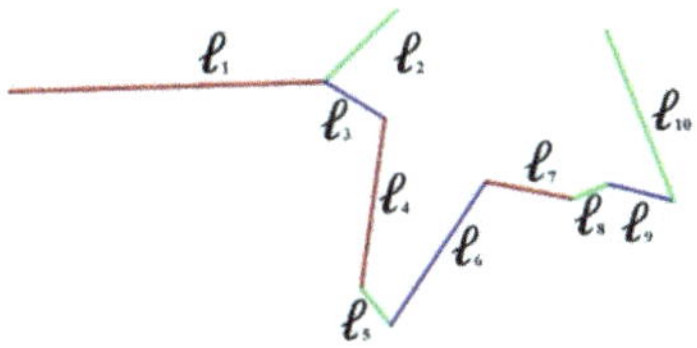

Fig. 1. Illustration of a L linear network with $M = 10$ line sections

For a linear network L, the point processes $\boldsymbol{X}$ are a mechanism of randomness that produces a pattern of points as its outcome. Thus, the number of points on $B \subset L$ is a random variable. Figure 2 shows a (finite, simple) point pattern $\boldsymbol{x}$ on L is a finite set $\boldsymbol{x} = \{\boldsymbol{x}_1, \boldsymbol{x}_2, \ldots, \boldsymbol{x}_n\}, \boldsymbol{x}_i \in L, i = 1, 2, \ldots, n$ of distinct points $\boldsymbol{x}_i \in L$, where $n \geq 0$ and point $\boldsymbol{x}_i$ is the space position on L, and the number of points n is not predefined. For any set $B \subseteq L$, let $N(\mathbf{X} \cap B)$ be the number $\boldsymbol{x}$ points lying in B.

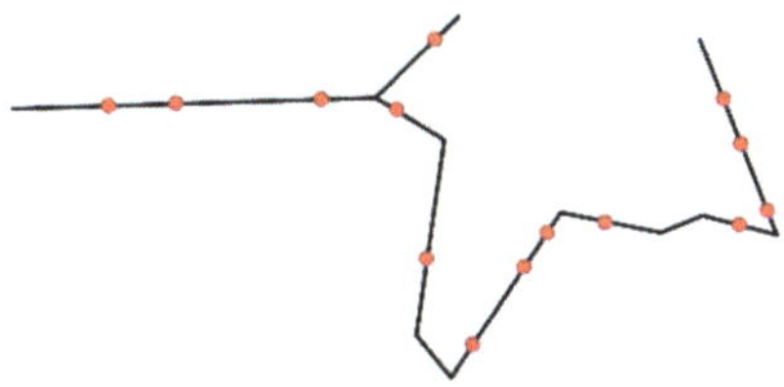

Fig. 2. Illustration linear network L with point pattern $\boldsymbol{x}$

Within a linear network, point process $\boldsymbol{X}$ is an inhomogeneous Poisson process, with intensity $\lambda(\boldsymbol{u}) : L \to [0, \infty)$, $\boldsymbol{u} \in B \subset L$ which is not constant or spatially variable. The intensity function of the nonstationary point process forms a loglinear model that depends on parameters $\boldsymbol{\theta}$ and is influenced by spatial covariates $z(\boldsymbol{u})$, written as follows [13],

$$\lambda(\boldsymbol{u}) = \lambda(\boldsymbol{u}; \boldsymbol{\theta}) = \exp\left(\boldsymbol{\theta}^T z(\boldsymbol{u})\right) \tag{1}$$

where $\boldsymbol{z}(\boldsymbol{u}) = (z_1(\boldsymbol{u}), z_2(\boldsymbol{u}), \ldots, z_p(\boldsymbol{u})\ )^T$ is the covariate vector and $\boldsymbol{\theta}$ is the regression parameter of size p.

2.2 Homogeneity Testing

The homogeneity test for the point process on a linear network is used to determine whether the intensity exhibits a homogeneous pattern. This allows for estimation of parameters that align with the distribution characteristics of the point pattern being studied. One of the homogeneity tests that can be used is the Cumulative Distribution Function (CDF) test. The hypothesis of the homogeneity test is formulated as follows:

H$_0$: $F_{0,j}(z) = \hat{F}_j(z)$ (homogeneous data intensity)

H$_1$: $F_{0,j}(z) \neq \hat{F}_j(z)$ (inhomogeneous data intensity) where

$$\hat{F}_j(z) = \frac{1}{n}\sum_{i=1}^{n} I\{z_{ij} \leq z\} \tag{2}$$

and

$$F_{0,j}(z) = \frac{\left|\{u \in L : \mathbf{Z}_j(u) \leq z\}\right|}{|L|} \tag{3}$$

The test statistic used is the Kolmogorov-Smirnov in Eq. (4) [12].

$$D = \max\left|\hat{F}_j(z) - F_{0,j}(z)\right| \tag{4}$$

2.3 Parameter Estimation

We maximize the corresponding log-likelihood function to estimate the parameter $\boldsymbol{\theta}$ [12]

$$\ell(\boldsymbol{\theta}) = \log L(\boldsymbol{\theta}) = \sum_{u \in \boldsymbol{x}} \log \lambda(\boldsymbol{u}; \boldsymbol{\theta}) - \int_B \lambda(\boldsymbol{u}; \boldsymbol{\theta}) d\boldsymbol{u} \tag{5}$$

where the integral term is discretized through the application of the Berman-Turner scheme in Eq. (4)

$$\int_L \lambda(\boldsymbol{u}; \boldsymbol{\theta}) d\boldsymbol{u} \approx \sum_{j=1}^{n+d} \lambda(\boldsymbol{u}_j; \boldsymbol{\theta}) w_j \tag{6}$$

where $j = 1, 2, \ldots, n + d$, n represent the count of data points, d represents the count of dummy points, and w_j are the quadrature weights with the sum $\sum_j w_j = |L|$. Then substitute (6) into (5) as Eq. (7)

$$\ell(\boldsymbol{\theta}) \approx \sum_{j=1}^{n} \log \lambda(\boldsymbol{u}_j; \boldsymbol{\theta}) - \sum_{j=1}^{n+d} \lambda(\boldsymbol{u}_j; \boldsymbol{\theta}) w_j \tag{7}$$

and I_j is defined as an indicator variable that equals 1, if u_j is a data point, and 0, if u_j is a dummy point. Thus, the approximate log-likelihood can be expressed as follows.

$$\begin{aligned}\ell(\boldsymbol{\theta}) &\approx \sum_{j=1}^{n} I_j \log \lambda(\boldsymbol{\theta}; \boldsymbol{u}_j) + \sum_{j=1}^{d} I_j \log \lambda(\boldsymbol{\theta}; \boldsymbol{u}_j) - \sum_{j=1}^{n+d} \lambda(\boldsymbol{\theta}; \boldsymbol{u}_j) w_j \\ &= \sum_{j=1}^{n+d} \left[y_j \log \lambda(\boldsymbol{\theta}; \boldsymbol{u}_j) - \lambda(\boldsymbol{\theta}; \boldsymbol{u}_j)\right] w_j \end{aligned} \tag{8}$$

with $y_j = I_j/w_j$. Using the Berman-Turner scheme, a log-likelihood function can be constructed, as shown in Eq. (8), which corresponds to the log-likelihood of a weighted Poisson regression model, where y_j represents the response and w_j represents the weights. The Iteratively Reweighted Least Square (IRLS) approach, implemented in the lppm.lpp function of the spatstat.linnet R packages, is used to maximize the log- likelihood function. In general, the parameter estimation algorithm using IRLS is shown in Table 1.

Table 1. Iteratively reweighted least square algorithm

Step 1	Determine initial value $\tilde{\boldsymbol{\theta}}^{(0)}$, starting with $\tilde{\boldsymbol{\theta}}^{(0)} = 0$
Step 2	Calculate the *working response* y_j^* and weights v_j for each $q = 0, 1, 2, \ldots$ initial value $\tilde{\boldsymbol{\theta}}^{(0)}$ is $\tilde{\boldsymbol{\theta}}^{(q)}$ with $q = 0$ $y_j^* = \log \lambda(\tilde{\boldsymbol{\theta}}; \boldsymbol{u}_j) + \frac{(y_j - \lambda(\tilde{\boldsymbol{\theta}}; \boldsymbol{u}_j))}{\lambda(\tilde{\boldsymbol{\theta}}; \boldsymbol{u}_j)}$ and $v_j = w_j \lambda(\tilde{\boldsymbol{\theta}}; \boldsymbol{u}_j)$
Step 3	Obtain the estimator $\tilde{\boldsymbol{\theta}}^{(q+1)}$ starting with $q = 0$, substitute the working response and weights $\tilde{\boldsymbol{\theta}}^{(q=0)}$ from step 2 into the weights and working response with solution $\tilde{\boldsymbol{\theta}}^{(q+1)^T} = \left(z(\boldsymbol{u}_j)^T v_j\left(\tilde{\boldsymbol{\theta}}^{(q)}\right) z(\boldsymbol{u}_j)\right)^{-1} z(\boldsymbol{u}_j)^T v_j\left(\tilde{\boldsymbol{\theta}}^{(q)}\right) y_j^*\left(\tilde{\boldsymbol{\theta}}^{(q)}\right)^*$
Step 4	Check the convergence of $\tilde{\boldsymbol{\theta}}^{(q+1)}$ with criterion $\tilde{\boldsymbol{\theta}}^{(q+1)} - \tilde{\boldsymbol{\theta}}^{(q)} \leq \varepsilon$ with ε is a very small positive value. If fulfilled then the iteration process is complete, if not fulfilled then repeat step 3 until converged

2.4 Model Selection

The backward elimination method aims to identify the subset of covariates that produces the best and significant model with the lowest prediction error by removing covariates one by one from the estimated model [14]. This method also helps to address multicollinearity by eliminating redundant variables, thereby simplifying the model and aligning with the principle of parsimony. The process begins with a model that includes all covariates and gradually removes covariates until only the significant covariates remain, based on the smallest Bayesian Information Criterion (BIC) value.

$$BIC = BIC(\gamma) = -2\ell(\hat{\boldsymbol{\theta}}) + p\ \log(n) \tag{9}$$

where $\ell(\hat{\boldsymbol{\theta}})$ is the log likelihood function of the point process model in Eq. (8) and ρ is the number of parameters in the model, and n is the number of points in the linear network L.

3 Dataset

In this paper, we focus on the region of Nganjuk Regency in Western East Java. Nganjuk is an important transit area frequently traversed by vehicles traveling between Central Java and other regions of East Java, as well as in the opposite direction. Additionally, Nganjuk lies along the main Surabaya-Yogyakarta route, contributing to relatively high traffic levels that may increase the likelihood of road accidents (see Fig. 3).

Fig. 3. Map of the geographical area of Nganjuk regency

The road and transportation office of Nganjuk Regency provided the specific coordinate (longitude and latitude) for road accidents across the 1,944 confirmed cases reported in Nganjuk, Indonesia, from January 2018 to December 2020. The spatial covariates represent environmental factors that affect road accidents (such as distance to the closest traffic light) and road geometry factors (such as road types, number of paths and lines road, presence of road marking, presence of curb on the left and right sides of the road) (see Table 2).

Table 2. Spatial covariates associated in this study

Notation	Variable	Unit scale	Description
$\mathbf{z}_1$	Distance to the closest traffic light	Ratio	
$\mathbf{z}_2$	Road types	Nominal	0: Local 1: Collector 2: Arterial
$\mathbf{z}_3$	Number of paths	Nominal	1: one path 2: two paths
$\mathbf{z}_4$	Number of lines	Ratio	
$\mathbf{z}_5$	Presence of road marking	Nominal	0: No 1: Yes
$\mathbf{z}_6$	Presence of curb on the left side of road	Nominal	0: No 1: Yes
$\mathbf{z}_7$	Presence of curb on the right side of road	Nominal	0: No 1: Yes

The location of the traffic light is obtained from Nganjuk Regency transportation office, and the distance to the closest traffic light is calculated using the shortest-path distance by distfun.lpp function from the spatstat.linnet R package. Road environment factors are recorded by the road unit and Nganjuk Regency transportation office in 2020, while road geometry factors are sourced from Google Maps (https://www.google.com/maps) in 2020. Based on the Law of the Republic of Indonesia No. 2 on Roads, public roads are classified into arterial, collector, local and neighborhood roads according to their function [15]. This study focuses on arterial, collector and local roads (see Fig. 4).

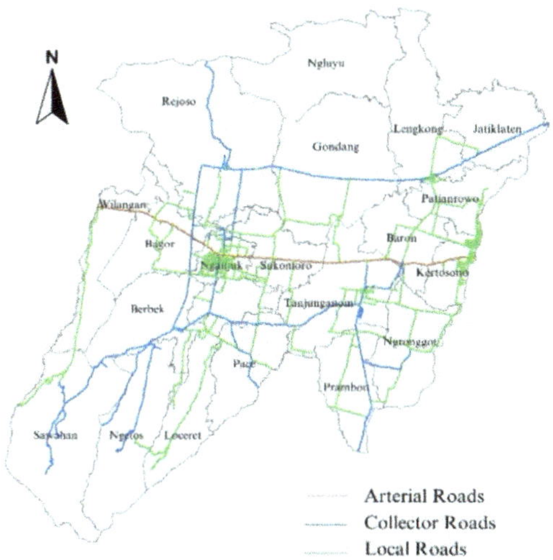

Fig. 4. Map of the road network in Nganjuk regency

4 Results and Discussion

4.1 Distribution of Traffic Accidents and Covariate Densities

Figure 5 highlights the distribution of traffic accidents sites in Nganjuk over a three-year period from 2018 to 2020.

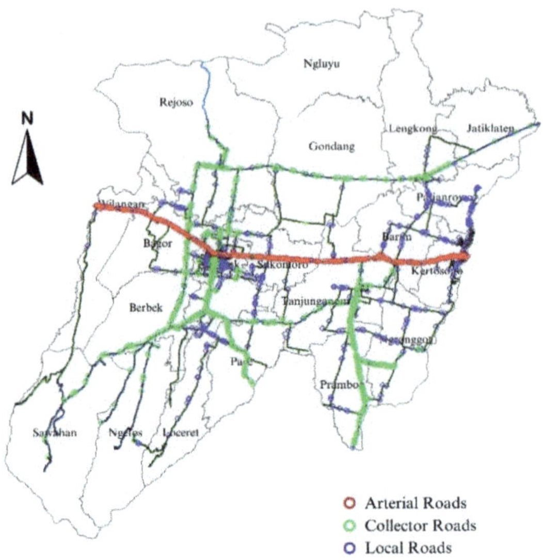

Fig. 5. Distribution of road traffic accident sites in Nganjuk regency over the period from 2018 to 2020

The distribution of road accidents in Nganjuk, shown in Fig. 5 mainly occurs on arterial roads (marked with red points), which serve as major routes connecting Nganjuk Regency with Madiun Regency as well as the border of Kediri and Jombang Regencies. The road sections passing through Wilangan, Bagor, Nganjuk, Sukomoro, and Kertosono districts are part of the arterial route with the highest accident density from 2018–2020, where accident locations are notably dense and overlapping. Additionally, accident locations are also distributed across local roads. For instance, on local roads in the Tanjung Anom, Prambon, and Nganjuk districts, the accident sites are also densely clustered, suggesting high accident intensity in these areas. Furthermore, other accident sites are scattered across surrounding roads.

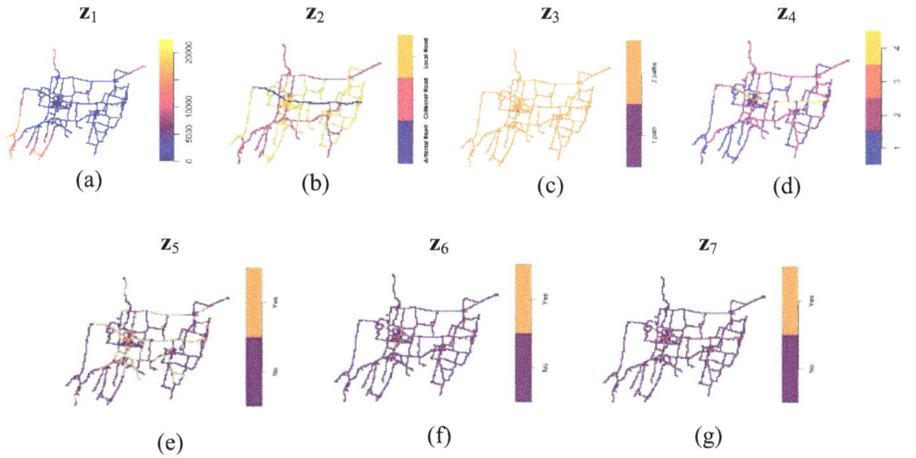

Fig. 6. Map of covariates **a** Distance to the closest traffic light **b** Road types **c** Number of paths **d** Number of lines **e** Presence of road marking **f** Presence of curb on the right side of the road **g** Presence of curb on the left side of the road

Figure 6 illustrates the covariates utilized in this study. Blue-colored road sections indicate proximity to traffic lights, typically located in the city center or in high-density intersections. In contrast, brighter-colored road sections (shifting toward yellow) indicate greater distances from traffic lights, often found in peripheral areas or on roads with lower traffic volume (See Fig. 6a). Figure 6b shows road types and colored by their level of importance: local roads (orange) are the most numerous and widespread, supporting accessibility at local and community levels; collector roads (pink) are fewer and serve as links connecting local roads to major roads, channeling traffic from smaller roads to major routes; and arterial roads (dark blue) are the fewest but largest and most prominent, facilitating fast and efficient regional mobility and economic activity. Most road sections consist of two paths, while arterial and collector roads may vary from one to three lanes, depending on width. Arterial roads generally have an average of four lanes. The majority of arterial and collector roads feature road markings, as shown in Fig. 6e. Nevertheless, there are instances where road markings have been removed or are no longer visible, potentially due to the effects of weathering or the lack of maintenance over an extended period of time. It is noteworthy that most existing roads lack curbs on either side.

4.2 Spatial Trend Detection

To determine whether the intensity of road accidents is homogeneous or inhomogeneous, a homogeneity test was conducted using the CDF and the Kolmogorov-Smirnov test statistic (see Table 3).

Table 3. Cumulative distribution function test results of accident data in Nganjuk regency

Description	D	P-value	Conclution
Distance to the closest traffic light	0.22713	$<2.2 \times 10^{-16}$	Inhomogen
Road types	0.32439	$<2.2 \times 10^{-16}$	Inhomogen
Number of paths	0.27851	$<2.2 \times 10^{-16}$	Inhomogen
Number of lines	0.01510	0.7492	Homogen
Presence of road marking	0.33345	$<2.2 \times 10^{-16}$	Inhomogen
Presence of curb on the left side of road	0.03521	0.0075	Inhomogen
Presence of curb on the right side of road	0.02679	0.1395	Homogen

The null hypothesis, which states that intensity is homogeneous, is rejected, indicating that accident intensities in Nganjuk Regency depend on road environment and geometry factors. Therefore, an inhomogeneous point process model is most appropriate. This study assumes that each road accident is an independent event unaffected by other accidents at different locations or times.

4.3 Modeling Result

The optimal model selection is performed using the backward elimination method based on the BIC value. Backward elimination is conducted by gradually removing insignificant covariates from the model (those with the highest p-value). The results of the model selection are presented in Table 4.

Table 4. Model selection with backward elimination

Step	Covariates in the model	Eliminated covariates	BIC
0	$z_1, z_2, z_3, z_4, z_5, z_6, z_7$		15343.35
1	$z_1, z_2, z_4, z_5, z_6, z_7$	z_3	15335.86
2	z_1, z_2, z_4, z_5, z_6	z_3, z_7	15334.37
3	z_1, z_2, z_4, z_5	z_3, z_6, z_7	15330.91

The risk of traffic accidents in Nganjuk Regency is described by an intensity function derived from the inhomogeneous Poisson point process model on a linear network, incorporating significant covariates as determined by the backward elimination method. The best model, as represented in Eq. (10) and the parameter estimates for the Poisson point process model are presented in Table 5.

$$\lambda(\boldsymbol{u}; \hat{\boldsymbol{\theta}}) = \exp\Big(\hat{\theta}_0 + \hat{\theta}_1 Z_1(\boldsymbol{u}) + \hat{\theta}_{2,1} Z_2(\boldsymbol{u}) + \hat{\theta}_{2,2} Z_2(\boldsymbol{u}) + \hat{\theta}_4 Z_4(\boldsymbol{u}) + \hat{\theta}_{5,1} Z_5(\boldsymbol{u})\Big)\Big) \quad (10)$$

Table 5. Parameter estimates $\hat{\boldsymbol{\theta}}$ of the inhomogeneous Poisson point process within a linear network for the road accidents in Nganjuk Regency data with backward method

Notation	Variable	$\hat{\boldsymbol{\theta}}$	Exp ($\hat{\boldsymbol{\theta}}$)	1/Exp ($\hat{\boldsymbol{\theta}}$)	Z_{val}	Significance
	Intercept	−4,1965	0.0150		−56.398	***
$\mathbf{z}_1$	Distance to the closest traffic light	−0.0018	0.9982	1.0018	−13.637	***
$\mathbf{z}_{2,1}$	Road type (collector)	0.8939	2.4445	0.4091	15.309	***
$\mathbf{z}_{2,2}$	Road type (arterial)	1.4780	4.3483	0.2299	17.105	
$\mathbf{z}_4$	Number of lines	0.1939	1.2140	0.8237	5.585	***
$\mathbf{z}_{5,1}$	Presence of road marking (there is a mark)	0.3491	1.4177	0.7054	5.662	***

Note The sign * represents the level of significance: * (0.1); ** (0.05); ***(0.01), while SE for the standard error of $\hat{\boldsymbol{\theta}}$

Table 5. considers the variable selection process using the backward method. We applied the backward method to determine a parsimonious model and to address multicollinearity. At a significance level of = 0.05, the results indicate that the covariates distance to the closest traffic light location ($\mathbf{z}_1$), road types ($\mathbf{z}_2$), number of lines ($\mathbf{z}_4$), and presence of road markings ($\mathbf{z}_6$) have a significant effect on the risk of traffic accidents in Nganjuk Regency. To interpret the effects of these factors, we consider the exponential function exp. ($\hat{\boldsymbol{\theta}}$) if the value is positive, and the 1/exp. ($\hat{\boldsymbol{\theta}}$) if the value is negative. Based on the model, the estimated accident intensity is 0.015 per 10 m if the location is on a local road with one lane, no road markings, and is at a point of high traffic congestion.

4.4 Effect of Road Geometry and Environmental Factors

Interestingly, the presence of road markings and the number of lanes on roads significantly increase the risk of traffic accidents in Nganjuk. Specifically, road markings are associated with a 42% increase in accident risk compared to unmarked roads. Although road markings are intended to enhance safety by providing clear guidance to drivers, this elevated risk can be explained by several factors. Road markings are frequently placed on complex, high-traffic roads where accident risks are inherently higher. Additionally, poorly maintained markings, such as those that are faded or obscured by dirt, may fail to provide effective guidance or even cause confusion, ultimately increasing the risk of accidents. Nonetheless, this does not imply that removing road markings would reduce accident rates, as they remain essential visual aids for safe navigation [16, 17]. Increasing the number of lanes on a road is also predicted to increase the risk of traffic accidents by 21%. This is because the more lanes used on a section of road, the wider the section of road, so the volume of traffic passing through the section of road will also be greater, increasing the potential for interactions between vehicles that can increase the risk of traffic accidents.

Parameter estimation results indicate that the risk of traffic accidents is 2.445 times higher on collector roads and 4.383 times higher on arterial roads compared to local roads. This increased risk is due to the primary function of arterial and collector roads, which accommodate medium to long-distance travel at higher average speeds than local roads. In addition, arterial and collector roads have higher traffic volumes resulting in increased vehicle interaction and, consequently, increased accident risk on these roads compared to local roads.

4.5 Predicted Risk Map

Based on the model results, predicted intensity maps are generated to provide an overview of road accident risk across all road sections in Nganjuk, considering road environment and geometry factors. This map serves as a basis for early accident risk assessment in Nganjuk (see Fig. 7)

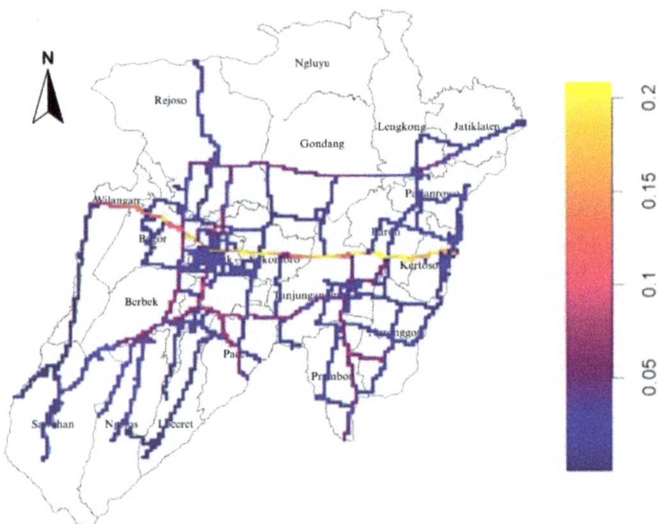

Fig. 7. Fitted intensity of road accident in Nganjuk Regency during 2018–2020 with intensity values represented by a color gradient

Figure 7 depicts the intensity mapping of the optimal model to predicting accident risk in Nganjuk, highlighting areas in the lightest color with the highest accident hazard, mainly along arterial and collector roads, which align with the pattern shown in Fig. 4. This is attributed to the high traffic volumes on these roads, influenced by environmental and road factors.

4.6 Methodological Consideration

The primary strength of this study is its use of high-resolution spatial data, allowing precise, location-level analysis of traffic accidents and providing a detailed view of accident risk in Nganjuk. By applying a spatial point process on a linear network, this approach identifies accident black spots and reveals spatial patterns influenced by factors such as environmental conditions and road geometry. The use of a parsimonious variable selection method, employing backward elimination, prevents overfitting and improves computational efficiency while maintaining accuracy. This approach is adaptable beyond district-level analysis to provincial or national levels by accounting for regional differences.

These results should be interpreted cautiously, considering several limitations. This study assumes that traffic accidents are independent events, given that each accident generally arises from unique causes that are not directly related to other incidents. Nonetheless, the accident locations in Nganjuk Regency show dense clustering, especially along arterial and collector roads, possibly due to overlapping incidents from 2018 to 2020; when visualized, it may appear as if all accidents took place simultaneously, though they span a range of time. Therefore, future research could consider temporal effects in modeling traffic accident risk. Due to the large number of variables, an interesting approach for future studies is the variable selection based on the regularization method and logistic-based approximation could offer valuable comparisons to the Berman-Turner scheme [18–21]. A more comprehensive analysis could support effective accident prevention strategies in Nganjuk Regency.

5 Conclusion

This paper presents an estimation technique for a point process on a linear network with log-linear intensity, using the Berman-Turner scheme to approximate the log-likelihood function within a generalized linear model framework. Findings reveal a non-homogeneous pattern in road accidents, with most accidents on arterial and collector roads. Stepwise variable selection shows that proximity to traffic lights, road types, number of lanes, and the presence of road markings significantly impact accident risk in Nganjuk Regency, with road markings and lane numbers increasing accident risk by 42% and 21%, respectively. These results underscore the importance of environmental and road geometry factors in assessing traffic accident risk. The high-resolution spatial model enables identification of high-risk sections for targeted safety interventions and can be expanded for wider applications by adjusting for regional factors. Future research could incorporate temporal dynamics and explore alternative variable selection methods, such as regularization, to further refine predictions. Overall, this study provides a strong foundation for developing effective accident prevention policies, supporting enhanced road safety and a reduction in accident rates.

Acknowledgement. The authors gratefully acknowledge financial support from the Institut Teknologi Sepuluh Nopember for this work, under project scheme of the Publication Writing and IPR Incentive Program (PPHKI) 2024. We also thank the reviewers for their constructive comments.

Data and Code Availability Data and code are available upon request.

References

1. WHO: Global Status Report on Road Safety 2018. World Health Organization (2018)
2. Khairina, R.L., Erwandi, D.: Gambaran Faktor Kegagalan Laten dan Kegagalan Aktif pada Kecelakaan Transportasi Darat di Indonesia Tahun 2019 – 2021. Natl. J. Occup. Healt Saf. (NJOHS). **3**(2), 099–106 (2022)
3. Lord, D., Washington, S., Ivan, J.: Poisson, Poisson-gamma and zero inflated regression models of motor vehicle crashes: balancing statistical fit and theory. Accid. Anal. Prev. **37**(1), 35–46 (2005). https://doi.org/10.1016/j.aap.2004.02.004
4. Malyshkina, N., Mannering, F.: Zero-state Markov switching count-data models: an empirical assessment. Accid. Anal. Prev. **42**(1), 122–130 (2010). https://doi.org/10.1016/j.aap.2009.07.012
5. ChikkaKrishna, N.K., Parida, M., Jain, S.S.: Identifying safety factors associated with crash frequency and severity on nonurban four-lane highway stretch in India. J. Transp. Saf. Secur. **9**(sup 1), 6–32 (2016)
6. Nambahu, B.B.T.: A.: Modeling of Road Traffic Fatalities in Namibia: a Generalized Linear Model Approach. Master Thesis. University of Namibia (2018)
7. Baddeley, A., Nair, G., Rakshit, S., McSwiggan, G., Davies, T.M.: Analysing point patterns on networks-a review. Spat. Stat. **42**, 100435 (2021). https://doi.org/10.1016/j.spasta.2020.100435
8. Ang, Q., Baddeley, A., Nair, G.: Geometrically corrected second order analysis of events on a linear network, with applications to ecology and criminology. Scand. J. Stat. **39**(4), 591–617 (2012). https://doi.org/10.1111/j.1467-9469.2011.00752.x
9. Rakshit, S., McSwiggan, G., Nair, G., Baddeley, A.: Variable selection using penalised likelihoods for point patterns on a linear network. Aust. N. Z. J. Stat. **63**(3), 417–454 (2021). https://doi.org/10.1111/anzs.12341
10. Chaudhuri, S., Juan, P., Mateu, J.: Spatio-temporal modeling of traffic accidents incidence on urban road networks based on an explicit network triangulation. J. Appl. Stat. **50**(16), 3229–3250 (2023)
11. Hasanah, A., Choiruddin, A. & Prastyo, D.: On the modeling of traffic accident risk in Nganjuk regency by Poisson point process on a linear network. In: AIP Conference Proceedings, 2639 No. 1, 050007 (2022)
12. Baddeley, A., Rubbak, E., Turner, R.: Spatial Point Patterns Methodology and Applications with R. CRC press (2015)
13. Møller, J., Waagepetersen, R.P.: Statistical Inference and Simulation for Spatial Point Processes. Chapman & Hall, Florida (2004)
14. Kassambara, A.: Machine Learning Essentials: Practical Guide in R, 1st ed. Sthda (2018)
15. Indonesia, U.-U.: (UU) Nomor 2 Tahun 2022 tentang Perubahan Kedua atas Undang-Undang Nomor 38 Tahun 2004 tentang Jalan. Secretary of State, Jakarta (2022)
16. Babić, D., Fiolić, M., Babić, D., Gates, T.: Road markings and their impact on driver behaviour and road safety: a systematic review of current findings. J. Adv. Transp. **2020**(1), 7843743 (2020)
17. Babić, D., Babić, D., Fiolic, M., Ferko, M.: Road markings and signs in road safety. Encyclopedia. **2**(4), 1738–1752 (2022)
18. Choiruddin, A., Yuni Susanto, T., Husain, A.M., Kartikasari, Y.: Kppmenet: combining the kppm and elastic net regularization for inhomogeneous cox point process with correlated covariates. J. Appl. Stat. **51**(5), 993–1006 (2024). https://doi.org/10.1080/02664763.2023.2207786
19. Choiruddin, A., Coeurjolly, J.F., Letué, F.: Adaptive lasso and Dantzig selector for spatial point processes intensity estimation. Bernoulli. **29**(3), 1849–1876 (2023)

20. Baddeley, A., Coeurjolly, A., Rubak, J., Waagepetersen, E.: Logistic regression for spatial Gibbs point processes. Biometrika. **101**(2), 377–392 (2014). https://doi.org/10.1093/biomet/ast060
21. Husain, A., Choiruddin, A.: Poisson and logistic regressions for inhomogeneous multivariate point processes: a case study in the Barro Colorado Island plot. In: Mohamed, A., Yap, B.W., Zain, J.M., Berry, M.W. (eds) Soft Computing in Data Science. SCDS 2021. Communications in Computer and Information Science, vol 1489, pp. 301–311. Springer, Singapore (2021). https://doi.org/10.1007/978-981-16-7334-4_22

SETAR and SETAR-Tree Methods for $PM_{2.5}$ Air Quality Forecasting

Dinda Ayu Safira, Heri Kuswanto(✉), and Muhammad Ahsan

Department of Statistics, Institut Teknologi Sepuluh Nopember, Surabaya 60111, Indonesia
heri_k@statistika.its.ac.id

Abstract. The air quality in DKI Jakarta has significantly deteriorated due to high air pollution, especially $PM_{2.5}$ particulate pollution, which has led to significant negative impacts on human health and considerable economic losses. $PM_{2.5}$ particulates have essential health effects as they can penetrate nasal hair filters and reach the respiratory tract. One way to address air pollution issues is by using time-series prediction based on historical data to forecast daily $PM_{2.5}$ levels. Such prediction models can provide early warnings when air quality reaches hazardous levels and aid in emission control planning or emergency actions. This study employs the SETAR and SETAR-Tree models to forecast $PM_{2.5}$ concentrations in DKI Jakarta. Concentrations of $PM_{2.5}$ are collected from air quality monitoring stations from January 2022 to November 2023. The modeling results indicate that SETAR-Tree outperforms SETAR, showing lower Mean Absolute Percentage Error (MAPE) values both in-sample and out-sample, thus demonstrating better performance in predicting $PM_{2.5}$ concentrations.

Keywords: Air Quality · Nonlinearity time series · SETAR · SETAR-tree

1 Introduction

Air pollution is an important problem that occurs due to several factors, such as urban and industrial development, coal-fired power plants, motor vehicles, and consumption of gasoline and diesel that emit pollutants in the form of particles and gases that have an impact on air pollution that endangers humans [1, 2]. There are seven parameters measured in the Air Pollution Standard Index, including carbon monoxide (CO), nitrogen dioxide (NO_2), sulfur dioxide (SO_2), ozone (O_3), hydrocarbons (HC), PM_{10} (particulate diameter $<10\,\mu m$), and $PM_{2.5}$ (particulate diameter $<2.5\,\mu m$) [3]. Currently, $PM_{2.5}$ concentrations in Jakarta have reached 3.8 times more than the annual limit set by the World Health Organization (WHO). If $PM_{2.5}$ continues to increase regularly, it can threaten the health of the population [1]. Currently, Jakarta is ranked 26th out of 100 Most Polluted Major City with an air quality index (AQI) classified as medium [4]. Fine particles or aerosols, sized up to 2.5 μm, can cause smog because they have high concentrations. $PM_{2.5}$ particles, which have a small diameter and large surface area, can carry a variety of toxic substances. These particles can penetrate the filtering of nasal hair and settle the airways by flowing and diffusing. Air exchange in the lungs can result in damage to

P. C. Rodrigues et al. (Eds.): ISBIS 2024, 13, pp. 70–85, 2027.
https://doi.org/10.1007/978-3-032-32458-0_6

various parts of the body [5]. Modeling and predicting $PM_{2.5}$ based on past data is one of the efforts that can be made to overcome air pollution in DKI Jakarta by estimating daily $PM_{2.5}$ concentration levels. This can serve as a warning and plan for emissions reductions when hazardous air quality is predicted [6, 7]. $PM_{2.5}$ shows nonlinear characteristics influenced by environmental factors. Therefore, nonlinear time series analysis, such as conventional Threshold Autoregressive (TAR) analysis, can provide an in-depth understanding of nonlinear time series data [8]. The conventional method of TAR is a type of nonlinear model that involves different AR functions, thus forming an AR regime-switching model with separate AR functions [9]. TAR is divided into two variations, Self-Exciting Threshold Autoregressive (SETAR) and Smooth Transition Autoregressive (STAR). The main difference between SETAR and STAR is defining transition function and regime. The SETAR model uses a single AR model for prediction, while the STAR model enables regime change by using logistic or exponential functions [10]. The SETAR model has been commonly used effectively in economic and environmental studies to analyze nonlinear time series. Previous research modeling Indonesia's export data with the SETAR model (2,1,1) resulted in Mean Absolute Percentage (MAP) [11], model performance comparison research Autoregressive Moving Average (ARMA) and SETAR find that the SETAR model outperforms the ARMA model in modeling national inflation [12], and air pollution modeling in Kozhikode district, Kerala, with SETAR model obtained a MAPE value of 0.6049 [13]. SETAR was then developed by Godahewa et al. (2023), who introduced a tree-based algorithm designed to improve prediction accuracy by minimizing the number of hyperparameters required. The algorithm integrates the principles of the TAR model with the concept of decision trees to create a time series forecasting model called SETAR-Tree.

Recent studies have further demonstrated the effectiveness of SETAR and SETAR-Tree models in diverse applications. For instance, Ashilla (2023) applied these models to forecast gold prices in Indonesia, showing that SETAR-Tree improved predictive accuracy compared to traditional SETAR [14]. Similarly, Katabba (2024) explored the use of SETAR-GA (Genetic Algorithm) and SETAR-Tree for forecasting Indonesia's export values, illustrating the flexibility of these models in handling nonlinear time series across various economic indicators [15]. These studies reinforce the versatility of SETAR-based methods in capturing complex dynamics in real-world data.

The concentration of $PM_{2.5}$ is a nonlinear phenomenon that fluctuates with time. Therefore, the SETAR and SETAR-Tree models effectively forecast $PM_{2.5}$ concentrations. Both methods can understand nonlinear patterns in historical $PM_{2.5}$ data and predict future $PM_{2.5}$ concentrations. Although this study focuses on $PM_{2.5}$ concentrations in DKI Jakarta, the SETAR and SETAR-Tree models have the potential to be applied to other cities or regions experiencing air quality challenges. Additionally, these models can be adapted to forecast other air pollution including NO_2, PM_{10}, and SO_2, providing a more comprehensive tool for managing air quality. This paper is organized as follows. Section 2 is a description of the data and research methodologies of the study. Section 3 presents the results and discussion, including comparisons of model performance. Section 4 summarizes the results and suggests future research directions.

2 Research Methods

2.1 Source Data and Research Variable

In this study, the data used are secondary data related to air quality obtained from the official website https://satudata.jakarta.go.id/. The research variable is one of the air quality parameters, namely $PM_{2.5}$, at the DKI4 station (Lubang Buaya) in Jakarta daily from January 2022 to November 2023.

2.2 Air Quality

Air quality is an essential thing for human health. However, air quality is currently deteriorating due to air pollution caused by various sources such as several sources of pollution, such as diesel, motor vehicles, gasoline, and coal power plants, thus potentially reducing the life expectancy of the population [1]. Air pollution is a combination of gases in the form of ozone (O_3), sulfur dioxide (SO_2), nitrogen dioxide (NO_2), carbon monoxide (CO), hydrocarbons (HC), and particulates in the form of PM10 (diameter particulates <10 μm), PM2.5 (particulate diameter <2.5 μm), as well as total suspended particulate (TSP) particles [16, 17].

2.3 Self-Exciting Threshold Autoregressive (SETAR)

The SETAR model is a variation of the TAR model that can be used to identify asymmetric phenomena, depict complex nonlinearities and capture data changes that linear models cannot capture. The TAR model assumes that the threshold value determines the regime. SETAR model is produced by considering the threshold variable to be the lag value of the time series itself. The SETAR model used in this study is a 2-regime SETAR model with the following model equation:

$$y_t = \begin{cases} \phi_0^{(1)} + \sum_{l=1}^{p_1} \phi_l^{(1)} y_{t-l} + \varepsilon_t^{(1)}, \textit{ if } y_{t-l} < T \\ \phi_0^{(2)} + \sum_{l=1}^{p_2} \phi_l^{(2)} y_{t-l} + \varepsilon_t^{(2)}, \textit{ otherwise} \end{cases} \tag{1}$$

where y_t is the the time series value at time- t, n is the number of lags in the time series, T is the regime determination threshold, d is the delay, $\phi^{(i)}$ are the AR parameters, and $\varepsilon^{(i)}$ are the errors in regime-i. The SETAR model assigns regimes based on lag values from time series. The first regime is determined from the training cases where the corresponding lag value is smaller than the threshold value (T). For the other instances where the matching lag value is larger than or equal to T, the other regime is identified [18].

In this study, the parameters of the SETAR model have been estimated by using the method of Ordinary Least Squares (OLS). For each regime, OLS minimizes the sum of the squares of the residuals between the observations and the predictions from the autoregressive structure. The estimation was performed using the tar() function from the tsDyn package in R, which applies OLS separately for each regime based on the identified threshold values

2.4 Self-Exciting Threshold Autoregressive—Tree (SETAR-Tree)

SETAR-Tree is an algorithm that adopts the concept of the SETAR model to determine regime separation, then conducts a grid search approach to obtain optimal lag and threshold for node separation. The illustration of SETAR-Tree construction can be seen in Fig. 1 [18].

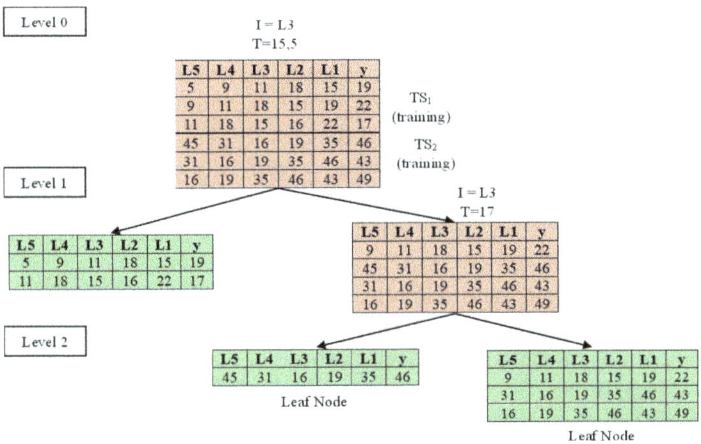

Fig. 1. Illustration of SETAR-tree construction with TS_1 and TS_2. *Source* Godahewa et al. [18]

Level 0 represents the root node formed from the matrix with training data TS1 and TS2. Then, the training cases are split into the child nodes using a 2-regime SETAR model, resulting in two child nodes for each tree node. A grid search approach is employed to determine the optimal lag (l) and threshold (T) for node splitting. If the appropriate lag (l) value is smaller than T and larger than or equal to T, the node will be divided into two separate child node groups.

The SETAR-Tree model utilizes the SETAR model for the root node and parent nodes, while it employs a linear Autoregressive (AR) model for the leaf nodes. The equations for the root node and parent nodes in the SETAR-Tree model are as follows:

$$y_t = \begin{cases} \phi_0^{(1)} + \sum_{l=1}^{L} \phi_l^{(1)} y_{t-l} + \varepsilon_t^{(1)}, \; if \; y_{t-l} < T \\ \phi_0^{(2)} + \sum_{l=1}^{L} \phi_l^{(2)} y_{t-l} + \varepsilon_t^{(2)}, \; otherwise \end{cases} \tag{2}$$

The SETAR-Tree model from the leaf node utilizes Autoregressive (AR):

$$y_t = \phi_1 y_{t-1} + \phi_2 y_{t-2} + \cdots + \phi_L y_{t-L} + \varepsilon_t \tag{3}$$

In the SETAR-Tree model, each node will only be split if the training data exhibits nonlinearity or a significant decrease in training error. Thus, the SETAR-Tree model employs a leaf-by-leaf approach to tree growth, where tree branches can have varying lengths. At level 1, only one node is divided to child nodes, while the other nodes remain intact and are considered leaf nodes because further splitting of those nodes does not meet the specified criteria. The node splitting process in the SETAR-Tree model is determined by two criteria: linearity testing and error reduction obtained from node splitting. If there are no nodes that need to be split, then the tree construction ends. Leaf nodes in the SETAR-Tree model can exist at different depths, as illustrated in As seen in Fig. 2, two leaf nodes are at level 2, while one is at level 1. Every leaf node has a model linked to it that was trained using the data instances that relate to that node. The same optimum lag and threshold that are used in the node separation procedure beginning at the root are used in testing to identify the correct leaf node for a particular test instance. Once the leaf node has been found, the trained model is used to create predictions for test data. One advantage of the SETAR-Tree model is its minimal need for hyperparameter tuning, as the default settings typically produce satisfactory results. By utilizing only a few key parameters to assess linearity and quantify error reduction in node separation, the model achieves reliable performance without requiring significant external adjustments to its hyperparameters. SETAR-Tree can automatically adapt and deliver accurate predictions with default settings, making it an efficient and practical solution for time series forecasting problems. [18].

All computations and modeling were performed using R programming language, particularly leveraging the TSA and forecast packages for time series analysis.

3 Result and Discussion

3.1 Overview of Research Variables

The description of $PM_{2.5}$ concentration can be summarized as descriptive statistics (Table 1).

Table 1. Descriptive statistics

Minimum	Median	Mean	Maximum
33	98	97.28	287

The lowest $PM_{2.5}$ concentration was recorded on November 26, 2023, at 33 $\mu m/m^3$, while the highest was on September 28, 2023, at 287 $\mu m/m^3$. The average $PM_{2.5}$ concentration at DKI4 station (Lubang Buaya) in Jakarta from January 2022 to November 2023 was 97.8 $\mu m/m^3$. The pattern of $PM_{2.5}$ concentration data is presented in Fig. 2.

3.2 Checking Stationarity of Variance and Mean

A stationarity checks on the $PM_{2.5}$ concentration plot indicates high variability and non-stationary data. A logarithmic transformation is carried out to address the non-stationarity of the variance, making the data more stationary. Table 3 shows the Augmented Dickey-Fuller (ADF) test results on the $PM_{2.5}$ data, confirming that the time series is stationary with respect to the mean after log transformation (Table 2 and Fig. 3).

Below is the plot of the transformed data.

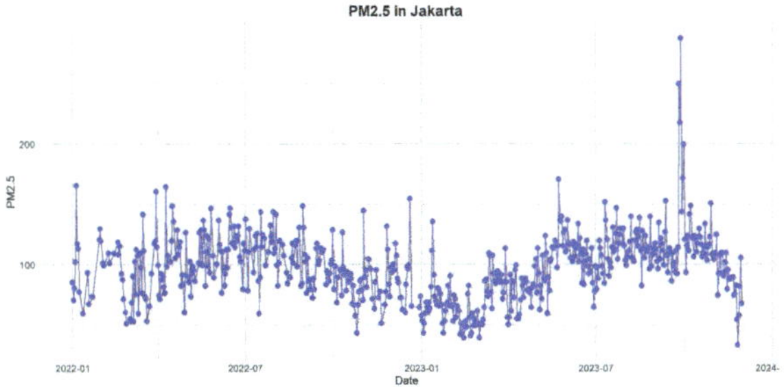

Fig. 2. Pattern of $PM_{2.5}$ concentration data

Table 2. Augmented dickey-fuller test

Augmented dickey-fuller test	
Dickey-Fuller	p-value
−3.7319	0.0224

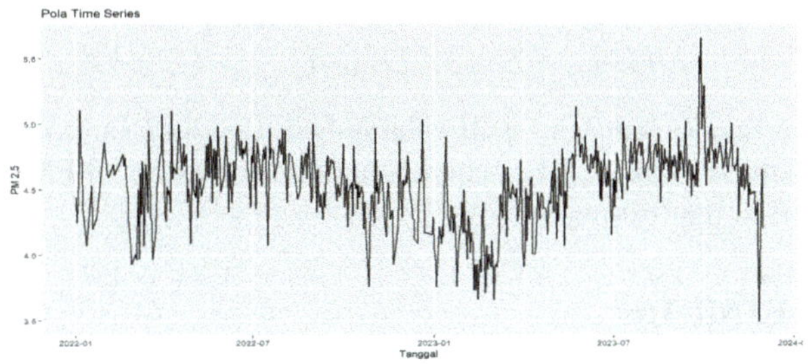

Fig. 3. Plot of data transformation

3.3 Modeling SETAR

The SETAR modeling in this study employs a 2-regime SETAR with a single threshold. A grid search approach is conducted to determine the optimal parameter values for delay and threshold based on the criterion of the smallest AIC. Scenarios are performed with each p_1 and p_2 having a maximum lag value of 10 and delay (2 to 10) (Table 3).

The smallest MAPE value is 3.2522 with a delay of 6, where p1 is lag 9 and p2 is lag 8, forming a SETAR (2,9,8) model with parameter estimation using OLS as follows.

Based on Table 4, the SETAR (2,9,8) model has some parameters that are not significant with a significance level of 0.05. Therefore, a grid search with a maximum lag value of 3 is conducted (Table 5 and Fig. 4).

The plot of the grid search results shows the smallest AIC value.

Based on the second grid search results, the smallest AIC value (with significant parameters) is obtained for the SETAR (2,3,1) model, with parameter estimation using OLS as follows.

Table 3. Grid search for SETAR model

d	p_1	p_2	r	RMSE	MAPE (%)
2	5	9	4.673	0.1945	3.2980
3	9	8	4.745	0.1947	3.2819
4	2	8	4.533	0.1978	3.3853
5	9	6	4.787	0.1952	3.3023
6	**9**	**8**	**4.691**	**0.1929**	**3.2522**
7	8	3	4.7	0.1965	3.3013
8	5	3	4.718	0.1971	3.3259
9	8	3	4.7	0.1966	3.3178
10	8	5	4.727	0.1953	3.2930

Based on Table 6, the SETAR (2,3,1) model has significantly estimated all parameters with p-values less than the significance level (0.05). The equation for the SETAR (2,3,1) model is as follows.

$$\hat{Y}_t = \begin{cases} 0.7152 + 0.5250Y_{t-1} + 0.1137Y_{t-2} + 0.2064Y_{t-3}, \textit{ if } Y_{t-2} \leq 4.736198 \\ 1.9988 + 0.5715Y_{t-1}, \textit{ if } Y_{t-2} > 4.736198 \end{cases} \tag{4}$$

The prediction results from the well-established model on both in-sample and out-of-sample data with SETAR (2,3,1), when compared to historical $PM_{2.5}$ concentration data, are presented in the following (Fig. 5).

3.4 Modeling SETAR-Tree

The SETAR-Tree model is an extension of the conventional SETAR model that utilizes the SETAR concept to determine regime partitioning. Node splitting is done by selecting the optimal lag and threshold through a grid search approach. This study uses a 2-regime SETAR model. Godahewa used lag 10 as the default parameter in the SETAR-Tree algorithm [18]. Therefore, this research conducts a grid search with lags ranging from 2 to 10, selecting the optimal lag based on the smallest AIC value (Table 7).

Based on the grid search results, the smallest AIC value is obtained for the SETAR-Tree model with lag 9, with the following parameter estimation.

Based on Table 8, the SETAR-Tree model with lag 9 forms four parent nodes and six leaf nodes. The equations for the parent nodes are presented in Eqs. (5)–(9).

Root Node:

$$\widehat{Y}_t = \begin{cases} \begin{matrix} 0.6798Y_{t-1} + 0.2511Y_{t-2} - 0.0426Y_{t-3} \\ -0.0308Y_{t-4} + 0.1704Y_{t-5} - 0.1366Y_{t-6} \\ +0.1928Y_{t-7} - 0.0501Y_{t-8} + 0.2417Y_{t-9} \end{matrix}, & \textit{if } Y_{t-1} \leq 4.37639 \\ \begin{matrix} 0.3375Y_{t-1} - 0.1437Y_{t-2} + 0.2996Y_{t-3} \\ -0.0949Y_{t-4} - 0.0114Y_{t-5} + 0.5143Y_{t-6} \\ -0.0781Y_{t-7} + 0.2189Y_{t-8} - 0.0003Y_{t-9} \end{matrix}, & \textit{if } Y_{t-1} > 4.37639 \end{cases} \tag{5}$$

Table 4. Parameter estimation of SETAR (2,9,8) model

No	Regime	Parameter	Estimate	p-value
1	Lower regime	$\phi_0^{(1)}$	0.6396	0.0057
		$\phi_1^{(1)}$	0.5199	0.0000
		$\phi_2^{(1)}$	0.1424	0.0182
		$\phi_3^{(1)}$	0.0560	0.3581
		$\phi_4^{(1)}$	−0.0146	0.8115
		$\phi_5^{(1)}$	0.1105	0.0634
		$\phi_6^{(1)}$	−0.0896	0.2230
		$\phi_7^{(1)}$	−0.0427	0.4920
		$\phi_8^{(1)}$	0.0780	0.1848
		$\phi_9^{(1)}$	0.0957	0.0748
2	Upper regime	$\phi_0^{(2)}$	21.310	0.0001
		$\phi_1^{(2)}$	0.3597	0.0000
		$\phi_2^{(2)}$	−0.0289	0.6884
		$\phi_3^{(2)}$	0.2798	0.0001
		$\phi_4^{(2)}$	−0.0791	0.2733
		$\phi_5^{(2)}$	0.0997	0.1764
		$\phi_6^{(2)}$	−0.2489	0.0083
		$\phi_7^{(2)}$	0.0468	0.4859
		$\phi_8^{(2)}$	0.1213	0.0616

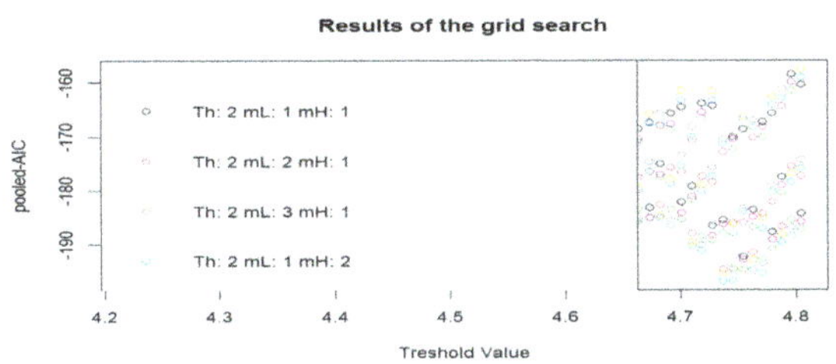

Fig. 4. Grid search plot

Table 5. Grid search for SETAR model

d	p_1	p_2	r	AIC
2	**3**	**1**	**4.736198**	**−196.8907**
2	3	1	4.744932	−196.7582
2	1	2	4.465908	−195.9316
2	1	2	4.477337	−195.8856
2	1	2	4.454347	−195.8245
2	3	1	4.770685	−195.3987
2	3	2	4.736198	−195.2571
2	2	2	4.477337	−194.9444
2	2	2	4.465908	−194.9114
2	3	2	4.744932	−194.8706

Table 6. Parameter estimation of SETAR (2,3,1) model

No	Regime	Parameter	Estimation	p-value
1	Lower regime	$\phi_0^{(1)}$	0.7152	0.0002
		$\phi_1^{(1)}$	0.5250	0.0000
		$\phi_2^{(1)}$	0.1137	0.0315
		$\phi_3^{(1)}$	0.2064	0.0002
2	Upper regime	$\phi_0^{(2)}$	1.9988	0.0000
		$\phi_1^{(2)}$	0.5715	0.0000

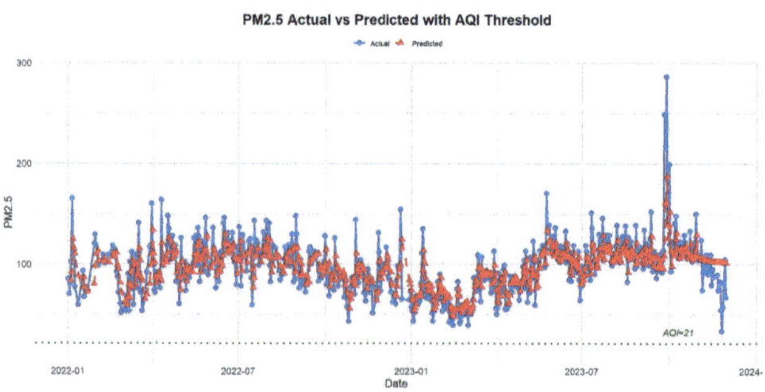

Fig. 5. SETAR (2,3,1) prediction

Table 7. Grid search for SETAR-tree model

Model	Depth	Leaf model	AIC	RMSE	MAPE
Lag 2	3	1	−67.97	0.2002	3.4366
		2	−7.02		
		3	−103.07		
		4	−19.65		
		5	−3.26		
Lag 3	3	1	−5.80	0.1949	3.3469
		2	−1.27		
		3	−79.55		
		4	−129.83		
		5	−5.70		
Lag 4	2	1	−69.57	0.1994	3.4056
		2	−128.40		
		3	−4.01		
Lag 5	2	1	−19.2	0.1934	3.2452
		2	−207.0		
		3	−23.0		
Lag 6	2	1	−17.30	0.1944	3.2863
		2	−191.60		
		3	−2.99		
Lag 7	2	1	−14.67	0.1938	3.2810
		2	−193.49		
		3	−1.46		
Lag 8	3	1	−13.6	0.1885	3.2059
		2	−16.0		
		3	−18.2		
		4	−172.6		
Lag 9	**5**	**1**	**−0.06**	**0.1806**	**3.0186**
		2	**−16.04**		
		3	**−111.25**		
		4	**−10.90**		
		5	**−115.60**		
		6	**−34.37**		

(continued)

Table 7. *(continued)*

Model	Depth	Leaf model	AIC	RMSE	MAPE
Lag 10	3	1	−5.95	0.1805	3.0876
		2	3.43		
		3	−14.39		
		4	−109.39		
		5	−102.21		

Parent Node 1:

$$\widehat{Y_t} = \begin{cases} 0.3375Y_{t-1} - 0.1437Y_{t-2} + 0.2996Y_{t-3} \\ -0.0949Y_{t-4} - 0.0114Y_{t-5} + 0.5143Y_{t-6} & , \; if \;\; Y_{t-6} \le 4.38 \\ -0.0781Y_{t-7} + 0.2189Y_{t-8} - 0.0003Y_{t-9} \\ 0.3849Y_{t-1} + 0.0866Y_{t-2} + 0.2001Y_{t-3} \\ +0.0292Y_{t-4} + 0.0896Y_{t-5} + 0.0394Y_{t-6} & , \; if \;\; Y_{t-6} > 4.38 \\ +0.1729Y_{t-7} - 0.0594Y_{t-8} + 0.0556Y_{t-9} \end{cases} \tag{6}$$

Parent Node 2:

$$\widehat{Y_t} = \begin{cases} 0.3849Y_{t-1} + 0.0866Y_{t-2} + 0.2001Y_{t-3} \\ +0.0292Y_{t-4} + 0.0896Y_{t-5} + 0.0394Y_{t-6} & , \; if \;\; Y_{t-2} \le 4.73 \\ +0.1729Y_{t-7} - 0.0594Y_{t-8} + 0.0556Y_{t-9} \\ 1.2248Y_{t-1} + 0.0473Y_{t-2} - 1.1133Y_{t-3} \\ -0.1418Y_{t-4} - 0.1702Y_{t-5} + 1.1278Y_{t-6} & , \; if \;\; Y_{t-2} > 4.73 \\ +0.4570Y_{t-7} - 0.3563Y_{t-8} - 0.1674Y_{t-9} \end{cases} \tag{7}$$

Parent Node 3:

$$\widehat{Y_t} = \begin{cases} 1.2248Y_{t-1} + 0.0473Y_{t-2} - 1.1133Y_{t-3} \\ -0.1418Y_{t-4} - 0.1702Y_{t-5} + 1.1278Y_{t-6} & , \; if \;\; Y_{t-3} \le 4.54 \\ +0.4570Y_{t-7} - 0.3563Y_{t-8} - 0.1674Y_{t-9} \\ 0.3912Y_{t-1} + 0.1659Y_{t-2} + 0.19206Y_{t-3} \\ -0.1312Y_{t-4} + 0.2220Y_{t-5} + 0.0054Y_{t-6} & , \; if \;\; Y_{t-3} > 4.54 \\ -0.1519Y_{t-7} + 0.1973Y_{t-8} + 0.0991Y_{t-9} \end{cases} \tag{8}$$

Parent Node 4:

$$\widehat{Y_t} = \begin{cases} 0.3912Y_{t-1} + 0.1659Y_{t-2} + 0.19206Y_{t-3} \\ -0.1312Y_{t-4} + 0.2220Y_{t-5} + 0.0054Y_{t-6} & , \; if \;\; Y_{t-2} \le 4.99 \\ -0.1519Y_{t-7} + 0.1973Y_{t-8} + 0.0991Y_{t-9} \\ 0.6843Y_{t-1} + 0.8571Y_{t-2} - 0.6795Y_{t-3} \\ +0.0797Y_{t-4} + 0.5658Y_{t-5} - 0.8127Y_{t-6} & , \; if \;\; Y_{t-2} > 4.99 \\ -0.1269Y_{t-7} + 0.0858Y_{t-8} + 0.2834Y_{t-9} \end{cases} \tag{9}$$

Table 8. Parameter estimation of SETAR-tree model

Level	Leaf model	Optimum lag	Optimum threshold	Parameter (Lag)	Estimation
Level 0	1	L1	4.37639	L1	0.6798
				L2	0.2511
				L3	−0.0426
				L4	−0.0308
				L5	0.1704
				L6	−0.1366
				L7	−0.1128
				L8	0.1430
				L9	0.0961
Level 1	2	L6	4.38	L1	0.3375
				L2	−0.1437
				L3	0.2996
				L4	−0.0949
				L5	−0.0114
				L6	0.5143
				L7	−0.0781
				L8	0.2189
				L9	−0.0003
Level 2	3	L2	4.73	L1	0.3849
				L2	0.0866
				L3	0.2001
				L4	0.0292
				L5	0.0896
				L6	0.0394
				L7	0.1729
				L8	−0.0594
				L9	0.0556
Level 3	4	L3	4.54	L1	1.2248
				L2	0.0473
				L3	−1.1133
				L4	−0.1418
				L5	−0.1702

(continued)

Table 8. (*continued*)

Level	Leaf model	Optimum lag	Optimum threshold	Parameter (Lag)	Estimation
				L6	1.1278
				L7	0.4570
				L8	−0.3563
				L9	−0.1674
Level 4	5	L3	4.99	L1	0.3912
				L2	0.1659
				L3	0.1920
				L4	−0.1312
				L5	0.2220
				L6	0.0054
				L7	−0.1519
				L8	0.1973
				L9	0.0991
Level 5	6			L1	0.6843
				L2	0.8571
				L3	−0.6795
				L4	0.0797
				L5	0.5658
				L6	−0.8127
				L7	−0.1269
				L8	0.0858
				L9	0.2834

The following is an illustration of the SETAR-tree that is formed (Fig. 6).

The prediction results from the well-established model on both in-sample and out-of-sample data with SETAR-Tree, when compared to historical $PM_{2.5}$ concentration data, are presented in the following (Fig. 7).

3.5 Comparison Between SETAR and SETAR-Tree

Based on the model evaluation, SETAR-Tree outperforms SETAR in predicting $PM_{2.5}$ concentrations in DKI Jakarta. With an in-sample RMSE of 0.1806 and an out-of-sample RMSE of 0.2885, SETAR-Tree yields lower prediction errors than SETAR. This is further evident from the in-sample MAPE of 3.0186% and the out-of-sample MAPE of 4.8268%, which are lower than SETAR. These results indicate that SETAR-Tree exhibits superior performance in forecasting $PM_{2.5}$ concentrations, with lower error rates in both in-sample and out-of-sample models. Beyond the case of $PM_{2.5}$ in DKI Jakarta, the

Fig. 6. Illustration of SETAR-tree

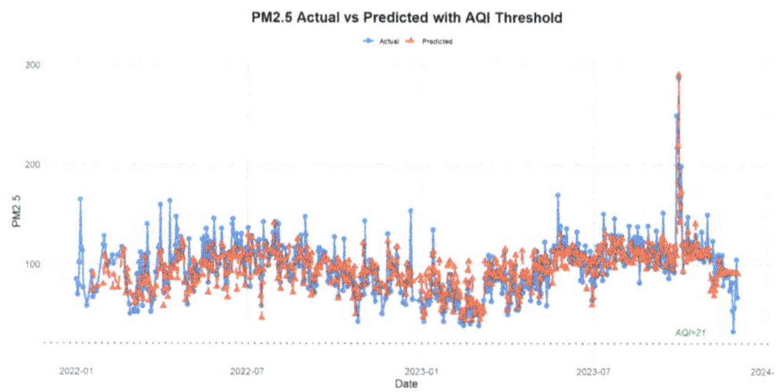

Fig. 7. SETAR-tree lag 9 prediction

flexibility of the SETAR-Tree model allows for potential adaptation to other air quality parameters like PM_{10} or NO_2, which also exhibit nonlinear behavior. Applying this approach to other cities facing air pollution, especially urban areas with rapid industrial development, could yield valuable insights and further validate the robustness of these models (Table 9).

Table 9. Evaluating the results of SETAR and SETAR-tree models

Model		RMSE	MAPE (%)
SETAR (2,3,1)	*In Sample*	0.2030	3.4625
	Out Sample	0.3102	5.0161
SETAR-tree	*In Sample*	0.1806	3.0186
	Out Sample	0.2885	4.8268

4 Conclusion

The SETAR-Tree model consistently performs better in the prediction of $PM_{2.5}$ concentrations in DKI Jakarta than the SETAR model. With lower RMSE and MAPE, both in-sample, and out-of-sample, SETAR-Tree provides more accurate and reliable estimates for air quality planning and regional decision-making. Thus, implementing SETAR-Tree can effectively address air pollution issues, protect public health, and support environmental sustainability in DKI Jakarta. Future research could explore the applicability of the SETAR and SETAR-Tree models to other regions and various air pollutants. This would help to generalize the findings and provide broader insights into how these models perform in different environmental contexts, aiding policymakers in diverse regions to manage air quality more effectively.

Acknowledgments. The authors would like to express their gratitude to the Ministry of Education, Culture, Research, and Technology of the Republic of Indonesia for funding this research under the "Master Program of Education Leading to a Doctoral Degree for Excellent Graduates (PMDSU) Batch VII," through Grant Number 038/E5/PG.02.00.PL/2024 and local Grant Number 1797/PKS/ITS/2024.

References

1. Greenstone, M., Fan, Q.: Indonesia's worsening air quality and its impact on life expectancy. Air Qual Life Index, 1–10 (2019)
2. Gusnita, D.: Pencemaran logam berat timbal (pb) di udara dan upaya penghapusan bensin bertimbal. Ber Dirgant. **13**, 95–101 (2012)
3. Kehutanan KLH dan: Peraturan Menteri Lingkungan Hidup dan Kehutanan Nomor 14 Tahun 2020 tentang Indeks Standar Pencemar Udara, Jakarta (2020)
4. IQAir: Live Most Polluted Major City Ranking (2024). https://www.iqair.com/world-air-quality-ranking (accessed February 27, 2024).
5. Xing, Y.F., Xu, Y.H., Shi, M.H., Lian, Y.X.: The impact of $PM_{2.5}$ on the human respiratory system. J. Thorac. Dis. **8**, E69–E74 (2016). https://doi.org/10.3978/j.issn.2072-1439.2016.01.19
6. Dong, Y., Wang, H., Zhang, L., Zhang, K.: An improved model for $PM_{2.5}$ inference based on support vector machine. In: 2016 IEEE/ACIS 17th IEEE/ACIS International Conference on Software Engineering, Artificial Intelligence, Networking and Parallel/Distributed Computing. SNPD 2016, pp. 27–31. https://doi.org/10.1109/SNPD.2016.7515873
7. Xayasouk, T., Lee, H.M., Lee, G.: Air pollution prediction using long short-term memory (LSTM) and deep autoencoder (DAE) models. Sustain, 12 (2020). https://doi.org/10.3390/su12062570
8. Tsay, R.S., Chen, R.: Nonlinear Time Series Analysis. John Wiley & Sons, New Jersey (2019)
9. Tong, H.: Non-linear Time Series: a Dynamical System Approach. Clarendon Press, Oxford (1993)
10. Zhou, J., Ågren, A.: Smooth Transition Autoregressive Models a Study of the Industrial Production Index of Sweden a Thesis. Uppsala Universitet (2010)
11. Riyansyah, H.N.G.P., Saputro, D.R.S., Winarno, B.: Identifikasi model self-exciting threshold autoregressive Dengan switching two regime (Kasus Pada data Ekspor Agrikultur Di Indonesia). Barekeng J Ilmu Mat Dan Terap. **14**, 511–522 (2020). https://doi.org/10.30598/barekengvol14iss4pp511-522

12. Putri, T., Irhamah.: Peramalan return Saham Bank Central Asia genetic algorithm. J Sains Dan Seni ITS. **5**, 1–6 (2016)
13. Lineesh, M.C.: Time series analysis and forecasting of air quality index. AIP Conf Proc, 2336 (2021). https://doi.org/10.1063/5.0045753
14. Ashilla, A.F.: Peramalan Harga Emas Indonesia Menggunakan SETAR dan SETAR-Tree. Institut Teknologi Sepuluh Nopermber (2023)
15. Katabba, Y.I.: Peramalan Nilai Ekspor Indonesia Menggunakan SETAR-GA dan SETAR-Tree. Institut Teknologi Sepuluh Nopember (2024)
16. Cohen, A.J., Brauer, M., Burnett, R., Anderson, H.R., Frostad, J., Estep, K., et al.: Estimates and 25-year trends of the global burden of disease attributable to ambient air pollution: an analysis of data from the global burden of diseases study 2015. Lancet. **389**, 1907–1918 (2017). https://doi.org/10.1016/S0140-6736(17)30505-6
17. Rita, R., Lestiani, D.D., Hamonangan, E., Santoso, M., Yulinawati, H.: Kualitas Udara (Pm10 Dan Pm2.5) Untuk Melengkapi Kajian Indeks Kualitas Lingkungan Hidup. Ecolab. **10**, 1–7 (2016). https://doi.org/10.20886/jklh.2016.10.1.1-7
18. Godahewa, R., Webb, G.I., Schmidt, D., Bergmeir, C.: SETAR-Tree: a Novel and Accurate Tree Algorithm for Global Time Series Forecasting, vol. 112. Springer, US (2023). https://doi.org/10.1007/s10994-023-06316-x

Robust Regression Model on Toddler Diarrhea Case in East Java Province: Maximum Likelihood and Generalized Maximum Likelihood Estimations

Yuliana Susanti(✉), Hasih Pratiwi, Andreas Rony Wijaya, Respatiwulan, Sri Sulistijowati Handajani, and Muhammad Bayu Nirwana

Study Program of Statistics, Faculty of Mathematics and Natural Sciences, Universitas Sebelas Maret, Surakarta, Indonesia
yulianasusanti@staff.uns.ac.id

Abstract. Diarrhea is an infectious disease of the gastrointestinal tract that poses significant health challenges throughout the world, including in Indonesia. In East Java Province, diarrhea cases in toddlers have increased, namely 241.523 cases in 2019, making it the second highest after West Java. This disease contributes significantly to the death rate of children aged 29 days to 59 months in children. A multiple linear regression prediction model for diarrhea cases is needed by considering the factors that influence it, such as the number of children in a household with good food management, families that have access to adequate sanitation/healthy latrine facilities, adequate drinking water facilities. Inadequate, and malnutrition in toddlers. Least squares method is an approach to estimating multiple regression model parameters with four assumptions, however, diarrhea cases in East Java have outliers and their distribution is not normal, so they require robust regression estimation methods, such as Maximum Likelihood Estimation (M) and General M Estimation (GM). This study aims to model the factors that significantly influence toddler diarrhea cases in East Java using robust regression with M and GM estimations. The results of this study show that the M and GM estimations robust regression model have value of adjusted R-squared and AIC respectively 84.16% and 99.74%, and a value of *AIC* are 673.3446 and 629.0898. The GM estimation has the largest adjusted R-squared and the smallest AIC, so the GM estimation is better to use than the M estimation.

Keywords: Diarrhea · Robust regression · M Estimation · GM Estimation

1 Introduction

Disease is a condition of weakness or reduced performance of a part of the body that causes interference with a person's physical or mental function. This can be caused by various factors, such as genetics, lifestyle, environment, and many more. Illness can vary from mild to severe. Correct diagnosis and appropriate treatment are essential to overcome or manage the disease. Every person has the right to receive health by the

P. C. Rodrigues et al. (Eds.): ISBIS 2024, 13, pp. 86–99, 2027.
https://doi.org/10.1007/978-3-032-32458-0_7

nation's national goals as regulated in Law Number 36 of 2009 with one of the articles in article 8 which reads "Every person has the right to obtain information about their health data including the actions and treatment they have received or will receive from health workers. East Java Province is a province that makes a significant contribution to the number of cases of toddler diarrhea in Indonesia. Based on the data from the Ministry of Health of Indonesia, in 2018, East Java Province had 232,398 cases of toddler diarrhea, followed by Central Java with 178,197 [1]. Cases of toddler diarrhea in East Java Province increased in 2019 with the number of toddler diarrhea reaching 241,523 and ranking second after West Java.

The greatest prevalence of diarrhea was in the infant age group at 10.6% and toddlers at 12.3%, while in the general group, it was 8% (Basic Health Research, 2018) [2]. Diarrhea is the second leading cause of death after pneumonia in babies aged 29 days–11 months, which is around 9.8%, and, in children, aged 12 – 59 months account for 4.5% of total deaths in 2022. Indonesia is still inadequate in terms of sanitation.

According to Basic Health Research (2010) [3], approximately 116 million people do not have access to adequate sanitation. This measure of environmental health consists of household suitability, provision of clean water, feces disposal, rubbish disposal, and waste disposal. Poverty is related to the inability to achieve minimum needs outside of income (non-income factors), such as health, education, water, and adequate sanitation.

Therefore, as a form of preventive action to prevent cases of diarrhea in toddlers, a regression analysis model can be used to build using factors that influence diarrhea cases in toddlers, especially in East Java Province. Regression analysis is a statistical analysis method used to determine the relationship between the response variable and predictor variables. One method that can be utilized to estimate parameters is using the Ordinary Least Squares (OLS) in regression tests (Burton and Alexander, 2021) [4]. However, the data on toddler diarrhea cases used contained outliers which caused the assumption of normality to not be met, so a method was needed that could handle data containing outliers without having to discard the data, namely through the use of robust regression.

The robust regression method will produce a regression equation model resistant to outliers [5]. Robust regression analysis provides an alternative to the least squares method regression model when fundamental assumptions, such as normality assumptions, are not met by the nature of the data. This method is essential for analyzing the data affected by outliers so that the result against outliers [6].

There are several estimation methods in robust regression, such as estimation: Maximum Likelihood Type (M), Scale (S), Method of Moment (MM), and Generalized M (GM). The M estimation is one of the robust regression estimation methods. The letter M identifies that the estimate M is the maximum likelihood type. According to Montgomery et al. [7], the principle of M estimation is to minimize the error function ρ. Research on robust regression with data in the form of the number of maternal deaths.

has also been carried out by Araswati [8]. The research results show that the number of maternal deaths in Indonesia in 2020 is influenced by the number of patient hypertension in pregnancy, percentage of pregnant women who receive services first visit during pregnancy, the percentage of births assisted by personnel health, and the number of HIV positive pregnant women was 98.2%.

The MM estimation was introduced by Yohai [9]. The MM estimation is a combination of the S estimation method and the M estimation method. Wilcox [10], the GM estimate is an extension of the M estimate when the M estimate is less sensitive to outliers in the predictor variables. Research related to M estimation, GM estimation, and high breakdown estimation points that have been applied to real cases using a procedure bootstrapping was carried out by Lee [11]. The results of this research can be concluded that M estimation and GM estimation gave better results appropriate than the Least Squares Method (OLS) when there is an assumption of normality which was violated.

Kusuma et al. [12] have carried out depth index modeling poverty in Indonesia in 2019 using a robust regression model estimation of M with Huber weighting. The research results show that variables which has a significant effect on the poverty depth index in Indonesia in 2019 is the percentage of poor people, Gini ratio and percentage households that use lighting with an electric source (40% to lower).

Aristiarto et al. [13] have carried out a robust regression analysis of GM estimates on the poverty severity index for provinces in Indonesia in 2021 using regression analysis are the variables percentage of poor people, human development index, and the proportion of households with self-owned house status is variables that have a significant effect on the poverty severity index in Indonesia in 2021. We are stated that GM estimation is able to handle the influence of outliers and produces the value adjusted R squared of 95.87%.

Subzar et al. [14] have carried out a comparison of robust regression methods GM estimation using various weights in the robust regression method for estimators to population means based on random sampling simple without replacement in case of outliers. From the results of that research. It was concluded that the GM estimation method with Mallow's weighting, GM estimation method with Schweppe weighting, and GM estimation method with SIS weighting is better when compared with OLS and M estimation methods with Huber weighting.

Fauzan et al. [15] must determine the robust regression model with Least Trimmed Square (LTS) estimation and Generalized M (GM) estimation to overcome the problems, we were stated that the regression model is robust with GM estimation and can produce a precision (adjusted R squared) of 100%.

Arya Said et al. [16] have compared the accuracy of the Robust Estimation Method Regression Model of Moment (MM) and Generalized-M (GM) Estimation in Modeling the Closing Price of Technology Sector Stocks Year. The analyst continues using MM estimator and GM estimator then compute and compare and AIC to find the best model. This research concludes that GM estimator model was the best model and Book Value (BV), Price to Book Value (PBV), Debt to Equity Ratio (DER), Return on Equity (ROE) dan Net Profit Margin (NPM) influences closing price tech company's stock.

This study aims to develop a robust regression model for the number of diarrheas in toddlers in East Java 2021 data based on the influencing factors, used estimation methods in robust regression are maximum likelihood (M) estimation, and generalized M (GM) estimation.

The organization of this article is divided into four sections. Section 1 contains the research background, previous studies, and research objectives. Section 2 outlines the research methodology of this study, specifically focusing on the M-estimation and

GM-estimation algorithms. Section 3 presents the results and discussion regarding the application of the M-estimation and GM-estimation algorithms to the issue of diarrheal disease. Finally, the last section provides the conclusions of this study.

2 Research Methods

The method in this research is to carry out robust regression modeling of M, and GM estimates for data on the number of diarrhea in toddlers in East Java 2021, including the number of diarrhea in toddlers in East Java (y), the number of toddlers with diarrhea with a place to manage food that meets health requirements (x_1), families with access to proper sanitation facilities/healthy latrines (x_2), the number Drinking water facilities are adequate (x_3), and the number of children under five is malnourished (x_4), taken from the Indonesian Ministry of Health [17].

2.1 Multiple Linear Regression Model

According to Montgomery and Peck [18], a multiple linear regression model with k predictors is

$$y = \beta_0 + \beta_1 x_1 + \beta_2 x_2 + \ldots + \beta_k x_k + \varepsilon \tag{1}$$

with

y : the value of the response variable.
x_k : the value of the predictor variable at the kth.
ε error ($\varepsilon \sim N\left(0, \sigma^2\right)$).
The parameter model $\beta_j, j = 0, 1, 2, \ldots, k$, are called the regression coefficients.
W may write the sample model corresponding to (1) as

$$y_i = \beta_0 + \beta_1 x_{i1} + \beta_2 x_{i2} + \ldots + \beta_k x_{ik} + \varepsilon_i = \beta_0 + \sum_{k=1}^{p} \beta_k x_{ik} + \varepsilon_i, i = 1, 2, \ldots, n \tag{2}$$

The Eq. (2) in matrix form is

$$y = X\beta + \varepsilon \tag{3}$$

with the estimated values for **y** and **ε** using OLS are

$$\hat{y} = X\hat{\beta} \text{and} \hat{\varepsilon} = y - \hat{y} = y - X\hat{\beta}.$$

2.2 M Estimation

According to Montgomery et al., [19] the basic principle of M-estimation is to minimize the residual function ρ which can be written in Eq. (4), The estimate M is an estimate that minimizes an error function of ρ, Zhang et al., [20].

$$\hat{\beta}_M = min \sum_{i=1}^{n} \rho(e_i) \tag{4}$$

The obtained estimator $\hat{\beta}_M$ is not scale invariant, so $u_i = \frac{e_i}{\hat{\sigma}}$ ^ will be used instead of e_i , with $e_i = y_i - \sum_{j=0}^{k} x_{ij}\beta_j$, so that Eq. (4) becomes

$$\hat{\beta}_M = min \sum_{i=1}^{n} \rho(u_i) = \sum_{i=1}^{n} \rho\left(\frac{e_i}{\hat{\sigma}}\right) = \sum_{i=1}^{n} \rho\left(\frac{y_i - \sum_{j=0}^{k} x_{ij}\beta_j}{\hat{\sigma}}\right) \tag{5}$$

with the chosen estimate for σ is

$$\hat{\sigma} = \frac{median|e_i - median(e_i)|}{0,6745} \tag{6}$$

The function ρ is the Huber weighting function.

$$\rho(u_i) = \{\frac{1}{2}(u_i)^2 c|u_i| - \frac{c^2}{2} \qquad , |u_i| \le c, |u_i| > c \tag{7}$$

with = 1,3450 and $u_i = \frac{u_i}{\hat{\sigma}_M}$.

Equation (5) is minimized by partially reducing $\hat{\beta}_M$ to β to obtain,

$$\sum_{i=1}^{n} X_{ij}\psi\left(\frac{Y_i - \sum_{j=0}^{p} x_{ij}\beta_j}{\hat{\sigma}_M}\right) = 0, j = 0, 1, \ldots, k. \tag{8}$$

with ψ is ρ' and X_{ij} is the i -th observation on the j -th predictor variables.

Equation (5) can be solved by defining a weighting function for the $i-$ th observation on the j -th predictor variable [21],

$$w_{iM} = \{1 \frac{c}{|u_i|} \qquad , |u_i| \le c, |u_i| > c, \text{ c } = 1,3450 \tag{9}$$

The following is the algorithm used in this research. Algorithms Estimating model uses the M estimate,

1. Estimate regression coefficients on the data using OLS.
2. Determining the error $e_i = y_i - \widehat{y_i}$
3. Calculate $\hat{\sigma}$

$$\hat{\sigma} = \frac{median|e_i - median(e_i)|}{0,6745}$$

4. Calculate value $u_i = \frac{e_i}{\hat{\sigma}}$
5. Calculate the weighted value w_i , using weighted Hubr.

$$w_{iM} = \{1 \frac{c}{|u_i|} \quad , |u_i| \le c, |u_i| > c$$

6. Estimating parameters $\hat{\beta}_M$ using the weight value of w_{iM}
7. Repeat steps 1–6 to obtain a convergent value of $\hat{\beta}_M$.
8. Test the significance of the M estimation robust regression model.
9. Calculate the adjusted R-square and the Akaike Information Criterion (AIC) value of the M estimation robust regression model.
10. Conclude from the analysis results and interpret the regression model obtained.

2.3 GM Estimation

According to Wilcox [10], in general, GM estimation can be defined by

$$\begin{aligned} \hat{\beta}_{GM} &= min \sum_{i=1}^{n} w_i \rho\left(\frac{e_i}{v(x_i)}\right) \\ &= \sum_{i=1}^{n} w_i \rho\left(\frac{y_i - \sum_{j=0}^{k} x_{ij}\beta_j}{v(x_i)\hat{\sigma}}\right) \end{aligned} \tag{10}$$

with $v(x_i)$ as the weight function for the variable x_i . According to Lin [22], the basic idea for GM estimation is to limit the influence of outlier in variable x_i using the weighting function w_i . Then the Eq. (10) can be solved by using a decrease in β_j, and equated to zero, then obtained

$$\begin{aligned} n \sum_{i=1}^{n} w_i \rho' \left(\frac{y_i - \sum_{j=0}^{k} x_{ij}\beta_j}{v(x_i)\hat{\sigma}}\right) &= 0 \\ \sum_{i=1}^{n} x_{ij} w_i \psi \left(\frac{y_i - \sum_{j=0}^{k} x_{ij}\beta_j}{v(x_i)\hat{\sigma}}\right) &= 0 \end{aligned} \tag{11}$$

According to Anderson et. al. [23], the weights used are Schweppe weights with $w_i = \sqrt{1 - h_{ii}}$ and $v(x_i) = w_i$, then obtained,

$$\begin{aligned} w_i &= w_i \frac{\psi\left(\frac{u_i}{v(x_i)}\right)}{(u_i)} \\ &= \frac{w_i}{u_i} \psi\left(\frac{u_i}{v(x_i)}\right) \end{aligned}$$

$$w_i = \frac{\sqrt{1 - h_{ii}}}{u_i} \psi\left(\frac{u_i}{\sqrt{1 - h_{ii}}}\right) \tag{12}$$

where $u_i = \frac{e_i}{\hat{\sigma}}$, with $\hat{\sigma} = 1,48M_i$, and M_i is the median of $(n - k)$ largest of e_i and $\psi(x) = max\{-K, min(K, x)\}$ is the Huber influence function with $K = 2\sqrt{\frac{k+1}{n}}$, and k: number of predictor variables.

The following is the algorithm used in this research. Algorithms Estimating model uses the GM estimate.

1. Estimate regression coefficients on the data using OLS.
2. Determine the error $e_i = y_i - \widehat{y_i}$
3. Determine the value M_i which is the median of $(n - k)$.
4. Determining the estimated value of $\hat{\sigma} = 1,48M_i$.
5. Determining the value of $u_i = \frac{e_i}{\hat{\sigma}}$.
6. Determining the value of the weight $w_i = \frac{\sqrt{1-h_{ii}}}{u_i}\psi\left(\frac{u_i}{\sqrt{1-h_{ii}}}\right)$.
7. Estimating parameters $\hat{\beta}_{GM}$ using the weight value of w_i .
8. Repeating steps 1–7 to obtain a convergent value of $\hat{\beta}_{GM}$
9. Testing the significance of the parameters of the GM estimation robust regression model.
10. Calculate the adjusted R-square and the Akaike Information Criterion (AIC) value of the GM estimation robust regression model.
11. Conclude from the analysis results and interpret the regression model obtained.

2.4 Model Selections

Selection of a better model can be done in several ways, including by looking at the adjusted coefficient of determination value and the Akaike Information Criterion (AIC) value. Selection of the best model on data based on the most significant adjusted R-square and the smallest AIC value.

3 Results and Discussion

Parameter estimation results with OLS for data the number of diarrhea in toddlers in East Java (y_i), the number of toddlers with diarrhea with a place to manage food that meets health requirements (x_1), families with access to proper sanitation facilities/healthy latrines (x_2), the number Drinking water facilities are adequate (x_3), and the number of children under five is malnourished (x_4) is done with the help of R-studio software in Table 1.

Based on Table 1, the estimated OLS parameters are obtained, namely

$$\widehat{y_{OLS}} = -571.7 + 343.4x_1 + 0.01034x_2 - 110.0x_3 + 0.8252x_4 \tag{13}$$

The value of $F_{\text{OLS}} = 19.46$ and p-value $= < 2.62\text{e-}8 < 5\%$, indicates that the linear regression model (13) fits with the data. It means that the predictor variables significantly affect the dependent variable simultaneously. The adjusted R-square value is 0.6662, which means that 66.62% of the number of toddler diarrhea in East Java Province (y) is influenced by places that manage food that meets health requirements (x_1), families with access to proper sanitation facilities/healthy latrines. (x_2), the number of adequate drinking water facilities (x_3), and the number of malnourished children under five (x_4) while 33.38% is influenced by other variables that have not been included in the model. The $|tcount|$ value for all variables predictor have p-value $< 5\%$, this means that all predictor variables affect the response variable, so it can be concluded

Table 1. Parameter estimation with OLS

Coefficients	Estimate	t value	Pr (> |t|)
(Intercept)	−571.7	−0.64	0.5239
X_1	343.4	2.73	0.0099
X_2	0.01034	2.89	0.0067
X_3	−110.0	−3.52	0.0013
X_4	0.8252	2.75	0.0096
F-count: 19.46 on 4 and 33 DF, p-value: < 2.62e-8			
Adjusted R-squared: 0.6662			

that giving several toddlers with diarrhea a place to manage food that meets health requirements (x_1), families with access to proper sanitation facilities/healthy latrines (x_2), the number drinking water facilities are adequate (x_3), and the number of children under five is malnourished (x_4), have a significant effect on the number of toddler diarrhea. Furthermore, it can be done with normality, homoscedasticity, autocorrelation, and multicollinearity tests.

The results of the classical assumption test (normality test, homoscedasticity test, autocorrelation test, and multi-correlation test) on the data, it can be seen that all classical assumptions are met except the normality assumption which is caused by outliers in the data. Outlier detection is done using the difference in fitted value (DFFITS). If the comparison value of $|DFFITS|$ is greater than $2\sqrt{\frac{k+1}{n}} = 2\sqrt{\frac{4+1}{34}} > 0.6488857$ then it can be identified that the data is an outlier. Based on the identification results, it can be seen that observation 15th is the outlier in the data, so robust regression is used, the iteration results of the estimation of M, and GM are presented in Tables 2 and 3. Each value from every iteration of the M-estimation and GM-estimation algorithms is displayed graphically in Fig. 1 and 2.

Based on Table 2 and 3, the parameter estimates for the robust regression model estimated M at the 18-th iteration, and estimated GM at the 33-th iteration, respectively, to obtain robust regression models (14–15),

$$\widehat{y_M} = -258.9063 + 3.358959x_1 + 0.009172527x_2 - 0.8471052x_3 + 0.6550499x_4 \quad (14)$$

$$\widehat{y_{GM}} = -257.1 + 3.666x_1 + 0.009418x_2 - 0.9350x_3 + 0.6001x_4 \quad (15)$$

The parameter significance test was carried out using the simultaneous F-test and partial t-test. The parameter estimation and analysis results using robust regression using M and GM estimation are shown in Table 4.

Table 4 shows that the F_M count values for M estimates $= 50.15$; and count values for F_{GM} estimates $= 3.646e + 04$ with all the p -values $< 5\%$, which means the predictor variables have significantly affected the response variable. The p-values for all predictor variables in both the strong regression models with M and GM estimates are all $< 5\%$, which means that all the predictor variables for both models are partially significant.

Table 2. Value of $\hat{\beta}$ Iterations of estimation of M estimation

Iterations	$\hat{\beta}_0$	$\hat{\beta}_1$	$\hat{\beta}_2$	$\hat{\beta}_3$	$\hat{\beta}_4$
1	−338.7362	3.424004	0.009327671	−0.9408811	0.7264347
2	−277.9543	3.390723	0.009204891	−0.8756664	0.6764906
3	−265.3294	3.370195	0.009184501	−0.8571896	0.6625692
4	−261.0855	3.362965	0.009176986	−0.8507150	0.6577221
5	−259.6855	3.360402	0.009174152	−0.8484102	0.6560143
6	−259.1874	3.359481	0.009173115	−0.8475770	0.6553984
7	−259.0079	3.359148	0.009172739	−0.8472757	0.6551759
8	−258.9430	3.359027	0.009172603	−0.8471667	0.6550954
9	−258.9195	3.358984	0.009172554	−0.8471273	0.6550663
10	−258.9110	3.358968	0.009172536	−0.8471131	0.6550557
11	−258.9080	3.358962	0.009172530	−0.8471079	0.6550519
12	−258.9069	3.358960	0.009172528	−0.8471061	0.6550506
13	−258.9065	3.358960	0.009172527	−0.8471054	0.6550501
14	−258.9063	3.358959	0.009172527	−0.8471052	0.6550499
15	−258.9063	3.358959	0.009172526	−0.8471051	0.6550498
16	−258.9063	3.358959	0.009172526	−0.8471050	0.6550498
17	−258.9062	3.358959	0.009172526	−0.8471050	0.6550498
18	−258.9062	3.358959	0.009172526	−0.8471050	0.6550498

Selection of the best model on data the number of diarrhea in toddlers in East Java (y_i), the number of toddlers with diarrhea with a place to manage food that meets health requirements (x_1), families with access to proper sanitation facilities/healthy latrines (x_2), the number Drinking water facilities are adequate (x_3), and the number of children under five is malnourished (x_4) is based on the most significant adjusted R-square value and the smallest AIC value. The adjusted R-square and AIC values for OLS estimated M, and GM can be seen in Table 5.

Table 5 shows that the M estimation robust regression model has a value of adjusted R-squared by 84.16% with a value of *AIC* by 673.3446, and the GM esti-mation robust regression model has a value of adjusted R-squared by 99.74% with a value of *AIC* by 629.0898.

A robust regression model using GM estimates is better used when compared with M estimates, this is because this model has the largest adjusted R-square value = 99.74% and the smallest AIC value = 629.0898. The robust regression model with GM estimates is the best, i.e.,

$$\widehat{Y_{GM}} = -257.1 + 3.666X_1 + 0.009418X_2 - 0.9350X_3 + 0.6001X_4.$$

Table 3. Value of $\hat{\beta}$ Iterations of estimation of GM Estimation

Iterations	$\hat{\beta}_0$	$\hat{\beta}_1$	$\hat{\beta}_2$	$\hat{\beta}_3$	$\hat{\beta}_4$
1	-3.799×10^2	3.450	9.999×10^{-3}	-9.366×10^{-1}	7.044×10^{-1}
2	-3.318×10^2	3.588	9.763×10^{-3}	-9.258×10^{-1}	7.911×10^{-1}
3	-2.997×10^2	3.637	9.669×10^{-3}	-9.257×10^{-1}	6.888×10^{-1}
4	-2.812×10^2	3.643	9.625×10^{-3}	-9.285×10^{-1}	6.913×10^{-1}
5	-2.719×10^2	3.645	9.595×10^{-3}	-9.303×10^{-1}	6.932×10^{-1}
6	-2.678×10^2	3.647	9.572×10^{-3}	-9.313×10^{-1}	6.944×10^{-1}
7	-2.660×10^2	3.649	9.552×10^{-3}	-9.320×10^{-1}	6.953×10^{-1}
8	-2.653×10^2	3.651	9.534×10^{-3}	-9.324×10^{-1}	6.959×10^{-1}
9	-2.646×10^2	3.653	9.518×10^{-3}	-9.326×10^{-1}	6.964×10^{-1}
10	-2.639×10^2	3.655	9.502×10^{-3}	-9.328×10^{-1}	6.968×10^{-1}
11	-2.633×10^2	3.657	9.487×10^{-3}	-9.330×10^{-1}	6.972×10^{-1}
12	-2.626×10^2	3.659	9.474×10^{-3}	-9.332×10^{-1}	6.976×10^{-1}
13	-2.619×10^2	3.660	9.462×10^{-3}	-9.334×10^{-1}	6.979×10^{-1}
14	-2.612×10^2	3.661	9.452×10^{-3}	-9.335×10^{-1}	6.982×10^{-1}
15	-2.606×10^2	3.662	9.444×10^{-3}	-9.337×10^{-1}	6.984×10^{-1}
16	-2.600×10^2	3.663	9.437×10^{-3}	-9.338×10^{-1}	6.986×10^{-1}
17	-2.595×10^2	3.663	9.431×10^{-3}	-9.339×10^{-1}	6.987×10^{-1}
18	-2.591×10^2	3.664	9.427×10^{-3}	-9.340×10^{-1}	6.989×10^{-1}
19	-2.588×10^2	3.664	9.424×10^{-3}	-9.341×10^{-1}	6.989×10^{-1}
20	-2.585×10^2	3.665	9.422×10^{-3}	-9.342×10^{-1}	6.990×10^{-1}
21	-2.583×10^2	3.665	9.421×10^{-3}	-9.343×10^{-1}	6.990×10^{-1}
22	-2.581×10^2	3.665	9.420×10^{-3}	-9.344×10^{-1}	6.991×10^{-1}
23	-2.580×10^2	3.665	9.420×10^{-3}	-9.345×10^{-1}	6.991×10^{-1}
24	-2.578×10^2	3.665	9.420×10^{-3}	-9.345×10^{-1}	6.991×10^{-1}
25	-2.577×10^2	3.665	9.419×10^{-3}	-9.346×10^{-1}	6.991×10^{-1}
26	-2.576×10^2	3.665	9.419×10^{-3}	-9.347×10^{-1}	6.991×10^{-1}
27	-2.575×10^2	3.665	9.419×10^{-3}	-9.347×10^{-1}	6991×10^{-1}
28	-2.574×10^2	3.665	9.419×10^{-3}	-9.348×10^{-1}	6991×10^{-1}
29	-2.573×10^2	3.665	9.419×10^{-3}	-9.348×10^{-1}	6991×10^{-1}
30	-2.573×10^2	3.665	9.418×10^{-3}	-9.349×10^{-1}	6991×10^{-1}
31	-2.572×10^2	3.666	9.418×10^{-3}	-9.349×10^{-1}	6991×10^{-1}
32	-2.571×10^2	3.666	9.418×10^{-3}	-9.350×10^{-1}	6991×10^{-1}
33	-2.571×10^2	3.666	9.418×10^{-3}	-9.350×10^{-1}	6991×10^{-1}

The interpretation of the regression model of GM estimation is that an increase in a place to manage food that meets health requirements will increase 3666 the number of Diarrhea in toddlers per thousand children, an increase in the number of drinking water facilities are adequate will increase 9.418 the number of diarrhea in toddlers per thousand children; each increase in proper sanitation facilities will lower 935 the number of diarrhea in toddlers per thousand children, and an each and the number of

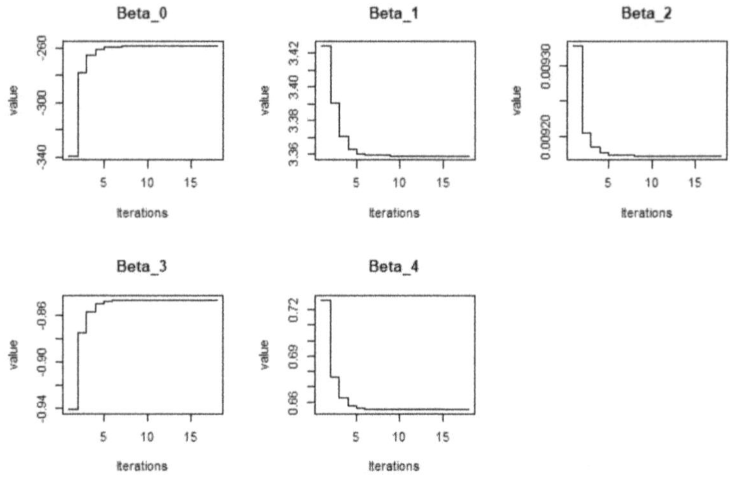

Fig. 1. Value of $\hat{\beta}$ Iterations of estimation of M Estimation

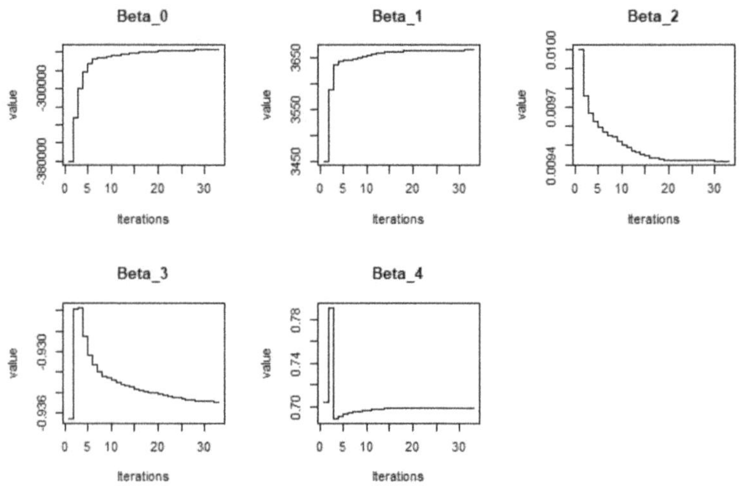

Fig. 2. Value of $\hat{\beta}$ Iterations of estimation of GM Estimation

children under five is malnourished 600.1 the number of diarrhea in toddlers per thousand children. The GM estimation can reduce outlier data from five to one outlier data. The adjusted R-square value for GM estimation is 99,74%, meaning that the independent variable (x_1, x_2, x_3, x_4) affects the dependent variable (y) by 99.74% and other variables influence the remaining 0.36%. The adjusted R-square GM is 99.74, the largest compared to the adjusted R-square other estimates (estimated M and the estimated AIC value of GM is 629.0898 the smallest compared to the AIC values of another estimate (estimated M).

Table 4. The parameter estimation and analysis results using robust regression using M, and GM estimation.

Robust Estimation	Coefficients	Estimate	T value	Pr(>|t|)
M estimation (18 iterations)	(Intercept)			
	x_1	−258.9063	−0.514	0.610979
	x_2	3.358959	4.709	4.34e-05
	x_3	0.009172527	4.518	7.57e-05
	x_4	−0.8471052	−4.767	3.66e-05
		0.6550499	3.842	0.000526
	F_M-count values=50.15 on 4 and 29 DF, p-value: <1.435e-13,			
	Adjusted R-square = 84.16, AIC = 673.3446			
GM estimation (33 iterations)	(Intercept)			
	x_1	−2.571e+02	−11.65	3.07e-13
	x_2	3.666e+00	144.75	2e-16
	x_3	9.418e-03	59.09	2e-16
	x_4	-9.350e-01	-52.70	2e-16
		6.991e-01	145.08	2e-16
	F_{GM}-count values=3.646e+04 on 4 and 29 DF, p-value: < 2.2e-16,			
	Adjusted R-square=99.97, AIC = 629.0898			

Table 5. Adjusted R-square, AIC value, and Outlier for Models with M and GM Estimations.

Estimation	Model	Adjusted R^2	AIC	Number of significant independent variables
OLS Estimation	M Estimation	66.62%	716.3424	4
M Estimation	GM Estimation	84.16%	673.3446	4
GM Estimation		99.74%	629.0898	4

4 Concluding Remarks

We obtained the convergent robust regression prediction model with M estimates obtained at the 18th iteration, and GM estimates received at the 38th iteration.

The results show that the M estimation robust regression model has a value of adjusted R-squared by 84.16% with a value of *AIC* by 673.3446, and the GM estimation robust regression model has a value of adjusted R-squared by 99.74% with a value of *AIC* by 629.0898. The best robust regression model is a robust regression model with GM estimates because this model has the largest adjusted R-square value = 99.74% and the smallest AIC value = 629.0898.

The best robust regression model for diarrhea data in East Java in 2021 is a model using GM estimates, i.e.

$\widehat{y_{GM}} = -257.1 + 3.666x_1 + 0.009418x_2 - 0.9350x_3 + 0.6001x_4.$

The results of the partial t-test analysis show that each predictor variable (X_1, X_2, X_3, X_4) significantly affected the number of diarrheas in toddlers in East Java.

Acknowledgment. The researcher would like to thank the Research and Community Service Institute, Universitas Sebelas Maret for providing financial support through the Research Grant Number: 194.2 UN27.22/PT.01.03/2024.

References

1. Imran Pambudi.: Laporan Kinerja 2022. Kementerian Kesehatan RI, (2023)
2. Kementerian Kesehatan RI.: Hasil Utama Riset Kesehatan Dasar (2018)
3. Trihono.: "Riset Kesehatan Dasar", Kementerian Kesehatan Republik Indonesia, (2010)
4. Burton, Alexander L.: OLS (Linear) regression. The encyclopedia of research methods in criminology and Criminal Justice **2** (2021): 509–514
5. Susanti, Y., Pratiwi, H., Handajani, S.S., Liana, T., Estimation, M., Estimation, S., Estimation, MM.: Int. J. Pure Appl. Math., **91**(2014)
6. Draper, N.R., Smith, H.: Applied regression analysis. John Wiley & Sons, Inc, (1998). https://doi.org/10.1002/9781118625590
7. Montgomery, D.C., Peck, E.A., Vining, G.G.: Introduction to Linear Regression Analysis, 3rd edn. John Wiley & Sons Inc, New York (2001)
8. Araswati, N.: Pemodelan Regresi Robust Estimasi M Fungsi Pembobot Huber da-lam Menangani Pencilan (Studi Kasus: Pemodelan Junlah Kematian Ibu di Indonesia). Skripsi Universitas Lampung (2022)
9. Yohai, V.J.: High breakdown point and high-efficiency robust estimates for regression. Annu. Stat. **15**(20), 642–656 (1987)
10. Wilcox, R.R.: Introduction to Robust Estimation and Hypothesis Testing. Academic Press, San Diego (2005)
11. Lee, SM., Pun, M.C.: On M Out of N bootsrapping for non-standard M-estimation with nuisance parameters. J. Amer-Ican Stat. Assoc. p. 1185 – 1197 (2006)
12. Kusuma, I., Susanti, Y., dan Subanti, S.: Pemodelan Kemiskinan di Indone-sia Menggunakan Analisis Regresi Robust. Seminar Nasional Aplikasi Sains & Teknologi. Jurusan Statistika FMIPA UNS (2021)
13. Aristiarto, R., Susanti, Y., Susanto, I.: Analisis Regresi Robust Estimasi GM pada Indeks Keparahan Kemiskinan Provinsi-Provinsi di Indonesia. Seminar Nasional Riset dan Inovasi Teknologi. **7**(1), 205–209 (2023)
14. Subzar, M., Al-Omari, A.I., Alanzi, A.R.A.: The robust regression methods for estimating of finite population mean based on SRSWOR in case of outliers. J. Comput., Mater. & Contin. **65**, 125–138 (2020)
15. Fauzaan Nabil, Yuliana Susanti, Etik Zukhronah.: Robust regres-sion analysis of GM estimation on the poverty gap index of indonesian provinces. journal.ibrahimy.ac.id/index.php/icorhestech, **1**(1), p. 369~374 (2024)

16. Said, A., Susanti, Y., Sugiyanto.: Perbandingan ketepatan model regresi robust estimasi method of moment (MM) dan Estimasi Generalized-M (GM) dalam Memodelkan Harga Penutupan Saham Sektor Teknologi Tahun," SainsMath J. MIPA Sains Terap., **3**(1), pp. 40–51, (2024)
17. Ministry of Health, "Profil Kesehatan Indonesia 2021," In Pusdatin.Kemenkes. Go. Id. http://www.kemkes/go/id
18. Draper, N.R., Smith. H.: Applied regression analysis. John Wiley & Sons, Inc, (1998)
19. Montgomery, D.C., Peck, E.A.: Introduction to linear regression analysis, 2nd edn. John Wiley & Sons Inc, New York (1992)
20. Zhang, K., Janson, L., Murphy, S.: Statistical inference with m-estimators on adaptively collected data. Adv. Neural. Inf. Process. Syst. **34**, 7460–7471 (2021)
21. Ronchetti, E.M., Huber, P.J.: Robust statistics. John Wiley & Sons, Hoboken, NJ, USA (2009)
22. Lin, S.W.: A comparative study of robust estimates in regression. In: 11th Annu. Conf. Asia Pacific Decis. Sci. Institute. Hongkong, pp. 569–572, (2006)
23. Anderson, David, R., Thomas, A. Williams, James, J. Cochran.: Statistics for business & economics. Cengage Learning, (2020)

Classification Analysis on Social Media Cyberbullying in Indonesia

Arum Handini Primandari[1(✉)], Rini Aprilianty Riadi[1], Ayundyah Kesumawati[1], and Dedi Rosadi[2]

[1] Universitas Islam Indonesia, Yogyakarta 55584, Indonesia
primandari.arum@uii.ac.id
[2] Universitas Gadjah Mada, Yogyakarta 55281, Indonesia

Abstract. This study addresses the issue of cyberbullying on social media in Indonesia, which has significant psychological and physical effects on victims. To aid in detecting and preventing cyberbullying victimization, a machine learning system should be built as it provides promising results. Based on data collected from Instagram and YouTube, the system classifies comments as cyberbullying or non-cyberbullying. The tree-based ensemble model, including Random Forest, AdaBoost, and XGBoost, was employed for classification. In handling the imbalance dataset, the Synthetic Minority Oversampling Technique (SMOTE) and SMOTE Edited Nearest Neighbor (SMOTE-ENN) were used. After tuning the hyperparameter for the three models with SMOTE-ENN, the result on the average of precision, recall, and f1-score is over 95% each.

Keywords: Cyberbullying · Indonesia language · Tree-based model

1 Introduction

The way people communicate has changed significantly in the last few decades. Today's technological advances allow humans to easily exchange information through social media networks. Today, these digital tools can transcend the world's physical boundaries in human interaction and behavior without having to conduct face-to-face meetings [1]. However, the impact of these rapid technological advances has led to the emergence of bullying behavior on social media as insulting comments. Thus, a new term, "cyberbullying," emerged. Cyberbullying is behavior carried out repeatedly to humiliate or jeopardize someone using digital technology in phones such as chat, email, and social media [2]. The impact of cyberbullying is certainly self-defeating, ranging from emotional (anger, fear, self-blame, etc.), psychological (low self-esteem, depression, suicide, etc.), to physical (eating disorders, and others) [3].

P. C. Rodrigues et al. (Eds.): ISBIS 2024, 13, pp. 100–116, 2027.
https://doi.org/10.1007/978-3-032-32458-0_8

The urgency of the technology utilization in the information exchange has prompted the government to issue the ITE Law. Law Number 19 of 2016 is an amendment to Law Number 11 of 2008 concerning Information and Electronic Transactions, Article 27 paragraph (3) UU ITE, which contains: "Every person who intentionally and without rights distributes and/or transmits and/or make accessible Electronic Information and/or Electronic Documents with defamatory and/or defamatory content." Those who meet the elements as referred to in Article 27 paragraph (3) of Law 19/2016 shall be punished with imprisonment for a maximum of four years and/or a maximum of IDR750.000.000,00.

The current rules governing behavior on social media make use of modern technology, specifically artificial intelligence, to identify comments that involve cyberbullying through the analysis of human language. However, there is currently no specialized tool available to detect comments that violate the ITE Law, particularly in relation to cyberbullying in Indonesia. Therefore, the development of technology to identify cyberbullying comments is essential. Additionally, this technology should help users exercise caution when posting comments. The implementation of artificial intelligence is one of the potential solutions to address the pressing issue of cyberbullying.

The random forest algorithm randomly combines the outputs of multiple decision trees to generate the final outcome as classification or prediction [4]. It was successfully implemented in text classification, such as sentiment analysis [5,6]. In addition, random forests have been employed for feature selection, classification, and regression tasks, demonstrating their versatility and effectiveness in a range of situations.

Weak learners were employed in the Random Forest algorithm modification, such as AdaBoost and XGBoost, to produce a strong predictive model. Traditional Boosting Tree models just use the information from the first derivative. XGBoost has been used in sentiment analysis to reliably categorize the sentiments expressed in textual data. AdaBoost show a good performance in classifying imbalance data. In 2021, Elnadree et al. studied how well sentiment analysis systems work by using the Word2Vec method along with XGBoost and random forest classification algorithms [7]. The outcomes showed high levels of performance. This emphasizes how important XGBoost is as a useful tool for sentiment classification jobs.

Research in 2020 by Talpur and O'Sullivan intended to detect cyberbullying to generate features from Twitter content by utilizing a common information technique [8]. In 2020, Stephenie, et all aimed to analyze sentiment from Tokopedia (the 5 top marketplace in Indonesia) product reviews for how Tokopedia customers respond to product quality and seller deliveries [9]. It suggests that the Random Forest method can properly predict Tokopedia product reviews with parameters mtry = 73 and ntree = 50. The greater the accuracy, the better the performance of the classification model.

The Natural Language Processing (NLP) is a computational technique that aims to analyze text and naturally present text for a particular purpose to discuss language like every day human language. NLP studies how everyday human language is practiced and determines which parts are essential (according to the research target). The result of this research is a prediction engine. This research's output is a prototype that is the initial model to develop a program. In addition to that, this research will put this prototype on a website that will later be accessible to a larger community, especially in Indonesia. It is hoped that this research can help the public, mainly Indonesian, to be more careful in giving comments on social media as the ITE Law has regulated it. At the same time, the results of this research are expected to raise public awareness about the importance of being wise when using social media.

This article is organized into several sections: introduction, materials and methods, results and discussion, future development, and conclusion. The introduction provides background on the problem and explains the rationale for the chosen methodology. The materials and methods section details the data sources and research methodology, including a brief overview of balancing methods and ensemble models. The results and discussion section presents the findings from the analysis, which encompass data pre-processing, balancing using SMOTE and SMOTE-ENN techniques, classification analysis, predicting test data, and building a website prototype. Finally, the conclusion summarizes the results and the overall research process.

2 Material and Method

The data of this study is comments obtained from Instagram and Youtube of several domestic influencers. To get the sample of cyberbullying, we selected some accounts having controversial posts such as Kekeyi, Lucinta Luna, Ria Ricis, Rans Entertainment, Prabowo, Anies Baswedan, Deddy Corbuzier, so all. Even with the selection, non-cyberbullying comments still outnumber cyberbullying. In this case, we encountered an imbalanced dataset problem, which was later solved using SMOTE and SMOTE-ENN methods. The following. is the research flowchart.

1. Collect the data from social media utilizing web scraping, then store it in a desirable format.
2. Categorize every comment into cyberbullying or non-cyberbullying. The data labeling is done manually by native Indonesian speakers.
3. Perform text preprocessing; explain as follows:
   (a) Word normalization is the procedure of converting non-standard terms into standard words in accordance with the Indonesian dictionary (KBBI—*Kamus Besar Bahasa Indonesia*). Non-standard vocabulary may include acronyms, slang, and regional terms. The normalization procedure employs a lexicon established by the researcher, referencing the slang and regional language present in the comments.

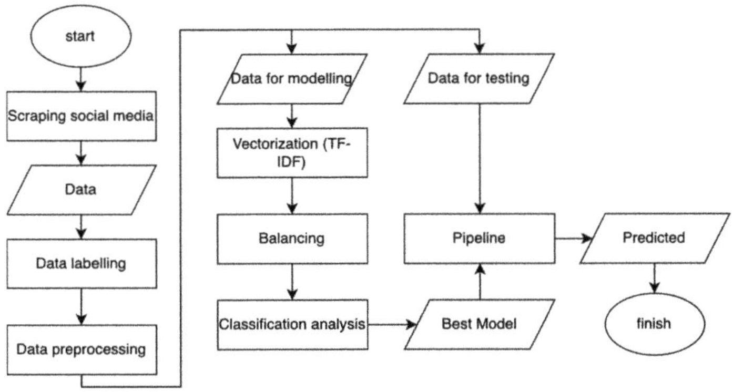

Fig. 1. Research flowchart

(b) Case folding is changing all the letter styles into lowercase.
(c) Remove punctuation is a process to remove all the punctuation as it was considered noise.
(d) Remove number is an action to remove all digits 0–9 as it does not give any meaningful information.
(e) Stopword removal is the removal of common words that appear in documents, such as pronouns and conjunctions. The researchers also added stopwords in cyberbullying cases, for example, "jokowi", "anies", "wow", "waduh", etc. [10]
(f) Tokenization is splitting the text into single words or phrases.
(g) Lemmatization is the grouping of different forms of the same word. This process will be carried out by employing the Python package "nlp-id" by the Kumparan team [11–14].

4. Calculate the Term Frequency-Inverse Document Frequency (TF-IDF) as a numeric text representation. It is used to weigh each word in a sentence in the document. The formula of TF-IDF define as follow [15–17].

$$W_{ij} = TF_{ij} * IDF_j = TF_{ij} * \left(ln \frac{N}{DF_j} + 1 \right) \tag{1}$$

where W_{ij} is the weight of the word or term j against document i, TF_{ij} is the number of occurrences of word or term j against document i, i is the document $(1, ..., N)$, and j is the word of the keyword $(1, ..., t)$.
5. Handle the imbalanced dataset by employing the SMOTE and SMOTE-ENN methods.
6. Build classification model using Random Forest, AdaBoost, and XGBoost classifier, which grows trees. A classifier's classification performance in relation to a set of test data is summarized by a confusion matrix. It is a two-dimensional matrix with the classifier's assigned class in one dimension and the object's actual class in the other. Classification measures that can be calculated using the values in the confusion matrix include accuracy, precision, recall, and f1-score [18,19].

7. After the best model is obtained, a pipeline is built to predict new data using the model. Testing data passed through the pipeline will result in a predicted category of whether a comment indicates cyberbullying (Fig. 1).

2.1 Synthetic Minority Oversampling Technique (SMOTE) and SMOTE Edited Nearest Neighbor (SMOTE-ENN)

Imbalanced data or unbalanced data is a condition when one class has significantly more objects than another class. The form of data imbalance occurs when the class ratio is 20:1, 100:1, 1000:1, or even up to 10000:1 for data classes whose objects are mostly named with major classes while others are named with minor classes. This imbalance results in the insensitive classification of minority data classes [20,21]. The SMOTE method is one solution to the imbalanced data problem, which is in principle different from the oversampling method.

The focus of the oversampling process is multiplying random observations. Meanwhile, the SMOTE method adds minor class data to the significant class by generating artificial data (synthetic minority). This artificial data is created based on k-nearest neighbors (KNN) where the number of KNN is determined by considering its ease of implementation. The formation between numerical and categorical scales will be different in the artificial data. The Euclidean distance measures proximity in numerical data. In contrast, categorical data is measured by the value of the occurrence numbers of the mode value.

The advantage of SMOTE compared to other methods is that it is easier to implement and interpret since it uses the basis of the KNN. In addition to that, SMOTE can produce good accuracy values compared to other methods in handling imbalanced data cases as it can reduce overfitting, which is a weakness of other oversampling techniques [22–24]. The following are the procedures for creating categorical data.

1. Choose the principal between the considered principal vectors and their KNN for nominal values. If there is the same value, then choose randomly.
2. Make this value sample data of the newly created class.

The Fig. 2 is an illustration of SMOTE. The blue square represents the minor class, while the lined box represents the major class. The synthesis sample formed is represented by a green square located between the minor and major classes. Formula calculation of the distance between minor classes examples with categorical scale variables was carried out using the Value Difference Metric (VDM) formula [25].

$$\Delta(X_i, X_j) = w_{x_i} w_{x_j} \sum_{i,j=1}^{N} \delta(x_i, x_j)^r \tag{2}$$

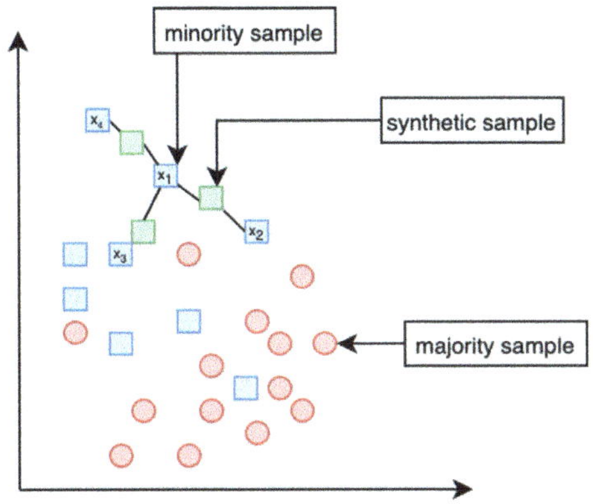

Fig. 2. SMOTE illustration

where $\Delta(X_i, X_j)$ is the distance between the observations X_i and X_j, w_{x_i}, w_{x_j} are the observed weight, N is the number of explanatory variables, r is the value of 1 or 2, value 1 means Manhattan distance formula or value 2 means Euclidean distance formula, $\delta(x_i, x_j)^r$ is the distance between categories with formula $\delta(V_1, V_2) = \sum_{i=1}^{n} |C_{1i}/C_1 - C_{2i}/C_2|^k$.

After creating a synthetic sample with SMOTE, the Edited Nearest Neighbor (ENN) as a cleaning method is processed by deleting samples that are noise from the majority class of its neighbors [26]. For every sample (including synthetic samples) in the dataset [27]:

1. Determine the k-nearest neighbors, which is often k=3.
2. Find out which class these neighbors belong to.
3. Eliminate the distinct sample's class from the majority class of its neighbors.

This stage aids in clearing out noisy data points and defining class boundaries, particularly in areas that overlap. The illustration for SMOTE-ENN is depicted in the Fig. 3 [28].

2.2 Random Forest Classification

The Classification and Regression Tree (CART) method is the basis of Random Forest that is widely considered as the development of the previous method by applying bootstrap aggregating (bagging) and random feature selection methods [29]. Bagging or Bootstrap Aggregating is a method based on the ensemble method, using a combination of several models. Random feature selection is a method to generate multiple versions and make a feature selection to get high accuracy and can be interpreted. The process of combining the outputs of several individual models is also known as ensemble learning. Each node in the decision tree works on a random subset of features to compute the result.

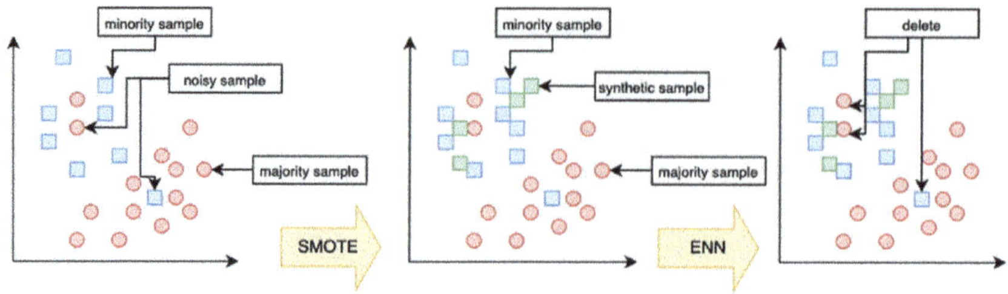

Fig. 3. SMOTE-ENN illustration

The fundamental principle of bagging is to diminish variance by averaging multiple noisy yet typically unbiased models. Trees are optimal selections for bagging due of their capacity to capture intricate relationships. The algorithm of random forest for classification define as follows [29,30]:

1. For $a = 1$ to A
   1. Draw a bootstrap sample B^* having size N from training set.
   2. Build random forest tree T_a to the data of bootstrap result, by iteratively repeating the procedures below for each tree's terminal node until the minimal node size n_{min} is reached.
      i. Choose randomly of m variables from p variables.
      ii. Select the best variables to split up among m variables. By default, $m = [\sqrt{p}]$ and the minimum size is one.
      iii. Split the node into two branches.

2. The ensemble tress output $\{T_a\}_1^A$
3. To make a classification out of new data x: Let $\hat{C}_a(x)$ be the predicted class of the ath tree. Then $\hat{C}_{rf}^A(x)$ is the majority vote $\{\hat{C}_a(x)\}_1^B$

Since the generated tree of bagging is identically (i.d) distributed, the expectation of average B tress is the same with any of them. In another word, the bias of the bagged tree is the same as that of the individual tree.

2.3 AdaBoost

Adaboost is a boosting method that combines weak learners into one strong learner. The algorithm gives high weights to misclassified instances so that the next tree focuses on more difficult classifications than the previous tree. This weighting is useful when the dataset is imbalanced because it can enhance the model's performance in classifying minor classes [31,32]. The Adaboost algorithm:

1. Assign equal weights to each training sample.
2. Iterative Training:
   (a) Train a Weak Learner: Use the weighted training data to train a weak learner (such as a decision tree).

(b) Determine Error: Determine the weak learner's weighted error rate.
(c) Update Weights: Make samples that were incorrectly classed heavier and those that were correctly classified lighter.
(d) Determine the Weak Learner's Weight: Determine the weak learner's weight by looking at its error rate.

3. Final prediction: each weak learner produces a prediction based on its importance in order to make a prediction on a new instance.

2.4 XGBoost

XGBoost is an ensemble development model of Random Forest using the boosting principle, which is to improve the performance of weak learners (trees). The residual from the n-1 tree is used as a training for the nth tree. The objective function of XGBoost consists of a loss function and regularization [33,34].

$$obj = \sum_{i=1}^{n} L(y_i, \hat{y_i}^{(t)}) + \sum_{i=1}^{t} \omega(f_t) \tag{3}$$

where y_i is the actual data, $\hat{y_i}^{(t)}$ is the predicted value, $L(y_i, \hat{y_i}^{(t)})$ is the loss function, and $\sum_{i=1}^{t} \omega(f_t)$ is the regularization. The common loss functions utilized in XGBoost are the sum squared error and logistic function. The function for regularization is as follows:

$$\Omega(f_t) = \gamma T + \frac{1}{2}\lambda \sum_{j=1}^{T} \omega_j^2 \tag{4}$$

where λ is the coefficient of its penalty, T is the number of leaf nodes, ω is the score obtained by leaf nodes. The parameters for avoiding overfitting are λ and γ. The Taylor series approximation on the first order derivatives of loss function. The final objective function:

$$obj = \frac{-1}{2} \sum_{j=1}^{T} \frac{G_j^2}{H_j + \lambda} + \lambda^T \tag{5}$$

where G_j and H_j represent the sum of the first and second partial derivatives of the leaf nodes prediction.

Although XGboost and Adaboost have similarities in improving weak learners for the next iteration, they differ in terms of algorithms, regularization, and handling overfitting. The Adaboost algorithm runs sequentially by giving higher weights to misclassified instances. The XGBoost algorithm is based on gradient boosting, which optimizes the loss function and regularization. XGBoost uses L1 and L2 regularization to avoid overfitting, while Adaboost does not. As a result, XGBoost tends to have better data capabilities with noise and outliers.

3 Results and Discussion

The initial stage carried out in this study was to preprocess the data and create categories, (cyberbullying and non-cyberbullying categories) based on the ITE Law. We define the cyberbullying activities as threats of violence or scaring and resulting in physical, psychological, and/or material harm using electronic platform [35]. It also contains obscene, rude, swear words, etc. in either Indonesian or regional languages [36,37]. The labelling process was done manually by native speaker, then validated by language expert.

The purpose of data preprocessing is to clean data from unessential elements. The steps for preprocessing data are case folding, removing punctuation and removing numbers, normalization, stopword, tokenizing, and stemming. The following Table 1 presents the data samples which will be analyzed.

Table 1. Example of comments

No	Comment	Class
1	*bajing memek kau urus anjing* (cursing words)	cyberbullying
2	*bangsat perek murah kampung sadar*(cursing words)	cyberbullying
3	*Bahagia bgt kalau sudah lihat kak ria ricis jdi ktwa senang n jdi ikt bahagia liatnya sehat slalu buat kk ricis n tim*	no-cyberbullying

The Fig. 4 portrays the comparison of the number of comment categorized as cyberbullying and non-cyberbullying, which was 4490 comments in total.

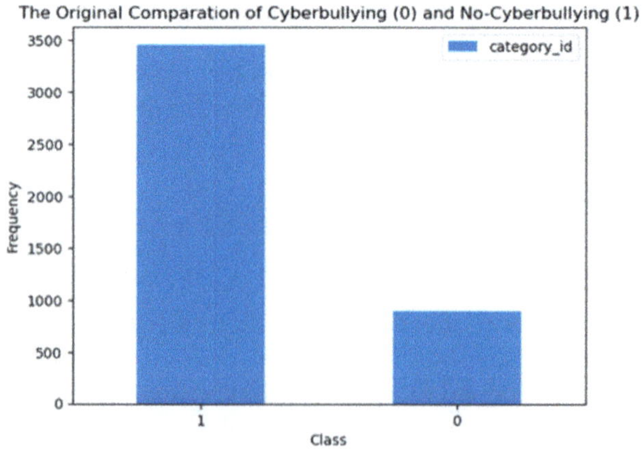

Fig. 4. The comparison of cyberbullying category

With 3,581 comments, the non-cyberbullying category outnumbers the cyberbullying category, which contains only 909 comments. These results clearly show a relatively large gap between the number of comments in the cyberbullying and non-cyber bullying categories. Since the data in this research was imbalanced data, a Synthetic Minority Oversampling Technique (SMOTE) analyst was carried out to solve this problem.

3.1 TF-IDF

After completing the data preprocessing, the TF-IDF was calculated as numeric representation of the text. It also can be considered as weight. The components in the TF-IDF consist of TF weights and IDF weights. The following Table 2 presents the result of the final calculation of the TF-IDF weighting. In this case, we used the minimum n-gram of one and the maximum n-gram of two. The example of 1-gram is abai (ignore), abang (big brother), zholim (cruel), zona (zone), etc., and for 2-gram/ bigram is abang-aku (my big brother), abai-komentar (ignore (the) comment), zholim rakyat (oppress (the) people), zona merah (red zone), etc. Bigrams form words into phrases so that it can provide a more nuanced understanding of text content.

Table 2. TF-IDF value

Abai (ignore)	*abai komentar* (ignore comment)	*abai netizen* (ignore netizen)	*Abang* (big brother)	...	*zuma mana* (zuma (game) where)
0	0	0	0	...	0
0	0	0	0	...	0
⋮	⋮	⋮	⋮	...	0
0	0	0	0	...	0

3.2 Handling Imbalanced Dataset

At this stage, the imbalance problem was handled using the Synthetic Minority Oversampling Technique (SMOTE). This method would help create synthetic or artificial data based on existing data to form balanced data. After SMOTE, each category contained 3,581 data which means 7,162 in total. Figure 5 presents the result of the SMOTE method. The x-label of 0 for cyberbullying and 1 for non-cyberbullying.

Unlike SMOTE, which equates the number of minority classes with the number of majority classes, the number of samples can likely differ on SMOTE-ENN. After going through the SMOTE procedure, SMOTE-ENN removes samples that are likely to be noisy or close to the decision boundary, which can help reduce the number of borderline or ambiguous samples. After several trials, the number of minority classes (cyberbullying) even exceeded the major class (no-cyberbullying) as shown in the following graph (Fig. 6).

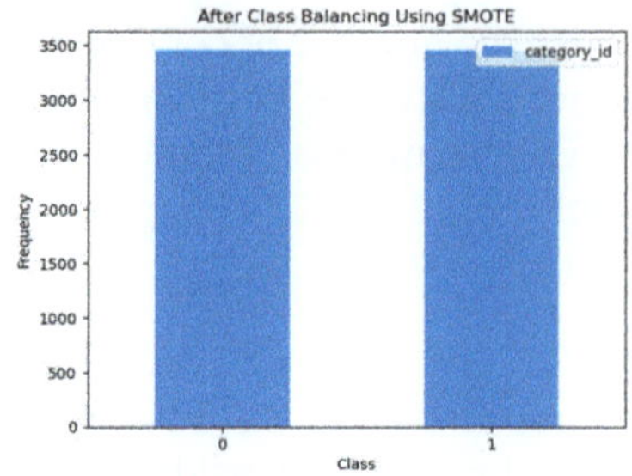

Fig. 5. The result of SMOTE

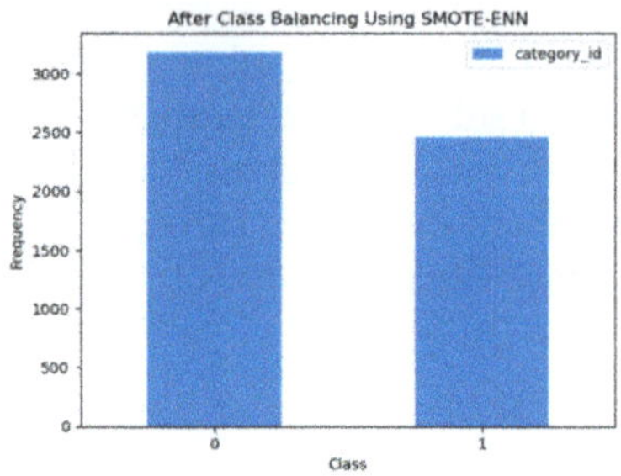

Fig. 6. The result of SMOTE-ENN

3.3 Classification Analysis

To construct the model, the data is divided into training and testing data with a ratio of 80:20. The ensemble learning used is the random forest, AdaBoost, and XGBoost. The following table compares the accuracy of each model on data with balancing and without balancing. Each model uses 5-fold cross-validation.

Based on Table 3, the accuracy value for data with SMOTE-ENN balancing is higher than without balancing and balancing using SMOTE. The average accuracy increase from utilizing SMOTE to SMOTE-ENN is about 2%. Compared to the unbalanced data, the average accuracy of using SMOTE is 4% higher and the average accuracy of using SMOTE-ENN is 6% higher.

Table 3. Comparison of ensemble model's accuracy

Model	Without balancing	SMOTE	SMOTE-ENN
Random Forest	0.886	0.923	0.951
AdaBoost	0.881	0.910	0.936
XGBoost	0.867	0.899	0.909

The tuning parameter employs grid search to find the best parameter's combination. For every model, the parameters were different according to its algorithm (Table 4).

Table 4. Grid search parameter for random forest

No	Parameter	Value
1	The number of decision tree (n_estimators)	100–150
2	The number of features/variables to consider when observing for the best split (max_features)	Square root or log base two of the number of samples (sqrt, log2)
3	The minimum number of samples required to split an internal node (min_samples_split)	2, 4
4	The bare minimum of samples that must be present at a leaf node. Only if a split point at any level leaves at least training samples in both the left and right branches will it be taken into account (min_samples_leaf)	1, 5
5	Bootsrap sample is Boolean input. If bootstrap samples are employed in tree construction, then it is true. If False, each tree is constructed using the entire dataset.	True, False

The best parameters for random forest are 150 trees, 1 minimal sample leaf, 4 minimal sample split, log base 2 of n samples for maximum features, and no bootstrap applied for generate every tree. It resulted on the average of precision, recall, and f1-score for more than 99%.

Adaboost uses fewer and simpler parameter combinations than the other two ensemble trees as it shown in Table 5. In addition to the number of trees and learning rate, there are parameters to control the depth of the base learner (weak learner).

Table 5. Grid search parameter for AdaBoost

No	Parameter	Value
1	The number of decision tree (n_estimators)	50, 100, 200
2	The learning rate	0.01, 0.1, 0.5, 1.0
4	The maximum depth for base learner (base_estimator_max_depth)	1, 2, 3, 4, 5

The best parameters for Adaboost are 200 ensemble trees, 1.0 for learning rate, and one for maximum depth of base learner. The accuracy and macro average for precision, recall, f1-score are 97% each.

he parameters utilized in XGBoost differ from those used in Random Forest. A gamma parameter as a regularization parameter adds a penalty when creating a new leaf node on the tree. This parameter determines the minimum loss reduction when partitioning leaf nodes. The higher the gamma value, the more conservative the model is in splitting. This means that XGBoost is more selective about the features used for separation. Features will be used when they have a significant impact on reducing errors (Table 6).

Table 6. Grid search parameter for XGBoost

No	Parameter	Value
1	The number of decision tree (n_estimators)	50, 100, 150
2	Gamma	0, 0.1, 0.2
3	The maximum of tree depth can grow (max_depth)	3, 5, 7
4	Boosting learning rate	0.01, 0.1, 0.2
5	The ratio of subsample to grow each individual tree (subsample)	0.6, 0.8, 1.0
6	The ratio of subsample columns to grow each individual tree (colsample_bytree)	0.6, 0.8, 1.0
7	The minimum sum of instance weight (hessian) needed in a node (the higher value can help avoiding the splits with too few data points)	1, 3, 5

The best parameter are 150 ensemble tree, 0 gamma, 5 maximum tree's depth, 0.2 for learning rate, 100% of subsample, 60% of columns subsample, and 1 for minimum sum of instance weight. The average of precision, recall, and f1-score are 97% each.

3.4 Predict New Data

To test the performance of the best model, a pipeline consisting of data preprocessing, vectorization, and models was created. Using 61 new data, the following are the results of the classification report. Based on Table 7, the precision of the cyberbullying class equals to one, means that every cyberbullying prediction made by the model is correct. However, the recall is low, meaning that only a few cyberbullying comments can be correctly predicted by the model. In the non-cyberbullying class, a recall value of one indicates that the model can identify all non-cyberbullying classes. However, with low precision, it indicates that some of the instances that were predicted to non-cyberbullying are actually cyberbullying comments.

3.5 Web Prototype

A web prototype is a website design for deploying a model. The following Fig. 7 is a landing page design for the website's home page. The purpose of the website

Table 7. Classification report on prediction of new data

Category	Precision	Recall	F1-score
Cyberbullying	1.00	0.31	0.47
Non-Cyberbullying	0.50	1.00	0.66
average macro	0.75	0.65	0.56

is to make it easier for users to use the model. In addition, the website can be an educational medium for users about cyberbullying, thereby increasing awareness to prevent it.

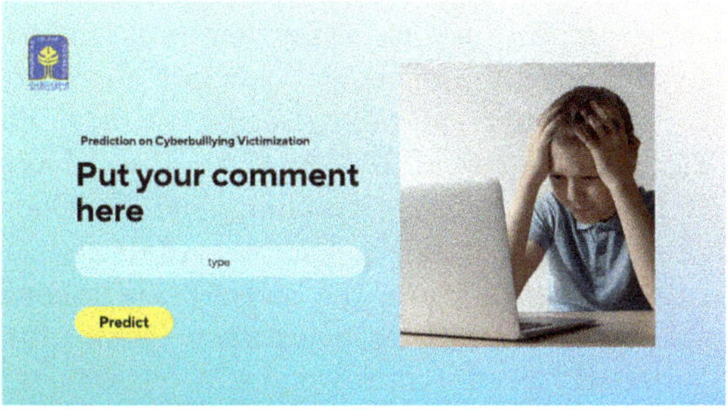

Fig. 7. Website prototype for home page

Users input their comments in the provided field and then press the "predict" button to start the prediction. After that, users are directed to the landing page for the results. On this page, as in Fig. 8, they will be shown the highest probability value generated by the model in predicting their comments.

4 Future Development

The development of future research is the model that can predict implicit cyberbullying victimization, such as subtle satire. In addition, it is expected to build more data normalization because the longer the Indonesian language, the more diverse terms, such as slang and new abbreviations.

5 Conclusion

as the number of majority classes. However, with SMOTE-ENN, noise from the SMOTE results is removed, causing the number of instances to decrease. This process effectively resolved the imbalance between comments classified as cyberbullying and those classified as non-cyberbullying, as it improved the accuracy of the predicted class.

Fig. 8. Website landing page for prediction result

The tuning parameters were set for every ensemble model to find the best combination to optimize model performance. Random Forest reached the highest measurement for the precision, recall, and f1-score average. The scores for both AdaBoost and XGBoost are identical. However, AdaBoost has simpler and fewer parameters than XGBoost. In terms of running time, XGBoost was the fastest among the three. Even though models such as AdaBoost and XGBoost can handle imbalanced datasets by nature, the method for balancing data, such as SMOTE and SMOTE-ENN, helps to raise accuracy. However, the testing results suggest that the model still needs improvement to classify minor classes. This may happen because the small number of samples provides a small corpus size. As a result, the model cannot recognize new words that appear in comments.

References

1. Lauw, H., Shafer, J.C., Agrawal, R., Ntoulas, A.: Homophily in the digital world: a livejournal case study. IEEE Internet Comput. **14**, 15–23 (2010). https://doi.org/10.1109/MIC.2010.25
2. Henson, B.: Bullying beyond the schoolyard: Preventing and responding to cyberbullying. Secur. J. **25**, 88–89 (2012). https://doi.org/10.1057/sj.2011.25
3. Bottino, S.M.B., Bottino, C.M.C., Regina, C.G., Correia, A.V.L., Ribeiro, W.S.: Cyberbullying and adolescent mental health: systematic review. Cad. Saude Publica **31**, 463–475 (2015). https://doi.org/10.1590/0102-311X00036114
4. Kumar Sharma, H., Kshitiz, K., Shailendra: NLP and machine learning techniques for detecting insulting comments on social networking platforms. In: Proceedings on 2018 International Conference on Advances in Computing and Communication Engineering, ICACCE 2018, pp. 265–272. Institute of Electrical and Electronics Engineers Inc. (2018). https://doi.org/10.1109/ICACCE.2018.8441728
5. Asgari, T., Daneshvar, A., Chobar, A.P., Ebrahimi, M., Abrahamyan, S.: Identifying key success factors for startups With sentiment analysis using text data mining. Int. J. Eng. Bus. Manag. **14**(2022). https://doi.org/10.1177/18479790221131612
6. Fikri, M.N.: The impact of fuzzy discretization's output on classification accuracy of random forest classifier. Int. J. Adv. Trends Comput. Sci. Eng. **9**, 3950–3956 (2020). https://doi.org/10.30534/ijatcse/2020/218932020

7. Elnadrey, R., Elsisi, A., Attwa, W.: International Journal of Computers and Information (IJCI) Performance investigation of features extraction and classification approaches for sentiment analysis systems. Int. J. Comput. Inf. (IJCI). **9**, 1–14 (2022)
8. Talpur, B.A., O'Sullivan, D.: Cyberbullying severity detection: a machine learning approach. PLoS ONE **15**, 1–19 (2020). https://doi.org/10.1371/journal.pone.0240924
9. Stephenie, Warsito, B., Prahutama, A.: Sentiment analysis on tokopedia product online reviews using random forest method. In: E3S Web of Conferences, vol. 202 (2020). https://doi.org/10.1051/E3SCONF/202020216006
10. Primartha, R., Adhi Tama, B., Arliansyah, A., Januar Miraswan, K.: Decision tree combined with pso-based feature selection for sentiment analysis. J. Phys.: Conf. Ser. (2019). https://doi.org/10.1088/1742-6596/1196/1/012018
11. Rianto, M., Wibowo, A.B., Santosa, E.P., P.I.: Improving stemming techniques for non-formal Indonesian sentences using incorbiz. ICIC Exp. Lett. **15**, 67–74 (2021). https://doi.org/10.24507/icicel.15.01.67
12. Hidayat, A.A., Pardamean, B.: Count time series modelling of twitter data and topic modelling: a case of Indonesia flood events. In: 3rd International Conference on Biospheric Harmony Advanced Research (2021)
13. Hidayat, R., Minati, S.: Comparative analysis of text mining classification algorithms for english and Indonesian qur'an translation. IJID (Int. J. Inf. Dev.) **8**, 47–51 (2019). https://doi.org/10.14421/IJID.2019.08108
14. nlp-id · PyPI, https://pypi.org/project/nlp-id/0.1.5/. Last accessed 2024/11/09
15. Wu, X., Fang, L., Wang, P., Yu, N.: Performance of using LDA for Chinese news text classification. In: IEEE (ed.) Proceeding of the IEEE 28th Canadian Conference on Electrical and Computer Engineering. pp. 1260–1264. , Halifax, Canada (2015). https://doi.org/10.1109/CCECE.2015.7129459
16. Qaiser, S., Ali, R.: Text mining: use of TF-IDF to examine the relevance of words to documents. Int. J. Comput. Appl. **181**, 25–29 (2018). https://doi.org/10.5120/ijca2018917395
17. Yahav, I., Shehory, O., Schwartz, D.: Comments mining with TF-IDF: the inherent bias and its removal. IEEE Trans. Knowl. Data Eng. **31**, 437–450 (2019). https://doi.org/10.1109/TKDE.2018.2840127
18. Ting, K.M.: Confusion matrix. In: Webb, G.I. (ed.) Encyclopedia of Machine Learning and Data Mining. pp. 260–261. Springer, Boston, MA (2017). https://doi.org/10.1007/978-1-4899-7687-1
19. Zeng, G.: On the confusion matrix in credit scoring and its analytical properties. Commun. Stat. Theory Methods. **49**, 2080–2093 (2020). https://doi.org/10.1080/03610926.2019.1568485
20. Chawla, N.V., Bowyer, K.W., Hall, L.O., Kegelmeyer, W.P.: SMOTE: synthetic minority over-sampling technique. J. Artif. Intell. Res. **16**, 321–357 (2002). https://doi.org/10.1613/jair.953
21. Fernández, A., García, S., Herrera, F., Chawla, N. V.: SMOTE for Learning from Imbalanced Data: Progress and Challenges, Marking the 15-year Anniversary, (2018). https://doi.org/10.1613/jair.1.11192
22. Shen, L., Lin, Z., Huang, Q.: Relay Backpropagation for Effective Learning of Deep Convolutional Neural Networks. Lecture Notes in Computer Science (including subseries Lecture Notes in Artificial Intelligence and Lecture Notes in Bioinformatics), vol. 9911, LNCS, pp. 467–482 (2015). https://doi.org/10.1007/978-3-319-46478-7_29

23. Geetha, R., Sivasubramanian, S., Kaliappan, M., Vimal, S., Annamalai, S.: Cervical cancer identification with synthetic minority oversampling technique and PCA analysis using random forest classifier. J. Med. Syst. **43**, 1–19 (2019). https://doi.org/10.1007/S10916-019-1402-6
24. Fernández, A., García, S., Herrera, F., Chawla, N.V.: SMOTE for learning from imbalanced data: progress and challenges, marking the 15-year anniversary. J. Artif. Intell. Res. **61**, 863–905 (2018). https://doi.org/10.1613/JAIR.1.11192
25. Barro, R.A., Sulvianti, I.D., Afendi, F.M.: Penerapan synthetic minority oversampling technique (smote) terhadap data tidak seimbang pada pembuatan model komposisi jamu. Xplore: J. Stat. **1**, 9–10 (2013). https://doi.org/10.29244/xplore.v1i1.12424
26. Wang, X., Ren, J., Ren, H., Song, W., Qiao, Y., Zhao, Y., Linghu, L., Cui, Y., Zhao, Z., Chen, L., Qiu, L.: Diabetes mellitus early warning and factor analysis using ensemble Bayesian networks with SMOTE-ENN and Boruta. Sci Rep. **13** (2023). https://doi.org/10.1038/s41598-023-40036-5
27. Muntasir Nishat, M., Faisal, F., Jahan Ratul, I., Al-Monsur, A., Ar-Rafi, A.M., Nasrullah, S.M., Reza, M.T., Khan, M.R.H.: A comprehensive investigation of the performances of different machine learning classifiers with SMOTE-ENN oversampling technique and hyperparameter optimization for imbalanced heart failure dataset. Sci Prog. 2022, (2022). https://doi.org/10.1155/2022/3649406
28. Yang, F., Wang, K., Sun, L., Zhai, M., Song, J., Wang, H.: A hybrid sampling algorithm combining synthetic minority over-sampling technique and edited nearest neighbor for missed abortion diagnosis. BMC Med. Inform. Decis. Mak. **22** (2022). https://doi.org/10.1186/s12911-022-02075-2
29. Breiman, L.: Random Forest. Berkeley (2001). https://doi.org/10.1007/978-1-4419-9863-7_612
30. Hastie, T., Tibsshirani, R., Friedman, J.: The Elemnts os Statistical Learning. Springer Science+Business Media, New York City, NY, USA (2009)
31. Roshan, S.E., Tanha, J., Hallaji, F., Ghanbari, M.R.: IMBoost: A New Weighting Factor for Boosting to Improve the Classification Performance of Imbalanced Data. Complexity. 2023, (2023). https://doi.org/10.1155/2023/2176891
32. Zhang, X., Yu, L., Yin, H.: An ensemble resampling based transfer adaboost algorithm for small sample credit classification with class imbalance. Comput. Econ. 1–28 (2024). https://doi.org/10.1007/S10614-024-10690-6/METRICS
33. Wu, Z., Zhao, J., Li, Y., Wang, Z., He, B., Chen, L.: A GAN-BO-XGBoost model for high-quality patents identification. Sci Rep. **14** (2024). https://doi.org/10.1038/s41598-024-60173-9
34. Frifra, A., Maanan, M., Maanan, M., Rhinane, H.: Harnessing LSTM and XGBoost algorithms for storm prediction. Sci Rep. **14** (2024). https://doi.org/10.1038/s41598-024-62182-0
35. Indonesia: Undang-Undang Republik Indonesia Nomor 19 Tahun 2016 Tentang Informasi Dan Transaksi Elektronik. Kementrian Sekretariat Negara Republik Indonesia,, Indonesia (2016)
36. Apa itu cyberbullying dan bagaimana menghentikannya? - UNICEF Indonesia, https://www.unicef.org/indonesia/id/child-protection/apa-itu-cyberbullying, Last accessed 2022/01/26
37. US Goverment: What Is Cyberbullying — StopBullying.gov, https://www.stopbullying.gov/cyberbullying/what-is-it, Last accessed 2022/01/27

Hybrid Approach for Signature Forgery Detection Using Convolutional Neural Network and Support Vector Machine

Yaumil Afwan and Sri Mulyana(✉)

Department of Computer Science and Electronics, Faculty of Mathematics and Natural Sciences, Universitas Gadjah Mada, Bulaksumur, Yogyakarta, Indonesia
yaumilafwan@mail.ugm.ac.id, smulyana@ugm.ac.id

Abstract. Signature forgery detection is essential for securing digital documents and transactions. However, existing methods have mainly focused on single-model approaches. This research aims to implement a hybrid approach using Convolutional Neural Network (CNN) and Support Vector Machine (SVM) to explore the potential of combining traditional and modern methods for signature verification systems. CNN is used to extract features from input signature images, while SVM is used to determine whether the features are genuine or forged. To ensure a robust learning process, the hybrid model will be compared to individual CNN and SVM models trained on the CEDAR and ICDAR 2011 SigComp datasets. Hyperparameter optimization is also performed, focusing on kernel type, learning rate and batch size. The results of this study suggest that the CNN model is still the most effective method in detecting forged and genuine signatures, as it achieved near-perfect accuracy (99.62% and 100%) on both datasets. The SVM model, while not as effective (93.75% and 85.80% on both dataset), can still be useful in certain scenarios. The hybrid model performs similarly to the CNN model (99.81% and 99.40% on both dataset), which combines the strengths of both models, may be a suitable alternative for specific applications.

Keywords: Convolutional neural network · Hybrid model · Image classification · Machine learning · Signature forgery · Support vector machine

1 Introduction

Signature forgery detection is an important area of research and application in finance, law, and government operations. Signatures have long been used as a traditional method of authentication [1]. A signature serves more than just as a mark; it represents consent, commitment, and the binding of legal obligations. Because of their inherent variability and complexity, handwritten signatures, in particular, present unique challenges in forgery detection.

Signature forgery detection is the process of distinguishing between genuine signatures, which are typically made by the authorized signer, and forged signatures,

P. C. Rodrigues et al. (Eds.): ISBIS 2024, 13, pp. 117–133, 2027.
https://doi.org/10.1007/978-3-032-32458-0_9

which are fraudulent imitations made by unauthorized individuals. Handwritten signature forgeries, according to [1], are classified based on distinguishing characteristics such as:

1. Random forgery. The signer uses the victim's name in their own style to create a simple forgery or random forgery.
2. Unskilled forgery. Occurs when the signer imitates the signature in their own style without knowing the spelling and without prior experience.
3. Skilled forgery. Without a doubt, the most difficult of all forgeries is created by professional impostors or individuals with experience in signature copying.

There are also two types of signatures: static and dynamic. Static signatures involve analyzing the static image of the signature, whereas dynamic signatures take into account the temporal aspects of signature creation, such as pressure applied and writing speed. Signature forgery detection frequently entails extracting features from signatures. Stroke direction, curvature, line thickness, and other geometric properties are examples of these characteristics.

Existing signature forgery detection methods frequently rely on handcrafted features and may struggle with the complex patterns and variations in genuine and forged signatures. Deep learning models, specifically Convolutional Neural Networks (CNN), have demonstrated promise in image-based tasks such as signature analysis. However, their application to signature forgery detection, particularly in conjunction with traditional methods such as Support Vector Machines (SVM), is still being researched.

While there are numerous applications for signature forgery detection, this study focuses on offline, static signature images. The CEDAR dataset and the ICDAR 2011 SigComp dataset will be used for training and evaluation. Furthermore, the research excludes hardware-based or specialized signature verification systems.

This research presents a far less-examined method, making it unique in the field of signature forgery detection. Although signature forgery detection is not new, this research attempts a hybrid method to detect fake signatures by merging the strength of two different machine learning techniques, namely CNN and SVM.

There are three main objectives of this research:

1. To implement a hybrid model for signature forgery detection.
2. To perform a thorough evaluation of the proposed hybrid model, as well as individual CNN-only and SVM-only models.
3. To advance understanding of signature forgery detection by providing insights into model behavior, feature importance, and potential applications.

2 Literature Review

Previous work on signature forgery detection has covered a wide range of techniques and methodologies.

Traditional methods have relied on feature-based approaches to distinguish between genuine and forged signatures, analyzing attributes such as stroke order, speed, and pen pressure [2]. For signature verification, notable examples include the use of histogram features [3] and Support Vector Machines (SVM) [4].

CNNs, for example, have been used to extract meaningful features from signature images, allowing for the accurate detection of forgeries [5]. Furthermore, research has investigated the use of real-time signatures [6], and has even led to the discussion of potential defensive strategies against adversarial attack methods such as Generative Adversarial Networks (GANs) and Robotic hands [7].

To improve accuracy and robustness, a hybrid system could leverage the strengths of both traditional and modern methods [8], which has been tested for image classification, namely classifying types of skin cancer [9]. The paper Deep Learning using Linear Support Vector Machines by Tang proposes an alternative to the traditional softmax layer in deep learning models, focusing on margin-based loss instead of cross-entropy loss. This approach shows a minor but consistent advantage over the conventional softmax layer [10]. Alexander et al. further explored this hybrid approach by combining CNN and SVM to classify Basal Cell Carcinoma (BCC), a common skin cancer [11]. This research will refer to this hybrid implementation rather than the more common approach of constructing separate models and feeding the CNN output into the SVM.

3 Research Methodology

This research aims to develop three models for signature forgery detection: CNN, SVM, and Hybrid CNN-SVM. The proposed research framework consists of two datasets that will be used to individually train and test the three aforementioned models. After the model has been trained and tested using the various metrics, it will then be analyzed further and compared with each other. The comparison results may show the effectiveness of the hybrid approach in detecting signature forgery. The proposed research framework can be observed in Fig. 1.

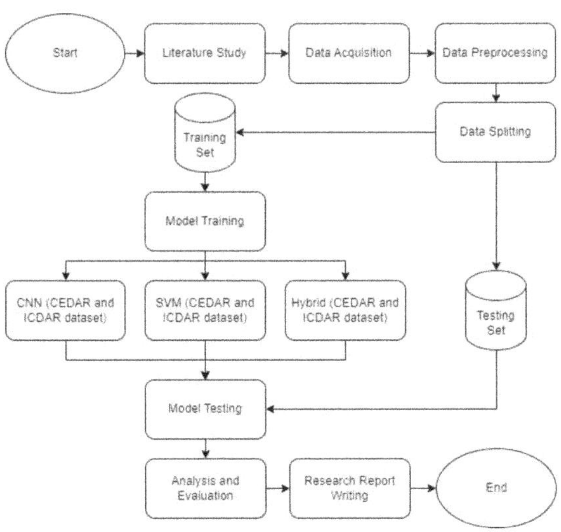

Fig. 1. Proposed research framework

3.1 Data Acquisition

Table 1 depicts the summary of dataset in this research. The CEDAR dataset is a collection of offline signatures that can be used for signature verification [12]. It was developed by the University of Buffalo's Center of Excellence for Document Analysis and Recognition (CEDAR).

The International Conference on Document Analysis and Recognition (ICDAR) 2011 SigComp dataset is a collection of offline and online signature samples used for signature verification [13]. The offline dataset comprises PNG images, scanned at 400 dpi, RGB color.

Table 1. Summary of dataset

Dataset	Size	File size (MB)	Format	Class	Source
CEDAR	2640 images	254	PNG	Genuine and Forged	Kaggle
ICDAR 2011 SigComp	2149 images	630	PNG	Genuine and Forged	Kaggle

3.2 Data Preprocessing

Data preprocessing is usually applied on input before further processing in machine learning. In this research, the signature images are preprocessed before training the models, to ensure generalization. This step includes resize and rescale (normalization). In this research, images from both datasets will be resized to 256 x 256 pixels, for standardization. Normalization is used to reduce computing time and can provide good training results because all pixel values have been normalized so they have the same range of values (between 0 and 1). This operation is both accessible through the ImageDataGenerator class in the tf_keras library [14].

3.3 Data Splitting

Table 2 contains the information regarding data splitting for each dataset. The CEDAR dataset will be divided into two subsets: 80% for training and the remaining 20% for testing. The ICDAR 2011 SigComp is already pre-split so data splitting is not necessary.

Table 2. Data split

Dataset	Training data	Testing data
CEDAR	2112 images	528 images
ICDAR 2011 SigComp	1649 images	500 images

3.4 Model Architecture

CNN Model

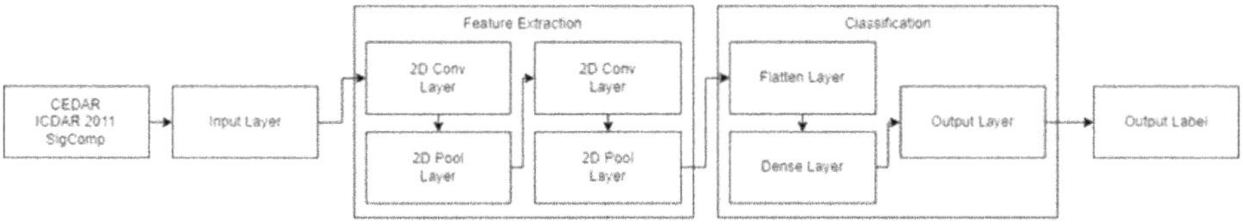

Fig. 2. CNN model architecture

A CNN is created as a standalone model for signature forgery detection. After loading the input image, it then passes through several convolution and pooling layers. ReLU will be used as the activation function in the convolution layer, with sigmoid as the output activation function. These layers further process the features and learn to classify them into either genuine or forged signatures. These stages are illustrated in Fig. 2, while Table 3 illustrates the layer composition in more detail.

Table 3. CNN model layer composition

Layer type	Output shape	Activation function
Input	256 × 256 × 3	
Conv2D_1 (16)	254 × 254 × 16	ReLU
Max Pooling2D_1	127 × 127 × 16	
Conv2D_2 (32)	125 × 125 × 32	ReLU
Max Pooling2D_2	62 × 62 × 32	
Conv2D_3 (64)	60 × 60 × 64	ReLU
MaxPooling2D_3	30 × 30 × 64	
Flatten	57600	
Dense (128)	128	ReLU
Dropout (0.5)	128	
Dense (Output)	2	Sigmoid

SVM Model

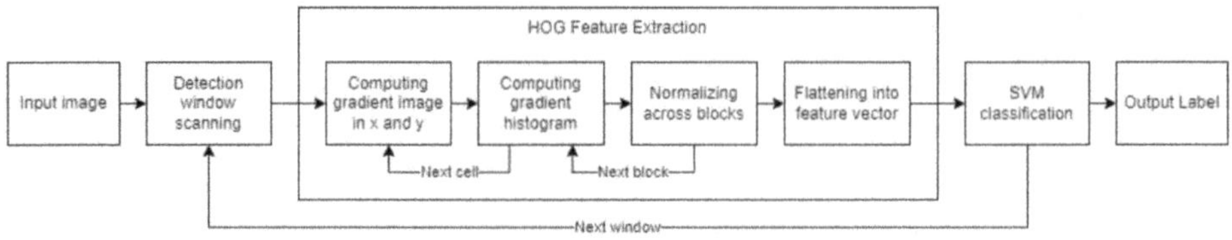

Fig. 3. SVM model architecture

Figure 3 depicts the stages of the SVM model. The signature image is first loaded, and then the Histogram of Oriented Gradient (HOG) descriptor is used to extract a feature vector from it. An SVM classifier is fed the feature vector. Based on the extracted features, the SVM attempts to find a decision boundary that best separates genuine and forged signatures in feature space. The SVM produces a binary classification decision: genuine or forged. It is determined by where the feature vector falls on the decision boundary. Figure 4 illustrates the HOG feature extraction on a sample signature image.

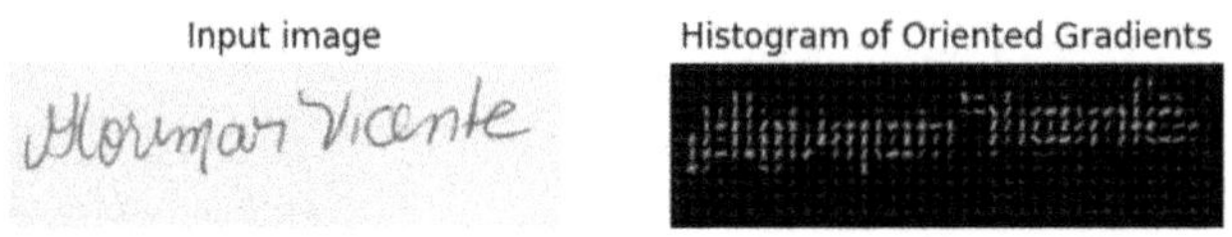

Fig. 4. Example of HOG operation on signature image

Hybrid (CNN-SVM) Model

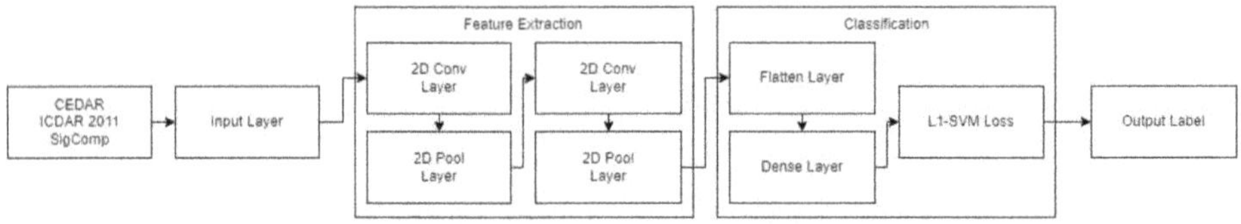

Fig. 5. Hybrid (CNN-SVM) model architecture

In the Hybrid (CNN-SVM) model, the architecture is similar to the CNN model up to the flatten layer. By implementing the fully connected SVM layer, the model will now generalize using the L1-SVM loss (using Linear activation and Hinge loss). Combining both approaches, CNN as the feature extractor and SVM as the classification. These stages are illustrated in Fig. 5, while Table 4 illustrates the layer composition in more detail.

Table 4. Hybrid (CNN-SVM) model layer composition

Layer type	Output shape	Activation function
Input	256 × 256 × 3	
Conv2D_1 (16)	254 × 254 × 16	ReLU
Max Pooling2D_1	127 × 127 × 16	
Conv2D_2 (32)	125 × 125 × 32	ReLU
Max Pooling2D_2	62 × 62 × 32	
Conv2D_3 (64)	60 × 60 × 64	ReLU
MaxPooling2D_3	30 × 30 × 64	
Flatten	57600	
Dense (128)	128	
Dropout (0.5)	128	
SVM Dense (Output)	2	Linear

3.5 Model Training

All three models will be trained model will undergo a supervised training process using the preprocessed dataset. Because the default parameters for software libraries are not optimal for all use cases, hyperparameter optimization techniques are necessary to fine-tune the performance of machine learning models [15]. Learning rates and batch size in CNN, as well as kernel types in SVM are all examples of hyperparameters. In this experiment, these hyperparameters will be tuned and performance will be documented per each training run.

3.6 Model Testing

The final models, which include CNN, SVM, and hybrid models, are evaluated on unseen data to determine their real-world applicability and generalization abilities. The results will be examined to ensure that the model is capable of detecting signature forgeries.

3.7 Analysis and Evaluation

The performance of all three models will be assessed and compared between the two datasets. Alongside confusion matrix, here will be four main performance metrics:

- Accuracy is a measurement of overall correctness.
- Precision will assess the model's ability to avoid false positives.
- Recall measures the ability to detect all instances of forgery.
- F1-score provides a balanced assessment by taking into account both false positives and false negatives.

4 Results and Discussion

4.1 Model Performance: CNN Model

Table 5. Training results for CNN model on CEDAR dataset

Learning rate	Batch size	Training		Validation		Training time
		Accuracy	Loss	Accuracy	Loss	
0.001	32	0.9735	**0.0757**	0.8769	0.4423	376.15
	64	0.9607	0.1176	0.8485	0.4258	364.44
	128	0.9162	0.2211	0.8712	0.3286	344.09
0.0001	32	0.9659	0.1232	0.9943	0.0556	376.28
	64	**0.9815**	0.0995	**0.9962**	**0.0428**	353.81
	128	0.9072	0.3046	0.9186	0.2636	336.18
0.00001	32	0.8059	0.4839	0.8277	0.4755	369.49
	64	0.7249	0.6073	0.6989	0.6116	361.6
	128	0.6804	0.6567	0.6515	0.6574	**334.56**

Table 6. Training results for CNN model on ICDAR dataset

Learning rate	Batch size	Training		Validation		Training time
		Accuracy	Loss	Accuracy	Loss	
0.001	32	**0.9982**	**0.0105**	**1.0000**	**0.0022**	290.77
	64	0.9812	0.0428	**1.0000**	0.0110	274.3
	128	0.9897	0.0347	0.9980	0.0108	276.76
0.0001	32	0.9782	0.0821	0.9880	0.0399	288.92
	64	0.9394	0.1824	0.9600	0.1214	279.27
	128	0.8751	0.3507	0.9280	0.2409	**259.99**
0.00001	32	0.6386	0.6589	0.7220	0.6441	287.31
	64	0.6822	0.6107	0.6880	0.6017	278.61
	128	0.6938	0.6415	0.6400	0.6383	261.34

For the CNN model, training is done twice on both datasets. Hyperparameters tested are learning rate and batch size with values of 0.001, 0.0001, 0.00001 and 32, 64, 128 respectively. Table 5 illustrates the training outcomes for the CNN model on the CEDAR dataset, showing discernible trends as the learning rate and batch size vary. Conversely, Table 6 showcases the training outcomes for the CNN model on the ICDAR dataset, portraying distinct performance characteristics compared to the CEDAR dataset. From the results, we obtain the best hyperparameter setting which is shown by Table 7.

Table 7. Specification for best CNN model

No.	Model name	Hyperparameter	
		Learning rate	Batch size
1	CEDAR-CNN-5	0.0001	64
2	ICDAR-CNN-1	0.001	32

The CEDAR-CNN-5 and ICDAR-CNN-1 model accuracy and loss plot are shown as Figs. 6 and 7, respectively.

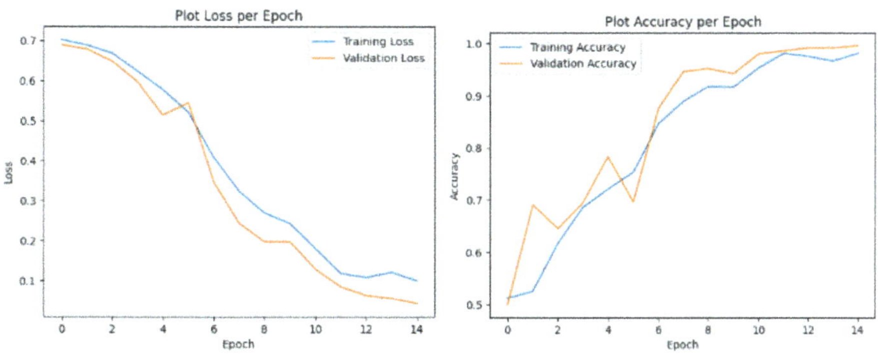

Fig. 6. CEDAR-CNN-5 loss and accuracy per epoch

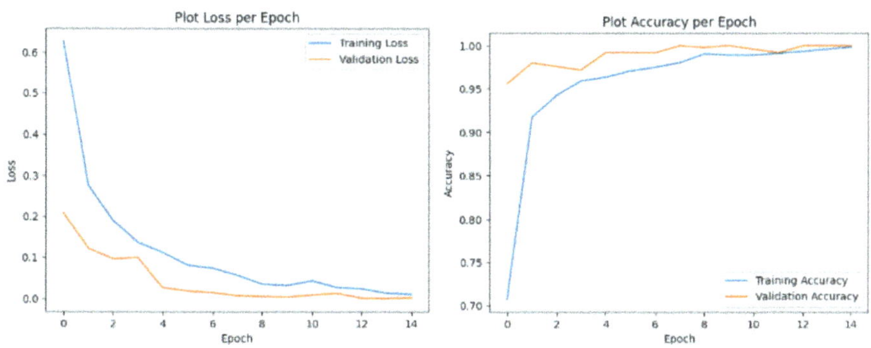

Fig. 7. ICDAR-CNN-1 loss and accuracy per epoch

We can infer from the plot above that the CNN model generalized well to the given dataset. During the training process, accuracy increases while loss decreases with each epoch, with values stabilizing between epochs 12 and 15. The graphs show that the CNN model converges faster on the ICDAR dataset than on the CEDAR dataset, implying that a smaller number of images may directly contribute to a faster learning process.

While there are minor changes in the above graphs, they do not indicate any discernible overfitting or underfitting.

4.2 Model Performance: SVM Model

The SVM model will test hyperparameters of three different kernel types, which are linear, polynomial and Radial Basis Function (RBF). After training is completed, the results are documented into Tables 8 and 9, with best values highlighted in bold.

Table 8. Training results for SVM model on CEDAR dataset

Kernel	Test accuracy	Training time
Linear	0.9261	**1589.33**
Polynomial	**0.9375**	1777.17
RBF	0.9223	1707.36

Table 9. Training results for SVM model on ICDAR dataset

Kernel	Test accuracy	Training time
Linear	0.852	**1254.95**
Polynomial	**0.858**	1316.61
RBF	0.856	1478.28

From the results, we can observe that the choice of kernel function significantly impacts the performance of the SVM model. The polynomial kernel achieves the highest test accuracy (0.9375), followed closely by the RBF kernel (0.9223) and then the linear kernel (0.9261). Non-linear kernels like polynomial and RBF are better suited for capturing complex relationships within the datasets compared to the linear kernel. The trade-off between training time and model performance requires researchers to balance these factors based on their specific requirements.

4.3 Model Performance: Hybrid Model

Table 10. Training results for Hybrid model on CEDAR dataset

Learning rate	Batch size	Training		Validation		Training time
		Accuracy	Loss	Accuracy	Loss	
0.001	32	0.9545	0.1242	0.8504	0.4348	361.84
	64	0.9820	0.0535	0.9053	0.2694	364.31
	128	0.9621	0.1170	0.8902	0.2508	**335.03**
0.0001	32	0.9920	**0.0395**	**0.9981**	**0.0069**	360.45
	64	**0.9924**	0.0553	0.9943	0.0202	361.02
	128	0.9342	0.2457	0.9659	0.1277	336.57
0.00001	32	0.7827	0.5727	0.7765	0.5509	368.93
	64	0.6402	0.8540	0.6534	0.8370	353.81
	128	0.6847	0.7855	0.6875	0.7713	343.07

Table 11. Training results for hybrid model on ICDAR dataset

Learning rate	Batch size	Training		Validation		Training time
		Accuracy	Loss	Accuracy	Loss	
0.001	32	**0.9921**	**0.0206**	0.9760	0.0488	286.47
	64	0.9921	0.0271	0.9860	0.0325	277.71
	128	0.9873	0.0454	**0.9940**	**0.0178**	262.33
0.0001	32	0.9703	0.0910	0.9740	0.0582	286.87
	64	0.9521	0.1266	0.9720	0.0607	279.19
	128	0.8975	0.2925	0.9260	0.1717	**258.41**
0.00001	32	0.7853	0.5521	0.7720	0.4995	286.04
	64	0.6622	0.8113	0.6020	0.7851	275.9
	128	0.5470	0.8967	0.5180	0.8955	262.44

For the Hybrid model, training is done twice on both datasets. Hyperparameters tested are learning rate and batch size with values of 0.001, 0.0001, 0.00001 and 32, 64, 128 respectively. Table 10 illustrates the training outcomes for the Hybrid model on the CEDAR dataset. Similarly, Table 11 presents the training results for the Hybrid model on the ICDAR dataset. We can observe a shift between the individual CNN model and Hybrid model. From the result, we obtain the best hyperparameter setting which are highlighted in Table 12.

Table 12. Specification for best hybrid model

No.	Model name	Hyperparameter	
		Learning rate	Batch size
1	CEDAR-Hybrid-4	0.0001	32
2	ICDAR-Hybrid-3	0.001	128

The CEDAR-Hybrid-4 and ICDAR-Hybrid-3 model accuracy and loss plot are shown below as Figs. 8 and 9, respectively.

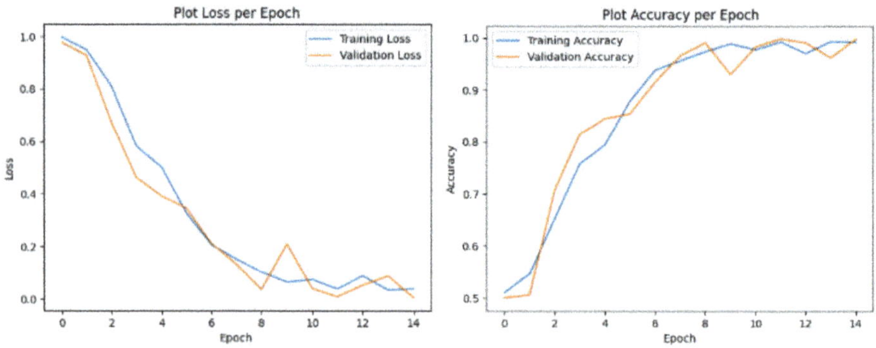

Fig. 8. CEDAR-hybrid-4 loss and accuracy per epoch

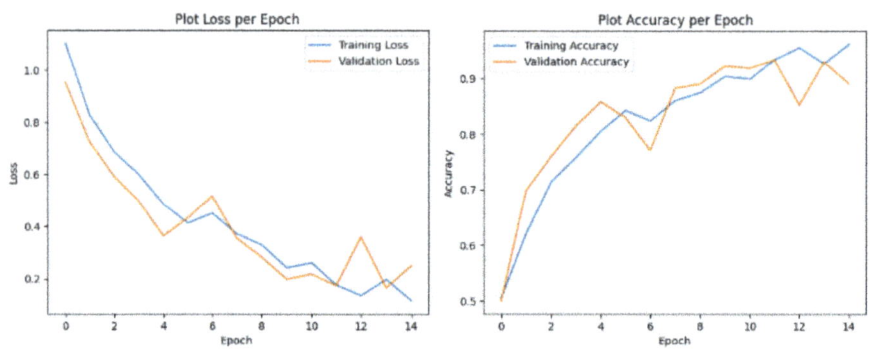

Fig. 9. ICDAR-hybrid-3 loss and accuracy per epoch

When we compare the graphs of the Hybrid and CNN models, we can see that the Hybrid model has greater volatility throughout the training phase. It is far less smooth than the CNN model. This demonstrates the inherent difficulties of merging

CNN and SVM components. The combination of these components may introduce additional sources of variation and nonlinearity, leading to more chaotic learning dynamics. Although the training and validation results are still satisfactory, there is also no evidence of overfitting, which occurs when training accuracy and loss increase but validation accuracy and loss remain constant.

4.4 Model Evaluation: CNN Model

Table 13 contains the confusion matrix of the CNN model. For the CEDAR dataset, the CNN model demonstrates exceptional accuracy, correctly classifying all forged and original signatures. Specifically, out of 264 original signatures, the model accurately predicts all (True Positives), while only misclassifying 2 forged signatures. Similarly, on the ICDAR 2011 SigComp dataset, the model achieves perfect classification, correctly identifying all forged and original signatures.

Table 13. CNN model confusion matrix

Dataset	Actual class	Predicted class	
		Forged	Original
CEDAR	Forged	262	2
	Original	0	264
ICDAR 2011 SigComp	Forged	248	0
	Original	0	252

On Table 14, the CNN model demonstrates high precision (1.00) and recall (0.99) for forged signatures, indicating minimal false positives and excellent ability to capture true positives. For original signatures, the model achieves equally impressive precision (0.99) and perfect recall (1.00), highlighting its capability to accurately classify both classes. On the ICDAR 2011 SigComp dataset, the model achieves perfect precision, recall, and F1-score for both forged and original signatures. Overall, the CNN model exhibits outstanding performance on both the CEDAR and ICDAR 2011 SigComp datasets, as evidenced by the perfect classification results and high evaluation metrics in the confusion matrix and classification report.

Table 14. CNN model classification report

Dataset	Class	Metrics			
		Pre	Rec	F1	Acc
CEDAR	Forged	1.00	0.99	1.00	1.00
	Original	0.99	1.00	1.00	
ICDAR 2011 SigComp	Forged	1.00	1.00	1.00	1.00
	Original	1.00	1.00	1.00	

4.5 Model Evaluation: SVM Model

We now move to Table 15, illustrating the confusion matrix of the SVM model. The SVM model on the CEDAR dataset correctly classified 236 of 260 forged signatures and 259 of 268 original signatures, but misclassified 24 forged signatures as original and 9 original signatures as forged. On the ICDAR 2011 SigComp dataset, the SVM model correctly identified 196 of 233 forged signatures and 233 of 267 original signatures, but misclassified 37 forged signatures and 34 original signatures.

Table 15. SVM model confusion matrix

Dataset	Actual class	Predicted class	
		Forged	Original
CEDAR	Forged	236	24
	Original	9	259
ICDAR 2011 SigComp	Forged	196	37
	Original	34	233

Table 16 houses the classification report of the SVM model. On the CEDAR dataset, the SVM model achieves high precision (0.96) for forged signatures, indicating minimal false positives, and recall of 0.91, suggesting the model captures a majority of true positives. Similarly, on the ICDAR 2011 SigComp dataset, the SVM model exhibits lower precision (0.85) and recall (0.84) for forged signatures compared to the CEDAR dataset. While the model achieves high accuracy and satisfactory performance metrics, there are some misclassifications, especially for forged signatures. Further optimization and experimentation are necessary to improve the SVM model's performance and reduce misclassifications.

Table 16. SVM model classification report

Dataset	Class	Metrics			
		Pre	Rec	F1	Acc
CEDAR	Forged	0.96	0.91	0.93	0.94
	Original	0.92	0.97	0.94	
ICDAR 2011 SigComp	Forged	0.85	0.84	0.85	0.86
	Original	0.86	0.87	0.87	

4.6 Model Evaluation: Hybrid Model

Table 17 portrays the confusion matrix of the Hybrid model. On the CEDAR dataset, the Hybrid model demonstrates exceptional accuracy, correctly classifying all 264 original signatures and all but one forged signature out of 264. Similarly, on the ICDAR 2011

SigComp dataset, the Hybrid model shows excellent performance, correctly identifying 246 out of 248 forged signatures and 251 out of 252 original signatures.

Table 17. Hybrid model confusion matrix

Dataset	Actual class	Predicted class	
		Forged	Original
CEDAR	Forged	263	1
	Original	0	264
ICDAR 2011 SigComp	Forged	246	2
	Original	1	251

Finally, classification report for the Hybrid model is included in Table 18. On the CEDAR dataset, the Hybrid model achieves perfect precision, recall, and F1-score for both forged and original signatures, indicating flawless classification performance. Similarly, on the ICDAR 2011 SigComp dataset, the Hybrid model demonstrates high precision, recall, and F1-score for both forged and original signatures, reflecting its superior classification capabilities.

Table 18. Hybrid model classification report

Dataset	Class	Metrics			
		Pre	Rec	F1	Acc
CEDAR	Forged	1.00	1.00	1.00	1.00
	Original	1.00	1.00	1.00	
ICDAR 2011 SigComp	Forged	1.00	0.99	0.99	0.99
	Original	0.99	1.00	0.99	

5 Conclusion

Based on the results of the experiment carried out, it can be concluded as follows:

1. This study has explored the use of Convolutional Neural Network (CNN), Support Vector Machine (SVM), and a combined Hybrid CNN-SVM model for detecting genuine and forged signature images.
2. The results of this study suggest that the CNN model is still the most effective method in detecting forged and genuine signatures, as it achieved near-perfect accuracy (99.62% and 100%) on both datasets. It also managed to achieve perfect precision and recall for the ICDAR dataset. The SVM model, while not as effective (93.75% and 85.80% on both dataset), can still be useful in certain scenarios.

3. The hybrid model which combines the strengths of both models performs similarly to the CNN model (99.81% and 99.40% on both dataset), it achieved perfect precision and recall for the CEDAR dataset, indicating that it may be more suitable alternative for specific applications, such as in this particular dataset.

The following are suggestions that can be implemented in further research, namely:

1. Further experiments can be carried out by comparing performance based on variations in the use of other hyperparameters such as other kernel settings in the SVM, batch normalization, the number of layers in the CNN architecture, etc. as well as its applicability to other domains beyond signature verification.
2. Further research can also explore other potential models and combination of algorithms outside of CNN or SVM.
3. This research uses two datasets (CEDAR and ICDAR 2011 SigComp) which is publicly available at kaggle.com, to divide the data into training data and test data. Further research can be carried out using additional data obtained independently or from other sources.

Acknowledgments. The dissemination and publication of this research were funded by the Department of Computer Science and Electronics, the Faculty of Mathematics and Natural Sciences, Universitas Gadjah Mada, Indonesia.

Disclosure of Interests The authors have no competing interests to declare that are relevant to the content of this article.

References

1. Hanmandlu, M., Mohd Yusof, M.H., Madasu, V.: Off-line signature verification and forgery detection using fuzzy modeling. Pattern Recogn. **38**, 341–356 (2005). https://doi.org/10.1016/j.patcog.2004.05.015
2. Soelistio, E.A., Hananto Kusumo, R.E., Martan, Z.V., Irwansyah, E.: A review of signature recognition using machine learning. In: 2021 1st International Conference on Computer Science and Artificial Intelligence (ICCSAI), 1, pp. 219–223 (2021). https://doi.org/10.1109/ICCSAI53272.2021.9609732
3. Tjahyanto, A., Rahardika, A.R., Shiddiqi, A.M.: An enhanced dynamic signature verification using the X and Y histogram features. Info. **12**(2), Article 2 (2021). https://doi.org/10.35970/infotekmesin.v12i2.668
4. Gunawan, G., Reswan, Y.: Desain Aplikasi Pengenalan Pola Tanda Tangan Menggunakan Metode Support vector machine (SVM). J. Media Infotama. **17**(1) (2021). https://doi.org/10.37676/jmi.v17i1.1311
5. Kao, H.-H., Wen, C.-Y.: An offline signature verification and forgery detection method based on a single known sample and an explainable deep learning approach. Appl. Sci. **10**(11), Article 11 (2020). https://doi.org/10.3390/app10113716
6. Gowri, P., Sivapriya, G., Karthick Raja, K., Kamaleshwar, N.K.J., Kesavaraj, N.: Real time signature forgery detection using machine learning. In: 2022 Second International Conference on Advances in Electrical, Computing, Communication and Sustainable Technologies (ICAECT), pp. 1–5 (2022). https://doi.org/10.1109/ICAECT54875.2022.9807905

7. Bird, J.J., Naser, A., Lotfi, A.: Writer-independent signature verification; evaluation of robotic and generative adversarial attacks. Inf. Sci. **633**, 170–181 (2023). https://doi.org/10.1016/j.ins.2023.03.029
8. Joodi, M., Saleh, M., Kadhim, D.: A new proposed hybrid learning approach with features for extraction of image classification. J. Robot. **2023** (2023). https://doi.org/10.1155/2023/9961421
9. Yohannes, R., Al Rivan, M.E.: Klasifikasi Jenis Kanker Kulit Menggunakan CNN-SVM. J. Algoritm. **2**(2), 133–144 (2022). https://doi.org/10.35957/algoritme.v2i2.2363
10. Tang, Y.: Deep learning using linear Support vector machines (2015). http://arxiv.org/abs/1306.0239
11. Ángeles Rojas, J.A., Calderon Vilca, H.D., Tumi Figueroa, E.N., Cuadros Ramos, K.J., Matos Manguinuri, S.S., Calderón Vilca, E.F.: Hybrid model of convolutional neural network and support vector machine to classify basal cell carcinoma. Comput. Y Sist. **25**(1), Article 1 (2021). https://doi.org/10.13053/cys-25-1-3431
12. Srinivasan, H., Srihari, S. N., Beal, M. J.: Machine Learning for Signature Verification (n.d.
13. Liwicki, M. et al.: Signature verification competition for online and offline skilled forgeries (SigComp2011). Int. Conf. Doc. Anal. Recognit. **2011**, 1480–1484 (2011). https://doi.org/10.1109/ICDAR.2011.294
14. Shanmugamani, R., Moore, S.: Deep learning for computer vision: expert techniques to train advanced neural networks using TensorFlow and Keras. Packt. (2018)
15. Raschka, S., Mirjalili, V.: Python Machine Learning: Machine Learning and Deep Learning with Python, Scikit-Learn, and TensorFlow 2, Third edn, Packt (2019)

Utilizing YOLOv7 Algorithm for Gossypium sp. Detection: An Implementation Study

Bianda Shafira Kartika Anggraini, Dina Tri Utari(✉), and R. B. Fajriya Hakim

Department of Statistics, Universitas Islam Indonesia, Yogyakarta 55584, Indonesia
dina.t.utari@uii.ac.id

Abstract. *Gossypium sp.*, commonly known as cotton, is versatile plant used for its fiber and seeds and holds medicinal properties. However, cotton cultivation is susceptible to various plant diseases, primarily affecting the leaves, reducing the production and quality of cottonseed and fiber. Early detection and identification of these diseases are crucial for effective pest control and increased production. Farmers rely on their experience to identify conditions that may not always be optimal. In this research, we propose utilizing the YOLO version 7 algorithm for real-time detection and classification of healthy and infected cotton leaves. The study focuses on two classes: healthy and infected. The model is configured with specific hyperparameters, including a batch size of 16, a network size of 416 × 416 pixels, 100 epochs, and a dataset split into 80% training data and 20% validation data. The implemented model achieves a mAP@IoU0.5 result of 97.5% and an F1-score of 94% at a confidence level of 54.8%. These results demonstrate the effectiveness of the YOLOv7 algorithm in accurately detecting and classifying healthy and infected cotton leaves in real time. By leveraging this technology, farmers can enhance disease identification and control measures, leading to improved production and quality of cottonseed and fiber.

Keywords: Image detection · *Gossypium sp.* · YOLOv7

1 Introduction

Gossypium sp. or cotton, is a highly valued plantation crop in Indonesia. It encompasses various species, including *Gossypium hirsutum*, which is traditionally used for medicinal purposes such as reducing fever, treating diabetes, menstruation, and coughing up blood [1]. Besides its medicinal uses, cotton is extensively cultivated for its fiber, a vital raw material for the textile ducts industry, including yarn, clothing and textile pro, and hospital cotton. Additionally, cotton seeds can be processed to produce oil, while cellulose-rich stalks can be utilized for paper pulp production [2]. However, cotton cultivation has risks, as the plants are susceptible to diseases that can significantly impact their productivity. Symptoms of these diseases are often visible on the leaves, which play a crucial role in cotton plants' growth and overall health [3]. Leaves are responsible for 80–90% of the diseases and pests that affect cotton plants, as they serve essential functions such as photosynthesis, transpiration regulation, and respiration [4, 5].

P. C. Rodrigues et al. (Eds.): ISBIS 2024, 13, pp. 134–151, 2027.
https://doi.org/10.1007/978-3-032-32458-0_10

Diseases affecting cotton plants can harm the quantity and quality of cotton fiber and seed [6]. For instance, bacterial blight has historically caused substantial yield losses in the USA, with an estimated 73,000 bales of cotton affected. The impact on cotton yields can be even more severe if leaf damage is followed by bacterial attacks on the fruit [7]. Currently, farmers primarily rely on visual observation to identify these diseases. However, their interpretations of disease symptoms are often based on personal experience, which may not always result in optimal disease identification. This can have significant implications for future crop yields. Therefore, accurate detection and identification of plant diseases are crucial steps that can facilitate early pest detection, disease control, and increased productivity [3].

Several studies have explored using different algorithms for detecting infected cotton plants. Kotian et al. utilized the transfer learning algorithm ResNet50 and the K-Nearest Neighbors algorithm to distinguish healthy and unhealthy cotton leaves [8]. Another study by Caldeira et al. compared the performance of GoogleNet, ResNet50, Support Vector Machines, Neuro-Fuzzy, Artificial Neural Networks, and K-Nearest Neighbors in detecting cotton plants, with Convolutional Neural Networks (CNNs) demonstrating 25% higher precision in detection [6]. With advancements in technology, artificial intelligence, particularly deep learning, has gained prominence in disease detection. Object detection using deep learning has been successfully applied to detect and classify healthy and infected cotton plants. Susa et al. conducted a study using YOLOv3 to detect and classify healthy and diseased cotton plants and leaves [9]. These studies highlight the potential of advanced algorithms, such as CNNs and YOLOv3, in accurately detecting and classifying healthy and infected cotton plants.

Recent progressions in computer vision and deep learning have facilitated the development of advanced algorithms capable of real-time item identification within complex agricultural environments. The YOLOv7 algorithm has surfaced as an exemplary solution due to its efficacy and accuracy in object recognition within the photographic studies conducted by Sun [10]. YOLOv7 represents a sophisticated single-stage framework for object detection that effectively reconfigures the detection process into a regression-oriented paradigm, thereby facilitating the swift processing of images while preserving high detection precision. This algorithm is particularly beneficial in agricultural contexts, where prompt decision-making is paramount. Its capability to execute real-time detection renders it appropriate for applications such as the autonomous surveillance of crops, wherein aerial drones or robotic systems may be utilized to evaluate plant vitality and detect complications such as pathogenic diseases or pest invasions [11]. The YOLOv7 framework has undergone extensive optimization for many applications, showcasing its adaptability across various sectors, such as traffic surveillance and agricultural evaluations. For example, contemporary research has indicated that YOLOv7 possesses the capability to proficiently identify diminutive and obscured targets within intricate field settings, rendering it an exemplary option for the detection of *Gossypium sp.*, where vegetation maybe closely clustered and partially concealed by foliage [12].

Furthermore, incorporating sophisticated methodologies, including attention mechanisms and multi-scale feature extraction, within the YOLOv7 architecture has significantly augmented its detection proficiency. These enhancements enable the algorithm to concentrate on prominent characteristics of the target entities, thereby improving detection accuracy under adverse conditions [13]. The utilization of YOLOv7 in the domain of *Gossypium sp.* detection not only aspires to elevate the precision of cotton plant identification but also endeavors to support the monitoring of their developmental stages and health statuses, ultimately contributing to the optimization of agricultural practices. The importance of employing YOLOv7 for detecting *Gossypium* species transcends the mere act of identification; it incorporates the potential for data-driven decision making within the agricultural sector. By harnessing real-time data acquired via YOLOv7, agricultural practitioners, including farmers and agronomists, can engage in informed decision-making concerning irrigation practices, fertilization strategies, and pest management, optimizing resource utilization and enhancing crop yield. Moreover, the capability to automate the monitoring process significantly decreases labor expenses and mitigates human errors, consequently augmenting the overall efficiency of agricultural enterprises [14].

In this implementation study, we propose utilizing the YOLOv7 algorithm for detecting and classifying healthy and infected cotton leaves. By training the model on a dataset consisting of labeled healthy and diseased cotton leaves, we aim to develop an efficient and accurate system for disease detection in cotton plants. The YOLOv7 algorithm offers the advantage of real-time detection, enabling timely intervention and disease control measures.

The motivation behind this research is to enhance disease identification in cotton cultivation by leveraging the capabilities of the YOLOv7 algorithm. By automating the detection process, we can reduce reliance on subjective human judgment and improve the efficiency of disease control measures. The implementation of YOLOv7 in this context has the potential to revolutionize cotton disease management, leading to increased productivity and improved crop quality.

2 Materials and Methods

2.1 Dataset

The data used in this study is secondary data obtained from the Kaggle website with the username Janmejaybhoi located in Burla, Odisha, India. The data is for cotton leaves found on plantations in India. The dataset used is entitled "Cotton Diseased Dataset" (www.kaggle.com/datasets/janmejaybhoi/cotton-diseasedataset).

2.2 You Only Look Once (YOLO)

The You Only Look Once (YOLO) algorithm, introduced by Joseph Redmon [15], significantly advances object detection. It utilizes the Darknet framework and is designed for real-time object detection using CNNs. The term real-time refers to the algorithm's ability to perform object detection in near-instantaneous time, achieved through techniques such as single-pass processing of input images and hardware optimization, such as GPU utilization, to enhance processing speed. Unlike traditional object detection methods, YOLO adopts a single neural network approach to detect objects in images.

This approach enables the network to simultaneously utilize features from the entire image to predict bounding boxes and object probabilities in a single evaluation [15] (Fig. 1).

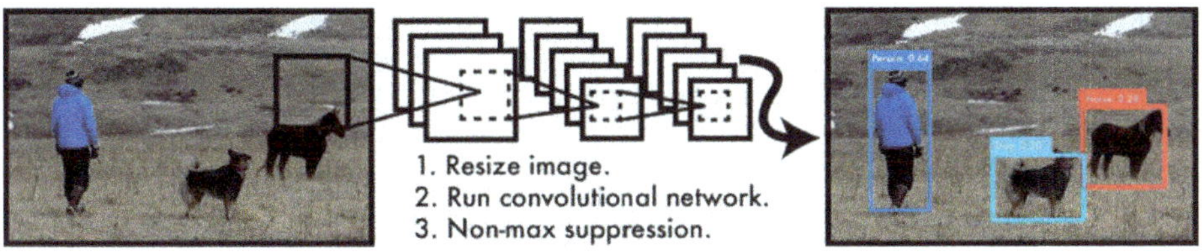

Fig. 1. Steps of YOLO algorithm [15].

The object detection process using YOLO involves three main steps:

1. Resize the input image,
2. Running a single convolutional network on the image,
3. Perform a threshold on the detection results based on the confidence value of the model.

YOLO divides the image input into *S*x*S* grids. If the center of an object falls within a grid cell, then the grid cell is responsible for detecting that object. Each grid cell will predict the bounding boxes that surround the object, and the number of bounding boxes in each grid will be determined by the parameter "*B*". Then the grid cell will also predict the confidence score for the box and the probability of the detected object class. The confidence score reflects the confidence level of the model in making detections and indicates how accurately the object is detected in the bounding box (Fig. 2).

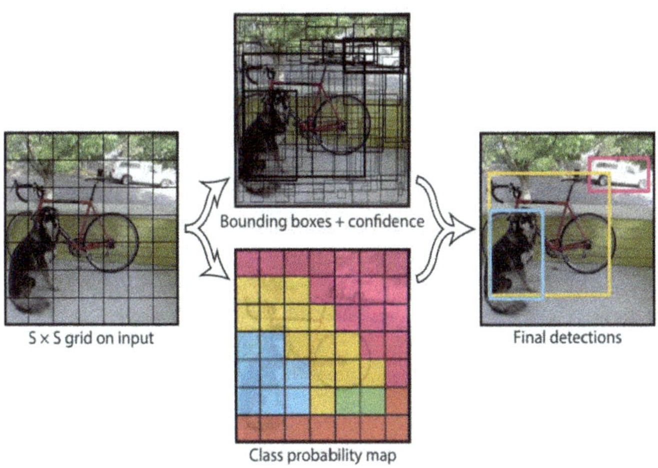

Fig. 2. The YOLO models.

Each predicted bounding box in the YOLO algorithm is represented by five values: *x*, *y*, *w*, *h*, and confidence. The (*x*, *y*) coordinates denote the bounding box's center relative to the grid cell's boundaries. These coordinates are normalized to a range between 0 and 1. Grid cells that do not contain objects have a confidence value of 0. The (*w*, *h*) values represent the absolute width and height of the bounding box in the entire image. The confidence score indicates the algorithm's confidence that the bounding box contains an object. Therefore, the YOLO prediction generates an output vector of [*S*, *S*, *B*x5 + *C*] where *C* is the labelled classes [15].

The YOLO algorithm will generate a confidence value for each box *B* as the probability value of the box that is believed to have an object, which will later be seen to what extent the prediction box and the actual object box in the image (ground truth box) overlap and is used to measure object detection accuracy using the Intersection Over Union (IoU) metric. Based on pre-trained datasets, IoU is an evaluation approach that quantifies the extent to which prediction and actual object boxes overlap (Fig. 3).

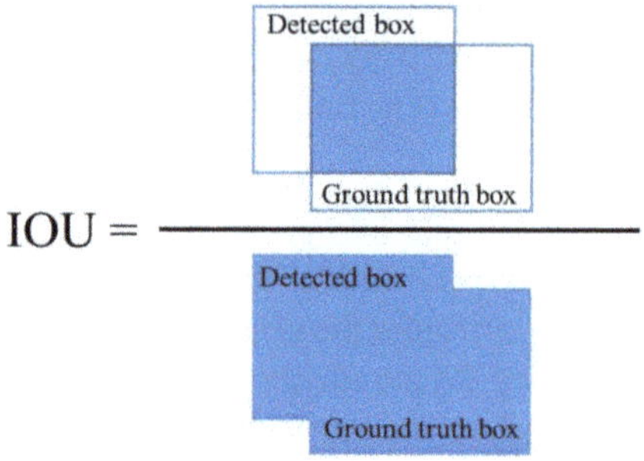

Fig. 3. Intersection Over Union (IoU) [16].

If no objects are detected in the bounding box, then the confidence score will be 0. The confidence score describes the level of confidence the model has in the existence of objects in the box. The following formula can express the calculation of the class confidence score [15]:

$$Confidence\ score = P(Class) * IoU_{pred}^{truth} \tag{1}$$

The YOLO detection network comprises 24 convolution layers and two fully connected layers. As shown in the figure below, some layers use 1 × 1 convolution as an alternative method to reduce the depth of feature maps. Utilizing 1 × 1 convolutions facilitates the network's optimization of input data processing, thereby enabling expedited inference durations while preserving the efficacy of detection performance [17]. The incorporation of 1 × 1 convolutions is of critical significance within this architectural framework. These layers facilitate the network's capacity for dimensionality reduction, thereby decreasing the number of parameters and the computational demands of subsequent layers. This characteristic is particularly advantageous for sustaining elevated frame rates during detection operations, as it minimizes the processing time required for each image [18]. Moreover, the amalgamation of 1 × 1 convolutions amplifies the network's capacity to learn intricate representations by allowing the model to effectively integrate features across various channels [19] (Fig. 4).

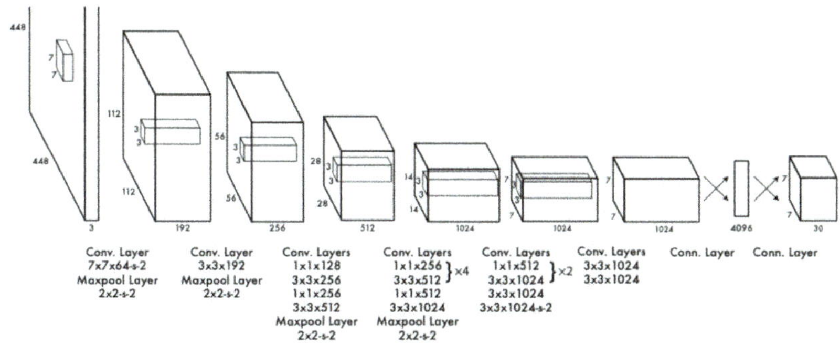

Fig. 4. The YOLO architectures [15].

YOLOv7 is the most recent version of the YOLO algorithm, created by WongKinYiu and Alexey Bochkovskiy (AlexAB) [20]. This iteration of the YOLO framework presents substantial improvements in detection precision and inference velocity, rendering it an exceptionally effective instrument for real-time object detection undertakings. Among all recognized real-time object detection methodologies, YOLOv7 attains a remarkable accuracy of 56.8% Average Precision (AP) while sustaining a processing rate of 30 frames per second (FPS) or greater on a GPU V100 [17]. These enhancements establish YOLOv7 as a premier option for many applications, particularly within the agricultural domain, where precise and prompt identification of crops and pests is paramount.

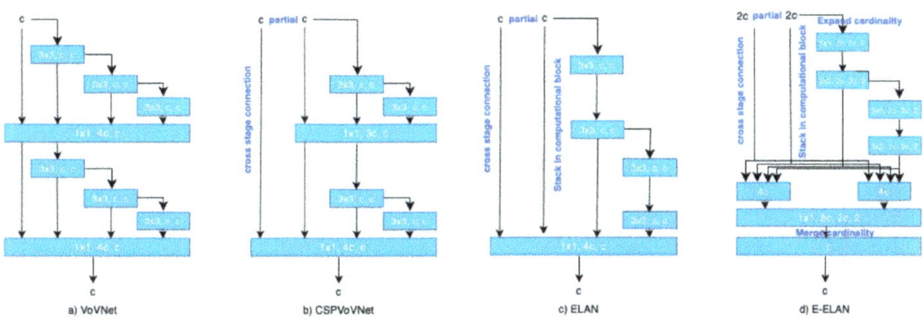

Fig. 5. The YOLOv7 architectures [20].

Figure 5 depicts the YOLOv7 architecture, which is based on the Efficient Layer Aggregation Network (ELAN) architecture with the concept of creating an expanded efficient network to get an Extended Efficient Layer Aggregation Network (E-ELAN). The number of parameters, computations, and computational density are the most important factors to consider while developing an efficient architecture. The CSPVoVNet architecture in Fig. 5b is a variant of the VoVNet design shown in Fig. 5a. The CSPoVNet design examines gradient routes to allow different layer weights to study distinct features, allowing faster and more accurate conclusions. In contrast, ELAN looks at a design strategy, "How to design an efficient network?" in Fig. 5c. As a result, deeper networks can successfully converge by managing the shortest and longest gradient pathways. E-ELAN extends the channels and cardinality of computational blocks to provide effective learning in deeper networks by applying group convolution [20].

YOLOv7 outperforms other object detection algorithms in terms of performance. YOLOv7 was tested on datasets like COCO (Common Objects in Context) and produced competitive results in averaging precision and IoU matrices. YOLOv7 reduces the number of parameters by up to 75%, needs 36% less computation, and achieves a higher average precision level (AP) of 1.5% compared to YOLOv4 [21].

3 Results and Discussions

This study uses data available on open-source data, namely the Kaggle website. This study uses cotton leaf data, which is divided into healthy cotton leaves and infected cotton leaves. There are 300 images collected, divided into 150 images of healthy cotton leaves and 150 images of infected or unhealthy cotton leaves; the image format used is .jpg. The images will train the model to distinguish between healthy and infected cotton leaves. The training and testing process will be carried out using images labeled and processed to produce a model capable of detecting and classifying the cotton leaves (Fig. 6).

(a) Healthy leaves (b) Infected leaves

Fig. 6. Dataset samples.

3.1 Data Labeling and Annotation

At this stage, labeling and annotation are carried out on the dataset. Labeling is done to label or tag class names for each object in the dataset to be used in the model training process, while annotation is done by providing a bounding box for each object to be detected. Labeling is divided into two classes: healthy and infected cotton leaves. This process uses labeling software. The first step is to open the dataset folder in the labeling software. Then, the labeling process begins by creating a bounding box using the "create rectbox" menu and creating a box that matches the object in the image. Furthermore, the label "healthy" is given to healthy cotton leaves, and "infected" is given to infected cotton leaves, as shown in Fig. 7.

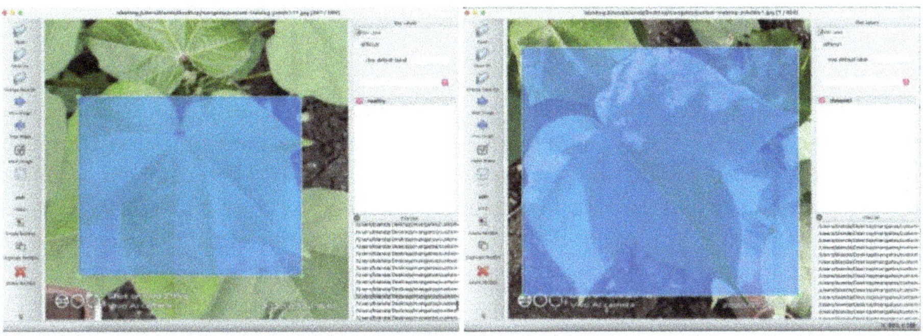

(a) Healthy leaves (b) Infected leaves

Fig. 7 Dataset labelling and annotation.

Labeling uses the YOLO format because the YOLO algorithm will be used when carrying out the training process. The result of the labeling is data containing information about the location of the bounding box and the label, which is stored in a file with.txt format. This file contains information about the object class, coordinates of the center of the bounding box (x-center and y-center), and the width and height of the bounding box. This information will be used in the model training process to recognize and differentiate between healthy and infected cotton leaves.

Figure 8 is an example of the results of the labeling that has been done. The number 0 indicates the class of the object. In this study, the number 0 is designated for infected cotton leaves, and the number 1 for healthy cotton leaves, then the bounding box center coordinates (green color) are shown at 0.657742 for the x-center and 0.574530 for the y-center. The numbers 0.574530 and 0.826339 indicate the width and height of the bounding box (yellow color).

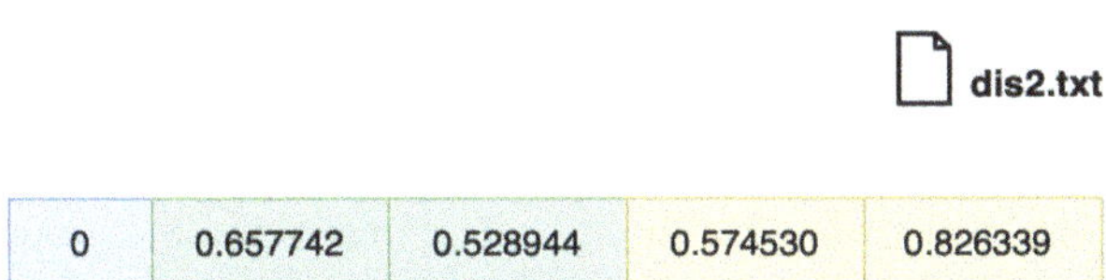

Fig. 8 Result of labelling and annotation.

The dataset will then be separated. The split dataset divides the percentage of data into training and validation data. The percentage employed in this study was 80:20, with 80% used for data training and 20% used for validation.

3.2 Model Hyperparameter Configuration

The model hyperparameters that will determine the model architecture during training must be configured to train the model. Several hyperparameters in the YOLOv7 algorithm must be modified.

1. Batch size

In machine learning, batch size refers to the sample dataset utilized in one iteration when training data. This study employed a batch size of 16, indicating that 16 images will be used in the model training process during each iteration. This decision optimizes computing efficiency and model convergence. A reduced batch size may produce noisier gradient estimates, improving the model's generalization capability. In contrast, an increased batch size might accelerate training but may lead to convergence on inferior solutions. We selected 16 since it offered a feasible compromise, enabling the model to learn efficiently while considering the available computational resources. An increased batch size can facilitate more reliable gradient estimations, potentially resulting in expedited convergence. Nevertheless, it concurrently demands a greater memory allocation, which may serve as a constraining factor contingent upon the computational resources employed for training [22].

2. Epoch

The epoch is a hyperparameter that controls how often the learning algorithm iterates over the training dataset. In this study, model training was done with 100 epochs. This quantity was selected based on initial trials, which suggested that 100 epochs would allow the model adequate time to learn from the data without overfitting. Future research may investigate the effects of differing epoch counts, especially under diverse environmental situations, to augment model resilience. In the context of YOLOv7 training, configurations frequently vary between 50 to 500 epochs, contingent upon the intricacy of the dataset and the particular application in question [23, 24].

3. Learning rate

The learning rate is one of the hyperparameters used to change the weight on the neural network to lessen the loss gradient. An initial learning rate of 0.01 was used in this investigation. An appropriately calibrated learning rate is crucial for optimal performance; future research may involve implementing learning rate scheduling to modify this parameter dynamically during training, hence improving the model's adaptability. An excessively elevated learning rate may induce the model to converge prematurely to a suboptimal outcome. In contrast, an inadequately low learning rate might lead to an extended training duration that risks becoming trapped in local minima [25].

4. Network size

The network size is the size of the image to be trained on the model. The configuration template's default network size is 416 × 416 pixels or 608 × 608 pixels. The training process in this study will be carried out on a network with a size of 416 × 416 pixels, which is a common default for YOLOv7 configurations. This dimension was used to balance preserving image detail and reducing computing demand. Experimenting with other network dimensions, such as 608 × 608 pixels, may provide insights into the model's capacity to identify cotton leaves with differing levels of detail, especially under diverse lighting and environmental conditions.

5. Class

The model's dependent variable, class label, is a category used to explain the label in the classification. This study employed two classes: infected cotton leaves, denoted by 0, and healthy cotton leaves, denoted by 1.

3.3 Training and Validation

Based on the previous explanation, the study was conducted with 100 epochs, with a batch size of 16. The input image size used was 416 × 416 pixels, and there were two classes: infected and healthy cotton leaves. Regularization is performed continuously through the Batch Normalization (BN) layer to update the model weights. The momentum factor is 0.937, and the decay rate is 0.0005. The initial vector is 0.01, and the augmentation coefficients of hue (H), saturation (S), and lightness (V) are 0.015, 0.7, and 0.4, respectively. With these settings, the results obtained will be explained as follows.

Figure 9 depicts the confusion matrix, often known as the mistake matrix. The confusion matrix is one of the matrices used to assess the effectiveness of the object detection model. This matrix contains true positives (TP), which are positive data anticipated to be accurate, false positives (FP), which are negative data predicted to be positive; false negatives (FN), which are negative data predicted to be positive; and true negatives (TN), which are negative data—successfully predicted [26].

The model obtained an accuracy value of 1 based on the confusion matrix. The prediction findings from the data identified as infected or diseased cotton leaves turned out to be accurately categorized. Similarly, the projected data for the classification of healthy cotton leaves can be appropriately classified. As a result, the model can correctly distinguish between healthy and sick cotton leaves. The value in Background FP, on the other hand, refers to a background object that does not belong to either class but is detected as such.

In Fig. 10, it can be seen a graph of the relationship between precision and confidence. Precision (positive predictive value) measures the goodness of a model in classification. Mathematically, precision is the ratio between true positives and the amount of data that is predicted to be positive [26].

$$Precision = \frac{TP}{TP + FP} \tag{2}$$

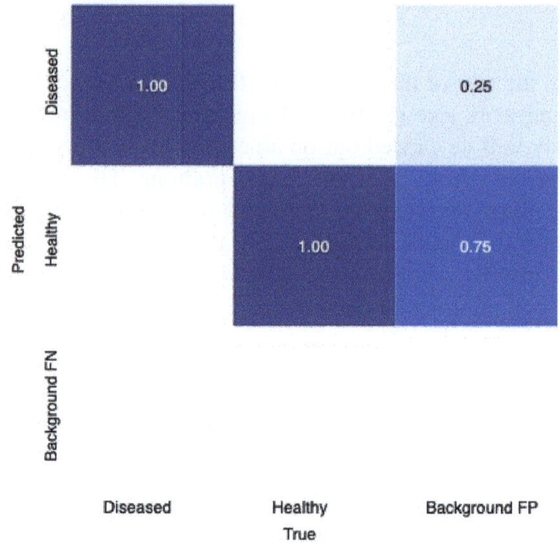

Fig. 9. Confusion matrix.

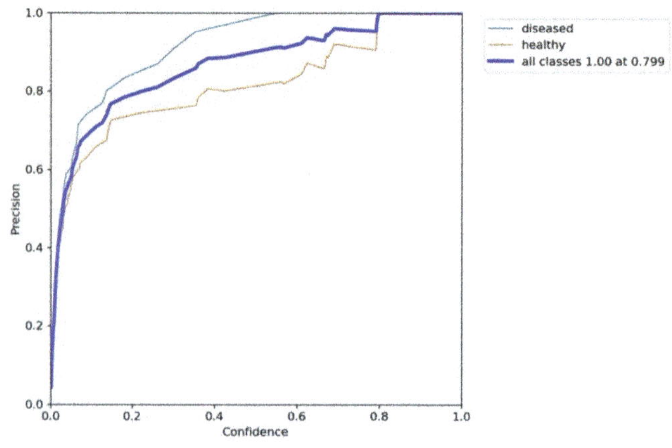

Fig. 10. Precision confidence curve.

Precision describes the accuracy with which a classification model can anticipate the class of an object. Meanwhile, confidence is the model's level of certainty about the validity of the provided label [26]. The greater the amount of confidence, the higher the confidence value.

The precision value attained in this investigation is 1.00, indicating that the model correctly labels items. The computed confidence value is 0.799, suggesting that the model is quite confident in the correctness of the label provided.

Figure 11 depicts the link between recall and confidence. Recall is the ratio of correct predictions to total correct and incorrect predictions. The model's confidence level in

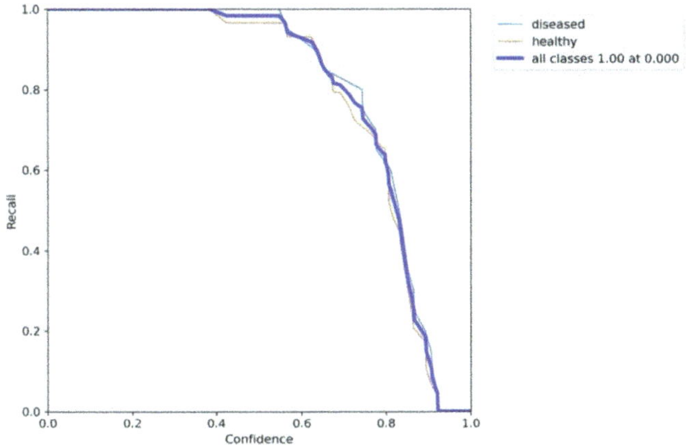

Fig. 11. Recall confidence curve.

the accuracy of its predictions is defined as its confidence level. The following is an example of recall [26].

$$Recall = \frac{TP}{TP + FN} \tag{3}$$

Recall indicates the extent to which the model can accurately classify all items. The higher the recall value, the better the model recognizes and categorizes items. The recall value for the entire class in this study was 1.00, with a confidence level of 0.000.

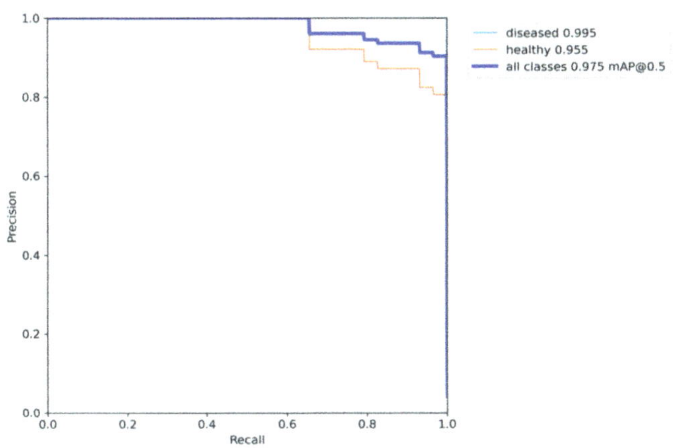

Fig. 12. Precision-recall curve.

A precision-recall curve is a plot of precision versus recall. Figure 12 depicts the link between precision and recall at various decision-making thresholds (thresholds). Even if the threshold values vary, a good model has high precision and recall values.

In the image above, using the mAP@0.5 matrix, a value of 0.975 is obtained, indicating that the model's average precision in finding the actual object in the image is 97.5%, indicating that the model is good at detecting objects with a reasonably high degree of accuracy. The mAP@0.5 (mean average precision at IoU 0.5) is an assessment matrix of object detection tasks that refers to calculating the average accuracy (AP) of each class of all objects at the IoU level of 0.5. This matrix computes a value by comparing the ground truth to the detected bounding box [27]. Average precision assesses the model's ability to recognize things accurately.

The matrix will be helpful when evaluating the model across a range of confidence levels. The trade-off between precision and recall emerges due to a shift in the classification's determination threshold. When the confidence and precision values are high, the recall value is usually low, and vice versa.

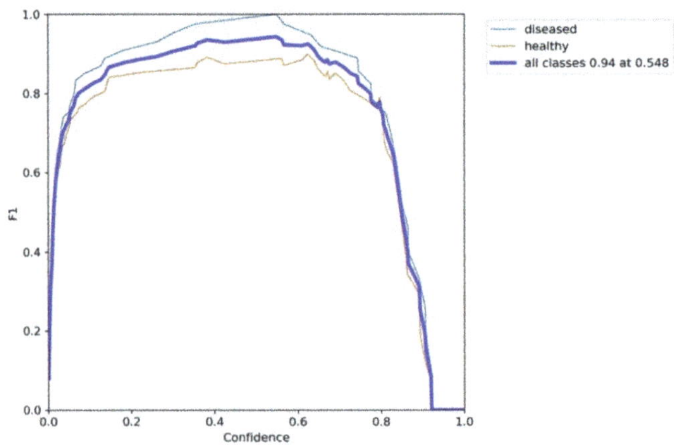

Fig. 13. F1-score curve.

The F1-score is a single statistic that combines precision and recall. The F1-score is a weighted average of precision and recall that provides an overall view of how well the model detects and predicts class. The F1-score is 1 for the best and 0 for the worst. Representationally, a high F1-score indicates that the precision and recall values are high. F1-score can be stated as follows [26].

$$F1 = 2 \times \frac{Precision \times Recall}{Precision + Recall} \tag{4}$$

In this investigation, the F1-score in Fig. 13 was 0.94 with a confidence of 0.548 for all classes or 94% with a confidence of 54.8%. As a result, the model in this investigation offers a fair mix of precision and recall. The mAP@0.5 and F1-score are alternative performance measurements to assess an object detection system's capability. The mAP@0.5 emphasizes object detection accuracy, whereas the F1-Score emphasizes object detection accuracy and the ability to discover things in images [26].

Figures 14 and 15 show the outcomes of model validation after it has gone through the training procedure. The model can detect objects in the dataset based on its received

Fig. 14. Validation 1.

Fig. 15. Validation 2.

validation photos. Each object also contains the results of model detection, indicating whether the leaves are healthy or diseased, as well as the prediction values obtained.

3.4 Testing

Testing was performed in this study to examine training and validation results using data other than the dataset used. This test aims to determine how far the trained model can recognize objects with a high level of accuracy. Images of cotton leaves were utilized in this test, gathered from various sources in different places, and the following results were produced.

(a) Testing 1 (b) Testing 2

(c) Testing 3 (d) Testing 4

Fig. 16. Testing result.

The testing data in Fig. 16a and b came from the same place as the training and validation datasets in India. Figure 16a Shows the object detection results and the accuracy level. Objects can be detected accurately, particularly infected cotton leaves, with an accuracy rate of 75%. healthy cotton leaves may be spotted with an accuracy rating of 94% and 51% in Fig. 16b.

Figure 16c shows testing results for cotton leaves from plantations in the area of Tangerang, Indonesia. The detection procedure findings demonstrate that the cotton leaves in the image are identified as healthy with a 76% accuracy rate. Even if the cotton leaf in the image has holes, this does not necessarily mean that it is diseased with a disease or infested with pests.

Cotton leaves from plantations in the Boyolali, Indonesia were used for the test results in Fig. 16d. The detection test results using an image of folded cotton leaves reveal that the model's recognition performance on cotton leaves in Fig. 16d could be more optimal. This reflects the model's difficulty in detecting objects with varied shapes, where the model's competence drops.

While our model exhibits encouraging outcomes under controlled conditions, we recognize the imperative of evaluating the YOLOv7 model in real-world environments to gauge its effectiveness comprehensively. Factors like diverse ambient conditions, lighting scenarios, and occlusions can substantially affect detection accuracy. Executing field testing will yield critical data regarding the model's resilience and flexibility, facilitating additional improvements and optimizations to the training methodology. By including these practical assessments, we intend to create a highly efficient instrument for farmers and agricultural professionals, guaranteeing its relevance across various agricultural settings.

4 Conclusions

The CNN architecture with YOLOv7 algorithm is used in this work to determine the status of cotton leaves, both infected and healthy. This experiment uses batch sizes of 16 and 100 epochs and a network size of 416x416 pixels. The dataset contains 300 cotton leaf images, with 80% for training and 20% for validation. According to the implementation findings, the YOLOv7 produced an F1 value of 94% with a confidence level of 54.8%. Furthermore, the mAP score achieved at the 0.5 threshold is 97.5%, suggesting a high level of accuracy in correctly recognizing and categorizing items. However, while testing using test data, there were variances in the accuracy scores, and certain items were not successfully detected. Image and video quality, varied lighting circumstances, background differences, and the size and form of items in the image can all influence these variations. Nonetheless, the results show that the final model can detect and classify items with a high degree of accuracy. However, accuracy issues persist under specific settings.

References

1. Halimat, A. et al.: Ethnobotanical survey of medicinal plants used in the treatment of gastrointestinal tract infections in Ebiraland Kogi state, Nigeria. ~ 38 ~ J. Med. Plants Stud. **8**, 38–44 (2020)
2. Worku, L.A., Bachheti, A., Bachheti, R.K., Rodrigues Reis, C.E., Chandel, A.K.: Agricultural residues as raw materials for pulp and paper production: overview and applications on membrane fabrication. Membranes (Basel). **13**, 228 (2023)

3. Bhimte, N.R., Thool, V.R.: Diseases detection of cotton leaf spot using image processing and SVM classifier. In: 2018 Second International Conference on Intelligent Computing and Control Systems (ICICCS), pp. 340–344. IEEE (2018)
4. Hilbert, I., Schleicher, T., Amera, T., Hennenberg, K.: The Cotton Supply Chain in Ethiopia, Freiburg (2018)
5. Wang, S., Alseekh, S., Fernie, A.R., Luo, J.: The structure and function of major plant metabolite modifications. Mol. Plant. **12**, 899–919 (2019)
6. Caldeira, R.F., Santiago, W.E., Teruel, B.: Identification of cotton leaf lesions using deep learning techniques. Sensors. **21**, 3169 (2021)
7. Pinckard, J.A., Ashworth, L.I., Snow, J.F., Rusell, T.E., Roncandori, R.W., Sciumbato, G.L.: Boll rots. In: Compendium of Cotton Diseases, pp. 20–24. American Phytopathological Society (1981)
8. Kotian, S., Ettam, P., Kharche, S., Saravanan, K., Ashokkumar, K.: Cotton leaf disease detection using machine learning. SSRN Electron. J. (2022)
9. Susa, J.A.B., Nombrefia, W.C., Abustan, A.S., Macalisang, J., Maaliw, R.R.: Deep learning technique detection for cotton and leaf classification using the YOLO algorithm. In: 2022 International Conference on Smart Information Systems and Technologies (SIST), pp. 1–6. IEEE (2022)
10. Sun, Y., Li, Y., Li, S., Duan, Z., Ning, H., Zhang, Y.: PBA-YOLOv7: an object detection method based on an improved YOLOv7 network. Appl. Sci. **13**, 10436 (2023)
11. Ren, L., Li, Z., He, X., Kong, L., Zhang, Y.: An underwater target detection algorithm based on attention mechanism and improved YOLOv7. Comput. Mater. Contin. **78**, 2829–2845 (2024)
12. Zeng, Y., Zhang, T., He, W., Zhang, Z.: YOLOv7-UAV: an unmanned aerial vehicle image object detection algorithm based on improved YOLOv7. Electronics (Basel). **12**, 3141 (2023)
13. Chen, J. et al.: Authenticity identification method for calligraphy regular script based on improved YOLOv7 algorithm. Front. Phys. **12** (2024)
14. Wang, W. et al.: Improved YOLOv7-based algorithm for detecting foreign objects on the roof of a Subway vehicle. Sensors. **23**, 9440 (2023)
15. Redmon, J., Divvala, S., Girshick, R., Farhadi, A.: You only look once: unified, real-time object detection. In: 2016 IEEE Conference on Computer Vision and Pattern Recognition (CVPR), pp. 779–788. IEEE (2016)
16. Mahdi, F.P., Motoki, K., Kobashi, S.: Optimization technique combined with deep learning method for teeth recognition in dental panoramic radiographs. Sci. Rep. **10**, 19261 (2020)
17. Deng, F. et al.: Real-time citrus variety detection in orchards based on complex scenarios of improved YOLOv7. Front. Plant Sci. **15** (2024)
18. Morales-Aranibar, L. et al.: Comparative analysis of key fiber characteristics in white Pima cotton (Gossypium barbadense L.): native accessions from the Peruvian Amazon. Agrosystems, Geosci. Environ. **7** (2024)
19. Wu, D. et al.: Detection of Camellia Oleifera fruit in complex scenes by using YOLOv7 and data augmentation. Appl. Sci. **12**, 11318 (2022)
20. Wang, C.-Y., Bochkovskiy, A., Liao, H.-Y.M.: YOLOv7: trainable bag-of-freebies sets new state-of-the-art for real-time object detectors (2022)
21. John, A., Devika, V.L., V, G.S., Sakhir, N.: Leaf disease detection & correction using YOLO V7 with GPT3 integrated
22. Shaheen, H., Singh, M.P.: Skin lesion classification using HG-PSO and YOLOv7 based convolutional network in real time. Proc. Inst. Mech. Eng. H. **237**, 1228–1239 (2023)
23. Tan, S.X., Ong, J.Y., Goh, K.O.M., Tee, C.: Boosting vehicle classification with augmentation techniques across multiple YOLO versions. JOIV: Int. J. Inform. Vis. **8**, 45 (2024)
24. Qiu, Y., Lu, Y., Wang, Y., Jiang, H.: IDOD-YOLOV7: image-Dehazing YOLOV7 for object detection in low-light foggy traffic environments. Sensors. **23**, 1347 (2023)

25. Tomas, J.P.Q., Doma, B.T.: Classifying motorcycle rider helmet on a low light video scene using deep learning. Int. J. Adv. Comput. Sci. Appl. **15** (2024)
26. Kuznetsova, A., Maleva, T., Soloviev, V.: Using YOLOv3 algorithm with pre- and post-processing for apple detection in fruit-harvesting robot. Agronomy. **10**, 1016 (2020)
27. Padilla, R., Passos, W.L., Dias, T.L.B., Netto, S.L., da Silva, E.A.B.: A comparative analysis of object detection metrics with a companion open-source toolkit. Electronics (Basel). **10**, 279 (2021)

Classification of Lung Cancer Disease in CT-Scan Images Using CNN with SMOTE and SMOTE-ENN Resampling Techniques

Regita Diah Pramesti[1], Sri S. Handajani[1](✉), Winita Sulandari[1], Hasih Pratiwi[1], Hilman F. Pardede[2], and Vicky Zilvan[2]

[1] Faculty of Mathematics and Natural Sciences, Sebelas Maret University, Surakarta, Indonesia
rr_ssh@staff.uns.ac.id

[2] Research Center of Artificial Intelligence and Cyber Security, National Research and Innovation Agency, Bandung, Indonesia

Abstract. The classification of lung cancer plays an important role in the medical field, as it allows for early detection and more effective treatment. Convolutional Neural Networks (CNN) are the most common type of neural networks used to detect and classify objects in image data. Classification using CNN can have problems when the amount of data is imbalanced. This could be fatal because the model would tend to be in the majority class, so it could not predict well in the minority class. The study aims to implement and compare CNN's performance with SMOTE and SMOTE-ENN resampling techniques on the classifying of lung cancer diseases with imbalanced data problems. SMOTE makes a new synthesis sample in the minority class, so the number is balanced. Meanwhile, SMOTE-ENN adds an ENN technique to remove the sample that is considered noise from the SMOTE results. The suggested method was evaluated using a confusion matrix. The data used was imaging data taken from Kaggle, which is 416 normal lung data and 70 lung cancer data. The results of the study showed that both methods were successful in dealing with data imbalances. The matrix evaluation indicated that the accuracy of the SMOTE-ENN model was 95% higher, while the accuracy of the SMOTE model was 93%.

Keywords: Lung cancer · Convolutional neural network · Imbalance Dataset · SMOTE · SMOTE-ENN

1 Introduction

Lung cancer is ranked 3rd with the highest number of cases in Indonesia, with 34,783 cases in 2020 [1]. These cancer cells can spread to the lymphatic, bone, liver, and brain systems. Individuals at risk of lung cancer, such as people who are frequently exposed to pollution or active or passive smokers, are advised to perform early detection with CT scans. CT scans are more effective than chest X-rays because they are more sensitive to detecting abnormalities or nodules with a size of at least 3 mm [2].

P. C. Rodrigues et al. (Eds.): ISBIS 2024, 13, pp. 152–162, 2027.
https://doi.org/10.1007/978-3-032-32458-0_11

Artificial Intelligence (AI), refers to the capability of machines to exhibit intelligent behavior akin to human actions [3]. In achieving that goal, AI uses the approach of machine learning, where machines are designed to learn from data without the need for explicit instructions from the user. In machine learning, algorithms analyze patterns and relationships in given data and then use that information to make predictions or decisions. Deep learning is a leading area in machine learning, which is very effective for tasks like image classification. In the health context, the Convolutional Neural Network (CNN) model is one of the most popular deep learning methods due to its remarkable ability to analyze and interpret medical images [4].

Convolutional Neural Network (CNN) is an algorithm for deep learning introduced by Fukushima in 1998. In the last few years, CNN has been successful in many image classification tasks, such as facial recognition, object detection and localization, image characterization, and age prediction [5]. Kalaivani et al. (2020) conducted a study on deep learning-based lung cancer detection and classification with an accuracy of 90%. The study explains that CNN's biggest advantage over other algorithms in machine learning is its ability to execute its own feature engineering [6].

Classification of images using CNN in the detection of lung cancer disease is problematic when the amount of data from normal people and affected people is imbalanced. This is fatal because models tend to be in the majority class, so they can't predict well or fail to identify the minority class. A mistake in diagnosing a disease that should be diagnosed with lung cancer turned out to be normal, causing patients not to get treatment quickly and with severe consequences such as death. In dealing with data imbalances, resampling is a technique that can be used by removing some of the data from the majority class or adding some data to the minority class using the data duplication process. Synthetic Minority Over-sampling Technique with Edited Nearest Neighbors (SMOTE-ENN).

Synthetic Minority Oversampling Technique (SMOTE) was first introduced by Chawla et al. in 2002 [7]. The research concludes that SMOTE can address the data imbalance problem by proving the increasing accuracy of class classification. The oversampling performance completed with SMOTE is that it randomly took samples from the minority class and replicated them to make new synthetic data [8]. Introduced the surrounding environment in the minority sample, so this technique can increase the number of samples in the minority class that are similar to the original data. In a study conducted by Anshori and Riana [9], using SMOTE to address imbalances in life expectancy data for lung cancer patients after thoracic surgery resulted in a significant improvement, namely increasing the average accuracy of 48.72–73.50%. The study also mentions that SMOTE succeeded in optimizing levels of imbalanced data.

The Synthetic Minority Oversampling Technique with Edited Nearest Neighbors (SMOTE-ENN) merges the SMOTE oversampling method with the under-sampling approach of Edited Nearest Neighbors (ENN). According to Mansourifar and Shi [10], the problem with the SMOTE technique is that the data synthesis results are biased. However, the problem can be solved with the ENN technique. Arisandi [11] compared the classification model using SMOTE-ENN resampling and without re-sampling in patients with heart failure. The results showed that the model using the SMOTE-ENN resampling technique increased the accuracy value in the minority class by 90%, whereas without the resampling, it only obtained an accurate value of 10%.

Based on the background described earlier, the study aims to implement and compare CNN's performance with SMOTE and SMOTE-ENN resampling techniques to classify lung cancer diseases with imbalanced data problems. The results of the method are evaluated using the confusion matrix to determine the best method's performance.

2 Literatur Review

2.1 Lung Cancer

Lung cancer occurs in cells of the airway wall of the lung organ, which divide uncontrollably and form a dense mass known as a tumor. Normal lung function can be disrupted as these cells develop.According to the Global Burden of Cancer (Globocan) in 2020 [1], in Indonesia, the number of cases of lung cancer ranks third with a total of 34,783 cases, after breast cancer and cervical cancer. Early detection is a prerequisite for preventing this. People who are at risk of lung cancer, such as active or passive smokers or people who are frequently exposed to smoke or pollution, should perform early detection with CT Scan. CT scans are more effective than chest x-rays because they are more sensitive to detecting abnormalities or nodules with a size of at least 3 mm [2].

2.2 Preprocessing Data

Data preprocessing is an early stage in data analysis that aims to prepare raw data before using it in further analysis processes. The primary purpose is to clean, transform, and organize data so that it can be used effectively by a machine learning model or algorithm [12]. In this study, data preprocessing includes some of the following methods:

Resize is the process of changing the size of the image to the desired size. This is useful when the image data has an inconsistent size and needs to be adjusted to have a uniform dimension before being inserted into a model or machine learning algorithm. In this study, the data was resized to 128 × 128 pixels.

The Normalization process changes the image pixel value range to a smaller or standard range. The aim is to produce images that have a uniform pixel distribution, which can help in model training by improving convergence and performance. The process is to change the pixel intensity value of the image from the range 0–255 to 0–1. Selanjutnya, untuk mencapai rentang 0–1 yaitu dengan mengalikan setiap nilai piksel dengan $\frac{1}{255}$ As described in Fig. 1.

2.3 Convolutional Neural Networks (CNN)

Convolutional neural networks are the most common type of neural network used to detect and classify objects in image data. The CNN algorithm has an architecture that consists of two components As described in Fig. 2. At the feature learning stage, the image is inserted for extraction, and then the value is studied on the image. The result

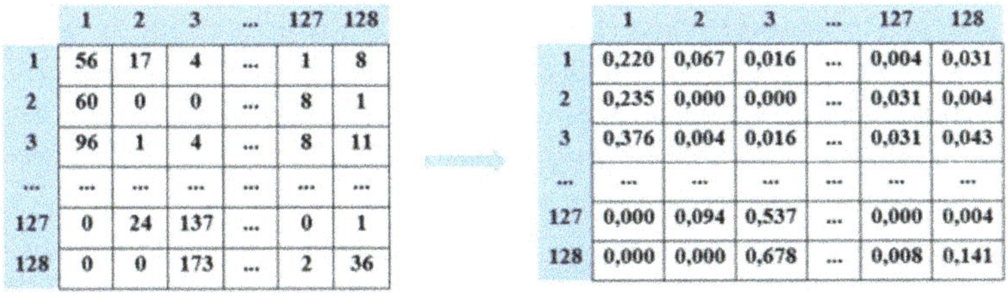

	1	2	3	...	127	128
1	56	17	4	...	1	8
2	60	0	0	...	8	1
3	96	1	4	...	8	11
...	...	...	...	...	...	...
127	0	24	137	...	0	1
128	0	0	173	...	2	36

	1	2	3	...	127	128
1	0,220	0,067	0,016	...	0,004	0,031
2	0,235	0,000	0,000	...	0,031	0,004
3	0,376	0,004	0,016	...	0,031	0,043
...	...	...	...	...	...	...
127	0,000	0,094	0,537	...	0,000	0,004
128	0,000	0,000	0,678	...	0,008	0,141

Fig. 1. Illustration of the normalization process

of the feature learning stage in CNN results in a series of feature maps containing representations of various aspects and patterns in the input data, such as edges, textures, shapes, and objects [13]. This feature is produced through a series of convolution layers, activation functions, and pooling layers. In this study, the ReLU (Rectified Linear Unit) activation function was employed to add non-linearity to the model, enabling the network to understand more complex representations.

The classification phase in the CNN architecture begins with a flattened layer, which is to align the feature maps resulting from the feature learning phase into a one-dimensional vector. The vector then passes through several fully connected layers, in which every neuron is linked to all neurons in the preceding layer, enabling the analysis of intricate feature combinations. In the last layer, the softmax activation function is used to generate a probability for each class, and the category with the highest probability is selected as the final prediction. This phase allows CNN to combine and interpret traits studied to produce accurate classifications.

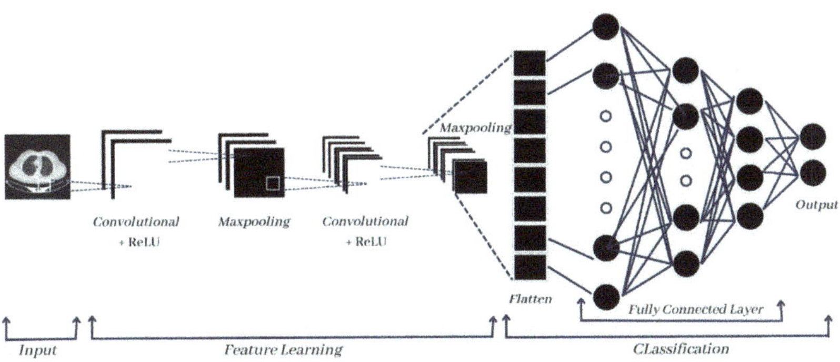

Fig. 2. Convolutional neural network architecture

2.4 Synthetic Minority Oversampling Technique (SMOTE)

SMOTE is one of the methods used in many research studies and succeeds in dealing with imbalanced data. The SMOTE method works by searching for the number of nearest neighbors as *k* of any data in the minority class [14]. After that, this method produces a synthetic data sample to the extent that the amount of data in the minority class is equal to that in the majority class. SMOTE performs oversampling by creating new synthesized data based on the Euclidean distance between the existing minority data and its nearest neighbors [7]. Using this distance calculation, SMOTE creates a new sample that is not only a duplication of existing data from minorities but also a new variation that helps machine learning models learn better patterns from minority classes, thereby improving the accuracy and generalization of models in the face of unbalanced data. In Fig. 3 explains how Smote works in generating new data.

In this study, the imblearn.over_sampling library available in Python is used to implement the SMOTE method. This study uses the default value of k,5 [15]. In SMOTE, k refers to the number of nearest neighbors used to form synthetic samples from the minority class. Specifically, each synthetic sample is generated by combining the characteristics of existing samples with the characteristics of k nearest neighbor samples. The default value of 5 was chosen because it has been extensively tested and is generally considered effective in producing synthetic samples that can well represent the minority class.

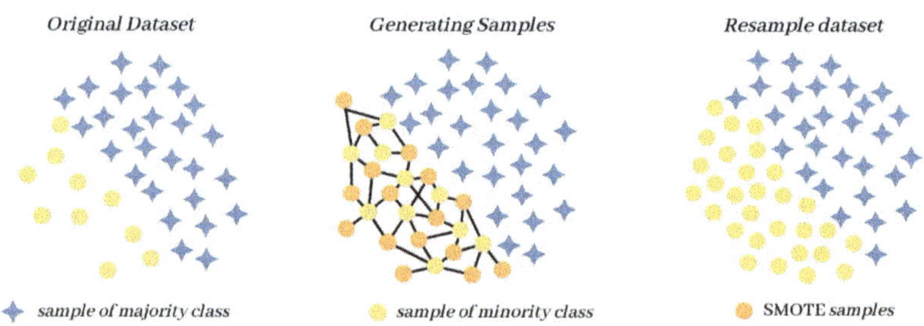

Fig. 3. How SMOTE works to generate new data

2.5 Synthetic Minority Oversampling Technique with Edited Nearest Neighbors (SMOTE-ENN)

SMOTE-ENN is a method to address class imbalance in classification data by combining SMOTE (Synthetic Minority Oversampling Technique) with edited nearest neighbors (ENN). The process involves two steps. First, oversampling is performed using SMOTE, where minority samples are selected to generate synthetic samples based on the Euclidean distance between minority samples and their nearest neighbors. Then, ENN is utilized to remove synthetic samples that are biased or inconsistent with the original data. A synthetic sample is considered biased if it is more similar to majority neighbors than minority neighbors, In this case, it is removed as described in Fig. 4. By employing this approach, SMOTE-ENN can help increase the number of minority samples while reducing noise in the dataset, resulting in a more balanced and better dataset for classification models [16].

This research uses the imblearn.over_sampling library that is available in Python. The library functions to implement the SMOTE-ENN method. In SMOTE-ENN also uses the default value of k, which is 5, in the SMOTE method and uses a value of k of 3 for the ENN method [15].

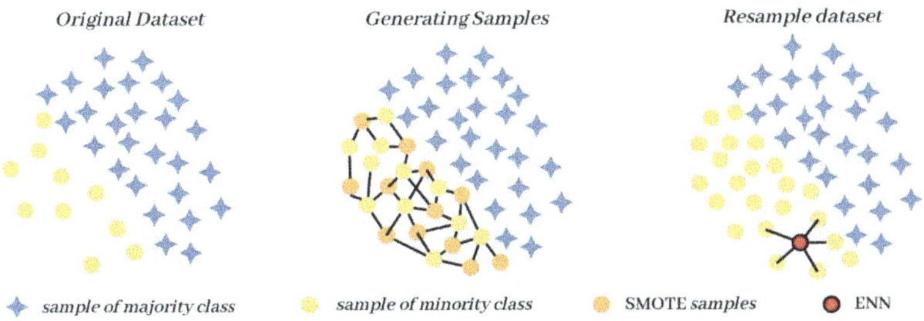

Fig. 4. How SMOTE-ENN works to generate new data

2.6 Confusion Matrix

A confusion matrix is used to evaluate classification. The confusion matrix helps to understand our model's success in classifying and the types of mistakes made in the model. Each row represents an instance in the actual class, while the matrix column represents the instance within the predicted class [17]. The confusion matrix is composed of four elements: true positive (TP), false positive (FP), false negative (FN), and true negative (TN) [10]. Figure 5 explains the four components. The confusion matrix is used to compute various evaluation metrics, including accuracy, precision, recall, and F1-scores as shown in Eqs. (1–4) [18].

The ratio of accurate predictions to total predictions, or accuracy [19], shows how frequently the algorithm correctly identifies patients as either cancerous or not.

$$\text{Accuracy} = \frac{TP + TN}{TP + TN + FP + FN} \tag{1}$$

The model's recall gauges how well it can identify cancer instances that have already occurred [19]. For instance, the model's recall is 90% if it successfully detects 90 out of 100 cancer cases.

$$\text{Precision} = \frac{TP}{TP + FP} \tag{2}$$

Precision indicates how accurate a cancer diagnosis is for a patient [19]. The precision is 75% if the algorithm correctly predicts 60 out of 80 patients to have cancer.

$$\text{Recall} = \frac{TP}{TP + FN} \tag{3}$$

The F-Score, which balances cancer prediction accuracy and detection, is the harmonic mean of recall and precision [19]. In situations where the balance of both is crucial, it offers a more trustworthy evaluation overall.

$$\text{F1-Score} = \frac{2 \times \text{Precision} \times \text{Recall}}{\text{Precision} + \text{Recall}} \tag{4}$$

		True/Actual Class	
		Positive (P)	*Negative* (N)
Predicted class	*True* (T)	*True Positive* (TP)	*False Positive* (FP)
	False (F)	*False Negative* (FN)	*True Negative* (TN)
		P = TP + FN	N = FP + TN

Fig. 5. Confusion matrix

3 Experimental Setup

3.1 Dataset

The dataset utilized in this study comprises secondary data from CT scans of both lung cancer patients and healthy individuals. This data set is obtained from Kaggle's website concerning to the source, namely Mahimkar [20]. Data was collected from the Iraqi State Educational Oncology Hospital in 2019. The study focuses on two main categories, normal patients and patients with lung cancer. The total data used consists of 416 normal patient data and 70 lung cancer patients.

3.2 Method

Figure 6 describes the method that is used. In the first stage, the data undergoes SMOTE and SMOTE-ENN processes to address the data imbalance. Following this, the data is preprocessed by splitting it into training and testing sets with an 80:20 ratio. The next stage involves classification using the CNN method. The structured approach ensures that the model is trained on a balanced dataset, allowing it to learn more effectively and improve classification accuracy. By utilizing SMOTE and SMOTE-ENN to enhance the minority class representation before splitting the data, the subsequent CNN classification is better equipped to identify patterns and make accurate predictions on both training and testing datasets.

The choice of batch size and epoch values is essential for training the CNN model with SMOTE and SMOTE-ENN resampling algorithms. By guaranteeing that weight updates take place regularly and at the appropriate intervals, the batch size of 32 serves to increase the training process's stability and effectiveness. In the meantime, the choice of 30 epochs helps to maximize the model's capacity to fully identify patterns in the data without leading to overfitting.

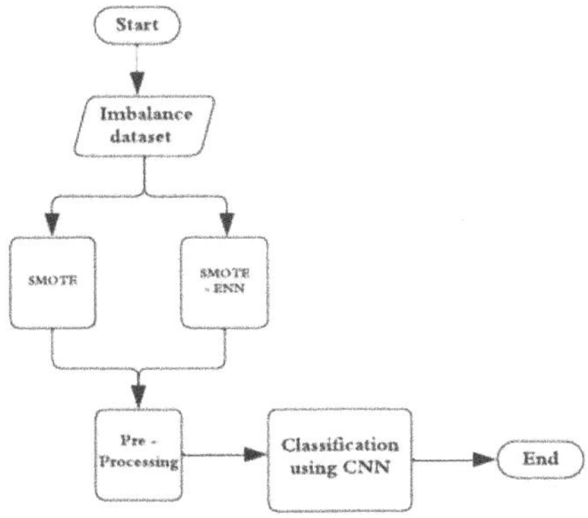

Fig. 6. Flowchart of the research procedure

4 Results and Discussion

Table 1 presents an example of synthetic results from SMOTE and SMOTE-ENN alongside the original data. The new data generated by both methods closely resembles the original data, demonstrating that they create synthetic samples by combining attributes from the minority class with those of their nearest neighbors. Both SMOTE and SMOTE-ENN effectively enhance the representation of the minority class while preserving the underlying data distribution, ensuring the generated samples are relevant and realistic for the classification task.

The amount of data resulting from the SMOTE and SMOTE-ENN techniques is different because SMOTE only adds a synthetic sample to a minority class to balance the datasets. By contrast, SMOTE-ENN does not only add synthetical samples but also removes samples that are considered to be noise or outliers using the ENN algorithm. Therefore, SMOTE-ENN produces less data than SMOTE as shown in Fig. 7. This approach helps improve the quality of the dataset by ensuring that the remaining samples are more representative of the true distribution, thereby enhancing the model's ability to generalize and perform better on unseen data.

After the data is balanced, the next step is to conduct classification using CNN. Table 2 shows the evaluation results, indicating that the CNN model with the SMOTE-ENN resampling technique outperforms the model that uses SMOTE alone. The performance improvement achieved by SMOTE-ENN is attributed to the effective combination of two techniques: SMOTE and ENN. This synergy enables SMOTE-ENN to address data imbalance issues more effectively, leading to enhanced overall evaluation metrics.

Moreover, by not only generating synthetic samples for minority classes but also removing noise and outliers, SMOTE-ENN contributes to a more robust dataset. This refinement allows the CNN model to learn more accurately from the data, thereby increasing its ability to generalize to unseen data. Consequently, the model's predictions become more reliable, making SMOTE-ENN a valuable technique for improving classification performance, particularly in imbalanced datasets.

Table 1. Example illustration between original data, with synthetic results SMOTE, and SMOTE-ENN

Original Data	SMOTE	SMOTE-ENN
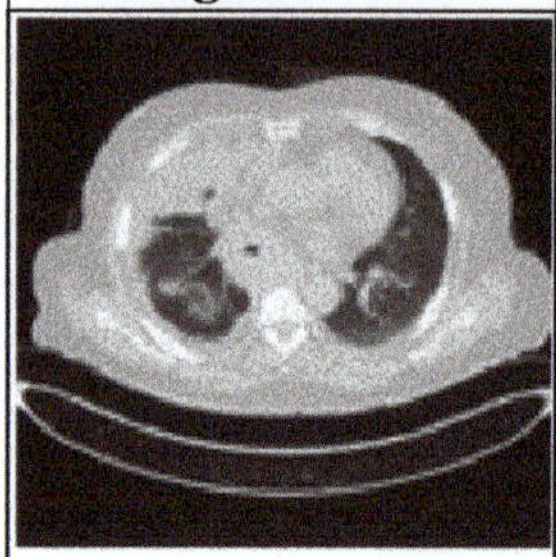	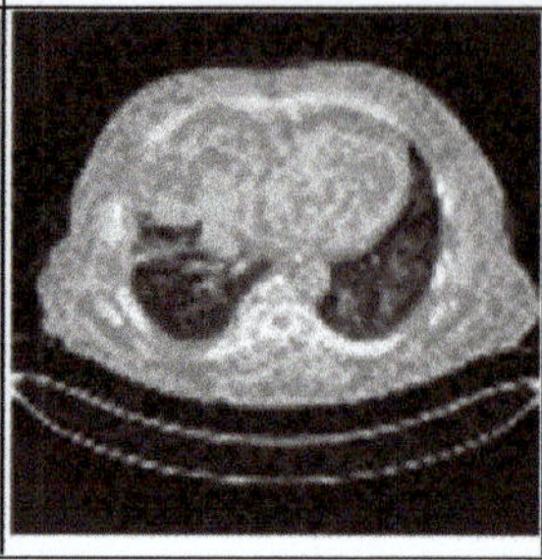	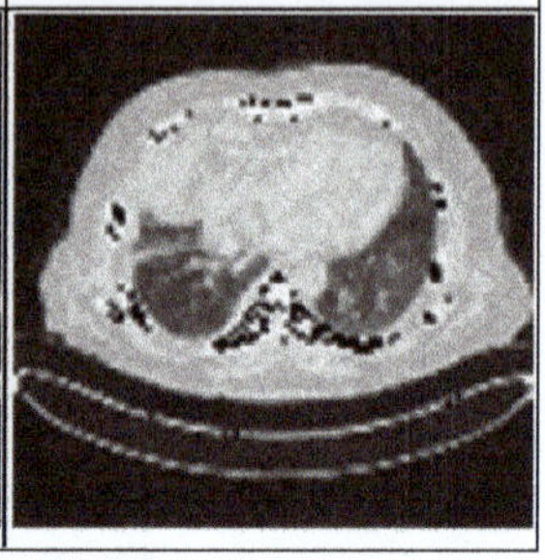

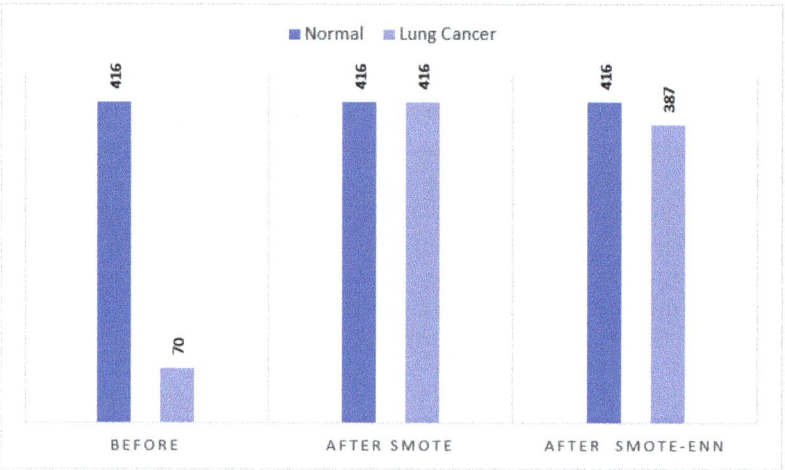

Fig. 7. Comparison of the amount of data before and after SMOTE and SMOTE-ENN

Table 2. Evaluation metrics obtained from the two algorithm models

Algorithm models	Categories	Evaluation metrics			
		Precision (%)	Recall (%)	F1-Score (%)	Accuracy (%)
CNN + SMOTE	Normal	99	87	92	93
	Cancer	88	99	93	
CNN + SMOTE-ENN	Normal	100	90	95	95
	Cancer	91	100	95	

5 Conclusion

SMOTE and SMOTE-ENN resampling techniques are effective for addressing imbalanced data problems. The difference between the two lies in the amount of synthetic data generated: in SMOTE-ENN, the number of synthetic samples tends to be lower. This is because SMOTE-ENN incorporates an additional step, the Edited Nearest Neighbors (ENN) technique, to remove samples considered as noise. The SMOTE-ENN method is superior across all evaluation metrics, achieving an accuracy of 95%, while SMOTE reaches only 93%. This suggests that combining SMOTE and ENN significantly improves the classification of lung cancer through CT-Scan imaging, reinforcing its usefulness in handling imbalanced data.

However, caution is essential when applying these models to medical data, as the stakes are high. Medical data is sensitive and poses significant risks in cases of misclassification, which can lead to serious consequences in clinical decision-making and patient safety. Therefore, despite the enhanced accuracy that SMOTE-ENN offers, rigorous model validation and continuous monitoring are crucial to ensure the reliability and accuracy of outcomes in medical applications.

Based on the research conducted, researchers recommend future studies to use larger datasets to enhance model reliability and generalization. Additionally, they suggest exploring advanced and latest resampling techniques to gain new insights and improve handling of data imbalance. Incorporating these cutting-edge methods can further enhance model performance.

Acknowledgments. This research has produced beneficial analytical results, and the authors would like to express their gratitude to Sebelas Maret University for funding this research. We would also like to extend our thanks to Aditya Mahimkar for providing-the published data, which has been instrumental in the analysis and development of the desired model. Additionally, we appreciate the support and insights from our colleagues and peers, which have greatly contributed to the success of this research. Their encouragement and feedback were invaluable throughout the process.

References

1. World Health Organization.: Global Cancer Observatory (2022). https://gco.iarc.who.int/media/globocan/factsheets/populations/360-Indonesiafact-sheet.pdf. Last accessed 25 Sept 2023
2. Joseph, J., Rotty, L.W.A.: Kanker Paru: Laporan Kasus. Med. Scope J. **2**(1), 17–25 (2020)
3. McLeod, R., Schell, G.P.: Management Information Systems. Upper Saddle River, New Jersey (2007)
4. Toraman, S., Alakus, T.B., Turkoglu, I.: Convolutional capsnet: a novel artificial neural network approach to detect COVID-19 disease from X-ray images using capsule networks. Chaos, Solitons Fractals. **140**, 110122 (2020)
5. Chen, H., Chen, A., Xu, L., Qiao, H., Lin, Q., Cai, K.: A deep learning CNN architecture applied in smart near-infrared analysis of water pollution for agricultural irrigation resources. Agric. Water Manag. **240** (2020)
6. Kalaivani, N., Maimaran, N., Sophia, S., Devi, D.: Deep Learning Based Lung Cancer and Classification. IOP Publishing (2020)

7. Chawla, N.V., Bowyer, K.W., Hall, L.O., Kegelmeyer, W.P.: SMOTE: Syntethics minority over-sampling technique. J. Artif. Intellegence Res. **16**, 321–357 (2002)
8. Pradipta, G.A., Wardoyo, R., Musdholifah, A., Sanjaya, I.N.H., Ismail, M.: SMOTE for Handling Imbalance Data: A Review. Institute of Electrical and Electronic Engineering (2021)
9. Anshori, I.F., Riana, S.: Prediksi Harapan Hidup Pasien Kanker ParuParu Pasca Operasi Bedah Thoraks Menggunakan Boosted Neural Network Dan Smote. J. Infomedia: Tek. Inform., Multimed. Jar. **6**(1), 9–15 (2021)
10. Mansourifar, H., Shi, W.: Deep Syntetics Minority over Sampling Technique. Cornell University (2020)
11. Arisandi, R.: Perbandingan Model Klasifikasi Random Forest dengan Resampling dan Tanpe Resampling Pada Pasien Penderita Gagal Jantung. J. Gaussian. **1**(12), 136–145 (2023)
12. Alasadi, S.A., Bhaya, W.S.: Review of data preprocessing techniques in data mining. J. Eng. Appl. Sci. **12**(16), 4102–4117 (2017)
13. Dhillon, A., Verma, G.K.: Convolutional neural network: a review of models, methodologies, and applications to object detection. Prog. Artif. Intell. **9**, 85–112 (2019)
14. Blagus, R., Lusa, L.: SMOTE for High-dimensional Class-imbalance Data. Research Article. **14**(106), 1471–2105
15. Sir, Y.A., Soepranoto, A.H.H.: Data resampling approach for handling class imbalance issues. Comput. J. Inform. **10**(1), 31–38 (2022)
16. Xu, Z., Shen, D., Nie, T., Kou, Y.: A hybrid sampling algorithm combining M-SMOTE and ENN based on random Forest for medical imbalanced data. J. Biomed. Inform. **107** (2020)
17. Tharwat, A.: Classification assessment methods. Appl. Comput. Inform. **17**(1), 168–192 (2021)
18. Liang, J.: Confusion matrix. POGIL Act. Clear. House. **3**(4) (2022)
19. Is, H., Tuncer, T.: Interaction-based behavioral analysis of twitter social network accounts. Appl. Sci. **9**, 1–15 (2019)
20. Mahimkar, A.: IQ-OTH/NCCD—Lung Cancer Dataset (2021). https://www.kaggle.com/datasets/adityamahimkar/iqothnccd-lung-cancer-dataset. Last accessed 30 Aug 2023

When Self-Citations Bother You: A Case Study on Google Scholar

Kartick Chandra Mondal[1,2](✉), Ari Kusumastuti[3], Ananya Pal[2], Isika Samanta[2], and Ansh Kumar[2]

[1] Department of Computer Science and Engineering, SRM University - AP, Amaravati 522240, India
kartickjgec@gmail.com
[2] Department of Information Technology, Jadavpur University, Kolkata 700106, West Bengal, India
[3] Universitas Islam Negeri Maulana Malik Ibrahim Malang, Malang, Indonesia

Abstract. Referring to previously published articles plays a pivotal role in academics. This processing of referring articles is also known as the citation. Self-citation occurs in an article when an author references another of their previous publications. This can be a legitimate way to reference earlier findings. However, excessive self-referencing could be seen as an effort to artificially enhance citation metrics and the perceived influence of an author's contributions. Therefore to uphold the research integrity and quantify the self-citation, a framework is proposed and called a self-citation detector, pinpointing and emphasizing potential instances of misuse. Different statistical indexes, namely, *diversity index*, *falsity index*, and *self to other ratio*, are proposed in this article. The use of them in the proposed framework intends to assess the credibility of both the publication being cited and the author publishing the article. For this purpose, we used Google Scholar data generated using SerpAPI to demonstrate the occurrence and extent of self-citation.

Keywords: Referencing · Self-citation · Google Scholar · Statistical Index

1 Introduction

In an era where the dissemination of knowledge spans vast digital landscapes, the need to ensure the authenticity of academic contributions has never been more pressing. Referencing is a licit way to acknowledge not only the origin of the information but also the previously published articles relevant to the context. This is also known as citing a related article or a citation on an article. Citing previously published articles helps authors give proper credit to other authors in an unambiguous manner, thereby mitigating the plagiarism concerns. At the same time, it facilitates the reader to explore suggested articles for further insights. Proper and lawful citation enhances the significance and importance of

P. C. Rodrigues et al. (Eds.): ISBIS 2024, 13, pp. 163–174, 2027.
https://doi.org/10.1007/978-3-032-32458-0_12

both the referenced and referencing articles within the research domain. This led to the concept of the citation count of any article a quantitative way of measuring the quality of the article. Therefore, this phenomenon has steered to an increase in the citation count, artificially elevating the status of a specific article. While self-citation is a legitimate and often necessary practice, excessive and strategic self-citation has the potential to compromise the integrity of research metrics and the perceived influence of an author's work [2].

The self-referencing in scholarly publications raises concerns about its potential misuse. The need to develop a self-citation detector and quantify it arises from the above phenomenon. Firstly, the academic community relies heavily on citation metrics as a quantitative measure of an author's impact and the significance of their contributions. When authors engage in excessive self-citation, there is a risk of artificially inflating these metrics, leading to an inaccurate assessment of an individual's scholarly influence. This distortion can have far-reaching consequences, impacting academic evaluations, funding decisions, and even the perceived reputation of academic institutions. Secondly, excessive self-citation may be driven by the desire to boost the visibility and recognition of an author's body of work. Authors may strategically reference their publications to create an illusion of widespread acknowledgment and influence. This not only undermines the fairness of academic evaluations but also hampers the organic development of scholarly conversations and the advancement of collective knowledge within a field.

A self-citation detector represents a crucial advancement in maintaining the integrity of scholarly research. Its significance lies in its ability to systematically and objectively address concerns surrounding self-citation misuse within academic publications [6]. Instead of relying solely on subjective judgment, this tool utilizes specific indices to evaluate the credibility of citations, distinguishing between appropriate self-referencing and instances where self-citation is employed inappropriately. By doing so, the self-citation detector acts as a support against the manipulation of citation metrics, ensuring that research evaluations are conducted fairly and accurately. In an age where quantitative indicators wield significant influence in academia, implementing such a detector becomes indispensable. Its presence not only upholds fairness in academic assessments but also cultivates an environment where the true impact of research is faithfully represented. Moreover, the adoption of a self-citation detector contributes to the advancement of knowledge and the pursuit of scientific excellence on a collective scale. By accurately reflecting the influence and contributions of scholarly work, it fosters an ecosystem where researchers are motivated to produce high-quality, impactful research, thus driving the progress of their respective fields.

The proposed framework as shown in Fig. 1 encompasses several key components to identify and mitigate excessive self-citation effectively. These components include:

1. **User-Friendly Interface**: To facilitate the implementation of the framework, a user-friendly interface is proposed. This interface would enable

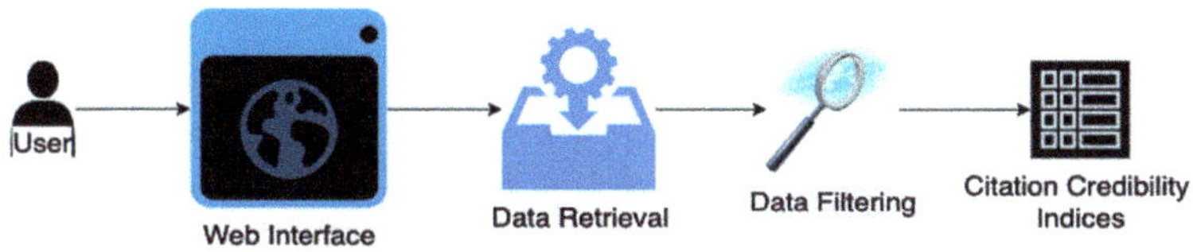

Fig. 1. Block diagram of the proposed framework.

researchers, journal editors, and peer reviewers to input a publication and receive a detailed analysis of its citation patterns. The interface could highlight potential areas of concern, empowering stakeholders to make informed decisions about the validity and impact of a given piece of research.

2. **Data Retrieval**: To demonstrate the practical application of the framework, Google Scholar data has been utilized, and extracted through SerpAPI. The data retrieval is done by downloading API search results via Postman. It allows for a systematic analysis of self-citation patterns across a wide range of publications, providing a comprehensive overview of the prevalence and extent of the issue.
3. **Citation Credibility Indices**: The heart of the framework lies in developing specific indices designed to evaluate the credibility of citations within a publication. These indices may consider factors such as the diversity of sources cited, the decency of the references, and the impact factor of the journals from which the citations are drawn. By employing a multi-dimensional approach, the framework aims to distinguish between legitimate self-referencing and instances where self-citation may be employed inappropriately.

The rest of the paper is organized as follows: Sect. 2 explains the important available indices used in the article in addition to some major research work on self-citations. Section 3 presents a detailed exposition of the framework and working procedure of the proposed approach. It also presents the necessary explanation of the proposed indices for detecting self-citation and its use in the proposed framework. Section 4 illustrates the experimental setup of the work and its result and discussion in the context of self-citation. The work concludes in Sect. 5.

2 Related Indices

In this section, we have presented some available citation metrics that have been used to measure the bibliometric impact of individual authors, researchers, academics, and scholars.

1. **h-Index**: The H-index, or Hirsch index [8], attempts to measure both the scientific productivity and the apparent scientific impact of the scientists. The index is based on the scientists' most cited papers and the number of citations that they have received from other people's publications. The index

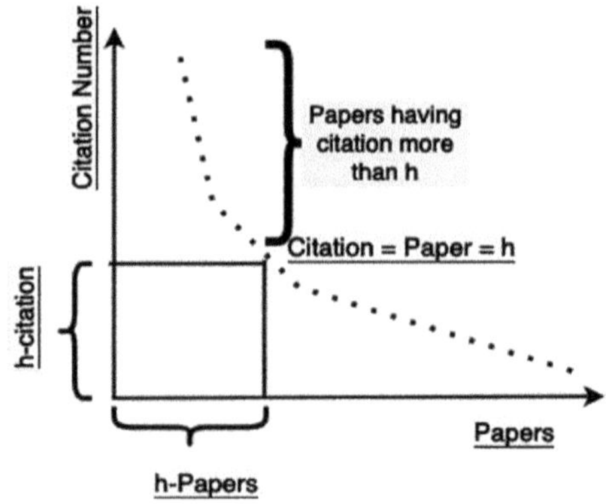

Fig. 2. Citation metric h-index.

Publication Number	Citation Number	
1	85	
2	70	
3	43	
4	30	
5	10	$\xleftarrow{i10\ Index} = 5$
6	9	
7	8	$\xleftarrow{h\ Index} = 7$
8	7	
9	6	
10	1	

Fig. 3. Calculating h-index & i10-index.

can also be applied to the productivity and impact of a group of scientists. It is presented in the Fig. 2.

Hirsch states, "A scientist has index h' if h' number of papers have at least h citations each". For example, a scholar with an h-index of 7 had published at least 7 papers, each of which has been cited at least 7 times. Figure 2 and 3 represent the computation of the h-index for better understanding.

2. **i10-Index**: The i10-index [4] can be found in Google Scholar and gives the value of the total number of publications of an author that has at least 10 citations. It was introduced by Google in 2011 and used to help gauge the productivity of a scholar. It can be easily boosted via multiple co-authors and collaborative papers in distinct domains. The i10-index of an author is 5 means only 5 of his papers have been cited at least ten times in other publications. Figure 3 represents the computation of the i10-index for better understanding.

2.1 Dynamics of Self-citation in Scholarly Research

The use of citation indexes has become increasingly prevalent in evaluating the scholarly output of researchers, institutions, and even entire countries. However, the conventional approach to calculating citation statistics often overlooks the influence of self-citations, which can distort perceptions of research impact. This article synthesizes findings from multiple studies to delve into the multifaceted nature of self-citation and its implications across various disciplines. Research has been conducted on the development of new citation metrics to address the issue of self-citation [3]. It introduces the Citation Impact Discerning Self-citations (CIDS) web-based service, which aims to provide more accurate citation statistics by accounting for self-citations. The assessment of CIDS reveals that self-citations significantly impact both the number of citations and the h-index at the individual level, emphasizing the need to consider them in research evaluations.

A study on the scientific production of Norway examines the prevalence and patterns of self-citation [1]. It reveals that while self-citation constitutes a substantial portion of all citations, its percentage decreases over longer citation periods. Additionally, the study finds a positive correlation between the number of self-citations and the number of authors, suggesting that self-citation behavior varies across disciplines and influences citation rates differently. Another study explores the incentives behind self-citation by investigating its impact on citations received from others [5]. It reports a positive relationship between self-citation and citations from others, indicating that authors who cite themselves more frequently tend to receive more citations from external sources. This finding challenges the assumption that self-citation is inherently manipulative and underscores its role as a legitimate aspect of scientific communication. A comparative analysis of self-citation patterns across six disciplines reveals discipline-specific variations [9]. While physical sciences exhibit a higher proportion of self-citations compared to social sciences and humanities, there are no significant differences in the coverage of self-citations versus citations to others within disciplines. This suggests a consistent pattern of self-citation behavior across disciplines despite varying citation practices.

Ioannidis discusses case studies of extreme self-citation practices and emphasizes the need to distinguish between appropriate and inappropriate self-citation [7]. The article underscores the potential distortion of scientific literature caused by inappropriate self-citation practices, particularly coercive-induced self-citation, which may originate from reviewers, scientific advisors, or funding agencies. While self-citation serves as a legitimate means of acknowledging one's contributions and building upon previous work, it can also be misused to inflate citation metrics and distort the scientific corpus. Understanding the complexities of self-citation is essential for devising fair and robust evaluation criteria in research assessments. Future studies should focus on dissecting the impact of different types of self-citation and exploring interventions to mitigate their potential misuse. By promoting transparency and integrity in citation practices, academia can foster a more reliable and impactful scientific discourse.

3 Proposed Approach

At first, data will be fetched from Google Scholar using SerpAPI to get our desired data. Here, pegianation is used to collect one by one all the data as the desired data is spread over multiple pages. After collecting the data related to a particular author's profile, it is kept in a simple json file. A preprocessing is done on the complete dataset to make it suitable for the index calculation. Then, a simple procedure for detecting and calculating the self-citations is followed. Here, we can apply many advanced procedures to detect the self-citation mentioned in Sect. 2.1, which is kept as a future study in our research. The detailed workflow of the project is shown in the Fig. 4.

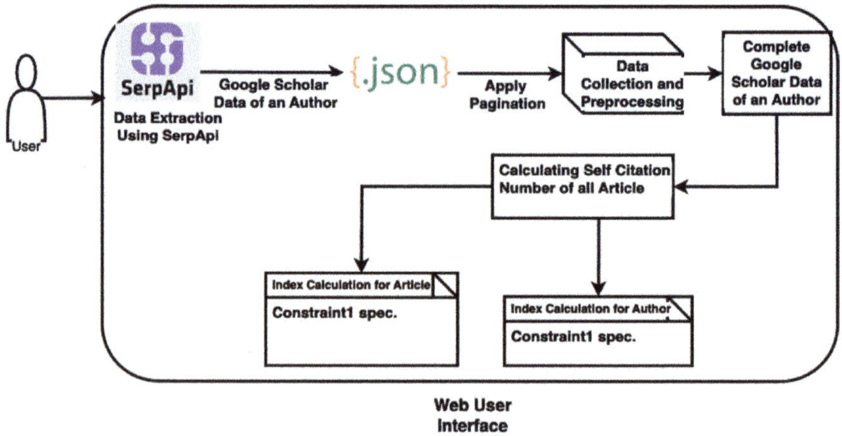

Fig. 4. Detailed workflow of the proposed approach.

3.1 Calculating Self-citations

The collected data from SerpAPI provides the author ID and a list of publications of a particular author. At the same time, we have also collected the complete information of a list of articles that have cited any particular article for the same author. The complete information comprises the title as well as the list of authors who have worked on it along with their author IDs. We iterate through the list of articles, and compare their authors with the author in question, by comparing their IDs. If the author in question is found on any of the articles from the list, then those articles are deemed as self-cited articles, while others are considered as other citations. So, the other citation is basically the difference between the total citation and the self-citation calculated in the previous step. At the end of the processing, a table is generated showing the complete list of publications with the total number of citations, number of self-citations, and number of other citations, for each particular publication. Later, these are summed up individually to find out the occurrences of total citations, self-citations, and other citations, for the author in question. The sample of the final table can be seen as presented in Table 1.

Table 1. Generated self citation table

Title	Total citation	Self citation	Other citation
Article 1	50	20	30
Article 2	40	10	30
Article 3	30	5	25
Article 4	20	0	20
Article 5	10	1	9
Total #	**150**	**36**	**114**

3.2 Proposed Statistical Indexes

Our proposed approach evaluates two main categories of indices based on different citation values generated by using the process mentioned in Sect. 3.1. One index is called the *Diversity Index* and the other index is called the *Falsity Index*. The diversity index can be evaluated by using the formula present in Eq. 1. The diversity index value finds how much diversity of citations is present in the article. If an article has low self-citation, the diversity index value will be near to 1. This signifies the article citations are diversified and not concentrated on the author itself. A diversity index value equal to 0 signifies that there is no integrity in the article in case of citing the article and all the citations are self-citation.

$$Diversity\ Index = \frac{Other\ Citations}{Total\ Citations} \tag{1}$$

whereas, the falsity index can be evaluated by using the formula present in Eq. 2. It means if the self-citation value is equal to the total number of citations present in the article or near that value, the falsity index value will be equal to 1 or near 1. So, we can say the article has no integrity and is falsely popularized as far as the citation is concerned when the falsity index value is higher. The falsity index can also be applicable to other bibliographic indices in the domain of referencing, for example, h index or i10 index. We have considered these two indices as these index values are present in current case study data, Google Scholar. It can be used on any index where citation count is used to evaluate the corresponding index value. In this case, it identifies the genuineness of the index value calculated using the actual citation numbers presented in the authors' profile.

$$Falsity\ Index = \frac{Self\ Citations}{Total\ Citations} \tag{2}$$

These two indices (diversity and falsity indices) can be applicable to both articles as well as to the author who publishes those articles. However, the diversity index and falsity index presented in Eqs. 1 and 2 can be directly applied to the article published by an author. Whereas, in case of an author, the aggregate values of self-citation, other-citation, and total citation of each article published by the author are used. So, the *Author Diversity Index* and *Author Falsity Index* can be evaluated by using the Eqs. 3 and 4. These author indexes (i.e., diversity as well as falsity) can also be applicable to any institution's or organization's citation information to identify the diversity and falsity practices followed by the institute's or organization's employees during the citation of published articles.

$$Author\ Diversity\ Index = \frac{Aggregated\ Other\ Citations}{Aggregated\ Total\ Citations} \tag{3}$$

$$Author\ Falsity\ Index = \frac{Aggregated\ Self\ Citations}{Aggregated\ Total\ Citations} \tag{4}$$

To effectively compare these authors' extent of their self-citation, we proposed a key metric called the Self-Other Ratio. The formula for this Self-Other ratio is given in Eq. 5

$$Self\ Other\ Ratio = \frac{Self\ Citations}{Other\ Citations} \tag{5}$$

This ratio provides insight into the relative prevalence of self-citations compared to other citations.

- Ratio is equal to 0 when all are other citation
- Ratio is less than 1 when other citation > self-citation
- Ratio is equal to 1 when other citations = self-citation
- Ratio is greater than 1 when other citation < self-citation
- Ratio is undefined or ∞ when all are self-citation.

Simply put, the higher the Self-Other Ratio for an author, the more pronounced their tendency to cite their work rather than relying on external citations.

4 Result and Discussion

4.1 Experimental Setup

The free version of SerpAPI gives limited access to fetching data from Google Scholar. At the same time, we need a significant amount of citations where we can show the variation of our index values. So, keeping that in mind, we have chosen two random Google Scholar authors' data where the list of publications is not too high but a significant number of citations can be seen in those articles.

The author's data (Publications, citations, etc.) is downloaded in JSON format using SerpAPI and Postman. This data is then fetched into the web page for processing and output is obtained. Two types of JSON files are collected using SerpAPI from Google Scholar. One is for the publication record of an

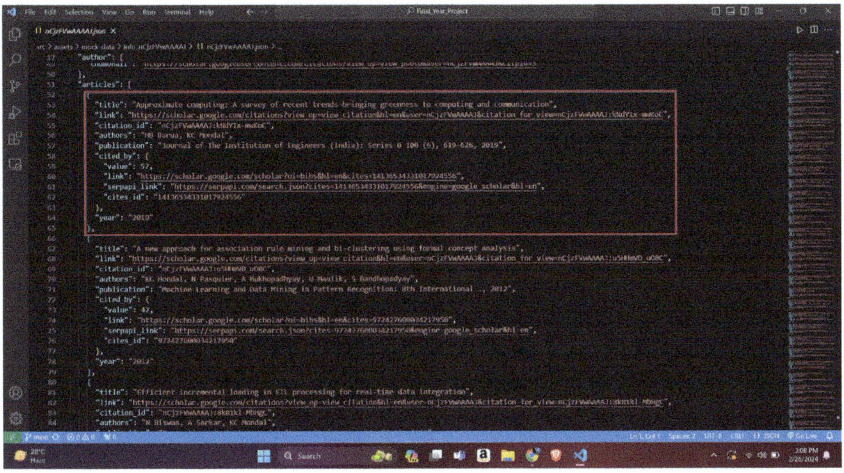

Fig. 5. JSON file having data of all publications by an author.

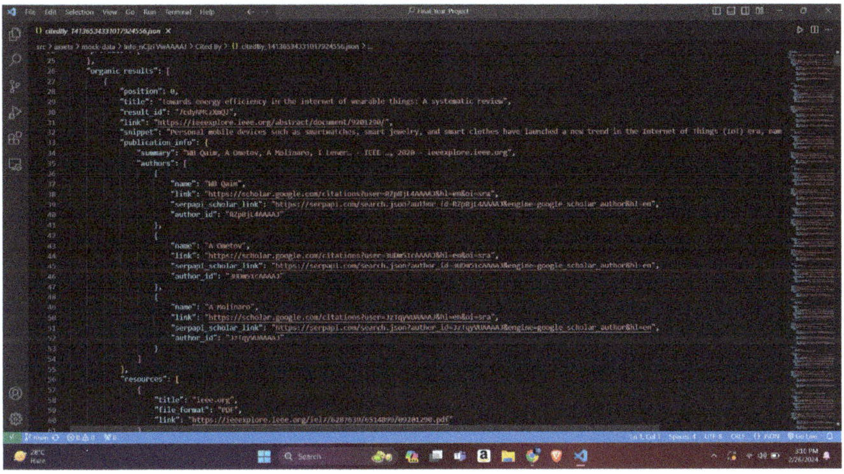

Fig. 6. JSON file fetched from cited by API of SerpApi.

author which is shown in Fig. 5. Another is for the 'cited by' information which is shown in Fig. 6 These JSON files are then downloaded and preprocessed. After preprocessing these JSON files, the data are stored in a structured way for further processing.

The final tabular dataset is used to execute our Java programs to find the values of different mathematical functions as well as our index values. We have developed a prototype of the approach and deployed it as a web service of the same concept. Although there are many improvements and logical correctness are need to be done for detecting self-citation as well as making the system work automatically on the available Google Scholar data, our system can run on static data collected from Google Scholar.

Table 2. Proposed index values for anonymous author 1. Data are collected from the Google Scholar.

Article	Total citation	Self citation	Other citation	Diversity index	Falsity index	Self other ratio
Article 1	57	2	55	0.96	0.04	0.04
Article 2	42	16	26	0.62	0.38	0.62
Article 3	18	0	18	1	0	0
Article 4	17	9	8	0.47	0.53	1.13
Article 5	15	13	2	0.13	0.87	6.5
:	:	:	:	:	:	:
:	:	:	:	:	:	:
h Index	10	4	9	0.9	0.4	–
i10 Index	13	1	9	0.7	0.08	–
For Author	444	73	371	**0.84**	**0.16**	**0.2**

4.2 Discussion

As we have mentioned earlier, we have used two Google Scholar author information. The final outcome of all the indexes of all the articles for both author profiles are very large and a sample of the output is presented in this paper. Tables 2 and 3 present the outcomes of the experiments done on our prepared datasets for two anonymized authors. The last row of Tables 2 and 3 shows the diversity index and falsity index values for the author. Whereas, the last two columns of Tables 2 and 3 represent the diversity index and falsity index values, respectively, for each published article by the author.

As mentioned in the previous section, diversity and integrity index values can also be calculated for different bibliographic indices. Here, since Google Scholar data contains only the h-index and i10 index, we have also shown how these two indices can be evaluated using self and other citations found for each article. After calculating the self-citation and other citation values for each article, we calculated the h-index and i10 index values using the self-citation numbers and other citation numbers available for each article. Then we apply the formula presented above to find the diversity index and falsity index of each bibliographic index (h and i10). Usually, the summation of the diversity index and falsity index value is equal to 1. Since, both these index values for bibliographic indexes do not directly lie on citation but the actual count of citation number, the above principle of summation equal to 1 does not follow in this case.

By examining the change in these indices from total citations to other citations, we gain valuable insight into the influence of self-citation on the overall

Table 3. Proposed index values for anonymous author 2. Data are collected from the Google Scholar.

Article	Total citation	Self citation	Other citation	Diversity index	Falsity index	Self other ratio
Article 1	64	2	62	0.97	0.03	0.03
Article 2	29	0	29	1	0	0
Article 3	15	9	6	0.4	0.6	1.5
Article 4	12	4	8	0.67	0.33	0.5
Article 5	10	9	1	0.1	0.9	9
:	:	:	:	:	:	:
:	:	:	:	:	:	:
h Index	11	6	9	0.82	0.55	–
i10 Index	17	0	8	0.47	0	–
For Author	411	85	326	**0.79**	**0.21**	**0.26**

citation metrics of each author. In essence, while the Self-Other Ratio is a relative parameter for comparing self-citation practices, the h-index and i-10 index provide a quantitative measure of citation impact. Together, these indices offer a comprehensive understanding of the role of self-citation in shaping the scholarly profile of each author.

5 Conclusion

Integrating a self-citation detector into research assessment frameworks signifies a significant advancement in the ongoing quest for diversity, integrity, and reliability within scholarly communication. By incorporating such a tool, the scholarly community takes a proactive stance against practices that may compromise the integrity of citation numbers and metrics. However, implementing a self-citation detector is just one facet of a multifaceted approach to safeguarding the scholarly discourse. To harness its potential, researchers must navigate the intricate web of scholarly databases with finesse. This necessitates strategically deploying sophisticated data extraction methods capable of discerning subtle nuances in citation patterns. Indeed, the strategic utilization of databases lies at the heart of the detector's effectiveness. As it sifts through vast repositories of scholarly literature, it relies on the precision and depth of data extraction techniques to distinguish between legitimate self-citations and instances of manipulation. This strategic approach enhances the detector's accuracy and underscores the importance of meticulous curation in maintaining the integrity of research assessment processes. Integrating a self-citation detector represents more than a technological innovation—it embodies a collective commitment to honesty, transparency, and excellence in scholarly research. By embracing these principles and leveraging cutting-edge tools, researchers pave the way for a future where the integrity of academic discourse remains steadfastly preserved. Prototype of the implementation is available at https://self-citation-detector.vercel.app/home.

References

1. Aksnes, D.W.: A macro study of self-citation. Scientometrics **56**(2), 235–246 (2003)
2. Amjad, T., Rehmat, Y., Daud, A., Abbasi, R.A.: Scientific impact of an author and role of self-citations. Scientometrics **122**, 915–932 (2020)
3. Couto, F., Pesquita, C., Grego, T., Veríssimo, P.: Handling self-citations using google scholar. Cybernet. Int. J. Scientometrics, Informetrics Bibliometrics **13**(01) (2009). ISSN 1137-5019
4. Dhamdhere, S.: Cumulative citations index, h-index and i10-index (research metrics) of an educational institute: a case study. Int. J. Lib. Inf. Sci. **10**, 1–9 (2018)
5. Fowler, J.H., Aksnes, D.W.: Does self-citation pay? Scientometrics **72**(3), 427–437 (2007). Sep
6. Hyland, K.: Self-citation and self-reference: Credibility and promotion in academic publication. J. Am. Soc. Inf. Sci. **54**, 251–259 (2003)
7. Ioannidis, J.P.: A generalized view of self-citation: Direct, co-author, collaborative, and coercive induced self-citation. J. Psychosom. Res. **78**(1), 7–11 (2015)
8. Sangam, S., Mogali, S.: The concept of h-index. PEARL J. Lib. Inf. Sci. **3**. 1–4 (2009)
9. Snyder, H., Bonzi, S.: Patterns of self-citation across disciplines (1980–1989). J. Inf. Sci. **24**(6), 431–435 (1998)

Comparative Forecasting of Domestic Flight Activity Patterns in Indonesia During and Post-COVID-19 with XGBoost and ARIMA

Zahra Maharani Putri Sumarna, Rohmatul Fajriyah(✉), Yoel Christopher Tjen, and Fandy A. Ariady

Department of Statistics, Universitas Islam Indonesia, Jln. Kaliurang KM 14.5, Sleman, Yogyakarta, Indonesia
{20611077,23928001,23928007}@students.uii.ac.id, 966110101@uii.ac.id

Abstract. In the aviation sector, the operational efficiency and service quality of airports rely heavily on flight activity, which is crucial for economic vitality and societal connectivity. The COVID-19 pandemic has caused significant disruptions to flight forecasting, emphasizing the need for reliable forecasting methods during uncertain times. This study investigates flight activity forecasting in Indonesia during both the pandemic and post-pandemic periods, comparing two forecasting methods: eXtreme Gradient Boosting (XGBoost) and Autoregressive Integrated Moving Average (ARIMA). XGBoost, known for its robustness in predictive analytics, was found to provide highly accurate forecasts during the pandemic, capturing dynamic fluctuations in flight activity. Post-pandemic, as conditions stabilized, XGBoost continued to deliver precise predictions. For comparison, ARIMA was also applied; while it performed reasonably well during the pandemic, its inability to meet the white noise assumption and difficulty in handling the volatile pandemic data made it less reliable than XGBoost. During the post-pandemic period, ARIMA performed better but still lagged behind XGBoost in following the data patterns. The results showed that XGBoost outperformed ARIMA in both periods. This study highlights XGBoost as a more resilient and dependable tool for flight activity forecasting in Indonesia, especially during periods of uncertainty.

Keywords: Flight activity · Forecasting · XGBoost · ARIMA

1 Introduction

Transportation, defined as the movement of people or goods using human-, animal-, or machine-powered vehicles [1], plays a vital role in daily life and is essential for Indonesia's economic, social, and political integration [2]. Given Indonesia's vast archipelago, air transportation is particularly crucial and preferred over sea transportation [3]. From January to August 2023, domestic air passenger traffic rose by 22.46% year-on-year to 41.6 million, significantly higher than the 13.2 million sea passengers during the same period.

P. C. Rodrigues et al. (Eds.): ISBIS 2024, 13, pp. 175–190, 2027.
https://doi.org/10.1007/978-3-032-32458-0_13

The increase in passenger numbers requires enhanced airport services. According to Sims [4], long-term airport planning begins with documenting infrastructure, forecasting aviation activity, and planning service improvements. Analyzing flight frequency is key for airport load management and supporting passenger activities [5, 6]. Despite its importance, forecasting often overlooks uncertainty, which is crucial during events like COVID-19, a significant disruptor to aviation [7, 8]. Research highlights the pandemic's impact on flight numbers, underscoring the need to incorporate uncertainty in aviation forecasting.

This study forecasts aviation activity in Indonesia using daily domestic flight data from 2020 to 2022, divided into two phases. The first phase, the pandemic period in this study, began on January 1, 2020, when COVID-19 was confirmed transmissible, leading to global emergency measures [9, 10]. It ends on July 21, 2022, when restrictions began easing [11]. The second phase, the post-pandemic period, spans from July 22 to December 31, 2022, as mobility restrictions relaxed and the aviation industry began returning to pre-pandemic activity. This division accounts for significant differences in conditions between the two periods, affecting data patterns.

This study uses time series data to forecast aviation activity in Indonesia, focusing on daily domestic flight frequencies from 2020 to 2022. Time series forecasting is effective in uncertain conditions, as it requires only one variable and is faster and more economical than other methods [4]. The XGBoost model, known for its scalability and effectiveness with complex, nonlinear data [12–14], will be used alongside the ARIMA model, which is widely applied in time series analysis, including in disease predictions [15]. The research aims to analyze trends in flight activity during and after the COVID-19 pandemic and compare the effectiveness of XGBoost and ARIMA for forecasting.

This study has several limitations: it uses secondary data, focuses on two forecasting methods, and applies a univariate model, excluding external factors that may affect flight activity. These constraints could impact the generalizability and precision of the results.

2 Material and Methods

2.1 Data and Variables

The dataset in this study records flight activities in Indonesia from 2020 to 2022, provided by AirNav Indonesia. Data storage is handled in Microsoft Excel, while RStudio is used for all stages of data processing, from preprocessing to analysis.

The primary variable for forecasting analysis is the daily number of flight activities, representing the "gate-to-gate" journey, covering departure to arrival. This analysis focuses exclusively on domestic flights, where both origin and destination airports are within Indonesia.

2.2 Descriptive Statistics

According to Maizar et al. [16], statistics is a versatile science that can be broadly applied. This field encompasses the study of planning, collecting, analyzing, processing, interpreting, drawing conclusions, and presenting data, with the analysis results potentially being numerical or non-numerical. Generally, statistics is divided into two categories: descriptive statistics (deductive statistics) and inferential statistics (inductive statistics). Descriptive statistics involve methods for collecting, tabulating, depicting, processing, and analyzing data, and interpreting the results with explanations that are easier to understand [17]. In descriptive statistics, the methods are limited to the simple collection, processing, presentation, and analysis of data, such as calculating the mean, mode, proportion, and so on [18].

2.3 eXtreme Gradient Boosting (XGBoost)

XGBoost or eXtreme Gradient Boosting was developed by Chen and Guestrin [19]. This method can be used for various analytical functions, including regression, classification, ranking, and time series forecasting. XGBoost follows a similar process to Gradient Boosting (GB); however, it differs in how the initial prediction values are determined. In Gradient Boosting, this value is computed as the mean of the actual values of the target feature, whereas XGBoost assigns a randomly initialized prediction value, which is typically set to 0.5 by default [20].

The tree-building process relies on computing the loss function (or residual calculation). Once the residuals are determined, the subsequent step in XGBoost involves generating trees and evaluating the similarity score [20].

$$similiarity\,score = \frac{(Sum\ of\ residuals)^2}{Number\,of\ residuals + \lambda} \tag{1}$$

Here, λ represents a regularization factor that is initially set to 0 by default.

The computation of the similarity score in Eq. 1 serves to determine the gain, which is subsequently utilized for pruning trees in XGBoost.

$$gain = LeftSimiliarity + RightSimiliarity + RootSimiliarity \tag{2}$$

The tree pruning in XGBoost uses the calculation shown in Eq. 3.

$$gain - \gamma \tag{3}$$

When Eq. 3 yields a positive outcome, the branch remains intact. Conversely, if the outcome is negative, the branch is pruned. There is an exception: if the first branch's result is positive but the root's calculation is negative, the root is not removed. Tree building ends with pruning. After pruning, the output prediction for each leaf is calculated using Eq. 4.

$$Output = \frac{sum\ of\ residuals}{number\,of\ residuals + \lambda} \tag{4}$$

The process of modeling using the XGBoost approach consists of these stages [21]:

1. Feature Selection

   The procedure for selecting features with XGBoost includes data preprocessing, extracting relevant features, and selecting them based on their importance scores.

2. Model Training
   Training is conducted using the chosen features and predefined parameters, following the previously outlined model-building process
3. Parameter Optimization
   Optimization is carried out to minimized the error between predicted values and actual outcomes.

The selection of hyperparameter values in the XGBoost approach significantly influences model performance, requiring careful tuning to develop a reliable forecasting model. These parameters are categorized by function, such as those under the "booster" category, where max_depth controls tree depth, with higher values leading to more complex models and a greater likelihood of overfitting, while min_child_weight sets the minimum observation weight in a child node, promoting a more conservative model. Gamma determines the minimum loss reduction needed for a split, with higher values restricting complexity. To mitigate overfitting, subsample limits the proportion of training data used per boosting iteration, and colsample_bytree regulates the fraction of feature columns selected for each tree. In the command-line parameter category, the number of estimators defines the total trees in the ensemble, shaping the model's ability to fit the data.

2.4 ARIMA

ARIMA models are designed to handle stationary as well as non-stationery time series, enabling precise predictions derived from historical observations of a single feature [22].

Represented as ARIMA (p, d, q), the model consists of three key parameters: *p* denotes the autoregressive component, *d* represents the differencing order, and q corresponds to the moving average component. The differencing step is applied to convert a non-stationary series into a stationary one. Meanwhile, seasonal ARIMA models are specifically formulated to identify recurring seasonal patterns that standard ARIMA models may not capture. Based on their complexity, seasonal models can be classified as either additive (basic seasonal) models or multiplicative seasonal models. In a simple seasonal model, the relationship is expressed as Alim et al. [15]:

$$X_t = S_t + T_t + I_t \tag{5}$$

where S_t, T_t, and I_t represent seasonal variation, trend, and random fluctuations, respectively. For a seasonal ARIMA model, the non-seasonal components are generally identified first, followed by the seasonal elements. After performing seasonal differencing or trend differencing, the time series can often be made stationary and then fitted.

To verify stationarity, the augmented Dickey-Fuller (ADF) test can be used. The autocorrelation function (ACF) and partial autocorrelation function (PACF) graphs help in identifying potential values of *p*, *q*, *P*, and *Q* according to the Box-Jenkins order selection method. Various ARIMA models are then fitted using the conditional sum of squares approach, and the model that best fits the data is determined. The model with the smallest corrected Akaike Information Criterion (AICc) value is regarded as the optimal choice [23]. Lastly, the Ljung-Box test is applied to the residuals to check for white noise.

2.5 Forecast Accuracy Metrics: MAPE and RMSE

Mean Absolute Percentage Error (MAPE) and Root Mean Squared Error (RMSE) are widely utilized metrics for assessing forecasting performance. MAPE quantifies the mean absolute percentage deviation between observed and predicted values, expressed as a percentage, using the formula:

$$MAPE = \frac{1}{n}\sum_{t=1}^{n}\left|\frac{A_t - F_t}{A_t}\right| \times 100\% \tag{6}$$

where n represents the total number of observations, A_t is actual value at time t_t, and F_t is predicted value at the same time point.

RMSE, on the other hand, measures the average magnitude of errors by computing the square root of the average squared discrepancies between actual and predicted values, with larger errors penalized more. Its formula is

$$RMSE = \sqrt{\frac{1}{n}\sum_{t=1}^{n}(A_t - F_t)^2} \tag{7}$$

3 Result and Discussion

3.1 Preprocessing Data

The raw data consists of 4,028,503 individual flight records, each containing a total of 22 variables. Before analysis, the data must undergo preprocessing. Out of the 22 variables, 8 core variables will be selected, deemed sufficient to uniquely identify each flight record. The combination of these 8 variables ensures that each flight record is unique. These 8 variables are (Table 1):

Table 1. Eight selected variables

No.	Variable name	Description
1	ADEP	Aerodrome of departure/departure airport code
2	ADES	Aerodrome of destination/destination airport code
3	DOF	Date of flight/flight date
4	Flight number	Flight number
5	AC register	Aircraft registration number
6	Time in	Time the aircraft passes through a specified area or point
7	ADLO	Flight status
8	DOMINT	Type of flight (domestic or international)

The dataset is filtered to focus on domestic flights from 2020 to 2022. Records marked as international (DOMINT = "INT") and overflights (ADLO = "O") are removed, as well as duplicates, missing values, and data from 2019. This cleaning reduces the initial 4,028,503 records to 3,469,095.

After cleaning, data is aggregated by counting unique daily occurrences across eight selected variables, transforming the detailed records into a daily count of domestic flights in Indonesia. This final dataset represents the daily number of domestic flights, as shown in Table 2.

Table 2. Daily flight activity counts

Date	Number of flights
01/01/2020	3,713
02/01/2020	4,717
03/01/2020	4,824

After obtaining the daily flight activity counts, a check for missing values and outliers is performed. No missing values are found in the dataset. However, for outliers, they are replaced with the average of the immediately adjacent observations [7].

For the XGBoost analysis, the flight date data from Table 2 will be transformed into several features derived from time series indices. These features will encompass the day of the week, quarter, month, year, day of the year, and calendar day within the month. The details of these features are provided in Table 3.

Table 3. Time series features

Feature	Description	Values
dayofweek	Day position in a week during the forecasting period	1 (Monday)–7 (Sunday)
quarter	Quarter position in a year during the forecasting period	1 (Q1)–4 (Q4)
month	Month position in a year during the forecasting period	1 (January)–12 (December)
year	Year during the forecasting period	2020–2022
dayofyear	Day position in a year during the forecasting period	1 (1st January)–366 (31st December in a leap year)
dayofmonth	Day position in a month during the forecasting period	1–31

Table 4 illustrates example of domestic flight activity data during the pandemic after incorporating these time series features.

Table 4. Flight activity data with time series features

Flight date	*Dayof week*	*quarter*	*month*	*year*	*dayofyear*	*dayofmonth*	Number of flights
01/01/2020	1	1	1	2020	1	1	3,713

The final step in data preprocessing is to split the data. Using a temporal split, the data will be splitted into training and testing sets with the following proportions (Table 5).

Table 5. Data splitting proportions

Data split	XGBoost (70:30)		ARIMA (90:10)		Position
	During	Post	During	Post	
Training data	653	114	840	147	Earliest records
Testing data	280	49	93	16	Most recent records

The testing dataset for ARIMA is smaller than the one used for XGBoost due to the characteristic of ARIMA as a short-term forecasting method [15].

3.2 Descriptive Statistics

Figure 1 is a graph illustrating the trends in domestic flight activity in Indonesia from 2020 to 2022.

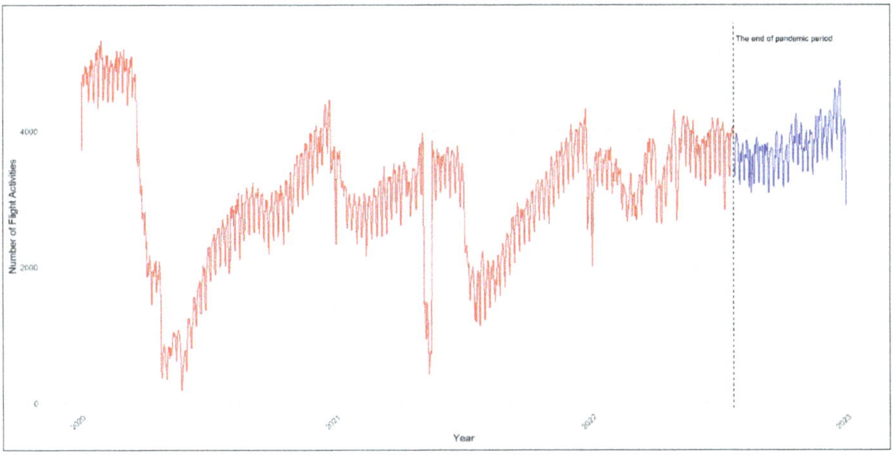

Fig. 1. Graph of domestic flight activities in Indonesia 2020–2022

In Fig. 1, two lines represent domestic flight activity during the pandemic and post-pandemic periods. The blue line reflects the number of domestic flights during the pandemic, from January 1, 2020, to July 21, 2022. The red line shows the trend in domestic flight activity after the pandemic, from July 22 to December 31, 2022. A vertical line divides the visualization, clearly separating the pandemic and post-pandemic periods.

The graph indicates that domestic flight activity in Indonesia from 2020 to 2022 experienced fluctuations. In early 2020, there was a sharp decline due to the COVID-19 pandemic when the government applied large-scale social restrictions (PSBB) to curb the virus's spread [24]. Following this steep drop, there was a gradual increase in flight activity as mobility restrictions were eased from May to December 2020. In early 2021, flight activity continued to fluctuate, with another significant decline in July and August 2021 due to a spike in COVID-19 cases, prompting the government to enforce emergency community activity restrictions (PPKM) [25].

As COVID-19 cases decreased, air transport in Indonesia began to recover, with a gradual increase in flight activity from August 2021 despite ongoing fluctuations. This upward trend continued through to the end of December 2022.

Figure 1 reveals distinct patterns in domestic flight activity across the pandemic and post-pandemic periods, illustrating the varying trends over these different times. The following graph provides a visual comparison of these patterns.

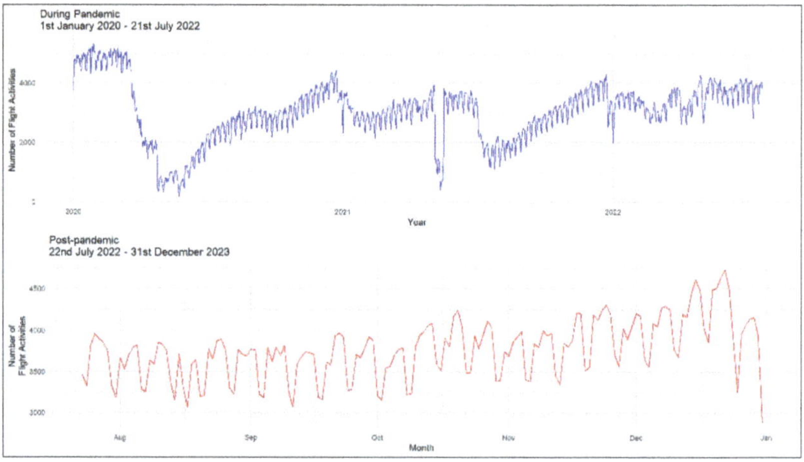

Fig. 2. Graph of domestic flight activities in Indonesia during and post-pandemic.

Figure 2 shows the pattern of domestic flight activity in Indonesia during the pandemic, characterized by random fluctuations. This randomness is due to independent influences that create non-systematic patterns. In this case, the independent influence is the COVID-19 pandemic, an unusual event that significantly impacted the aviation industry [8].

In contrast, the post-pandemic period exhibits a seasonal pattern, marked by recurring peaks and troughs at regular intervals [26].

3.3 Forecasting Flight Activities Using XGBoost

This research employs a rolling forecasting origin for cross-validation, partitioning data into an initial training window and a testing interval for each iteration. The training window, set to half the dataset, allows the model to capture data patterns before prediction, while a 10% subset of the test data supports incremental and precise model assessment. Settings such as fixedWindow for consistency, allowParallel for parallel processing, and customized verboseIter and returnData enhance model evaluation. Adjustments to the rolling origin also include multi-step errors to improve long-term prediction accuracy [27].

The cross-validation steps were integrated into the XGBoost model creation process. To develop the XGBoost model, hyperparameter tuning was conducted first to identify the best combination of parameters that would yield the lowest error rate. Table 6 lists the parameter values that were inputted for training and combination.

Table 6. Input parameters for XGBoost

Parameters	Values
Number of estimators	Range 100–200
Max_depth	Between 6, 15, and 20
Colsample_bytree	1
Subsample	1
Gamma	0
Min_child_weight	1
Learning rate	1

After all the parameters in Table 6 were combined and tested, the best parameters for the XGBoost model to forecast domestic flight activity in Indonesia during and post the pandemic were identified. These optimal parameters are shown in Table 7.

Next, we evaluate feature importance. Figure 3 below shows the feature importance for both during and post-pandemic period. This visualization provide insight into which features have the greatest influence on the model's predictions.

The feature importance analysis from the XGBoost model reveals distinct trends in daily domestic flight activity forecasting between the pandemic and post-pandemic periods. During the pandemic, the "dayofyear" feature was most influential (72% importance), highlighting the role of seasonal patterns likely influenced by fluctuating travel demand, pandemic-related policies, and weather. Post-pandemic, "dayofweek" became the leading feature (64% importance), indicating a shift toward routine and predictable travel patterns as flight operations stabilized.

Using the established XGBoost model, a forecast of domestic flight activity in Indonesia was carried out. The forecasting for the pandemic period was conducted from October 15, 2021, to July 21, 2022, covering a total of 280 data points, as the pandemic period officially ended on July 21, 2022. The forecast for the post-pandemic

Table 7. Best tuned parameters

Parameters	Values	
	During	Post
Number of estimators	105	100
Max_depth	6	6
Colsample by tree	0.5	0.5
Subsample	0	0
Gamma	1	1
Min_child_weight	1	1
Learning rate	1	1

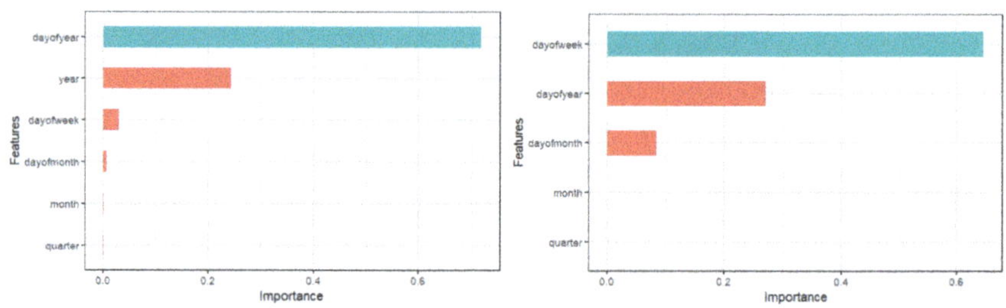

Fig. 3. Feature importance during (Left) and post-pandemic (Right).

period started from November 13, 2022, and continued through December 31, 2022. The forecasted results are illustrated in Figs. 4 and 5.

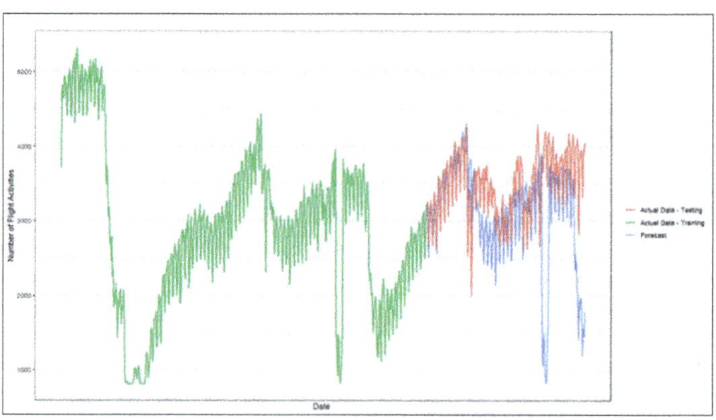

Fig. 4. Plot of during pandemic forecast using XGBoost.

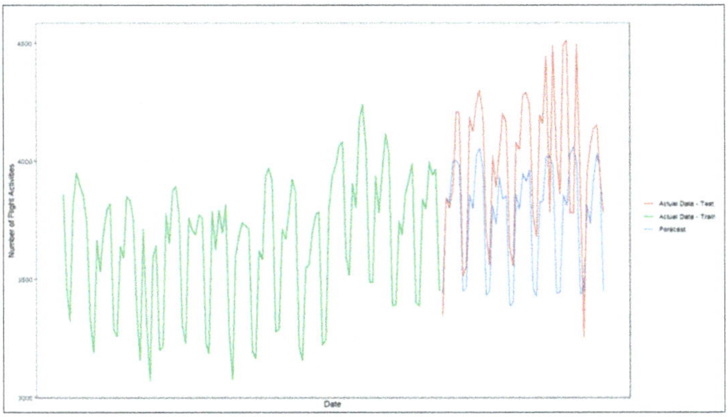

Fig. 5. Plot of post-pandemic forecast using XGBoost.

The forecast results from the XGBoost model are compared with the actual test data. In Fig. 4, the salmon-colored line represents the training data, the blue line shows the forecasted results, and the green line indicates the actual test data used for evaluation. While the forecast closely follows the actual data, some points show significant gaps. The MAPE and RMSE for this forecast is 14.6% and 842.17, suggesting good accuracy.

In Fig. 5, although some gaps remain, the forecasted values closely follow the pattern of the actual test data. The MAPE for this post-pandemic forecast is 6.6% and 309.2 indicating that the model's forecast accuracy is very good.

3.4 Forecasting Flight Activities Using ARIMA

Differencing once was performed on the during-pandemic data as the ADF test indicated the data was non-stationary (ADF test: $t = -2.9092$, $p > 0.05$). After differencing once, the data became stationary (ADF test: $t = -7.3974$, $p < 0.05$). For the post-pandemic data, no differencing was necessary as the ADF test showed the data was already stationary (ADF test: $t = -4.4462$, $p < 0.05$).

Model identification for ARIMA was performed using ACF and PACF plots (Fig. 6). For the during-pandemic data, the PACF plot showed no significant initial lags, suggesting $p = 2$ or $p = 3$ to capture potential longer-term dependencies or trends that might not appear in the first few lags. Additionally, seasonal peaks at lags 7, 14, and 21 indicated a periodicity of 7, further supporting these choices for p values. The ACF plot also showed no significant initial lags, suggesting $q = 1$ or $q = 2$ to account for periodic influences.

For the post-pandemic data, the ACF plot showed a significant initial lag at lag 1, with seasonal peaks similar to the during-pandemic data, suggesting $q = 1$. Similarly, the PACF plot had significant lags at the first two points, along with seasonal peaks, indicating $p = 2$.

With $d = 1$ for the during-pandemic period and $d = 0$ for the post-pandemic period, multiple model variations, including automated order selection methods, were evaluated to determine the best fit for each time frame. Tables 8 and 9 provide a comparison of AICc values and Ljung-Box test results.

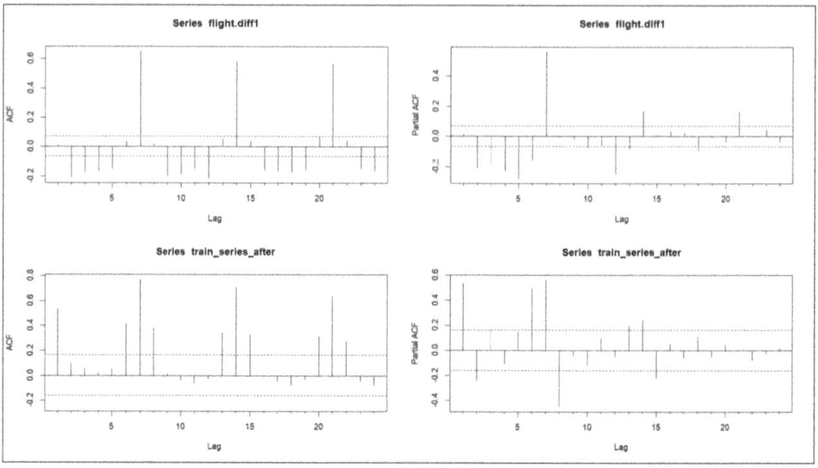

Fig. 6. ACF and PACF Plot for during (Top) and post-pandemic (Bottom).

Table 8. AIC and Ljung-Box test comparisons for ARIMA models (during pandemic)

Model	AICc	Ljung-Box X^2	Ljung-Box p-value
SARIMA(2,1,1)(1,0,1)$_7$	11381.75	51.16	0.0001508
SARIMA(2,1,2)(1,0,1)$_7$	11371.12	45.39	0.0009772
SARIMA(3,1,1)(1,0,1)$_7$	11383.75	51.37	0.0001407
SARIMA(2,1,1)(1,0,0)$_7$	11522.32	83.57	9.648e–10
SARIMA(2,1,2)(1,0,0)$_7$	11522.59	84.12	7.757e–10
SARIMA(3,1,1)(1,0,0)$_7$	11522.86	82.33	1.576e–09
SARIMA(3,1,2)(1,0,0)$_7$	11523.27	77.15	1.191e–08
ARIMA(5,1,0)	11859.94	432.10	<2.2e–16

Table 9. AIC and Ljung-Box test comparisons for ARIMA models post-pandemic)

Model	AICc	Ljung-Box X^2	Ljung-Box p-value
SARIMA(1,1,2)(1,1,2)$_7$	1741.29	11.914	0.919
SARIMA(2,1,1)(1,1,2)$_7$	1741.42	11.676	0.9268
SARIMA(1,1,2)(1,1,1)$_7$	1740.19	12.09	0.9129
ARIMA(0,1,1)	2063.71	364.37	<2.2e–16

Comparing the AICc and Ljung-Box p-values for each model (Tables 10 and 11) shows that for during pandemic period the SARIMA(2,1,2)(1,0,1)$_7$ model has the lowest AICc, indicating a better fit based on this criterion. However, all Ljung-Box p-values are less than 0.05, which suggests that none of the models pass the white noise test, indicating remaining autocorrelation in the residuals.

For the post-pandemic period, SARIMA$(1,1,2)(1,1,1)_7$ appears to be the best model, having the lowest AICc and a Ljung-Box p-value greater than 0.5, which suggests that this model meets the white noise assumption.

The estimated parameters of the SARIMA$(2,1,2)(1,0,1)_7$ and SARIMA$(1,1,2)(1,1,1)_7$ model are listed in Tables 10 and 11.

Table 10. Estimated parameters of SARIMA$(2,1,2)(1,0,1)_7$ for during pandemic

Parameter	Estimation	Std. Error	CI (lower bound) 95%	CI (upper bound) 95%
ar1	−0.5030	0.1586	−0.8139	−0.1921
ar2	0.3094	0.1475	0.0193	0.5995
ma1	0.4292	0.1472	0.1407	0.7177
ma2	−0.4786	0.1408	−0.7545	−0.2027
sar1	0.9959	0.0032	0.9897	1.0021
sma1	−0.9000	0.0335	−0.9650	−0.8350

Table 11. Estimated parameters of SARIMA$(1,1,2)(1,1,1)_7$ for post-pandemic

Parameter	Estimation	Std. Error	CI (lower bound) 95%	CI (upper bound) 95%
ar1	0.6874	0.1902	0.3149	1.0599
ma1	−1.0602	0.2615	−1.5734	−0.5470
ma2	0.1096	0.2193	−0.3210	0.5402
sar1	−0.0691	0.1179	−0.3013	0.1631
sma1	−0.8755	0.1045	−1.0816	−0.6694

After selecting the models, we applied SARIMA$(2,1,2)(1,0,1)_7$ to forecast the during-pandemic data and SARIMA$(1,1,2)(1,1,1)_7$ to forecast the post-pandemic data. Figures 9 and 10 display the forecast plots for each period.

Based on Fig. 7, it can be seen that the SARIMA$(2,1,2)(1,0,1)_7$ model does not closely follow the actual data pattern during the pandemic period. However, the model produces relatively low MAPE and RMSE values of 7.53% and 332.91, respectively.

For the post-pandemic period, as shown in Fig. 8, the SARIMA$(1,1,2)(1,1,1)_7$ model begins to better capture the pattern of the actual data, although there are still noticeable gaps and discrepancies. Nonetheless, the resulting MAPE and RMSE values are also relatively low, at 7.49% and 349.2, respectively.

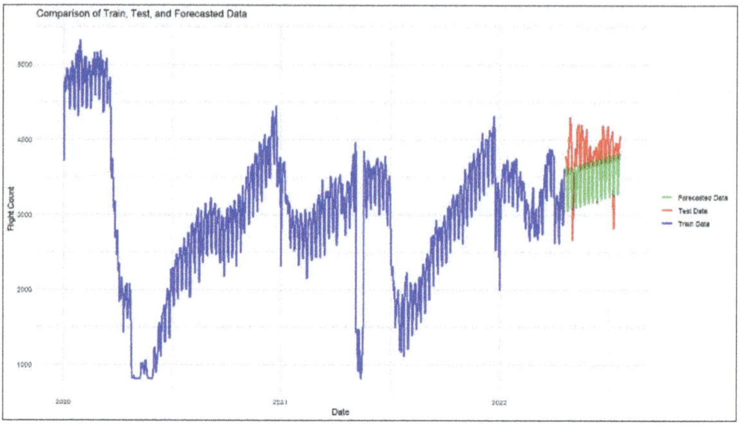

Fig. 7. Plot of during pandemic forecast using SARIMA.

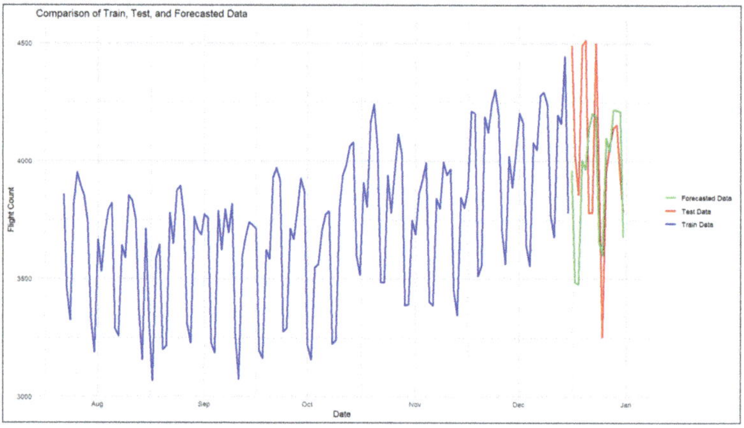

Fig. 8. Plot of post-pandemic forecast using SARIMA.

4 Conclusions

Forecasting was conducted on two different data patterns: during the pandemic, which was more fluctuating, and post-pandemic, which was more stable, using XGBoost and ARIMA methods. For the during-pandemic data, although the MAPE and RMSE of ARIMA were lower than those of XGBoost, the XGBoost model was better at following the actual data patterns, which were more complex and irregular. Additionally, the ARIMA model for the during pandemic period is not recommended for use, as it did not satisfy the white noise assumption. The presence of autocorrelation in the residuals indicates that the model failed to fully capture all patterns in the data. The complex and highly fluctuating nature of the pandemic data made it more suitable for a non-linear model like XGBoost, which can capture complex relationships between features.

On the other hand, for the post-pandemic data, which was more stable, XGBoost outperformed ARIMA both in evaluation metrics (MAPE and RMSE) and in its ability to follow the actual data pattern. XGBoost demonstrated greater flexibility in handling dynamic changes in the post-pandemic data, while ARIMA, although performing reasonably well, was less capable of capturing the short-term fluctuations and complexities in the data.

References

1. Sani, Z.: Transportasi: Suatu Pengantar. Universitas Indonesia (UI-Press), Jakarta (2010)
2. Perhubungan, K.: Peraturan Menteri Perhubungan No. Km.49. http://jdih.dephub.go.id/produk_hukum/view/UzAwdUlEUTVJRlJCU0ZWT0lESXdNRFU9 (2005)
3. Badan Pusat Statistik: BRS No. 66/10/Th. XXVI—Perkembangan Transportasi Nasional Agustus 2023. BPS (Issue 21). BPS, Jakarta (2023)
4. Sims, R.: A review and application of aviation forecasting for airport planners, vol. 397. Theses and dissertations. https://commons.und.edu/theses/397 (2016)
5. Hanif, B.: Pergerakan Pesawat Komersial Terhadap **5**(2), 151–156 (2019)
6. Wenzel, S., Kölker, K., Bießlich, P., Lütjens, K.: Approach to Forecast Air-Traffic Movements at Capacity-Constrained Airports, vol. 25. Aerospace Research Centre (2015)
7. Airport Cooperative Research Program (ACRP): Airport Aviation Activity Forecasting. Transportation Research Board, Washington DC (2007). https://doi.org/10.17226/23192
8. Wensveen, J.: Air Transportation: a Global Management Perspective, 9th edn. Routledge, New York (2023)
9. Huang, C., et al.: Clinical features of patients infected with 2019 novel coronavirus in Wuhan, China. Lancet. **395**(10223), 497–506 (2020). https://doi.org/10.1016/S0140-6736(20)30183-5
10. World Health Organization (WHO): Listings of WHO's response to COVID-19. https://www.who.int/news/item/29-06-2020-covidtimeline (2020)
11. Dyah: Pelajaran dari PPKM Level 1–4. Antara News (2021)
12. Eurocontrol: artificial intelligence: a new era for aviation. Skyw. Mag. (2019). https://doi.org/10.38179/ijcr.v3i1.203
13. Luo, J., Zhang, Z., Fu, Y., Rao, F.: Time series prediction of COVID-19 transmission in America using LSTM and XGBoost algorithms. Results Phys. **27**, 104462 (2021). https://doi.org/10.1016/j.rinp.2021.104462
14. Lv, C.X., An, S.Y., Qiao, B.J., Wu, W.: Time series analysis of hemorrhagic fever with renal syndrome in mainland China by using an XGBoost forecasting model. BMC Infect. Dis. **21**(1), 1–13 (2021). https://doi.org/10.1186/s12879-021-06503-y
15. Alim, M., Ye, G.H., Guan, P., Huang, D.S., Zhou, B.S., Wu, W.: Comparison of ARIMA model and XGBoost model for prediction of human brucellosis in mainland China: a time-series study. BMJ Open **10**(12), 1–8 (2020). https://doi.org/10.1136/bmjopen-2020-039676
16. Maizar, M., Mustika, I., Nabella, S.D.: Pengantar Statistik 1. Penerbit Media Sain Indonesia, Bandung (2022)
17. Silvia, V.: Statistika Deskriptif, 1st edn. Penerbit Andi, Kabupaten Sleman (2021)
18. Prihatiningsih, D.: Mudahnya Belajar Statistik Deskriptif. CV Sarnu Untung, Grobogan (2022)
19. Chen, T., Guestrin, C.: XGBoost: a scalable tree boosting system. In: Proceedings of the 22nd ACM SIGKDD International Conference on Knowledge Discovery and Data Mining, 13–17-Augu, pp. 785–794 (2016). https://doi.org/10.1145/2939672.2939785

20. Islam, S.F.N., Sholahuddin, A., Abdullah, A.S.: Extreme gradient boosting (XGBoost) method in making forecasting application and analysis of USD exchange rates against rupiah. J. Phys. Conf. Ser. **1722**(1) (2021). https://doi.org/10.1088/1742-6596/1722/1/012016
21. Ji, S., Wang, X., Zhao, W., Guo, D.: An application of a three-stage XGboost-based model to sales forecasting of a cross-border e-commerce enterprise. Math. Probl. Eng. **2019** (2019). https://doi.org/10.1155/2019/8503252
22. Kumar, M., Anand, M.: An application of time series Arima forecasting model for predicting sugarcane production in India. Stud. Bus. Econ. 81–94 (2015)
23. Liu, Q., et al.: Forecasting the seasonality and trend of pulmonary tuberculosis in Jiangsu Province of China using advanced statistical time-series analyses. Infect Drug Resist. (2019). https://doi.org/10.2147/IDR.S207809
24. Tuti, R.W., Nurmandi, A., Zahra, A.A.: Handling COVID-19 in the capital city of Jakarta with innovation policy: the scale of social restrictions policy. Heliyon **8**(5), e09467 (2022). https://doi.org/10.1016/j.heliyon.2022.e09467
25. BBC: Jokowi umumkan PPKM darurat di Jawa dan Bali 3–20 Juli 2021: 'Ini akan lebih ketat dari kebijakan pembatasan sebelumnya. BBC News Indonesia. https://www.bbc.com/indonesia/indonesia-57584375 (2021)
26. Primandari, A.H., Kartikasari, M.D.: Analisis Runtun Waktu dengan R. Universitas Islam Indonesia, Sleman Regency (2020)
27. Hyndman, R.J., Athanasopoulos, G.: Forecasting: Principles and Practice, 3rd edn. Melbourne, Australia. https://otexts.com/fpp3/ (2021)

Skin Disease Classification Using Hybrid Convolutional Neural Network

Alfito Putra Fajar Pratama(✉), Hasih Pratiwi, and Isnandar Slamet

Sebelas Maret University, Surakarta, Indonesia
alfito.ptr@gmail.com, hpratiwi@mipa.uns.ac.id

Abstract. Skin diseases have a variety of causes, including exposure to chemicals, sunlight, viruses, bacteria, and other factors. Classification of skin diseases is essential because of their similar symptoms, such as red rashes, itching, and burning. The similar symptoms of the diseases make it difficult to distinguish them visually. This research aims to classify skin diseases using a hybrid Convolutional Neural Network (CNN) method. The dataset used is MSLD v2.0, which is skin disease image data with 6 classes, namely monkeypox, cowpox, chickenpox, measles, HFMD, and healthy. Hybrid CNN is an integration between the CNN model and machine learning methods. This research uses three CNN models, namely EfficientNet, DenseNet, and ResNet, as feature extraction. The classification methods used include logistic regression, random forest, and XGBoost. Data augmentation is also applied to increase data variation. The highest performance results are obtained when using ResNet as a feature extraction and logistic regression as a classification method after going through the data augmentation process with an accuracy of 82% and a macro f1-score of 80%, which showed high performance in skin disease detection. Hybrid CNN with machine learning method shows the ability to feature extraction of skin disease images and achieves optimal performance.

Keywords: CNN · Feature extraction · Image classification · Machine learning · Skin disease

1 Introduction

Skin diseases are disorders that occur on the outermost layer of the body with various causes, including exposure to chemicals, sunlight, viruses, weak immune systems, microorganisms, fungi, and other factors [1]. Infections caused by fungi, viruses, and bacteria can cause various skin problems, which are characterized by symptoms such as red spots or rashes, itching, burning or hot sensations on the skin, pain when the rash is touched, swelling in the infected area, and sores or bumps.

The similar symptoms of skin diseases make it difficult to distinguish skin diseases visually. One skin disease that has visual similarities is smallpox. Smallpox is generally characterized by the appearance of a fluid-filled rash on the skin's surface, which causes itching [2]. Several types of smallpox can be contracted by humans, including chickenpox, cowpox, and monkeypox. Monkeypox is similar to chickenpox or measles, which

P. C. Rodrigues et al. (Eds.): ISBIS 2024, 13, pp. 191–204, 2027.
https://doi.org/10.1007/978-3-032-32458-0_14

is characterized by the progressive appearance of a rash that resembles red patches all over the body. Because of this, some people have difficulty distinguishing monkeypox from other diseases [3]. Measles also has similar symptoms with the appearance of a small red skin rash tightly and evenly distributed throughout the body [4].

Monkeypox Skin Lesion Dataset (MSLD) v2.0 is a skin disease dataset that includes images of various body parts. This dataset includes smallpox cases such as monkeypox, chickenpox, and cowpox and also has data with cases of measles, hand-foot-mouth disease, and healthy individuals. This dataset is publicly available and can be used to explore the potential of deep learning models in identifying and diagnosing various skin diseases [5].

Image classification technology can help analyze and identify skin diseases by distinguishing various conditions in images. Applicable deep learning techniques such as Convolutional Neural Network (CNN) can identify and extract features and classify objects independently. Some CNN models that have been specifically designed for image recognition tasks include DenseNet, ResNet, and EfficientNet models. These models have been tested in detecting images, such as in research conducted by [7] by applying EfficientNet and ResNet models in detecting skin cancer images, which resulted in an accuracy of 93.10%. The application of the DenseNet model in detecting image objects was carried out in research [8] in distinguishing the health level of rice plants. The study used 3 DensNet models, namely DensNet121, DensNet169, and DenseNet201. The final result got an accuracy of 91.67% using the DenseNet121 model.

There are several methods for classification, including Random Forest, Extreme Gradient Boosting, and Linear Regression. Random Forest is a versatile and effective method for classification and regression, excels in large-scale problems, and adapts to various data types [9]. Extreme Gradient Boosting is a technique for modeling a series of regression trees built sequentially with an iterative process where each subsequent tree attempts to correct the prediction error produced by the previous tree. This method is known for its excellence in classification and regression, as well as for its ability to be competitive, robust, and provide easy-to-interpret results [10]. Logistic regression is a technique used in machine learning to create classification models and can be applied to a variety of problems [11].

Hybrid machine learning involves integrating different approaches to overcome individual limitations and achieve synergistic effects [12]. Hybrid CNN integrates the CNN method for feature extraction combined with the classification method. CNN excels in learning complex and varied features [13]. The extracted features can then be processed using various classification methods, which contributes positively to the classification process. This research aims to classify skin diseases using the CNN hybrid method. The CNN method will be used for feature extraction and combined with a classification method, which is expected to make a positive contribution to accelerating the skin disease identification process.

2 Materials and Methods

This research uses Google Collaboratory to train the model. The research starts with data identification, data augmentation, image feature extraction, and model evaluation. The research flow can be seen in Fig. 1.

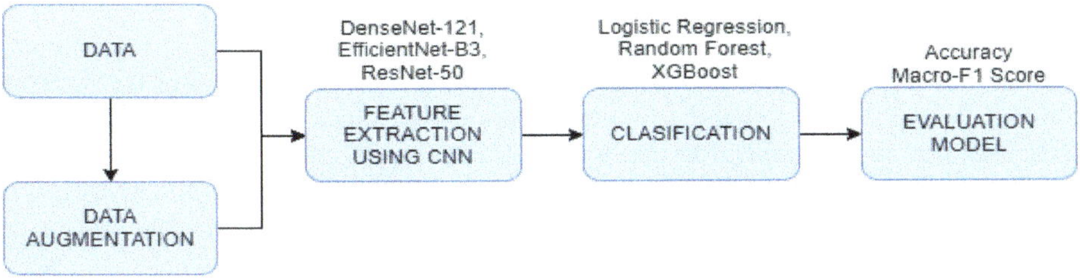

Fig. 1. Research flow

2.1 Dataset

The dataset used is a secondary dataset obtained through Kaggle, namely the Monkeypox Skin Lesion Dataset (MSLD) v2.0, which consists of six classes, where monkeypox has 284 data, chickenpox 75 data, measles 55 data, chickenpox 66 data, HFMD 161 data, and healthy 114 data. The sample of each class can be seen in Fig. 2.

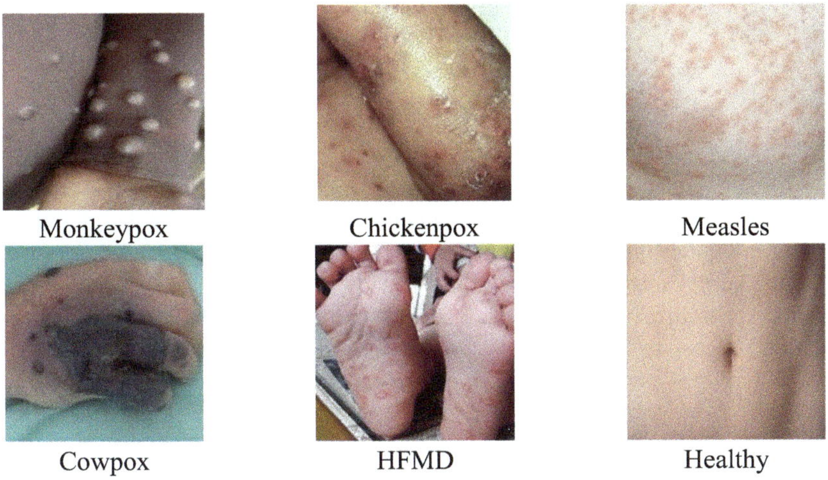

Fig. 2. Picture of skin disease

2.2 Data Augmentation

Data augmentation is a strategy that allows researchers to increase the diversity of data available to train models without the need to collect new data physically. Data augmentation techniques increase the size and quality of the dataset, resulting in better models and avoiding overfitting [14].

This research applies data augmentation to balance the number of samples per class. The augmentation applied is by rotating the image with a multiple of 90 degrees, image reflection, and performing color variations on each class so that the class becomes balanced.

2.3 Convolutional Neural Network (CNN) for Feature Extraction

The CNN method is a type of deep learning technique derived from Multi-layer Perceptron (MLP) and is used to handle two-dimensional data, such as audio or images [15]. CNN uses a convolution layer to apply convolution operations to an input using filters to extract important features from the input. An illustration of the convolution operation between an image input matrix and a 3 × 3 convolution kernel matrix can be seen in Fig. 3.

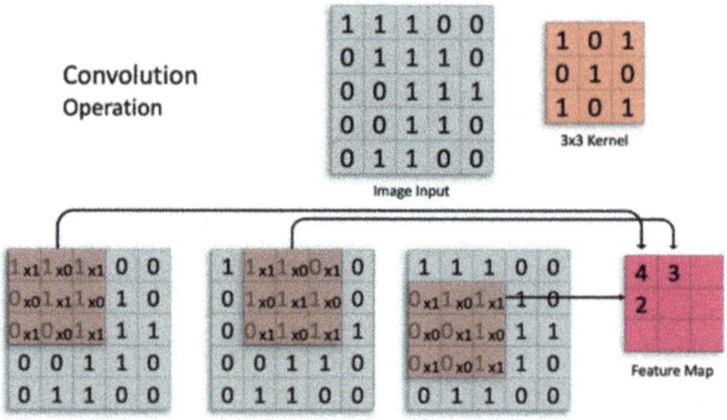

Fig. 3. Illustration of convolutional layer operation [15]

The kernel size becomes a hyperparameter that can be adjusted to obtain image characteristics. The kernel multiplies the input image according to its size, and the result is stored as a feature map. The kernel moves to get the next value; the size of the step taken by the kernel when moving is called a stride.

In this research, CNN is used as a feature extraction where the model ends with a flattening process to get a vector representation of the number of model extraction results. Flattening is a technique that transforms a matrix into a one-dimensional vector. This process is designed to take the feature map produced by the previous layer and convert it into a single-dimensional format, enabling further processing of the feature map.

2.4 Densely Connected Convolutional Networks (DenseNet)

Densely Connected Convolutional Networks (DenseNet) is an architecture that introduces a unique concept where each layer is directly connected to all other layers in a dense block. Specifically, each layer in DenseNet receives inputs from all previous layers and in turn, sends its outputs as inputs to all subsequent layers in the block. This aims to improve the flow of information between layers by treating the feature map of each previous layer as a separate input [16]. The DenseNet method has several variants, including DenseNet-121, DenseNet-169, DenseNet-201, and DenseNet-264, each of which has a different number of parameters, with DenseNet-264 having the largest number of parameters. This research uses DenseNet-121 as the feature extractor, and the architecture of DenseNet-121 can be seen in Fig. 4.

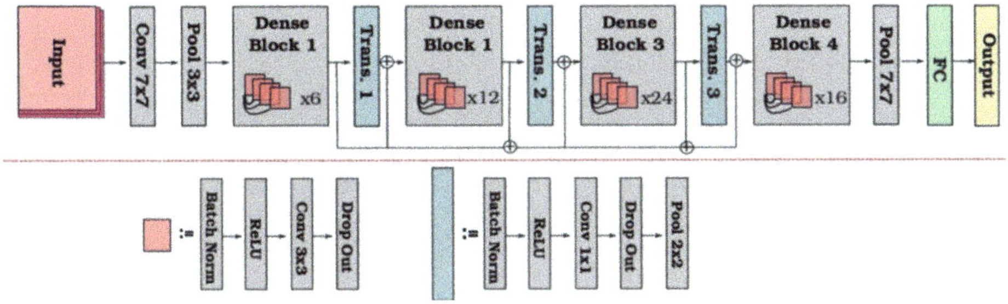

Fig. 4. DenseNet architecture [17]

2.5 Residual Networks (ResNet)

In 2016, Kaiming and his colleagues [18] made a significant contribution by introducing an innovative CNN architecture known as Residual Networks (ResNet). The ResNet method brings innovation by overcoming a common problem in CNN models, namely the vanishing gradient problem. This problem arises when the gradients in the deeper layers start to disappear, preventing the next layer from undergoing significant changes. This can lead to high time complexity and increase the risk of errors in model training [18].

The ResNet architecture is designed by composing several residual blocks with varying layers. There are variations of ResNet models with layers 18, 34, 50, 101, and 152. In this study, the authors chose to use ResNet with 50 layers, known as ResNet50. The architecture of ResNet-50 is shown in Fig. 5.

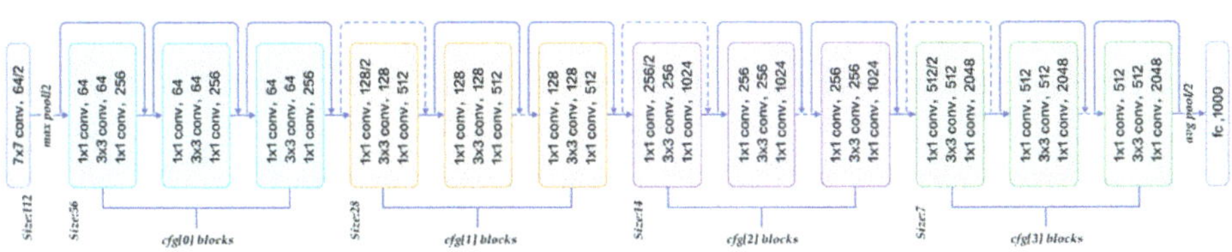

Fig. 5. ResNet-50 architecture [19]

2.6 EfficientNet-B3

EfficientNet is a family of CNNs developed by Google AI in 2019. EfficientNet aims to improve CNN accuracy while reducing computational load, which is achieved through various strategies, including improving the model architecture, using deeper and wider layers, and utilizing co-scaling to balance accuracy and efficiency. This architecture is based on improving the model architecture and the size of the input image, which is achieved by increasing the image resolution in addition to increasing the depth and width of the network layers. In addition, this architecture uses convolutions that can be separated based on the depth of the model, thus offering higher efficiency compared to standard convolutions [20]. The name EfficientNetB3 indicates that it is the third version of the EfficientNet family. The architecture of EfficientNet-B3 can be seen in Figs. 6 and 7.

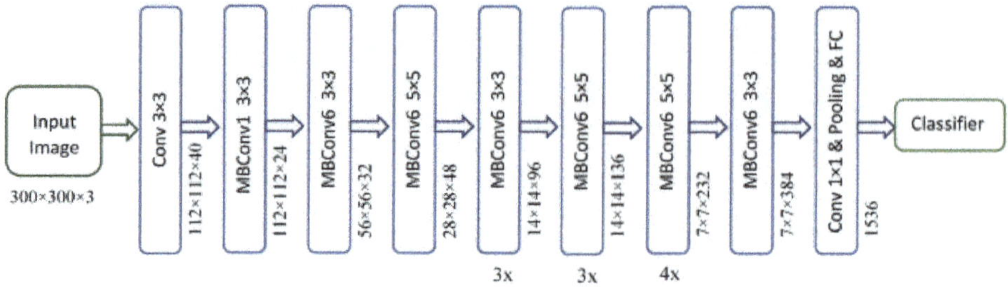

Fig. 6. Efficient-Net architecture [21]

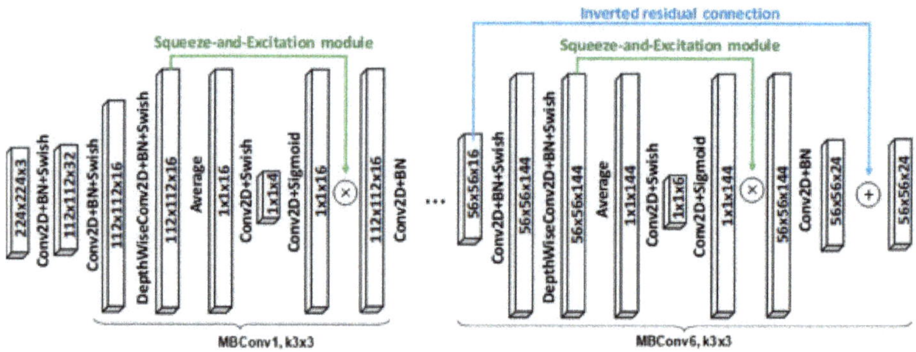

Fig. 7. MBConv blocks in the EfficientNet CNN model [22]

2.7 Logistic Regression

One of the traditional statistical techniques to handle classification problems is Logistic Regression (LR). The LR method generates probabilities to predict the class. Suppose $X_1, X_2, ..., X_p$ as predictor variables and Y as the response variable. The regression formula with Z value can be seen in Eq. (1),

$$Z_j = \beta_{0j} + \beta_{1j}X_1 + \beta_{2j}X_2 + \cdots + \beta_{2p}X_p \tag{1}$$

where

Z_j	:	linear value for class-j,
β_{0j}	:	Intercept for class-j,
$\beta_{1j}, \beta_{2j}, \ldots, \beta_{pj}$	:	coefficient for each feature $X_1, X_2, ..., X_p$ for class-j

The Z value obtained from Eq. (1) is then used in the logistic function to obtain the class probability. The logistic function is expressed in Eq. (2) [23].

$$P(Y) = \frac{1}{1 - e^{-(Z_j)}} forj = 1, \ldots, K \; and \; z = (z_1, \ldots, z_K) \tag{2}$$

2.8 Random Forest

Leo Breiman first presented Random Forest (RF) in 2001 [24]. This method consists of several decision trees, where each tree relies on a value taken freely and evenly across the trees in the group called a bootstrap. An ensemble method known as bootstrap aggregation or bagging is used to improve data classification accuracy effectively. Bagging algorithms can avoid diversity loss, increase classification speed, and reduce memory requirements. Bagging uses a bootstrap method or sampling technique with replacement on the original dataset n times to generate a training set [25]. The random forest classification step starts by bootstrapping the original dataset on a set of N features. Trees will be formed using this new data, generating random trees. Each tree will perform a prediction, and the final result will be determined based on majority voting, i.e. by selecting the prediction class that appears the most from each tree formed. The RF classification step can be seen in Fig. 8.

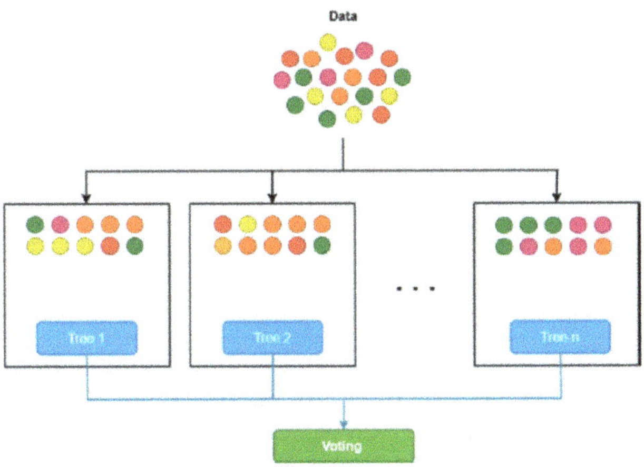

Fig. 8. RF Classification steps

2.9 Extreme Gradient Boosting

The Extreme Gradient Boosting (XGB) method is a method that uses a tree architecture with a boosting system. Boosting is one of the merging strategies that can turn some weak groupings into strong results. This classification technique involves creating a learning model based on some characteristics or prediction model, which is then used to classify new information by considering the previously generated weights. The ensemble concept with boosting works sequentially, where each model benefits from the previous model's error, and finally, the entire model is combined to form a stronger prediction [26]. The XGB algorithm can be seen in Fig. 9.

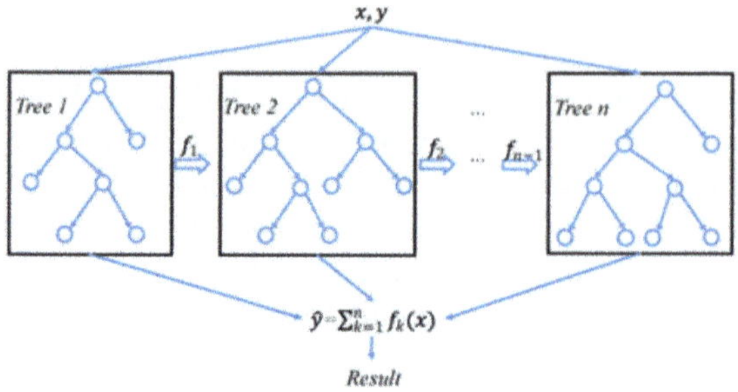

Fig. 9. XGB Architecture [27]

Based on Fig. 9. The XGB prediction can be formulated in Eq. (3) [27],

$$\hat{y} = \sum_{k=1}^{n} f_k(x_i) f_k \in F \tag{3}$$

where

$\hat{y}$	:	the final prediction for the$i$th instance i.e. the sum of the predictions of all trees,
n	:	total number of decision trees in the model,
f_k	:	kth predictor function or decision tree that is part of the XGB model,
x_i	:	i-th instance of the input data,
$f_k(x_i)$	:	the prediction generated by the kth decision tree for the i-th instance,
F	:	the space of all possible regression trees

The XGB model is a model that contributes to the final prediction through an iterative residual learning process.

2.10 Model Evaluation

The results of feature extraction of CNN models before entering the classification process will be divided. The dataset is divided into two parts, namely training data and test data. This division aims to evaluate the previously trained model so that its ability to predict new data that has never been involved in the training process can be measured. Using 80% of training data can produce more balanced and fair classification results and improve overall and per-class performance [28].

The Accuracy and f1-score metrics are used to see the model's capabilities. Accuracy measures the extent to which the classification model can make correct predictions on all evaluated data. The accuracy value can be calculated by considering the number of True Positive (TP) classes from the confusion matrix results. The accuracy value of all classes is expressed in Eq. (3).

$$accuracy = \frac{TP}{Total\ Data} \tag{4}$$

F1-score is a combination of precision and recall in a single metric. Higher F1-score values indicate better performance in maintaining a balance between precision and recall. The precision value can be calculated with Eq. (4), and the recall of each class can be calculated with Eq. (5). After obtaining the precision and recall values, a single F1-Score can be calculated by Eq. (6).

$$Precision(class\, n) = \frac{TP_n}{FP_n + TP_n} \tag{5}$$

$$Recall(class\, n) = \frac{TP_n}{TP_n + FN_n} \tag{6}$$

$$F1 - Score(class\, n) = 2 \times \frac{Precision_n \times Recall_n}{Precision_n + Recall_n} \tag{7}$$

After obtaining the f1-score value for each class, the next step is to calculate the average f1-score. The macro average with n being the number of f1-score classes is expressed in Eq. (7).

$$Macro\, F1 - Score = \frac{1}{n}\sum_{i=1}^{n} F1 - Score_i \tag{8}$$

3 Result

3.1 Data Augmentation

In this study, the model will be trained on both the original and augmented data. The dataset is divided into 80% for training and 20% for testing. The augmentation process is performed to increase the training data, ensuring that the dataset is balanced across all classes. Specifically, each class will be augmented to achieve a total of 300 samples, which helps to mitigate the issues arising from class imbalance. An example of the augmented data can be seen in Fig. 6, showcasing how the variations help create a more robust training set. The augmentation techniques employed include random rotations (0, 90, 180, and 270 degrees), reflections, color jittering (saturation adjustments in the range of 0.5 to 1.5), brightness and contrast adjustments (also in the range of 0.5 to 1.5), and synthetic blurring using a Gaussian kernel. An example of the augmented data can be seen in Fig. 6, showcasing how the variations help create a more robust training set (Fig. 10).

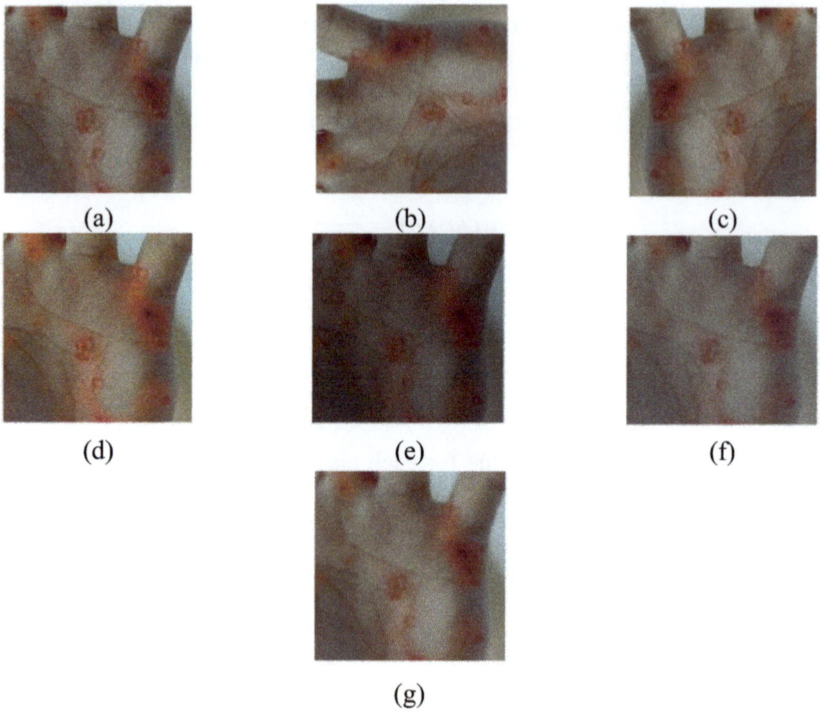

Fig. 10. Example of data augmentation results with (**a**) original image, (**b**) random rotations, (**c**) image re-flexion, (**d**) color saturation, (**e**) brightness, (**f**) contrast, and (**g**) blur.

Data distribution in the train data before and after augmentation can be seen in Table 1.

Table 1. Train data distribution before and after augmentation

Data	Monkeypox	Chickenpox	Measles	Cowpox	HFMD	Healthy
Before	227	60	44	52	128	91
After	300	300	300	300	300	300

3.2 Feature Extraction

The original dataset and the augmented dataset each go into the CNN model to perform feature extraction from each image in the dataset. These extracted features will then become the numerical representation of each image, which is used in the classification method. There are 3 CNN models used, namely DenseNet-121, EfficientNet-B3, and ResNet-50. The result of this feature extraction is a collection of numerical vectors that describe each image in our dataset. These vectors reflect relevant characteristics of the images, such as shape, texture, and pattern. Having this numerical representation allows us to proceed to the next stage. The length of the vectors generated by each model varies, with 50175 for Densenet-121, 75264 for EfficientNet-B3, and 100352 for ResNet-50. An example of the EfficientNet-B3 model extraction results can be seen in Table 2.

Table 2. EfficientNet-B3 Model Extraction Results Against Original Data

Sample Pictures	Representation of Extracted Numbers					
	1	2	...	75262	75263	75264
1	−0.23	−0.21	...	0.98	0.00	0.55
2	−0.26	−0.21	...	−0.24	−0.25	−0.28
⋮			...			
557	−0.19	−0.16	...	−0.28	−0.14	−0.17
558	−0.06	−0.14	...	−0.28	−0.05	0.41

The feature extraction results using Efficinet-B3 resulted in a numerical representation of 75264 numbers. These vectors reflect relevant characteristics of the images, such as shape, texture, and pattern. The extracted numeric representation columns will be the predictor variables in the classification process.

3.3 Classification

After the images go through the extraction process, the data is classified by the Logistic Regression (LR), Random Forest (RF), and Extreme Gradient Boosting (XGB) methods. Training data is used as model training data and will predict testing data as a model performance evaluation. The classification results of the original data can be seen in Table 3.

Table 3. The classification results using original data

Hybrid CNN models	Accuracy (%)	Precision (%)	Recall (%)	F1-Score (%)
DenseNet-121 + LR	59	49	49	49
DenseNet-121 + RF	57	52	37	37
DenseNet-121 + XGB	64	67	49	52
ResNet-50 + LR	81	86	74	78
ResNet-50 + RF	65	87	47	50
ResNet-50 + XGB	74	86	64	70
EfficientNet-B3 + LR	80	83	77	79
EfficientNet-B3 + RF	66	88	50	56
EfficientNet-B3 + XGB	71	78	61	65

Table 3 presents the hybrid CNN model results using the original data. Among the models, the Hybrid DenseNet-121 with RF achieved the lowest accuracy and macro f1-score, with accuracy at 57% and macro f1-score at 37%. The highest accuracy was obtained by the ResNet-50 with LR hybrid model, reaching 81%, while the highest macro f1-score was achieved by EfficientNet-B3 with LR, scoring 78%.

Furthermore, augmentation data is classified. The classification results are shown in Table 4.

Table 4. The classification results using augmented data

Hybrid CNN Models	Accuracy	Precision	Recall	F1-Score
DenseNet-121 + LR	61%	57%	58%	57%
DenseNet-121 + RF	57%	52%	50%	50%
DenseNet-121 + XGB	58%	54%	56%	54%
ResNet-50 + LR	82%	81%	82%	80%
ResNet-50 + RF	68%	70%	71%	70%
ResNet-50 + XGB	78%	81%	80%	80%
EfficientNet-B3 + LR	81%	81%	79%	80%
EfficientNet-B3 + RF	72%	74%	73%	73%
EfficientNet-B3 + XGB	73%	72%	70%	71%

Table 4 presents the hybrid CNN model results using the original data. Among the models, the Hybrid DenseNet-121 with RF achieved the lowest accuracy and macro f1-score, with accuracy at 57% and macro f1-score at 50%. The highest accuracy and macro f1-score was obtained by the ResNet-50 with LR hybrid model, reaching 82% accuracy and 80% macro f1-score. When augmentation was applied, it further enhanced the model's recall but tended to decrease precision. For example, the hybrid ResNet-50 with LR model shows an 8% improvement in recall but decreases precision by 5%. This trade-off highlights the model's improved ability to detect positive cases, albeit with an increase in false positives, which may be significant depending on the application context.

4 Conclusion

From the results and discussion above, several key conclusions can be drawn regarding the performance of hybrid CNN models with machine learning methods in classifying skin disease images. First, data augmentation improved the models' overall performance, as seen in increased accuracy and macro f1-scores across most models. Specifically, ResNet-50 with logistic regression demonstrated the highest accuracy at 82% and 80% of macro F1-score, reflecting the models' ability to accurately classify diverse skin conditions. In contrast, Hybrid DenseNet-121 consistently showed the lowest performance, indicating its limitations for this specific task. These findings suggest that careful selection of CNN architecture and classifiers can significantly impact model effectiveness in medical image classification applications.

To further improve the performance of hybrid CNN models in classifying skin disease images, several steps are recommended. First, increasing the amount of data would likely enhance model accuracy and generalization, as the current dataset is relatively small and may not capture the full diversity of skin conditions. Fine-tuning the models by adjusting hyperparameters could also help optimize performance and prevent overfitting. Overall, the use of hybrid CNN models presents a promising new approach to image classification, offering an innovative solution that combines deep learning's feature extraction capabilities with the precision of machine learning classifiers. Implementing these strategies could lead to more accurate and reliable skin disease classification, contributing to improved diagnostic support in medical applications.

References

1. Srisantyorini, T., Cahyaningsih, N.F.: Analisis kejadian penyakit kulit pada pemulung di tempat pengolahan sampah terpadu (TPST) kelurahan sumur batu kecamatan bantar gebang kota bekasi. J. Kedokt. Dan Kesehat. **15**(2), 135–147 (2019)
2. Trianita, M. N.: *Infeksi Kulit*. Alodokter. https://www.alodokter.com/infeksi-kulit (2023)
3. Thepade, S.D., Bang, S.V., Chaudhari, P.R., Dindorkar, M.R.: Covid19 identification from chest X-Ray images using machine learning classifiers with Glcm features. Electron. Lett. Comput. Vis. Image Anal. **19**(3), 85–97 (2020)
4. Srimenganti, I., Taufik, I., Mulyana, E.: Implementasi algoritma decision Tree(ID3) Untuk Penyakit Campak. 235–242 (2019) https://senter.ee.uinsgd.ac.id/repositori/index.php/prosiding/article/view/senter2018p26
5. Ali, S. N., Ahmed, Md. T., Jahan, T., Paul, J., Sani, S. M. S., Noor, N., Asma, A.N., Hasan, T.: A Web-based Mpox Skin Lesion Detection System Using State-of-the-art Deep Learning Models Considering Racial Diversity. IEEE J. Biomed. Health Inform. , XX, 1. http://arxiv.org/abs/2306.14169 (2023)
6. Soegeng, M.K., Liliana, Noertjahyana, A.: Penerapan convolutional neural network untuk klasifikasi kanker kulit melanoma pada dataset gambar Kulit. Infra, **9**(1) (2021)
7. Saputra, A.D., Hindarto, D., Santoso, H.: Disease classification on rice leaves using DenseNet121, DenseNet169, DenseNet201. Sinkron, **8**(1), 48–55. https://doi.org/10.33395/sinkron.v8i1.11906 (2023)
8. Biau, G., Scornet, E.: A random forest guided tour. TEST **25**(2), 197–227 (2016). https://doi.org/10.1007/s11749-016-0481-7
9. Friedman, J. H.: Greedy function approximation: a gradient boosting machine. Ann. Stat., **29**(5), 1189–1232 (2001). http://www.jstor.org/stable/2699986
10. Bonte, C., Vercauteren, F.: Privacy-preserving logistic regression training. BMC Med. Genomics **11**(S4), 86 (2018). https://doi.org/10.1186/s12920-018-0398-y
11. Reichstein, M., Camps-Valls, G., Stevens, B., Jung, M., Denzler, J., Carvalhais, N., Prabhat.: Deep learning and process understanding for data-driven Earth system science. Nature, **566**(7743), 195–204 (2019). https://doi.org/10.1038/s41586-019-0912-1
12. Ahlawat, S., Choudhary, A.: Hybrid CNN-SVM classifier for handwritten digit recognition. Procedia Comput. Sci. **167**, 2554–2560 (2020). https://doi.org/10.1016/j.procs.2020.03.309
13. Shorten, C., Khoshgoftaar, T.M.: A survey on image data augmentation for deep learning. J. Big Data **6**(1), 60 (2019). https://doi.org/10.1186/s40537-019-0197-0
14. Putra, E.W.S.: Klasifikasi citra menggunakan convolutional neural network (CNN) pada Caltech 101. Jurnal Teknik ITS, **5**(1). https://doi.org/10.12962/j23373539.v5i1.15696 (2016)

15. Celi, L.A., Majumder, M.S., Ordóñez, P., Osorio, J.S., Paik, K.E., Somai, M. (eds.): Leveraging data science for global health. Springer, Cham (2020). https://doi.org/10.1007/978-3-030-47994-7
16. Yusuf, A., Wihandika, R.C., Dewi, C.: Klasifikasi emosi berdasarkan ciri wajah menggunakan convolutional neural network. JPTIIK **3**(11), 10595–10604 (2020)
17. Radwan, N.: Leveraging sparse and dense features for reliable state estimation in urban environments (2019)
18. He, K., Zhang, X., Ren, S., Sun, J.: Deep Residual Learning for Image Recognition. In: *Proceedings of the IEEE Conference on Computer Vision and Pattern Recognition (CVPR)*, 770–778 (2016)
19. Rastogi, A.: *ResNet50*. Medium. (2022). https://blog.devgenius.io/resnet50-6b42934db431
20. Saputra, A.D., Hindarto, D., Rahman, B., Santoso, H.: Comparison of accuracy in detecting tomato leaf disease with GoogleNet VS EfficientNetB3. Sink.: J. Dan Penelit. Tek. Inform. **8**(2), 647–656 (2023)
21. Soleimanipour, A., Azadbakht, M., Rezaei Asl, A.: Cultivar identification of pistachio nuts in bulk mode through EfficientNet deep learning model. J. Food Meas. Charact. **16**(4), 2545–2555 (2022). https://doi.org/10.1007/s11694-022-01367-5
22. Lasloum, T., Alhichri, H., Bazi, Y., Alajlan, N.: SSDAN: multi-source semi-supervised domain adaptation network for remote sensing scene classification. Remote Sensing **13**(19), 3861 (2021). https://doi.org/10.3390/rs13193861
23. Kurt, I., Ture, M., Kurum, A.T.: Comparing performances of logistic regression, classification and regression tree, and neural networks for predicting coronary artery disease. Expert Syst. Appl. **34**(1), 366–374 (2008). https://doi.org/10.1016/j.eswa.2006.09.004
24. Breiman, L.: Random Forests. Machine Learning. Mach. Learn. **45**(1), 5–32 (2001). https://doi.org/10.1023/A:1010933404324
25. Tibshirani, R.J., Efron, B.: (1993). An introduction to the bootstrap. Monographs on statistics and applied probability **57** (1993)
26. Segura, D., Khatib, E.J., Barco, R.: Dynamic packet duplication for industrial URLLC. Sensors **22**(2), 587 (2022). https://doi.org/10.3390/s22020587
27. Wang, Y., Pan, Z., Zheng, J., Qian, L., Li, M.: A hybrid ensemble method for pulsar candidate classification. Astrophys. Space Sci. **364**(8), 139 (2019). https://doi.org/10.1007/s10509-019-3602-4
28. Gu, X., Angelov, P.P., Soares, E.A.: A self-adaptive synthetic over-sampling technique for imbalanced classification. Int. J. Intell. Syst. **35**(6), 923–943 (2020). https://doi.org/10.1002/int.22230

Comparison of ETAS and etasFLP for Fitting Space-Time ETAS Model to Large Earthquake Data

Annisa Auliya Rahman, Achmad Choiruddin(✉), and Hidayatul Khusna

Department of Statistics, Institut Teknologi Sepuluh Nopember, 60111 Surabaya, Indonesia
choiruddin@its.ac.id

Abstract. The space-time Epidemic-Type Aftershock Sequence (space-time ETAS) model is a widely employed analytical tool in the study of earthquake catalogs. It is a semi-parametric model that iteratively performs parametric and nonparametric estimation using maximum likelihood estimation and kernel estimators through a stochastic declustering algorithm. There are two `R` packages that perform such algorithms, although with different estimation techniques: (1) `ETAS` and (2) `etasFLP` packages. Previous work on small to medium datasets has shown that the `etasFLP` outperforms the `ETAS` in terms of parameter estimation and computing time. Nevertheless, there has been no discussion on its performance for fittig large datasets. This study compares the performance of the two `R` packages on several datasets of the Sumatra earthquake catalog. The results show that the `etasFLP` is a more preferred option for large datasets since it performs similarly to the `ETAS` but with faster computation. Application to the Sumatra earthquake indicates that the earthquake risk is higher in areas around the western coastline, especially around Nias Island and the Mentawai Islands.

Keywords: `ETAS` · `etasFLP` · Large dataset · Natural disasters · Space-time ETAS · Sumatra eartquake catalog

1 Introduction

An earthquake is a naturally occurring phenomenon characterized by sudden, rapid vibrations or shocks on the earth's surface. This is caused by the movement or shifting of rock layers within the earth's crust. This movement can be either the result of tectonic plate movement or volcanic activity, which in turn causes seismic waves that cause vibrations on the earth's surface [2]. To facilitate further study and support risk mitigation efforts, it is crucial to record information from each earthquake event in an earthquake catalog.

The space-time Epidemic-Type Aftershock Sequence (space-time ETAS) model is widely recognized as suitable method for earthquake modelling [17,18,28] and has been applied in numerous countries [1,9,13,14,16,25]. The

P. C. Rodrigues et al. (Eds.): ISBIS 2024, 13, pp. 205–218, 2027.
https://doi.org/10.1007/978-3-032-32458-0_15

space-time ETAS model represents a specific variant of the Hawkes point process, which can accommodate earthquake clusters consisting of background event and triggered event [11,20]. The model is based on seismological studies, such as the modified Omori law of aftershock frequency and the Gutenberg-Ritcher law of magnitude frequency [19]. Although the model offers various features, fitting the model and estimating the parameters of the space-time ETAS model is computationally and statistically challenging due to its complexity [4,12].

Since the space-time ETAS is a semi-parametric model, its estimation is done in two stages. The parametric component is estimated using Maximum Likelihood Estimation (MLE), while the nonparametric component is estimated using kernel estimator. Two `R` packages are available for estimating the space-time ETAS model: (1) `ETAS` [12] and (2) `etasFLP` [4]. These packages utilize different techniques for the estimation. The `ETAS` package uses the Davidon-Fletcher-Powell (DFP) algorithm in MLE process, while `etasFLP` employs either the standard Newton-type algorithm or BroydenFletcherGoldfarbShanno (BFGS) algorithm as an alternative [4,12,28]. For non-parametric estimation, both packages use a bivariate isotropic normal kernel function, but with different kernel estimators and bandwidth selection (see Sect. 3.2). Despite its different techniques, the two algorithms is still comparable [12].

As previously stated, the complexity of the space-time ETAS model makes the computational process challenging, such as in terms of convergence and computing time, which is also influenced by the amount of data. Previous work on small to medium datasets using simulated and real data has demonstrated that the `etasFLP` algorithm outperforms the `ETAS` algorithm in terms of parameter estimation as well as computing time [7]. However, there has been no discussion about the performance of the two algorithms on large datasets. Therefore, this study will aim to provide a comparison of the two algorithms on a variety of large datasets, in terms of both model performance and computing time. This study will utilize actual earthquake data from Sumatra, Indonesia, rather than simulated data, considering the long computing times that may be encountered.

The structure of the rest of the paper is organized as follows. Section 2 outlines the dataset used in this study, and Sect. 3 presents the space-time ETAS model along with the estimation methods using `ETAS` and `etasFLP`. The comparison of `ETAS` and `etasFLP` on several datasets explained in Sect. 4 and the conclusion presented in Sect. 5.

2 Dataset

This study applies the `ETAS` and `etasFLP` packages to earthquakes in Sumatra, Indonesia, a region with significant seismic activity [2]. Several factors contribute to Sumatra's high earthquake frequency, including the presence of active fault lines like the Sumatra Fault System (SFS) and Mentawai Fault System (MFS), as well as numerous volcanoes along the mainland [3,15,23].

The data for this study come from the United States Geological Survey (USGS), focusing on the weakest earthquakes (magnitude ≥ 4 and focal depth <70 km), as these earthquakes can be destructive, in Sumatra region (6.125°S – 5.806°N and 95.010°E – 108.545°E).

To evaluate and compare the performance of the two packages, the data set was divided according to time range and earthquake count as follows.

1. Dataset 1 is a catalog of Sumatra earthquakes during 2006–2023, with 5057 earthquake events.
2. Dataset 2 is a catalog of earthquakes in Sumatra during 1993–2023, with a total of 8673 earthquake events.

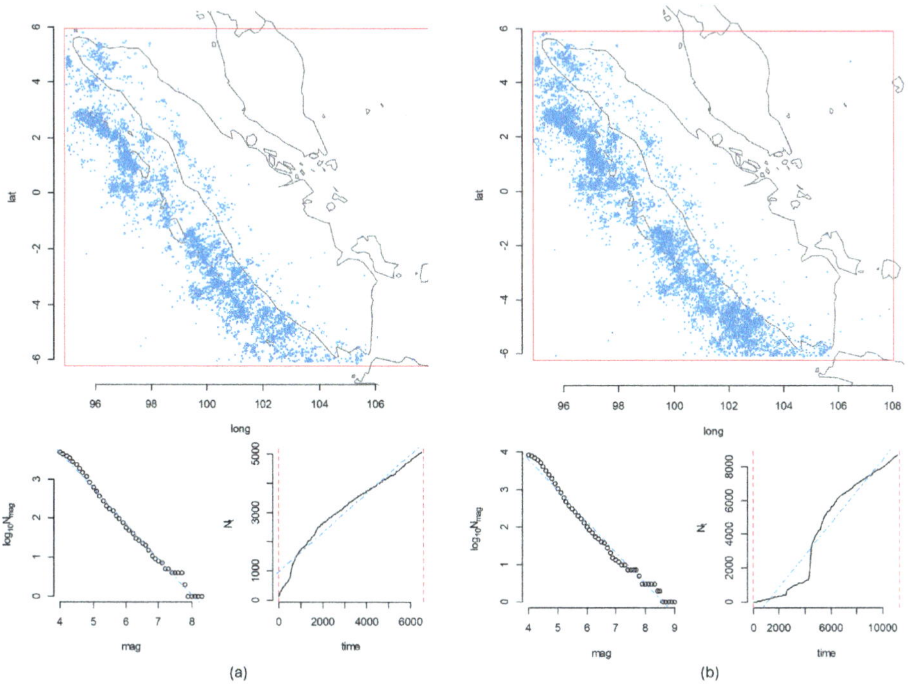

Fig. 1. Earthquake distribution (top); logarithm of frequency based on magnitude (bottom-left); cumulative frequency over time (bottom-right) for Sumatra earthquakes occurring during (**a**) 2006–2023 and (**b**) 1993–2023.

The distribution of earthquake occurrence in each dataset is shown in Fig. 1. The earthquake events in each dataset are concentrated in the western part of Sumatra, particularly around the small islands to the west. Completeness and stationarity over time are also examined to ensure that the algorithm converges [27,28] and to idenitify whether the earthquake patterns observed in Sumatra adhere to the Gutenberg-Richter law [12,19]. Figure 1 (bottom-left) illustrates a linear relationship between magnitude and the logarithm of the number of earthquakes, which is consistent with the Gutenberg-Richter law and completeness. Figure 2 (bottom-right) depicts a linear trend, indicating that earthquake occurrence is stationary in time for Dataset 1, but not for Dataset 2. This is to be expected, as Sumatra is known for its large earthquakes. A notable example is the Aceh earthquake of December 26, 2004, which had a magnitude of 9.1 M_w. The larger the magnitude, the more aftershocks are generated. Consequently, the occurrence of earthquakes in Sumatra is likely to exhibit non-stationary temporal patterns. Nevertheless, it is assumed throughout this study that all data sets are stationary.

3 Space-Time ETAS Model and Its Estimation Technique

3.1 Space-Time ETAS Model

The space-time ETAS model is a self-exciting point process, or to be more precise, a special form of the Hawkes process. The events are divided into separate processes: the background event of the cluster center and the triggered events inside each cluster. Each triggered events may then trigger further events [20]. The process can be depicted as in Fig. 2.

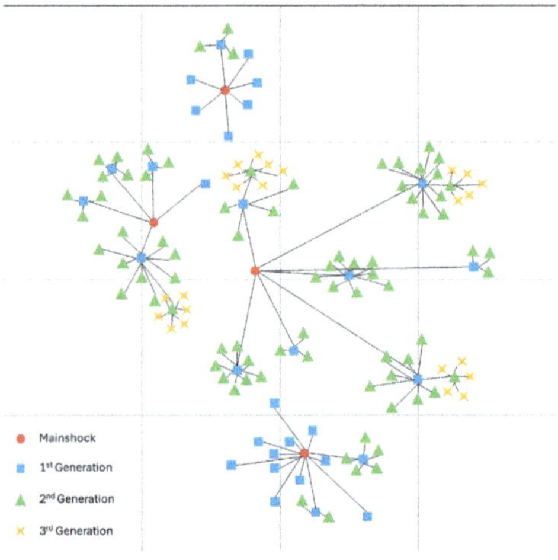

Fig. 2. Illustration of self-exciting point process with three generations.

Earthquake catalogs typically contains: time of occurrence (t), latitude (x) and longitude (y) of the epicenter, and magnitude (m); $(t_i, x_i, y_i, m_i; i = 1, 2, ..., n)$ on $R \times R^2 \times [m_0, \infty)$ [19]. Consider a space-time point process, denoted by $\mathbf{X}$, which occurs within a domain $Z = S \times T$. Here, T represents the time domain, while S denotes the two-dimensional space. The conditional intensity function indicates the probability of an earthquake within a given region and at a specific time, given the historical event $\mathcal{H}_t$ up to time t [12]. It is expressed as follows

$$\rho(t, x, y|\mathcal{H}_t)dtdxdy \approx P(\mathbf{X} \cap [t, t+dt] \times [x, x+dx] \times [y, y+dy] \neq \emptyset|\mathcal{H}_t).$$

Developed based on seismological laws and its statistical features, the space-time ETAS model has a conditional intensity function defined as [28]

$$\rho_{\beta,\boldsymbol{\theta}}(t, x, y, m|\mathcal{H}_t) = u_\beta(m)\lambda_{\boldsymbol{\theta}}(t, x, y|\mathcal{H}_t), \tag{1}$$

$u_\beta(m)$ is the probability density function for earthquake magnitude, applies the Gutenberg-Richter law, whereas $\lambda_{\boldsymbol{\theta}}(t, x, y|\mathcal{H}_t)$ describes background and aftershock rates, respectively.

$$u_\beta(m) = \beta \exp(-\beta(m - m_0)); \beta > 0, \tag{2}$$

$$\lambda_{\boldsymbol{\theta}}(t, x, y|\mathcal{H}_t) = \tilde{v}(x, y) + \sum_{i;t_i<t} \tau_i(t, x, y). \tag{3}$$

In Eqs. (2)–(3), m_0 denotes magnitude threshold, while the parameter β is defined as a parameter relating the magnitude of earthquakes to their frequency. The background rate, represented by the function $\tilde{v}(x, y) = \mu v(x, y)$, is stationary in time, μ is a parameter, and $\tau(t, x, y)$ is the aftershock rate that is composed of the several characteristics. The ETAS and etasFLP have distinct characteristics, yet still comparable. The $\tau(t, x, y)$ in ETAS expresses as (4) and encompasses the following characteristics [12].

$$\tau_i(t, x, y) = \zeta_{A,\alpha}(m_i)h_{c,p}(t - t_i)g_{d,\gamma,q}(x - x_i; y - y_i; m_i), \tag{4}$$

1. The expected number of aftershocks for an event with magnitude m_i, denoted as $\zeta_{A,\alpha}(m_i)$, is defined as

$$\zeta_{A,\alpha}(m_i) = A \exp[\alpha(m_i - m_0)],$$

   with $A, \alpha > 0$ are parameters that indicates the efficiency of an earthquake magnitude in generating aftershocks.
2. The function $h_{c,p}(t-t_i)$ is a temporal rate, represents the probability function of the time of occurrence of aftershocks resulting from the earthquake that occurred at time t_i. This function considers the modified Omori law and is expressed as [12,19]

$$h_{c,p}(t - t_i) = \frac{p-1}{c}\left(1 + \frac{t - t_i}{c}\right)^{-p}.$$

   The parameters of the modified Omori law are represented by $c > 0$ and $p > 1$, where p indicates the aftershock decay rate.

3. The function $g_{d,\gamma,q}(x-x_i;y-y_i;m_i)$ is a spatial rate, represents the aftershock location probability function produced by an earthquake of magnitude m_i at location (x_i, y_i).

$$g_{d,\gamma,q}(x-x_i;y-y_i;m_i) = \frac{q-1}{\pi d\exp(\gamma(m_i-m_0))}\left(1+\frac{(x-x_i)^2+(y-y_i)^2}{d\exp(\gamma(m_i-m_0))}\right)^{-q},$$

with $d, \gamma > 0$ and $q > 1$ is parameters related to the spatial influence of the mainshock.

Whereas, $\tau_i(t,x,y)$ (3) in `etasFLP` algorithm defined by [4]

$$\tau_i(t,x,y) = h(t-t_i|m_i)g(x-x_i;y-y_i;m_i).$$

The temporal rate is described by $h(t-t_i|m_i)$, while the spatial rate is explained by $g(x-x_i;y-y_i;m_i)$. These rates are expressed as follows

$$\tau_i(t,x,y) = \frac{\kappa_0\exp(\alpha-\gamma)(m_i-m_0)}{(c+t-t_i)^p}\left(d+\frac{(x-x_i)^2+(y-y_i)^2}{\exp(\gamma(m_i-m_0))}\right)^{-q}, \quad (5)$$

which is equivalent to (4) if κ_0 is reparameterized to [12]

$$\kappa_0 = \frac{1}{\pi}A(p-1)c^{p-1}(q-1)d^{q-1}. \quad (6)$$

The parametric components in the space-time ETAS model, namely β and $\boldsymbol{\theta} = (\mu, A, \alpha, c, p, d, \gamma, q)^\top$ (for `ETAS`) or $\boldsymbol{\theta} = (\mu, \kappa_0, \alpha, c, p, d, \gamma, q)^\top$ (for `etasFLP`), as well as the non-parametric component $v(x, y)$, will be estimated separately. Although both algorithms employ distinct techniques, in general, both `ETAS` and `etasFLP` employ a comparable algorithm for parameter estimation, namely stochastic declustering. Further explanations on parameter estimation with both algorithms can be found in Sect. 3.2.

3.2 Stochastic Declustering Algorithm

The parametric components, β and $\boldsymbol{\theta}$, are estimated by the MLE method using the log-likelihood function as follows [12,18]

$$\ell(\beta,\boldsymbol{\theta}|\mathcal{H}_t) = \sum_{i=1}^{n}\log\rho_{\beta,\boldsymbol{\theta}}(t_i,x_i,y_i,m_i|\mathcal{H}_t) - \int_{m_0}^{\infty}\int_T\iint_S \rho_{\beta,\boldsymbol{\theta}}(t,x,y,m|\mathcal{H}_t)dxdydtdm,$$

where n denotes the number of earthquake events. Given that (2) and (3) are independent and $\int_{m_0}^{\infty} u_\beta(m)dm = 1$, the log-likelihood is expressed as follows [12,28]

$$\ell(\beta,\boldsymbol{\theta}|\mathcal{H}_t) = \ell_1(\beta|\mathcal{H}_t) + \ell_2(\boldsymbol{\theta}|\mathcal{H}_t),$$

where

$$\ell_1(\beta|\mathcal{H}_t) = \sum_{i=1}^{n}\log u_\beta(m_i),$$

and

$$\ell_2(\boldsymbol{\theta}|\mathcal{H}_t) = \sum_{i=1}^{n} \log(\lambda_{\boldsymbol{\theta}}(t_i, x_i, y_i|\mathcal{H}_{t_i})) - \int_T \iint_S \lambda_{\boldsymbol{\theta}}(t, x, y|\mathcal{H}_t)dxdydt. \quad (7)$$

This results in a closed-form solution for β

$$\hat{\beta} = \frac{n}{\sum_{i=1}^{n}(m_i - m_0)}. \quad (8)$$

However, $\ell_2(\boldsymbol{\theta}|\mathcal{H}_t)$ has a complex function, necessitating the use of approximation and numerical method to estimate $\boldsymbol{\theta}$. The integral value in (7) will be initially approximated using radial partitioning and a coordinate transformation from Cartesian coordinates to polar coordinates (details on [4,12]), then proceed by numerical methods. The `ETAS` utilizes a Davidon-Fletcher-Powell (DFP) algorithm [12], whereas the `etasFLP` employs either a standard Newton-type algorithm or Broyden-Fletcher-Goldfarb-Shanno (BFGS) algorithm [4].

For the non-parametric function $v(x, y)$, both algorithm using kernel estimator with an isotropic bivariate normal kernel function [26], but with different kernel estimator and bandwidth selection. The `ETAS` employs an adaptive bandwidth that is selected based on the nearest neighbor distance [12], whereas the `etasFLP` utilizes a fixed bandwidth that is determined by the Forward Likelihood Predictive (FLP) approach [4].

The kernel estimator used in the `ETAS` algorithm is expressed as follows [12, 28]

$$\hat{v}(x, y) = \frac{1}{|T|}\sum_{i=1}^{n} w_i K(x - x_i, y - y_i; b_i) \quad (9)$$

where $|T|$ represents the length of the time period over which earthquake events are observed and w_i is the probability that event i is a background event, determined by the following function

$$w_i = \frac{\hat{\mu}\hat{v}(x_i, y_i)}{\lambda_{\hat{\boldsymbol{\theta}}}(t_i, x_i, y_i, m_i|\mathcal{H}_{t_i})}, \quad (10)$$

and $K(x, y; b)$ is a isotropic bivariate normal kernel function with an adaptive bandwidth b defined by

$$K(x, y; b_i) = \frac{1}{2\pi {b_i}^2} \exp\left(-\frac{1}{2{b_i}^2}\left(x^2 + y^2\right)\right).$$

The bandwidth b is selected based on the following function

$$b_i = \max\left(b_{\min}, r(i, n_p)\right),$$

where b_{min} is the bandwidth threshold to prevent bandwidth values that are too small and $r(i, n_p)$ is the distance between earthquake i and n_p–th nearby events.

Instead of (9), the `etasFLP` algorithm use the the kernel estimator defined as below [4]

$$\hat{v}(x,y) = \frac{\sum_{i=1}^{n} w_i K(x - x_i, y - y_i; \boldsymbol{B})}{\sum_{i=1}^{n} w_i}, \tag{11}$$

where w_i given by (10) and $K(x,y;\boldsymbol{B})$ is the isotropic bivariate normal kernel with two fixed bandwidths $\boldsymbol{b} = (b_x, b_y)$ as follows [24,26],

$$K(x,y;\boldsymbol{B}) = (2\pi)^{-1}|\boldsymbol{B}|^{-1/2} \exp\left(-\frac{1}{2}\begin{bmatrix}x\\y\end{bmatrix}^{\top} \boldsymbol{B}^{-1}\begin{bmatrix}x\\y\end{bmatrix}\right) \tag{12}$$

where $\boldsymbol{B}$ is a symmetric positive definite 2×2 matrix of bandwidth with zero elements of non-diagonal components. The bandwidths in the `etasFLP` are selected using the FLP approach (see [4]).

In the stochastic declustering algorithm, the parametric and non-parametric estimation processes are repeated iteratively until convergence is achieved. The parameter estimation steps of the space-time ETAS model using the stochastic declustering algorithm are generally summarized in Algorithm 1.

Algorithm 1 Stochastic declustering algorithm for estimating $\boldsymbol{\theta}$ and $u(x,y)$

1. Initialization
   - $\hat{\boldsymbol{\theta}}^{(0)}$.
   - $\hat{u}^{(0)}(x_i, y_i); i = 1, ..., n$.
   - The stopping criteria.
2. Estimating $\boldsymbol{\theta}$
   - Estimate the value of the integral in (7) using radial partitioning and transformation to polar coordinates [4,12].
   - Find $\hat{\boldsymbol{\theta}}^{(v)}$ by minimizing $E(\boldsymbol{\theta}) = -l_2(\boldsymbol{\theta}|\mathcal{H}_t)$ using DFP algorithm for `ETAS` and either a standard Newton-type or BFGS algorithm for `etasFLP`.
3. Estimating $v(x,y)$
   - Compute w_i using (10).
   - Revise the estimation of background intensity using (9) for `ETAS` or (11) for `etasFLP`, incorporating the estimated weights w_i and the chosen bandwidth.
4. Repeat steps 2 and 3 until the stopping criteria are satisfied.

---

4 Application of `ETAS` and `etasFLP`

4.1 Model Comparison

The two `R` packages applied to Dataset 1 and 2 were evaluated according to three criteria: parameter estimation, number of iterations, and computing time required to achieve convergence. In addition, Akaike Information Criterion (AIC) was used to assess model performance. The AIC value is calculated according to the following equation

$$\text{AIC}(\hat{\boldsymbol{\theta}}, df) = -2\ell_2(\hat{\boldsymbol{\theta}}|\mathcal{H}_t) + 2df$$

where $\ell_2(\hat{\boldsymbol{\theta}}|\mathcal{H}_t)$ is determined by (7) evaluated at $\hat{\boldsymbol{\theta}}$ and $df = 8 + tr(\mathbf{Q})$ represents the degrees of freedom, which include the number of parameters in $\hat{\boldsymbol{\theta}}$ and the complexity of the non-parametric kernel estimates. Here, $tr(\mathbf{Q}) = (2\pi)^{-1}\sum_i^n(b_i)^{-1}$ for the ETAS and $tr(\mathbf{Q}) = n(2\pi)^{-1}(b_x + b_y)^{-1}$ for the etasFLP [7].

All models use the same initial parameter value, follows Ogata [18]. However, since both packages operate within distinct spatial units and spatial unit transformations, the initial parameters of those containing spatial units are modified, resulting in the following adjustments: $\hat{\boldsymbol{\theta}}^{(0)} = (1, 0.01, 1, 0.01, 1.3, 10, 1, 2)^\top$. However, in Dataset 2, the ETAS algorithm did not converge. Therefore, the initial parameters for Dataset 2 is adjusted based on spatial unit transformation of ETAS until the results are able to converge. This results $\hat{\boldsymbol{\theta}}^{(0)} = (1, 0.01, 1, 0.01, 1.3, 123.45, 1, 2)^\top$ as initial parameters for Dataset 2.

Based on Table 1, it is observed that the standard error values for the parameters in etasFLP are generally larger than those in ETAS. This indicates that the parameter estimates from etasFLP have larger uncertainties compared to ETAS. Furthermore, as the two algorithms employ different coordinate transformations, the parameters containing spatial units, such as $\hat{\mu}, \hat{\kappa_0}, \hat{A}$ and $\hat{d}$, are not directly comparable. Nevertheless, the parameter estimates of c and q between the two algorithms exhibit markedly disparate values. While comparable estimation outcomes are observed for the parameters of $\hat{p}, \hat{\alpha}$, and γ. Concurrently, the parameter estimates for p, α, γ from both algorithms result in comparable estimation outcomes. The similarity of the parameter estimation results suggests that for some parameters, the two algorithms yield consistent results despite the differences in their approaches. The discrepancies in parameter estimates between the two algorithms may be due to differences in spatial unit transformations and estimation techniques employed by the two algorithms.

In addition to the parameter estimation results, we also compare their performance based on computing time, $-\ell_2(\hat{\boldsymbol{\theta}}|\mathcal{H}_t)$, and $\text{AIC}(\hat{\boldsymbol{\theta}}, df)$, as shown in Table 2. Table 2 reports that etasFLP has a higher maximum negative likelihood value, which is 5.69% larger for Dataset 1 and 6.68% larger for Dataset 2 than ETAS. This discrepancy might be due to the limitation of the etasFLP in reaching the maximum negative likelihood. The pursuit of the maximum negative likelihood will inevitably result in the selection of a bandwidth that is too small, thereby leading to the issue of under-smoothing. Consequently, we also undertake a comparison of the AIC in order to account for the accuracy and complexity of the model. The ETAS model exhibits a higher likelihood, yet it also considers a more complex model with an adaptive bandwidth, resulting in a higher number of degrees of freedom. The AIC values for ETAS and etasFLP

Table 1. Parameter estimates using ETAS and etasFLP algorithm

Estimate (SE)	Dataset 1 ETAS	Dataset 1 etasFLP	Dataset 2 ETAS	Dataset 2 etasFLP
$\hat{\mu}$	1.004 (0.001)	0.510 (0.011)	1.005 (0.008)	0.259 (0.007)
$\hat{A}$	0.174 (0.025)	0.008* (–)	1.803 (0.102)	0.050* (–)
$\hat{\kappa_0}$	0.800* (–)	0.680 (0.750)	0.706* (–)	1.143 (0.703)
$\hat{c}$	0.013 (0.038)	3.395 (0.409)	0.012 (0.027)	2.330 (0.160)
$\hat{p}$	1.089 (0.003)	1.473 (0.047)	1.014 (0.002)	1.250 (0.016)
$\hat{\alpha}$	1.518 (0.005)	1.580 (0.034)	1.181 (0.005)	1.192 (0.026)
$\hat{\gamma}$	0.807 (0.017)	1.182 (0.050)	0.881 (0.010)	1.058 (0.033)
$\hat{d}$	81.626 (0.036)	13.069 (2.737)	70.121 (0.023)	20.815 (2.698)
$\hat{q}$	2.202 (0.013)	2.968 (0.262)	2.055 (0.007)	2.631 (0.128)

*The value is converted using (6)

are comparable, although etasFLP exhibits a slightly higher AIC value of 4.92% for Dataset 1 and 5.73% for Dataset 2.

Furthermore, etasFLP is observed to be more efficient in terms of computing time. The results indicate that the computating time of etasFLP is 4.96% faster for Dataset 1 and 18.65% faster for Dataset 2 compared to that of the ETAS. Furthermore, an examination of the relationship between time and the number of events reveals that Dataset 1 is stationary in time, while Dataset 2 is not (see Sect. 2). This could be the reason for the slower computation time of both algorithms, besides the number of data. However, the etasFLP algorithm is generally better in handling this issue than the ETAS algorithm. The results indicate that etasFLP is a more preferable choice for large datasets, when fast computing time is required and the AIC value remains comparable to that of ETAS. This finding aligns with the conclusions of the previous study by Choiruddin et al. [7] and Jalilian [12].

4.2 Best Model Interpretation

Given that the etasFLP approach is the preferred methodology, we consider the interpretation of the space-time ETAS model with etasFLP on Dataset 2 with

Table 2. Computing time (in minutes), $-l_2(\hat{\boldsymbol{\theta}}|\mathcal{H}_t)$, and AIC($\hat{\boldsymbol{\theta}}, df$) of Sumatran earthquake obtained from `ETAS` and `etasFLP` algorithms

Dataset	Method	Computing time (mins)	$-l_2(\hat{\boldsymbol{\theta}}\|\mathcal{H}_t)$	AIC($\hat{\boldsymbol{\theta}}, df$)
`ETAS`	`ETAS`	192.98	63051.78	127400.00
	`etasFLP`	183.40	66632.00	133671.70
`ETAS`	`ETAS`	692.75	101941.30	206371.90
	`etasFLP`	563.53	108688.90	218203.60

the objective of developing a model that can accommodate observations with a longer temporal span. Nevertheless, the results of parameter estimation in Dataset 1 and 2 are quite similar, except for $\hat{\mu}, \hat{\kappa_0}, \hat{d}$. The estimated value of μ, 0.259, indicates that background earthquakes occur every 4 days on Sumatra. The mainshock is estimated to affect spatially up to 20.815 km^2 ($\hat{d}$). The $\hat{p}$ is greater than 1, indicating the stationary nature of the models. The values of $\hat{p}$ and $\hat{q}$ show that $\hat{q}$ is higher, indicating that temporal contagion is more persistent than spatial contagion in the Sumatra earthquakes. A lower $\hat{p}$ corresponds to less decay over time compared to space. The parameters $\hat{\alpha} = 1.192$ and $\hat{\gamma} = 1.058$ reflect the magnitude's efficiency in generating aftershocks. The parameter $\hat{\kappa_0}$, controlling the overall triggering intensity, is estimated to be about 1.143 events per day per km^2. These results can also be seen in Fig. 3.

As depicted in Fig. 3, the estimated background intensity is uniformly distributed along the western coast of Sumatra Island and parts of the mainland. The most intense areas are found near Nias Island. The estimated triggered intensity also reaches its highest levels around Nias Island and Mentawai Island. Typically, the northwestern region of Sumatra shows higher earthquake intensity, especially near Nias Island. These observations match the earthquake data primarily recorded along Sumatra Island's western coast. The area is located between an active subduction zone and the Mentawai Fault System (MFS), which heightens earthquake risks.

Moreover, the stochastic declustering algorithm is capable of estimating the probability of an event being a background event, as indicated by (10). Earthquake events with a probability greater than 0.95 are identified as mainshocks, as depicted in Fig. 4. The figure illustrates that the majority of earthquake events in Sumatra are derived events, with only 4.42% classified as background events. Aftershocks occur more frequently on small islands located to the west of Sumatra.

5 Conclusion

This paper compares the performance of `ETAS` and `etasFLP` on large datasets by applying them to the Sumatra earthquake catalog. The results show that `etasFLP` is the better choice for large datasets, with significantly faster computing and AIC values that remain comparable to `ETAS`, although with parameter

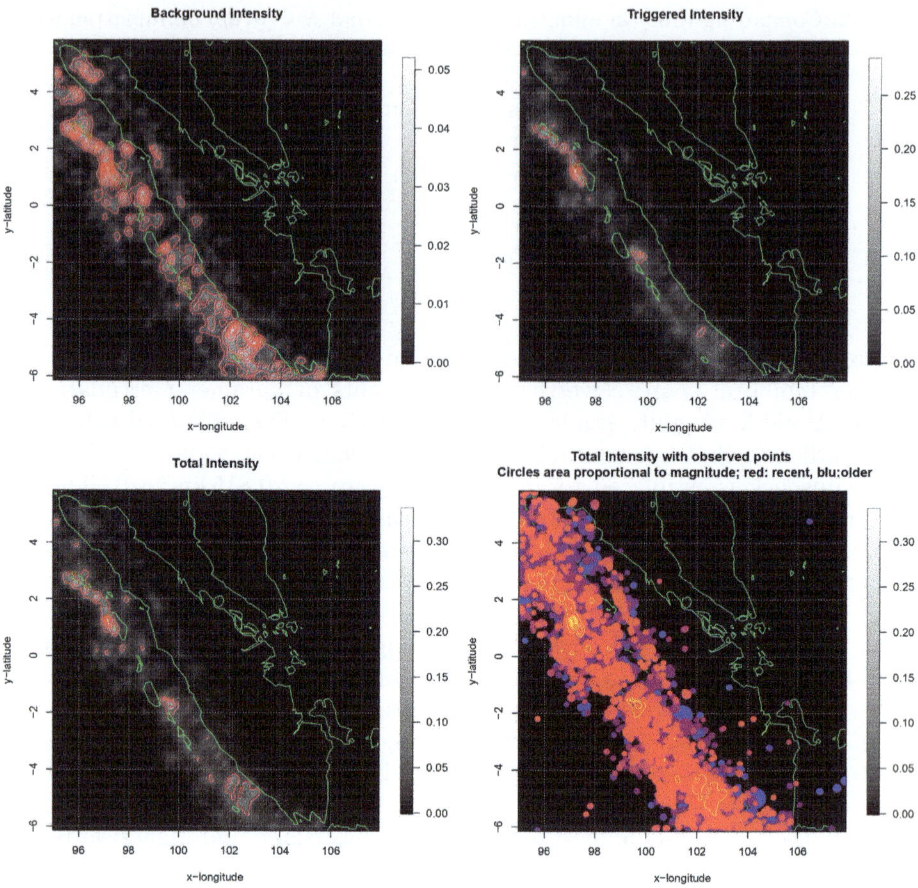

Fig. 3. Plot of estimated background intensity (top-left), triggered intensity (top-right), total intensity (bottom-left), total intensity with actual earthquake point (bottom-right) for Sumatra earthquake catalogue (1993–2023).

estimation results that are not as good as `ETAS` for some parameters. Moreover, with the same initial value, `etasFLP` has better convergence ability. We observe that time contagion has a greater persistence compared to space contagion in the case of Sumatra earthquakes. The highest earthquake intensities occur on Nias Island and Mentawai Islands.

It is important to note that neither algorithm ensures convergence and both are reliant on the initial estimates [10,22]. It may be beneficial to investigate the appropriate initial estimates, as exemplified by Schoenberg [21] for the earlier version of the ETAS model. Moreover, since the space-time ETAS model is primarily based on earthquake catalog data, we may in the future develop conditional intensity models that can incorporate geological factors such as faulting, subduction, and volcanoes. The ideas developed for Cox point processes with

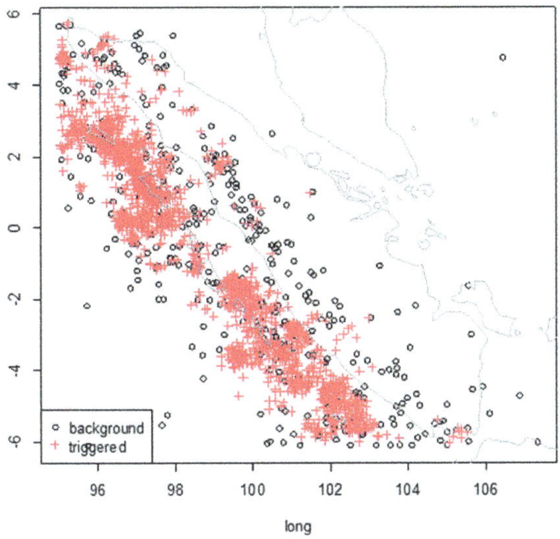

Fig. 4. Estimated background and triggered events of the Sumatran earthquake during 1993–2023 using stochastic declustering.

covariates [5,6,8] can be the basis for this development. Comparing several different spatial and temporal rate functions can also be done to improve the model, as was done by Ogata [18].

Acknowledgement. The authors gratefully acknowledge financial support from the Institut Teknologi Sepuluh Nopember for this work, under project scheme of the Publication Writing and IPR Incentive Program (PPHKI) 2024. We also thank the reviewers for their constructive comments.

References

1. Andreas, C., Choiruddin, A., Prastyo, D.D.: Modeling earthquake catalog in Sumatra by space-time epidemic-type aftershock sequences model: Combining Davidon-Fletcher-Powell and stochastic declustering algorithms. In: The International Conference on Data Science and Emerging Technologies, pp. 335–351. Springer (2023)
2. BMKG: Katalog gempabumi Indonesia: Relokasi hiposenter dan implikasi tektonik. Badan Meteorologi, Klimatologi, dan Geofisika (BMKG), Indonesia (2018)
3. Bradley, K.E., Feng, L., Hill, E.M., Natawidjaja, D., Sieh, K.: Implications of the diffuse deformation of the Indian Ocean lithosphere for slip partitioning of oblique plate convergence in Sumatra. J. Geophys. Res. Solid Earth **122**(1), 572–591 (2017)
4. Chiodi, M., Adelfio, G.: Mixed non-parametric and parametric estimation techniques in R package etasFLP for earthquakes' description. J. Stat. Softw. **76**, 1–29 (2017)
5. Choiruddin, A., Aisah, Trisnisa, F., Iriawan, N.: Quantifying the effect of geological factors on distribution of earthquake occurrences by inhomogeneous Cox processes. Pure Appl. Geophys. **178**(5), 1579–1592 (2021)

6. Choiruddin, A., Coeurjolly, J.F., Letué, F.: Adaptive lasso and Dantzig selector for spatial point processes intensity estimation. Bernoulli **29**(3), 1849–1876 (2023)
7. Choiruddin, A., Rahman, A.A., Andreas, C.: Algorithms for fitting the space-time etas model to earthquake catalog data: a comparative study. J. Agric. Biol. Environ. Stat. 1–18 (2024)
8. Choiruddin, A., Yuni Susanto, T., Husain, A., Mega Kartikasari, Y.: kppmenet: combining the kppm and elastic net regularization for inhomogeneous cox point process with correlated covariates. J. Appl. Stat. **51**(5), 993–1006 (2024)
9. Davoudi, N., Tavakoli, H.R., Zare, M., Jalilian, A.: Aftershock probabilistic seismic hazard analysis for Bushehr province in Iran using ETAS model. Nat. Hazards **100**, 1159–1170 (2020)
10. Dennis, Jr., J.E., Schnabel, R.B.: Numerical Methods for Unconstrained Optimization and Nonlinear Equations. SIAM (1996)
11. González, J.A., Rodríguez-Cortés, F.J., Cronie, O., Mateu, J.: Spatio-temporal point process statistics: a review. Spatial Stat. **18**, 505–544 (2016)
12. Jalilian, A.: ETAS: an R package for fitting the space-time ETAS model to earthquake data. J. Stat. Softw. **88**, 1–39 (2019)
13. Jiang, C.S., Zhuang, J.C.: Evaluation of background seismicity and potential source zones of strong earthquakes in the Sichuan-Yunan region based on the space-time ETAS model. Chin. J. Geophys. **53**(2), 305–317 (2010)
14. Lombardi, A.M.: The epistemic and aleatory uncertainties of the ETAS-type models: an application to the Central Italy seismicity. Sci. Rep. **7**(1), 11812 (2017)
15. McCaffrey, R.: The tectonic framework of the Sumatran subduction zone. Annu. Rev. Earth Planet. Sci. **37**, 345–366 (2009)
16. Nicolis, O., Chiodi, M., Adelfio, G.: Windowed ETAS models with application to the Chilean seismic catalogs. Spatial Stat. **14**, 151–165 (2015)
17. Ogata, Y.: Statistical models for earthquake occurrences and residual analysis for point processes. J. Am. Stat. Assoc. **83**(401), 9–27 (1988)
18. Ogata, Y.: Space-time point-process models for earthquake occurrences. Ann. Inst. Stat. Math. **50**, 379–402 (1998)
19. Ogata, Y.: Statistics of earthquake activity: models and methods for earthquake predictability studies. Annu. Rev. Earth Planet. Sci. **45**, 497–527 (2017)
20. Reinhart, A.: A review of self-exciting spatio-temporal point processes and their applications. Stat. Sci. **33**(3), 299–318 (2018)
21. Schoenberg, F.P.: Facilitated estimation of etas. Bull. Seismol. Soc. Am. **103**(1), 601–605 (2013)
22. Shanno, D.F.: Conditioning of quasi-newton methods for function minimization. Math. Comput. **24**(111), 647–656 (1970)
23. Sieh, K., Natawidjaja, D.: Neotectonics of the Sumatran fault, Indonesia. J. Geophys. Res. Solid Earth **105**(B12), 28295–28326 (2000)
24. Silverman, B.W.: Density Estimation for Statistics and Data Analysis. Routledge (2018)
25. Ueda, T., Kato, A.: Seasonal variations in crustal seismicity in San-in district, Southwest Japan. Geophys. Res. Lett. **46**(6), 3172–3179 (2019)
26. Wand, M.P., Jones, M.C., et al.: Multivariate plug-in bandwidth selection. Comput. Stat. **9**(2), 97–116 (1994)
27. Zhuang, J.: Next-day earthquake forecasts for the Japan region generated by the ETAS model. Earth Planets Space **63**(3), 207–216 (2011)
28. Zhuang, J., Ogata, Y., Vere-Jones, D.: Stochastic declustering of space-time earthquake occurrences. J. Am. Stat. Assoc. **97**(458), 369–380 (2002)

Forecasting Temperature Variations in Surakarta Using Semiparametric Penalized Fourier Series Estimator Based on Cosinus Function

Ihsan Fathoni Amri[1,4], Nur Chamidah[2,3](✉), and Toha Saifudin[2,3]

[1] Faculty of Science and Technology, Doctoral Study Program of Mathematics and Natural Sciences, Airlangga University, Surabaya, Indonesia
[2] Departement of Mathematics, Faculty of Science and Technology, Airlangga University, Surabaya, Indonesia
nur-c@fst.unair.ac.id
[3] Faculty of Science and Technology, Research Group of Statistical Modeling in Life Science, Airlangga University, Surabaya, Indonesia
[4] Department of Data Science, Faculty of Science and Agriculture, Universitas Muhammadiyah Semarang, Semarang, Indonesia

Abstract. This study addresses the challenge of accurately modeling temperature trends in urban settings, using a semiparametric approach that combines parametric and nonparametric methods to enhance model flexibility. A Penalized Fourier Series estimator was employed to capture temperature variations in Surakarta, based on data collected from January 1, 2024, to April 9, 2024. By setting the Fourier coefficient to 1, the model adopts a linear representation that balances simplicity and accuracy. The approach achieved a high prediction accuracy, with a Mean Absolute Percentage Error (MAPE) of 5.381 and a Generalized Cross Validation (GCV) score of 0.6044918, suggesting a 94.619% precision level. These findings demonstrate the effectiveness of the proposed method for climate adaptation planning. Future research could explore extending the model to other climatic variables or different regions to further validate its applicability.

Keywords: Temperature · Semiparametric model · Penalized Fourier Series · Forecasting

1 Introduction

Surakarta, as one of the central economic cities in Central Java, faces increasing challenges due to climate change affecting the city's temperature patterns [1]. Accurate analysis of temperature trends in Surakarta is critical to anticipate and manage potential environmental impacts [2]. The semiparametric method used in this study allows for greater flexibility in modeling temperature data, integrating both parametric and non-parametric components [3]. The parametric component in this analysis is approached

P. C. Rodrigues et al. (Eds.): ISBIS 2024, 13, pp. 219–231, 2027.
https://doi.org/10.1007/978-3-032-32458-0_16

by using temperature data from previous periods, enabling the model to leverage historical information in predicting future trends. Meanwhile, the nonparametric component is approached by considering time factors, covering changes that occur seasonally or annually which can affect temperature.

In the context of semiparametric methods, various types of estimators such as kernel estimators, local linear estimators, local polynomial estimators, spline estimators, Fourier series, and so on can be applied to address different aspects of the data model [4]. These estimators are typically chosen based on the characteristics of the data and the objectives of the analysis. One of the most common is the spline estimator, which is highly effective for modeling data with strong nonlinear patterns and requires flexibility in curve formation [5]. The kernel estimator is another option, used for smoothing data and assisting in identifying trends within noisy data [6]. The Fourier series estimator, utilized in this study, is particularly suitable for data exhibiting periodic or seasonal patterns, decomposing components that regularly recur over time [7]. Each of these estimators has its own strengths and limitations, allowing researchers to tailor the analysis based on the specific needs of the data and the research questions faced. Additionally, the semiparametric approach also allows for the combination of these estimators [8].

The user of Fourier series estimators in semiparametric methods provides advantages in analyzing complex temperature patterns, such as the fluctuations occurring in Surakarta [9]. By extracting seasonal components and trends from temperature data, this estimator enriches the analysis by capturing trigonometric polynomial concepts, revealing dynamics that may not be detected through conventional methods [10]. This is crucial as it can assist in climate adaptation planning and natural resource management. For example, extreme events such as heatwaves or sudden cold spells can have serious impacts on public health, productivity, and quality of life in the city.

Furthermore, this study aims to provide insights into the impact of other climatic variables on temperature [11]. Factors such as humidity, precipitation, and solar activity have traditionally been known to affect temperature, and by integrating these variables into the semiparametric model, predictions become more accurate [12]. This approach enables policymakers to formulate more precise strategies in responding to climate change, reducing the risk of natural disasters, and enhancing the city's preparedness for extreme conditions.

The impact of this analysis extends beyond the environmental sector to economic sectors that are sensitive to temperature changes [13]. In Surakarta, industries such as agriculture, fisheries, and tourism heavily rely on stable climatic conditions. Therefore, a deep understanding of temperature patterns and accurate predictions are crucial. For example, in agriculture, knowledge of optimal planting and harvesting periods can help farmers avoid losses due to extreme weather [14]. In tourism, planning events and outdoor activities can be adjusted to avoid periods of unfavorable weather [15].

The temperature analysis in Surakarta also has significant social implications. Drastic temperature changes can affect living conditions, particularly for vulnerable populations such as the elderly or those living in slum areas [16]. Government programs aimed at improving housing quality, public health, and city infrastructure should consider the results of this analysis to design effective and inclusive interventions.

At the implementation level, the findings of this study are hoped to be integrated into Geographic Information Systems (GIS) and other platforms used by the city government to monitor and manage environmental conditions. Through data integration, Surakarta can be more proactive and responsive to challenges posed by climate change [17]. For example, early warning systems can be developed based on the predictive models generated, providing citizens and policymakers with crucial tools to take action before natural disasters or other extreme conditions occur.

In conclusion, this research paves the way for the development of more evidence-based and scientific policies in response to climate change. Through the semiparametric approach and the use of Fourier series estimators, the temperature analysis in Surakarta not only aids in identifying current and future trends but also assists in formulating effective and efficient strategies for climate adaptation and risk mitigation that the city will face in the future.

2 Preliminaries

2.1 Modelling Approach

The analysis used to determine the functional relationship patterns between the response variable and predictor variables is regression analysis. When a case is found where the functional relationship of the response variable and predictor variable forms a specific pattern while others do not, a semiparametric regression approach is employed. The semiparametric regression model by [18]:

$$y_r = \beta_0 + \beta_1 y_{r-1} + g(t_r) + \varepsilon_r, \quad r = 1, 2, 3, \ldots, T \tag{1}$$

where

y_r = response variable.

β_0, β_1 = parametric component parameters.

$g(t_r)$ = unknown smooth function.

ε_r = zero mean and σ^2 variance normal random error.

r = at time.

T = size of sampel.

To unknown smooth function in Eq. (1), we use fourier series estimator. Modeling technique using Fourier series estimators to accommodate non-linear and periodic data quality, due to its ability to simulate unknown functional relationships and manage fluctuation patterns [19]. In this study $g(t_r)$ which is approximated by the following Fourier series function. The fourier series function given by Khairunnisa et al. [20]:

$$g(t_r) = \alpha_0 + \sum_{k=1}^{K} (a_k \cos\cos\ 2\pi k t_r) \tag{2}$$

where

$\gamma, \alpha_0, \alpha_k$ = parameter in nonparametric function.

k = fourier series estimators.

2.2 Results Interpretation

The final phase consisted of analyzing the outcomes using predefined standards, particularly focusing on the MAPE value, to identify the most precise and dependable model for forecasting the effects of severe weather on Surakarta's local environment. The criterion for selecting the best model was based on the MAPE value:

$$MAPE = \frac{1}{T}\sum_{r=1}^{T}\frac{|y_r - \hat{y}_r|}{y_r} \tag{3}$$

where

T = size of the sample.

$\hat{y}_r$ = the value predicted by the model for time point r.

y_r is the value observed at time point r.

The criteria for MAPE values are shown in the following Table 1:

Table 1. MAPE value criteria

MAPE	Definition
<10	Highly accurate
10–20	Accurate
20–50	Reasonable
>50	Inaccurate

2.3 Statistical Analysis

Here are the steps in statistical analysis using a semiparametric approach based on penalized Fourier series in English:

1. Collect temperature data.
2. Enter temperature data at time r, and temperature at time $r - 1$.
3. Create a scatter plot of the temperature variable at time r with the temperature at time $r - 1$.
4. Create a scatter plot of the temperature variable at time r with time (t_r)
5. Select an appropriate semiparametrik regression model to model the relationship between the response variable and the predictor variables.
6. Apply the semiparametrik regression model to the data to model the fungctional relationship between y_r, y_{r-1}, and r.

7. Optimize the model using Generalized Cross-Validation (GCV) techniques to select the best model parameters.
8. Use the Mean Absolute Percentage Error (MAPE) evaluation matrix to measure the accuracy of the model.
9. Select the model that shows the best performance based on the evaluation.
10. Use the selected model to make future predictions and validate the results with an additional data set.
11. Analyze the prediction results and report findings on temperature patterns.

The flowchart below (Fig. 1) outlines the process for analyzing and predicting temperature data. It starts with data collection and input, followed by creating scatter plots to visualize relationships between temperature and time. A semiparametric regression model is then selected, optimized using GCV, and evaluated with MAPE. The best-performing model is used for future predictions, and the results are analyzed to identify temperature patterns (Fig. 1).

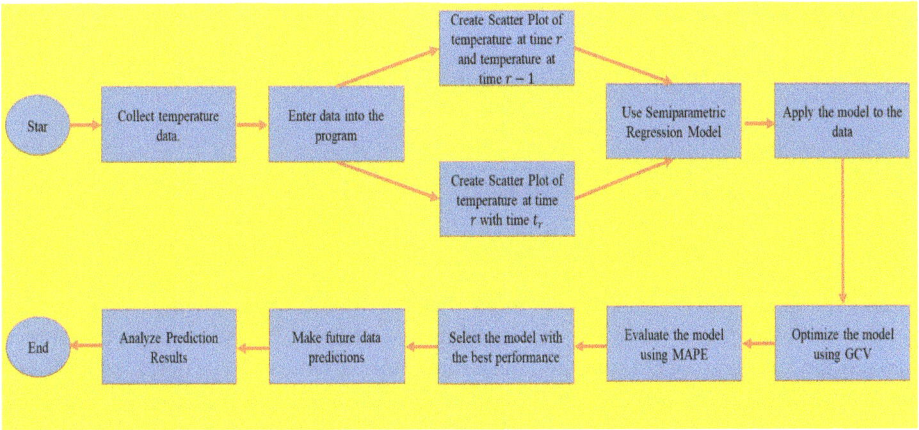

Fig. 1. Flowchart of forecasting temperature variations in Surakarta

2.4 Statistical Analysis

In the research section, the analysis results for temperature at period r are denoted as y_r, and temperature at period $r - 1$ as y_{r-1} in Surakarta, Indonesia. The data used consists of 100 time series data points from January 1, 2024, to April 9, 2024, sourced from NASA. The initial justification is to examine the correlation between temperature at r and temperature at period $r - 1$. Below are the correlation results between temperature at r and temperature at period $r - 1$:

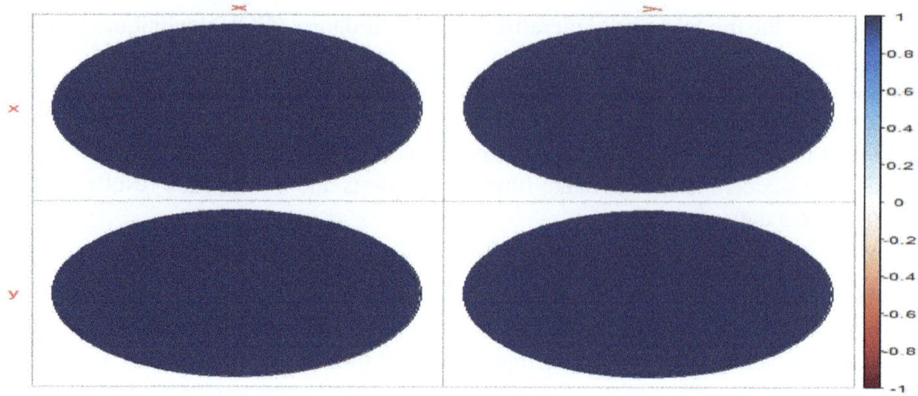

Fig. 2. Correlation plot between y_r dan y_{r-1}

Here are the correlation results in the confusion matrix between the temperature at r and the temperature at $r-1$:

Table 2. Confusion matrix between y_r dan y_{r-1}

	y_{r-1}	y_r
y_{r-1}	1.00000	0.99178
y_r	0.99178	1.00000

In Fig. 2 and Table 2, it can be seen that the image tends towards blue, with a correlation value displayed in the confusion matrix of 0.99178, indicating a correlation between the temperature at time r and the temperature at time $r-1$. Therefore, based on this justification, an analysis will be conducted to determine the functional relationship between the temperature at time r and the temperature at time $r-1$ by examining the scatter plot. Below is the scatter plot between the temperature at time r and the temperature at time $r-1$:

Fig. 3. Scatter plot between y_r dan y_{r-1}

Based on the above Fig. 3, it can be seen that the scatter plot forms a certain pattern. To strengthen the argument regarding the scatter plot above, a linearity test was conducted, and the RESET test result was less than 2e−16, indicating that the functional relationship between the temperature at time r and the temperature at time $r-1$ shows a linear pattern. Thus, it is proven that the scatter plot forms a certain pattern.

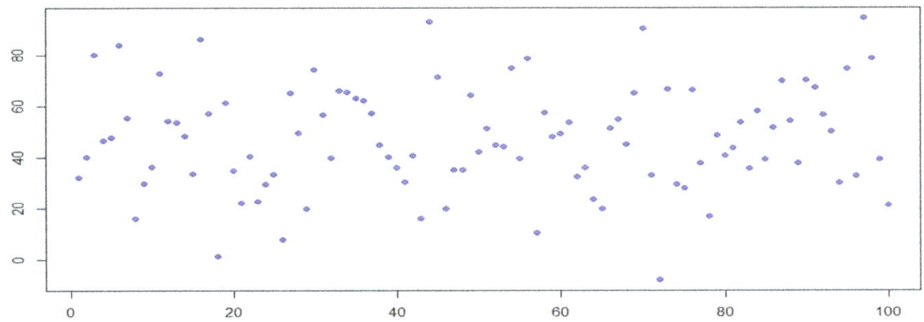

Fig. 4. Scatter plot between T (time) and y_r

Based on the assumption from the scatter plot, we can look at Figs. 3 and 4 the temperature at time r and the temperature at time $r-1$ form a certain pattern, while the temperature at time r with time (t_r) itself does not form a specific pattern, a semi-parametric approach using Fourier series estimator is used. To obtain the best semi-parametric model based on Fourier series, the search for the minimum Generalized Cross Validation (GCV) value is conducted using cosine functions applied to each Fourier coefficient. In this case, the Fourier coefficients are set to a maximum of 10. Below are the figures and GCV values for each Fourier coefficient:

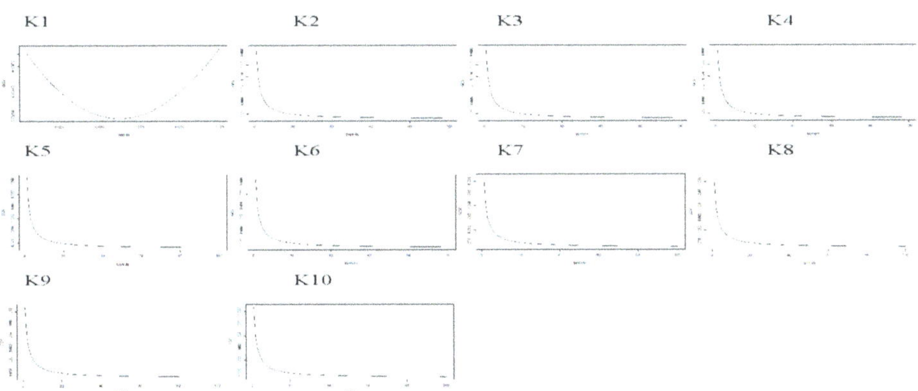

Fig. 5. GCV plot for $K = 1$ until $K = 10$

Based on the image above, it can be seen that each Fourier coefficient has its own minimum GCV value and corresponding lambda.

Table 3. GCV value and lambda for $K = 1$ until $K = 10$

K	Cosinus	
	GCV	Lambda
1	0.6044918	0.012
2	1.077302	99
3	1.077275	99
4	1.077353	99
5	1.077252	99
6	1.077358	99
7	1.077350	99
8	1.077173	99
9	1.077279	99
10	1.077328	99

In Fig. 5 and Table 3, it can be seen that the GCV value for each Fourier coefficient has a minimum GCV value from the cosine function, and it is apparent that the first Fourier coefficient has the best value compared to the other Fourier coefficients based on the smallest minimum GCV value. It can be concluded that the best semiparametric model lies in the first Fourier coefficient with a minimum GCV value of 0.6044918 and a lambda of 0.012. Therefore, the best semiparametric model based on the cosine function in the Fourier series estimator can be written as follows:

$$\hat{y}_r = 3.795 + 0.997\, y_{r-1} + 8,859 \cos \cos\; 2\pi t_r$$

Since the ultimate goal of this research is to make a prediction, it is necessary to determine the model's goodness-of-fit criteria, which in this study is measured using MAPE. The MAPE value for the best model is 5.381, meaning the accuracy of the semiparametric approach based on the Fourier coefficient model is 100–5.381 = 94.619. The forecasting results can be seen in the table below:

Table 4. Actual value versus forecasting value

Date	Forecasting value	Actual value
31-Mar-24	25.19	25.04
1-Apr-24	29.24	29.22
2-Apr-24	26.33	26.74
3-Apr-24	28.93	29.25
4-Apr-24	26.14	26.56
5-Apr-24	25.33	25.50

(continued)

Table 4. (*continued*)

Date	Forecasting value	Actual value
6-Apr-24	29.99	30.25
7-Apr-24	24.89	24.74
8-Apr-24	28.35	27.73
9-Apr-24	27.80	28.09

Based on Table 4, a comparison plot can be made between the actual temperature data and the forecasting data. The comparison plot can be seen in the image below with red is actual value and blue is forecasting value:

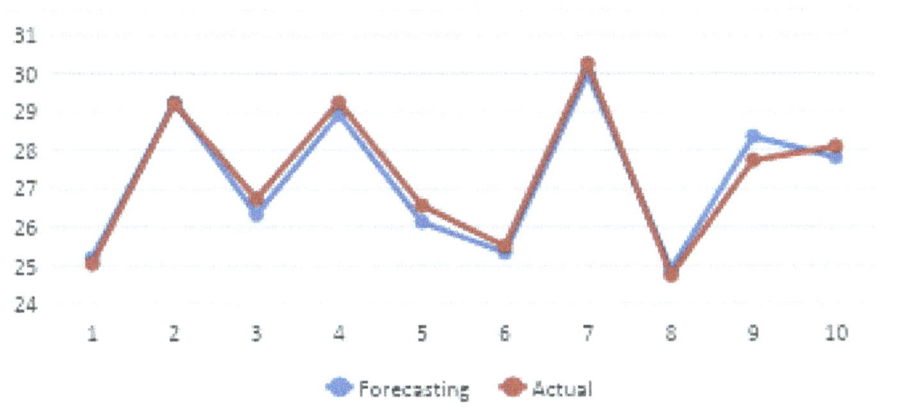

Fig. 6. Comparism plot for actual value versus forecasting value

Based on Table 4 and Fig. 6, it can be seen that the forecasted temperature values are not significantly different from the original temperature data. This means that the obtained forecasting can be used as a reference for predicting temperatures in future periods. This can serve as a basis for policies related to drastic climate changes, with the assistance of climate experts to interpret the forecasted values in detail.

3 Material and Method

3.1 Study Design Dan Data Collection

In the semiparametric study employing the Penalized Fourier Series estimator, temperature data from Surakarta were analyzed. The dataset comprises 100 observations spanning from January 1, 2024, to April 9, 2024. These data points were retrieved from the official NASA website, specifically from their data access viewer portal located at https://power.larc.nasa.gov/data-access-viewer/. For the purposes of model training and validation, the dataset was divided into two subsets: 90 observations were used for training the model, ensuring robust parameter estimation and model fit, and the remaining 10 observations were reserved for testing, allowing for an unbiased evaluation of the model's predictive performance. This research leverages the comprehensive temperature records available through this platform to conduct detailed temperature trend analysis over the specified period.

3.2 Research Variables

This section contains data sources, research variables, sampling techniques, data collection methods and data analysis methods. The data analysis method used must be described in detail. In this research, the dependent variable is the daily temperature in Surakarta. The independent variables include various factors that influence the temperature at period r, notably the temperature from the preceding period, $r - 1$. These variables are detailed in Table 5.

Table 5. Variable structure.

Notation	Variable	Detail
y_r	Temperature	Temperature at period r
y_{r-1}	Temperature	Temperature at period $r - 1$
$g(t_r)$	Time	Number of daily observations over a given period

4 Results and Discussion

In our study, we employed a semiparametric approach using the Fourier series estimator to analyze temperature patterns in Surakarta. The proposed model is expressed mathematically as:

$$\hat{y}_r = 3.795 + 0.997\, y_{r-1} + 8,859 \cos\cos\ 2\pi t_r$$

Where $\hat{y}_r$ represents the estimated temperature at time t, and the coefficients 3.795 and 8.859 denote the intercept and the amplitude of the cosine function, respectively. The Fourier coefficients were crucial in capturing periodic fluctuations within the dataset. Notably, the first Fourier coefficient was set to 1, aligning with our hypothesis that as the model approaches a linear form, the treatment of Fourier coefficients becomes redundant since their impact converges to a constant effect.

Upon analyzing the model's predictive accuracy, we observed a Mean Absolute Percentage Error (MAPE) of 5.381, which indicates a high accuracy level, as the model accounts for approximately 94.619% of the variability in the temperature data. This precision is reflected in the Generalized Cross Validation (GCV) value, which reached its minimum at 0.6044918 for the first Fourier coefficient. These metrics suggest that the model is highly reliable and efficient in forecasting, reducing overfitting while maintaining flexibility to adapt to the data's inherent patterns.

The close alignment of the Fourier series estimator with a coefficient of 1 to previous data periods supports the notion that more complex Fourier treatments may not provide additional benefits over simpler or linear models when the data structure allows it. This finding is pivotal as it simplifies the model, making it more interpretable and easier to implement while still capturing the essential dynamics of temperature variations in Surakarta.

In conclusion, our analysis demonstrates that a semiparametric approach, utilizing a simplified Fourier series estimator with a coefficient set to 1, provides a robust framework for forecasting temperature trends. This approach not only ensures high accuracy but also enhances the model's applicability for real-world scenarios, such as climate adaptation planning, where straightforward and reliable predictions are essential.

5 Conclusion

This study successfully applied a semiparametric approach using a Penalized Fourier Series estimator to model temperature trends in Surakarta. By setting the first Fourier coefficient to 1, a simplified model captured the core dynamics of temperature data, closely aligning with historical patterns. The model achieved a Mean Absolute Percentage Error (MAPE) of 5.381, reflecting a prediction accuracy of 94.619%, supported by a low Generalized Cross Validation (GCV) value of 0.604.

These results confirm that the semiparametric Fourier series model is both reliable and efficient for temperature forecasting, providing a simplified yet accurate approach. This has practical implications for Surakarta, where precise temperature predictions are essential for climate adaptation strategies and policy planning.

Future research could extend this model to include additional climatic variables, such as humidity, or test its applicability in other regions. Expanding the model could further enhance its utility in comprehensive climate analysis, supporting more informed decision-making at the local level. This study highlights the importance of advanced statistical methods in environmental analysis, aiding policymakers in developing data-driven strategies.

Acknowledgments. I would like to express my heartfelt gratitude to Universitas Muhammadiyah Semarang (UNIMUS) and Universitas Airlangga (UNAIR) for their unwavering support and resources that have greatly enriched my academic journey.

Disclosure of Interests. The authors declare no competing interests that are relevant to the content of this article. All data utilized in this study were obtained from publicly available sources, specifically the NASA data access viewer portal. No external funding was received for conducting this research. The semiparametric approach using the Penalized Fourier Series estimator, as described in the manuscript, was developed independently by the authors without any influence from external entities. All findings and opinions expressed herein are solely those of the authors and do not represent any institutional or organizational affiliations. Additionally, the authors would like to acknowledge the support from Universitas Muhammadiyah Semarang (UNIMUS) and Universitas Airlangga (UNAIR), and express gratitude to their supervisor Ibu Nur Chamidah and co-supervisor Bapak Toha Saifudin for their guidance and feedback.

References

1. Dewi, A.E., Maryono, M., Warsito, B.: Implementasi Program Kampung Iklim Di Kota Surakarta. In: Proceeding Biology Education Conference: Biology, Science, Enviromental, and Learning, pp. 221–228 (2019)
2. Handayani, M.N., Sasmito, B., Wijaya, A.P.: Analisis hubungan antara perubahan suhu dengan indeks kawasan terbangun menggunakan citra Landsat (studi kasus: kota Surakarta). Jurnal Geodesi Undip **6**, 208–2018 (2017)
3. Octavanny, M.A.D.: Pemodelan Indeks Pembangunan Kesehatan Masyarakat Provinsi Papua Dengan Regresi Semiparametrik Truncated Spline. In: Prosiding Seminar Nasional Matematika dan Statistika, pp. 29–41 (2023)
4. Husain, H., Budiantara, I.N., Zain, I.: Mixed estimator of spline truncated, Fourier series, and kernel in biresponse semiparametric regression model. In: IOP Conference Series: Earth and Environmental Science, p. 012046. IOP Publishing (2021)
5. Schuster, N.A., Rijnhart, J.J.M., Twisk, J.W.R., Heymans, M.W.: Modeling non-linear relationships in epidemiological data: the application and interpretation of spline models. Front. Epidemiol. **2**, 975380 (2022)
6. Martino, L., Read, J.: A joint introduction to Gaussian processes and relevance vector machines with connections to Kalman filtering and other kernel smoothers. Inf. Fusion **74**, 17–38 (2021)
7. Sahidah, S., Kuzairi, K., Mardianto, M.F.F.: Estimator Deret Fourier Dalam Regresi Nonparametrik Dengan Penalti Untuk Perencanaan Penjualan Produk Musiman. Zeta-Math J. **7**, 69–78 (2022)
8. Ampa, A.T., Budiantara, I.N., Zain, I.: Selection of optimal smoothing parameters in mixed estimator of kernel and Fourier series in semiparametric regression. In: Journal of Physics: Conference Series, p. 012035. IOP Publishing (2021)
9. Mersi, C.: Pemodelan Harga Cabai Merah dan Cabai Rawit dengan Pendekatan Regresi Nonparameterik Berdasarkan Estimator Deret Fourier (Studi Kasus di Bulog Surabaya) (2016)
10. Rizkia, D.P., Fitri, F., Permana, D., Fitria, D.: Modeling the gender development index of West Java Province using a Fourier series nonparametric regression approach. UNP J. Stat. Data Sci. **2**, 234–239 (2024)
11. Herdhyanti, A., Muflikhah, L., Cholissodin, I.: Prediksi Curah Hujan dengan Empat Parameter menggunakan Backpropagation (Studi Kasus: Stasiun Meteorologi Ahmad Yani). Jurnal Pengembangan Teknologi Informasi dan Ilmu Komputer **6**, 5862–5870 (2022)
12. Anandari, A.A.: Analisis Regresi Deret Fourier: Aplikasi Data Curah Hujan. CV Jejak (Jejak Publisher) (2023)
13. Ramadhan, Z.A., Emalia, Z.: Determinan fenomena perubahan iklim dalam perspektif sosial ekonomi di Pulau Jawa dan Pulau Sumatera. Jurnal STEI Ekonomi **32**, 111–122 (2023)
14. Apriani, A., Mustaqimah, U., Marlina, A.: Penerapan Arsitektur Biofilik Pada Pusat Pertanian Perkotaan Di Surakarta. Senthong **6** (2023)
15. Susanti, F.A.: Pengembangan Kawasan Heritage Loji Wetan Sebagai Kawasan Creative District Kota Surakarta dengan Pendekatan Arsitektur Simbiosis (2022)
16. Aprilina, D.O.: Hubungan antara paparan iklim kerja panas dengan dehidrasi dan kelelahan kerja pada tenaga kerja konstruksi di pt. pp urban proyek rehabilitasi pasar legi kota surakarta (2021)
17. Batu, R.B.L. et al.: Analysis of the implementation of the prohibition of littering waste in Law No. 32 of 2009 concerning environmental protection and management. Indonesian. J. Adv. Res. **2**, 1581–1594 (2023)

18. Chamidah, N., Lestari, B., Budiantara, I.N., Aydin, D.: Estimation of multiresponse multi-predictor nonparametric regression model using mixed estimator. Symmetry (Basel) **16**, 386 (2024)
19. Dani, A.T.R., Dewi, A.F., Ni'matuzzahroh, L.: Studi Simulasi dan Aplikasi: Estimator Deret Fourier pada Pemodelan Regresi Nonparametrik. In: Prosiding Seminar Nasional Matematika dan Statistika (2022)
20. Khairunnisa, L.R., Prahutama, A., Santoso, R.: Pemodelan Regresi Semiparametrik Dengan Pendekatan Deret Fourier (Studi Kasus: Pengaruh Indeks Dow Jones dan BI Rate Terhadap Indeks Harga Saham Gabungan. Jurnal Gaussian **9**, 50–63 (2020)

Self-exciting Threshold Autoregressive Model with Application to Data Inflow and Outflow for NTT Province and National Level

Veronika Kolo, Muhammad Sjahid Akbar(✉), and Setiawan

Department of Statistics, Faculty of Science and Data Analytics, Institut Teknologi Sepuluh Nopember, Surabaya 60111, Indonesia
m_sjahid_a@its.ac.id

Abstract. Money has an important role in the economy because it allows the transaction and exchange of goods and services. Therefore, the amount of money circulating in society has an impact on the economic condition of a country where when the amount of money circulating in society is too high, inflation occurs, and vice versa if the amount of money circulating in society is too low, deflation occurs. *Inflows* and *outflows* are important components in the management of currency by Bank Indonesia. BI conducts physical monitoring to ensure that the amount of currency in circulation is sufficient to meet the transaction needs of the community. Therefore, to manage currency stocks in the future, accurate estimates of *inflows* and *outflows* are needed as a reference for BI's policy in determining the amount of money supply. *Inflows* and *outflows* are influenced by many factors, one of which is local socio-cultural factors such as Eid celebrations, school holidays (in July), and Christmas or year-end holidays. Therefore, to manage currency stocks in the future, accurate estimates of *inflows* and *outflows* are needed as a reference for BI's policy in determining the amount of money supply. Economic and financial data has a nonlinear data pattern, so it is quite difficult if it is modeled linearly but nonlinear. One effective method to overcome nonlinear patterns is *Self Exciting Threshold Autoregressive* (SETAR). This method is able to capture nonlinear patterns in each regime with a separate AR model. The purpose of this study is to obtain the SETAR model and apply it to inflow and outflow data in NTT and National provinces. In this study, OLS was used to estimate the SETAR parameters. The SETAR models obtained are SETAR(2,12,12) and SETAR(2,12,11) for NTT's Inflow and Ouflow data, while for National Inflow and Outflow, namely SETAR(2,9,12) and SETAR(2,12,12) with MAPE of 1.67% and 8.9% for NTT and MAPE 29% and 4.6% for National.

Keywords: Inflow · Outflow · SETAR

1 Introduction

Money has a central role in the economy as a means of transaction to facilitate the exchange of goods and services, therefore money circulating in society has an impact on the economic condition of a country. If the money circulating in the community is

P. C. Rodrigues et al. (Eds.): ISBIS 2024, 13, pp. 232–253, 2027.
https://doi.org/10.1007/978-3-032-32458-0_17

too high, inflation will occur, while if the money circulating in the community is too low, it will cause deflation [1]. The amount of money in circulation is regulated by Bank Indonesia (BI) through the currency circulation policy as a transaction tool to drive the economy. The purpose of BI's policy is to maintain liquidity stability in the economy [2]. *Inflow* and *outflow* are important components in the management of currency by BI. Bank Indonesia conducts physical monitoring to ensure that the amount of currency in circulation is sufficient to meet the transaction needs of the community.

Inflows and *outflows* are influenced by many factors, one of which is local socio-cultural factors such as Eid celebrations, school holidays (in July), and Christmas or year-end holidays. In the *time series*, the Eid al-Fitr event called the effect of calendar variations Amalia et al. [3], found that a significant increase *in inflow* occurred in the month before Eid al-Fitr, while a significant increase in *outflow* occurred in the month before Eid al-Fitr. Significant changes *in inflows* and *outflows* also occur at the end of each year (December). This is influenced by the Christmas holidays and year-end holidays, hereinafter referred to as the seasonal effect [4]. BI through the *Open Market Committee* (OMC) holds a monthly agenda to project the currency in circulation, this forecast is carried out by BI with the aim of stabilizing the value of the rupiah [5]. However, with the case of multiple calendar and seasonal variations, it has become a special topic in the research of money circulation experience. Therefore, to manage currency stocks in the future, accurate estimates of inflows and outflows are needed as a reference for BI's policy in determining the amount of money supply.

The *Self Exciting Threshold Autoregressive* (SETAR) model is a development of the *Threshold Autoregressive* (TAR) model. The SETAR model can identify the same delay parameters at each *regime* and is a family of nonlinear time-sequence models with the same *delay parameters* for each *regime*. The SETAR model has the privilege of generating complex nonlinear dynamics and can generate data jumps that cannot be captured by other time series models [6]. The SETAR model shows better performance than other linear and nonlinear models [7]. The SETAR model is also determined by the autoregressive order (p), the number of regimes, the delay parameters, and the threshold. Compared to NN, the SETAR model has the privilege of being able to capture asymmetrical phenomena and data jumps that cannot be captured by the linear time series model [8]. Some successful studies using the SETAR model are Non-linear Currency Modeling with SETAR (Self-exciting Threshold Autoregressive) on EUR/USD, EUR/TRY, and USD/TRY Pairs [7]. Forecasting Bank Central Asia's Stock Return Using Self Exciting Threshold Autoregressive – Genetic Algorithm [9] and Exchange Rate Modeling Using the Regime Switching Model [10].

In this study, the *inflow* and *outflow data* used are in NTT province and data on a national scale. The researcher's consideration is that the inflow and outflow data in East Nusa Tenggara (NTT) have double seasonal cases (July and the end of the year) as well as calendar variations (Eid al-Fitr). The effect of calendar variations in NTT is not as high as during the year-end holidays, this is because the majority of NTT's population is Christian. National data is used because the majority of Indonesia's population is Muslim, so the increase in *outflow* and *inflow* occurs on the Eid al-Fitr holiday. The SETAR method is used to capture online data patterns.

2 Methodology

2.1 Terasvirta Nonlinearitas Test

The Terasvirta test is a nonlinearity detection test developed from *a neural network* model and belongs to the *Lagrange Multiplier (LM) type test group.* Terasvirta linearity test introduced by Terasvirta et al. [11]. The hypotheses tested in *the Terasvirta* test are as follows:

$H_0 : \theta_{01} = \theta_{02} = \cdots = \theta_{0q}$ (The data contains a linear pattern)

H_1 : *setidaknya terdapat satu* $\theta_{0q} \neq 0$ (The data contains a nonlinear pattern)
The procedure to obtain the statistical value of the F test is as follows.

(1) Regress at 1,,,..., and calculate the residual values and calculate the number of residual squares $Y_t Y_{t-1} Y_{t-p} \widehat{\varepsilon}_t$

$$SSR_0 = \sum \hat{\varepsilon}_t^2 \tag{1}$$

(2) Regress on 1,,,..., $\widehat{\varepsilon}_t Y_{t-1} Y_{t-p}$ and m additional predictors, and then calculate the residual and residual square sum $\widehat{v}_t$

$$SSR = \sum \hat{v}_t^2 \tag{1}$$

(3) Calculate test statistics

$$F_{hit} = \frac{SSR_0 - SSR/m}{SSR/(n-p-1-m)} \tag{3}$$

where N is the total observations, p is the number of predictors of the initial model and m is the additional predictor. If or if then the decision is rejected $F_{hit} > F_{\alpha;m.(n-p-1-m)} p - value < \alpha H_0$.

2.2 Threshold Autoregressive (TAR) Model

TAR is an alternative model for describing periodic time series. This model is motivated by several nonlinear characteristics commonly found in daily life such as the presence of asymmetry in the descending and ascending patterns of a process, the phenomenon of jumps, and amplitude dependence frequencies that cannot be captured by linear time series models. This model uses thresholds.

The TAR model can be written as follows:

$$y_t = \phi_0 + \sum_{i=1}^{p} \phi_1 y_{t-i} + \left(\alpha_0 + \sum_{i=1}^{p} \alpha_i y_{t-i}\right) I\left(\frac{y_{t-d} - \tau}{\delta}\right) + \varepsilon_t \tag{4}$$

with:

y_t = Time Series Data

d = parameter delay

τ = Location parameters

δ = parameter skala

$I(.)$ = Smoothing functions such as logistical, exponential, or indicator functions

ε_t = A random array of variables that are identical, independent, and follow a specific distribution with a mean of zero and a variant σ_a^2.

2.3 Self Exiting Treshold Autoregressive (SETAR) Model

The SETAR model is one of the nonlinear models of the time series. The SETAR model was first introduced by Tong in 1990. The SETAR model is a development of TAR. The movement between regimes is controlled by a variable called a threshold like the TAR model. The peculiarity of this model is that it can generate complex non-linear dynamics, capture asymmetrical phenomena and data jumps that cannot be captured by linear time series models [8].

SETAR k-regime model *(k; p 1, p2,..., pk; d)* have the following similarities.

$$y_t = \begin{cases} \phi_0^{(1)} + \sum_{i=1}^{p_1} \phi_i^{(1)} y_{t-i} + \varepsilon_t^{(1)}, & \text{jika } y_{t-d} \leq r_1 \\ \phi_0^{(2)} + \sum_{i=1}^{p_2} \phi_i^{(2)} y_{t-i} + \varepsilon_t^{(2)}, & \text{jika } r_1 < y_{t-d} \leq r_2 \\ \vdots & \\ \phi_0^{(k)} + \sum_{i=1}^{p_k} \phi_i^{(k)} y_{t-i} + \varepsilon_t^{(k)}, & \text{jika } r_{k-1} < y_{t-d} \end{cases} \quad (5)$$

k **is** nomor *regime* dalam model**;** d **is** panjang delay variabel *thresh;*p_k **is** orde *autoregressive* pada *regime* ke k dalam model**;** r_k **is** nilai *threshold* pada *regime* ke k. Nilai *threshold* memenuhi batas. Untuk setiap $-\infty = r_0 < r_1 < \ldots < r_{k-1} < r_k = \infty$ *regime* ke-,. Dalam masing-masing $k\varepsilon_t \sim N\left(0, \sigma_a^2\right)$ *regime* diasumsikan bahwa perilaku dinamis deret waktu mengikuti proses *autoregressive linear* [12].

The SETAR model can be estimated using *Ordinary Least Square* (OLS). Suppose the SETAR model is formed with a 2-regime or *SETAR*$(2; p_1, p_2)$ as explained by the Eq. (6).

$$y_t = \begin{cases} \phi_0^{(1)} + \sum_{i=1}^{p_1} \phi_i^{(1)} y_{t-i} + \varepsilon_t^{(1)}, & \text{jika } y_{t-d} \leq r_1 \\ \phi_0^{(2)} + \sum_{i=1}^{p_2} \phi_i^{(2)} y_{t-i} + \varepsilon_t^{(2)}, & \text{lainnya} \end{cases} \quad (6)$$

where y_t is the value of the time series at time, t r_k is the *threshold* value on *the regime* to, is the delay, kd $\phi_i^{(k)}$ is the AR parameter, and $\varepsilon_t^{(k)}$ is the *error* on the *regime* to k

Equation (6) can be described in Eqs. (7) and (8), respectively.

$$y_t = \phi_0^{(1)} + \sum_{i=1}^{p_1} \phi_i^{(1)} y_{t-i} + \varepsilon_t^{(1)} \quad (7)$$

$$y_t = \phi_0^{(2)} + \sum_{i=1}^{p_2} \phi_i^{(2)} y_{t-i} + \varepsilon_t^{(2)} \tag{8}$$

Tong and Lim [11], suggest a SETAR modeling procedure based on AIC is Akaike's Information Criterion (AIC). The procedure for the 2-regime model is illustrated $\boldsymbol{SETAR}(k; p_1, p_2; d)$, the first thing to do is to find the AR model order for each regime. Given a fixed value and, suppose is the maximum order for 2 separate AR linear models. Elections are subjective, Tong (1990) suggests with <. Based on the values that have been set, model with an AR model for each $drPPP = n^{\alpha}\alpha\frac{1}{2}r$ *regime.* The order to be chosen is as good as it looks so $P_jj = 1, 2$

$$AIC(\hat{p}_j) = \min_{0 \le p_j \le P} \left\{ n_j \ln\left[\frac{\|\hat{a}_j(p_j)\|^2}{n_j}\right] + 2(p_j + 1) \right\} \tag{9}$$

where is the number of observations in the AR model at n_j *the regime* to j, $\hat{a}_j(p_j)$ is the residual vector of $\boldsymbol{AR}(p_j)$, and $\|\mathbf{x}\| = (x',\mathbf{x})^{\frac{1}{2}}$ is the norm of the x vector. So

$$AIC(d, r) = AIC(\hat{p}_1) + AIC(\hat{p}_2) \tag{10}$$

Next is to look for the threshold value r. Suppose the fixed value and the variable value of a set of *dr potential* threshold candidates $R = \{r_1, r_2, ..., r_S\}$ and minimize the AIC in the candidates contained in. Therefore, the value is chosen $R\ \hat{r}$ from r so that

$$AIC(d, \hat{r}) = \min_{r \in R}\{AIC(d, r)\} \tag{11}$$

Since it can be any value in an interval, this step may require some replication based on existing potential candidates through *r the search grid.* To begin replication, [11] suggests using the sample percentile as the initial candidate. The last step is to look for delay d. Suppose $r\ D = \{1, 2, ..., T\}$ it becomes a potential candidate for *the delay d* parameter. So, the value $\hat{d}$ is selected using

$$\boldsymbol{AIC}(\hat{d}, \hat{r}) = \min_{d \in D}\left\{\frac{\boldsymbol{AIC}(d, \hat{r})}{(n - n_d)}\right\} \tag{12}$$

where $n_d = \max(d, P)$. Since the effective number of observations in the regulated AR varies as the value changes, it is best to normalize the AIC by the effective number of observations $d\ (n - n_d)$.

The data used in this study is secondary data obtained from Bank Indonesia for NTT Province and National. The data is divided into in-sample and out-sample data. The variables used in this study consist of independent variables which are inflow and outflow data from January 2010 to December 2023. The notation used to represent these variables can be seen in Table 1 below:

The general research steps in modeling SETAR 2-Regime are as follows:

1. Conducting Terasvirta nonlinear tests on inflow and outflow data.
2. If the data is nonlinear then continue in step (3), but if the result is not significant, indicating that the data is linear then a linear time series model is used.

Table 1. Notation and research variables

Variable	Variable Name	Operational Definition
y_{1t}	NTT inflow for the tth period	Bank activities to deposit money to BI
y_{2t}	NTT Outflow for the tth period	Banks withdraw money that is still in circulation (ULE)
y_{3t}	National Inflow for the tth period	Bank activities to deposit money to BI
y_{4t}	National Outflow for the tth period	Bank Activities to Withdraw Money That Is Still Fit for Circulation (ULE)

3. Plot PACF on inflow and outflow data to get optimal lag.
4. Determine the maximum order of AR(p) based on the PACF plot.
5. Determine the delay (d) and threshold parameters with the smallest AIC criteria.
6. Parameter estimation of the SETAR model with OLS.
7. Get the best SETAR model with the smallest MAPE value.

3 Results

In this study, the SETAR model used is the SETAR model with 1 threshold or known as the SETAR 2-regime model. The SETAR model with the Tong approach will be applied separately at each relevant time period for each inflow and outflow data and the results will be discussed based on descriptive statistical notation. For this purpose, the first is a nonlinear test (Tsay's Test) on each data in the province of NTT and National.

Table 2. Linearity tests

		Nonlinear Terasvirta	
		Statistical Tests	P-value
NTT	Inflow	3,27	0,002759
	Outflow	39,66	5,884e-15
National	Inflow	2,1838	0,03793
	Outflow	32,125	1,251e-12

Based on Table 2, the p-value is below 0.05. This means that inflow and outflow data are nonlinear.

Based on Table 3, the best model of NTT Inflow data is SETAR(2,12,12) with *a d* of 11 and a threshold value of 2,818925 NTT's outflow data is SETAR(2,12,12) with *a d* of 11 and a threshold value of 8,271718.

Graphs 1 and 2 illustrate the relationship between the delay (d) and the threshold value that triggered the change. The optimal d value and threshold are determined based on the smallest value of AIC. For the results of the NTT inflow data grid search, a delay

Table 3. Results of SETAR model identification in NTT

		SETAR Hyper parameters					
		m	Theshold delay	mL	mH	Threshold value	Pooled AIC
NTT	Inflow	12	11	12	12	2,818925	−904,4476
	Outflow	12	11	12	12	8,271718	15,69876

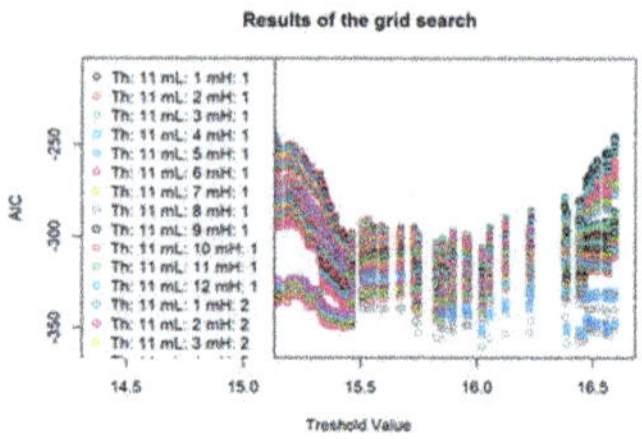

Graph 1. NTT inflow threshold and AIC value

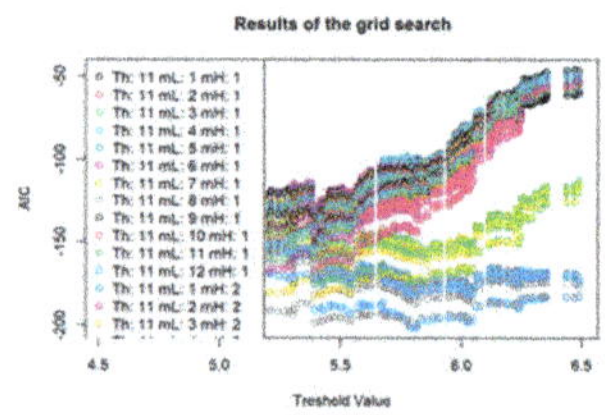

Graph 2. NTT outflow threshold and AIC value

of 11 was obtained with the smallest AIC value of −904,4476 while the results of the NTT outflow data grid search obtained a delay of 11 with the smallest AIC value of 15,69876.

Tables 4 and 5 are the results of the SETAR model estimation using ordinary least square (OLS). There are many parameters in the low regime and high regime that are not significant because the p-value is more than the significance level of 0.05. However, insignificant parameters are not included in the model with no influence in the model.

Table 4. Estimation of SETAR Model Parameters on Inflow and Outflow Data NTT

SETAR model													
Low regime													
Inflow	c	1	2	3	4	5	6	7	8	9	10	11	12
	0,77	0,31	0,12	−0,01	0,01	0,05	0,17	−0,01	−0,03	0,01	−0,01	−0,19	0,27
Outflow	3,82	−0,11	−0,01	−0,16	−0,20	−0,01	0,13	0,03	0,09	0,06	−0,35	0,18	0,90
		Estimation	Standard.Error	p-value									
Inflow	C	0,77	0,221374	0,000636									
	1	0,31	0,079403	0,000102									
	2	0,13	0,063729	0,045828									
	3	−0,01	0,058896	0,865758									
	4	0,01	0,060793	0,866298									
	5	0,05	0,061901	0,395591									
	6	0,17	0,05942	0,00394									
	7	−0,01	0,06045	0,779542									
	8	−0,03	0,061647	0,555288									
	9	0,01	0,059859	0,863121									
	10	−0,01	0,057789	0,930472									
	11	−0,19	0,058111	0,001622									
	12	0,27	0,085895	0,001771									
Outflow	C	3,82	2,402216	0,113684									
	1	−0,11	0,091649	0,206445									
	2	−0,01	0,111303	0,932345									
	3	−0,16	0,150582	0,26437									
	4	−0,20	0,191894	0,289586									
	5	−0,01	0,154388	0,928656									

(continued)

Table 4. *(continued)*

SETAR model				
Low regime				
	6	0,13	0,163774	0,423683
	7	0,03	0,123484	0,771854
	8	0,09	0,130418	0,484459
	9	0,07	0,23276	0,766761
	10	−0,35	0,318853	0,262719
	11	0,18	0,294564	0,520287
	12	0,90	0,070328	1,51E−25

Table 5. Estimation of SETAR model parameters on inflow and outflow data NTT

SETAR model													
High regime													
Inflow	c	1	2	3	4	5	6	7	8	9	10	11	12
	−0,46	−0,03	0,05	0,18	0,06	0,04	−0,01	−0,21	−0,08	−0,17	−0,32	0,97	0,66
Outflow	5,32	0,34	−0,02	−0,02	0,04	−0,07	−0,03	0,02	−0,04	−0,01	−0,05	0,14	0,08
		Estimation	Standard.Error	p-value									
Inflow	C	−0,46	1,106661	0,676746									
	1	−0,03	0,099172	0,747988									
	2	0,05	0,162741	0,717377									
	3	0,18	0,306824	0,541899									
	4	0,06	0,2628	0,817249									
	5	0,04	0,155961	0,770179									
	6	−0,01	0,269829	0,964382									
	7	−0,21	0,208012	0,314046									
	8	−0,08	0,195353	0,680939									
	9	−0,17	0,2101	0,419596									
	10	−0,32	0,368716	0,37358									
	11	0,97	0,379272	0,010962									
	12	0,66	0,326549	0,042372									
Outflow	C	5,32	1,734489	0,002542									
	1	0,34	0,070287	2,5E−06									
	2	−0,02	0,057758	0,648601									
	3	−0,02	0,054707	0,659013									
	4	0,04	0,053643	0,43753									
	5	−0,07	0,05555	0,207636									

(continued)

Table 5. (*continued*)

SETAR model				
High regime				
	6	−0,03	0,055949	0,533614
	7	0,023	0,057301	0,677218
	8	−0,04	0,055143	0,389721
	9	−0,01	0,053988	0,748871
	10	−0,05	0,059925	0,336535
	11	0,14	0,113931	0,216063
	12	0,08	0,111806	0,454437

The following is the SETAR(2,12,12) model with all parameters for the upper regime formed in the following NTT inflow data.

$$\hat{y}_{1t} = \begin{cases} 0.7734073^{(1)} + 0.3174768^{(1)}y_{t-1} + 0.1283928^{(1)}y_{t-2} \\ -0,00997^{(1)}y_{t-3} + 0,010254^{(1)}y_{t-4} + 0,052746^{(1)}y_{t-5} \\ +0.1741562^{(1)}y_{t-6} - 0,01695^{(1)}y_{t-7} - 0,03645^{(1)}y_{t-8} \\ +0,010339^{(1)}y_{t-9} - 0,00505^{(1)}y_{t-10} \\ -0.1867500^{(1)}y_{t-11} + 0.2737084^{(1)}y_{t-12} + \varepsilon_t^{(1)} \\ , if\, \mathrm{y}_{t-11} \leq 2,818925 \\ -0,46233^{(2)} - 0,03193^{(2)}y_{t-1} + 0,059024^{(2)}y_{t-2} \\ 0,187599^{(2)}y_{t-3} + 0,060842^{(2)}y_{t-4} + 0,04565^{(2)}y_{t-5} \\ -0,01207^{(2)}y_{t-6} - 0,21017^{(2)}y_{t-7} - 0,08049^{(2)}y_{t-8} \\ -0,17007^{(2)}y_{t-9} - 0,32912^{(2)}y_{t-10} \\ 0,977681^{(2)}y_{t-11} + 0,668874^{(2)}y_{t-12} + \varepsilon_t^{(2)}, jika\,\mathrm{y}_{t-11} > 2,818925 \end{cases}$$

The following is the SETAR Model(2,12,11) with all parameters for the upper regime formed on the NTT Outflow data, written as follows.

$$\hat{y}_{1t} = \begin{cases} 3,823517^{(1)} - 0,11632^{(1)}y_{t-1} - 0,00947^{(1)}y_{t-2} \\ -0,16874^{(1)}y_{t-3} - 0,20398^{(1)}y_{t-4} - 0,01385^{(1)}y_{t-5} \\ +0,131406^{(1)}y_{t-6} + 0,035873^{(1)}y_{t-7} + 0,091421^{(1)}y_{t-8} \\ +0,069172^{(1)}y_{t-9} - 0,35853^{(1)}y_{t-10} \\ 0,189848^{(1)}y_{t-11} + 0,903462^{(1)}y_{t-12} + \varepsilon_t^{(1)} \\ , if\, \mathrm{y}_{t-11} \leq 8,271718 \\ 5,329826^{(2)} + 0,344896^{(2)}y_{t-1} - 0,02638^{(2)}y_{t-2} \\ -0,02419^{(2)}y_{t-3} + 0,041764^{(2)}y_{t-4} - 0,07032^{(2)}y_{t-5} \\ -0,03491^{(2)}y_{t-6} + 0,023902^{(2)}y_{t-7} - 0,04758^{(2)}y_{t-8} \\ -0,01732^{(2)}y_{t-9} - 0,05779^{(2)}y_{t-10} \\ 0,141571^{(2)}y_{t-11} + 0,083865^{(2)}y_{t-12} + \varepsilon_t^{(2)}, jika\,\mathrm{y}_{t-11} > 8,271718 \end{cases}$$

Graphs 3 and 4 show the plot of time series data inflow data and outflow data in NTT province.

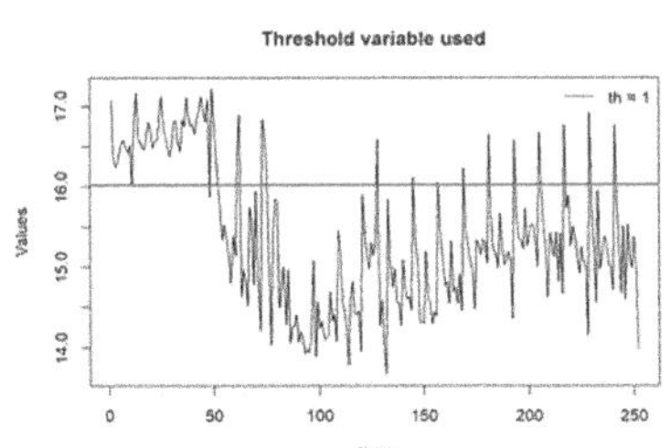

Graph 3. Threshold Data Inflow NTT

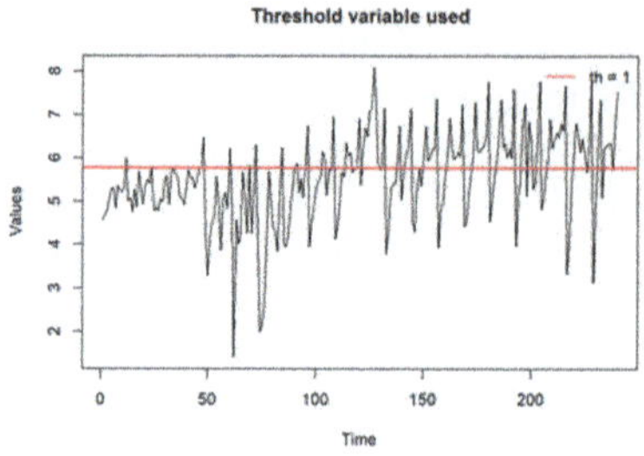

Graph 4. Threshold Data Outflow NTT

Graphs 3 and 4 show the threshold values used in dividing the 2-regime. The threshold value used in the NTT inflow data is 2.818925, while the threshold value used in dividing the regime in the National outflow data is 8.271718.

Table 6. Results of the identification of the SETAR model of National data

		SETAR Hyper parameters					
		m	Theshold Delay	mL	mH	Threshold Value	Pooled AIC
Nasional	Inflow	12	11	12	12	474,2608	1441,197
	Outflow	12	11	12	12	20,11257	−34.61601

Based on Table 6, the best model of National Inflow data is obtained, namely.

SETAR(2,12,12) with *d* of 11 and a threshold value of 474,2608. NTT's outflow data is SETAR(2,12,12) with *a d* of 11 and a threshold value of 20,11257.

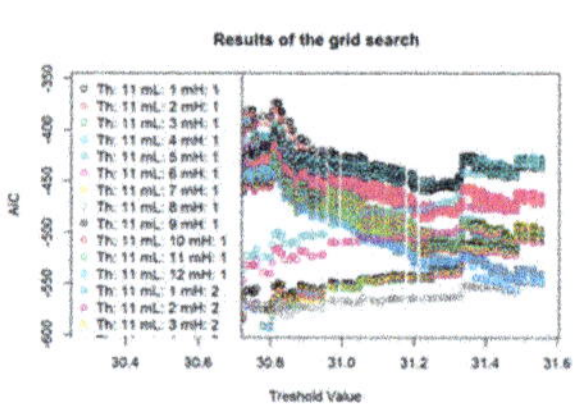

Graph 5. National Inflow threshold and AIC value

Graphs 5 and 6 show that the optimal d value and threshold are determined based on the smallest value of AIC. For the results of the national inflow data grid search, a delay of 11 was obtained with the smallest AIC value of 1441,197 while the results of the national outflow data grid search obtained a delay of 11 with the smallest AIC value of −34.61601 (Tables 7 and 8).

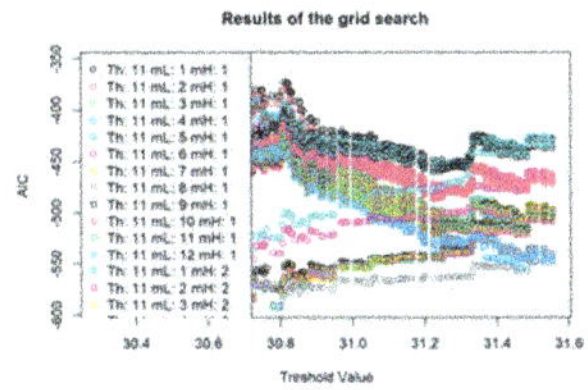

Graph 6. National Outflow threshold and AIC value

The following is the SETAR Model(2,9,12) with all parameters for the upper regime formed in the following National inflow data.

$$\hat{y}_{1t} = \begin{cases} 137,3429^{(1)} + 0,11153^{(1)}y_{t-1} + 0,213571^{(1)}y_{t-2} \\ +0,115056^{(1)}y_{t-3} + 0,092412^{(1)}y_{t-4} - 0,00055^{(1)}y_{t-5} \\ +0,012865^{(1)}y_{t-6} + 0,005471^{(1)}y_{t-7} + 0,076917^{(1)}y_{t-8} \\ +0,000523^{(1)}y_{t-9} - 0,11579^{(1)}y_{t-10} \\ +0,016344y_{t-11} + 0,089946^{(1)}y_{t-12} + \varepsilon_t^{(1)} \\ , if\, \mathrm{y}_{t-11} \leq 474,2608 \\ 255,6726^{(2)} - 0,36548^{(2)}y_{t-1} + 0,466695y_{t-2} \\ +1,612438y_{t-3} - 0,20794^{(2)}y_{t-4} - 0,2428^{(2)}y_{t-5} \\ +0,104831y_{t-6} - 0,35636^{(2)}y_{t-7} - 2,27208^{(2)}y_{t-8} \\ -0,24782^{(2)}y_{t-9} - 0,62258^{(2)}y_{t-10} \\ 2,021946^{(2)}y_{t-11} + 0,521562^{(2)}y_{t-12} + \varepsilon_t^{(2)} \\ , if\, \mathrm{y}_{t-11} > 474,2608 \end{cases}$$

The following is the SETAR Model(2,12,12) with all parameters for the upper regime formed in the following National inflow data.

$$\hat{y}_{1t} = \begin{cases} 6,930177^{(1)} - 0,13178^{(1)}y_{t-1} - 0,03765^{(1)}y_{t-2} \\ -0,0766^{(1)}y_{t-3} - 0,06648^{(1)}y_{t-4} + 0,017568y_{t-5} \\ +0,018745^{(1)}y_{t-6} - 0,00188^{(1)}y_{t-7} + 0,02543^{(1)}y_{t-8} \\ -0,00367^{(1)}y_{t-9} - 0,04544^{(1)}y_{t-10} \\ 0,30704y_{t-11} + 0,63488^{(1)}y_{t-12} + \varepsilon_t^{(1)} \\ , if\, \mathrm{y}_{t-11} \leq 20,11257 \\ 33,80005^{(2)} - 1,06742^{(2)}y_{t-1} - 0,62042^{(2)}y_{t-2} \\ -0,70689y_{t-3} - 0,49912^{(2)}y_{t-4} + -0,36479^{(2)}y_{t-5} \\ +0,000359^{(2)}y_{t-6} + 0,005836^{(2)}y_{t-7}0,054889^{(2)}y_{t-8} \\ 1,203721^{(2)}y_{t-9} + 0,252423y_{t-10} \\ 0,19505y_{t-11} + 0,840714^{(2)}y_{t-12} + \varepsilon_t^{(2)} \\ , if\, \mathrm{y}_{t-11} > 20,11257 \end{cases}$$

Graphs 7 and 8 show the threshold values used in dividing the 2-regime. The threshold value used in the National inflow data is 474,2608 while the threshold value used in dividing the regime in the national outflow data is 20,11257.

Table 7. Estimation of SETAR model parameters on national inflow and outflow data

SETAR model													
Low regime													
Inflow	c	1	2	3	4	5	6	7	8	9	10	11	12
	137,3	0,11	0,21	0,11	0,09	−0,00	0,01	0,00	0,07	0,00	−0,11	0,01	0,08
Outflow	6,93	−0,13	−0,03	−0,07	−0,06	0,01	0,01	−0,00	0,02	−0,00	−0,04	0,30	0,63
		Estimation	Standard.Error	p-value									
Inflow	C	137,3429	40,17416	0,000821									
	1	0,11153	0,065415	0,090389									
	2	0,213571	0,057949	0,000324									
	3	0,115056	0,056151	0,042299									
	4	0,092412	0,059917	0,125221									
	5	−0,00055	0,060849	0,992852									
	6	0,012865	0,063584	0,839941									
	7	0,005471	0,061072	0,928749									
	8	0,076917	0,057201	0,180874									
	9	0,000523	0,057599	0,992769									
	10	−0,11579	0,056461	0,042131									
	11	0,016344	0,055618	0,769289									
	12	0,089946	0,094655	0,343599									
Outflow	C	6,930177	1,863802	0,000288									
	1	−0,13178	0,048215	0,007072									
	2	−0,03765	0,044831	0,402386									
	3	−0,0766	0,043629	0,081305									
	4	−0,06648	0,047403	0,162978									
	5	0,017568	0,048296	0,716584									

(continued)

Table 7. *(continued)*

SETAR model				
Low regime				
	6	0,018745	0,048457	0,699458
	7	−0,00188	0,047425	0,968428
	8	0,02543	0,043766	0,562124
	9	−0,00367	0,043307	0,932608
	10	−0,04544	0,046934	0,334572
	11	0,30704	0,067475	1,14E-05
	12	0,63488	0,080593	7,89E-13

Table 8. Estimation of SETAR model parameters on inflow and outflow data seeds

High regime												
Constant	1	2	3	4	5	6	7	8	9	10	11	12
255,6	−0,36	0,46	1,61	−0,20	−0,24	0,10	−0,35	−2,27	−0,24	−0,62	2,02	0,52
33,80	−1,06	−0,62	−0,70	−0,49	−0,36	0,00	0,00	0,05	1,20	0,25	0,19	0,25
	Estimation	Standard.Error	p-value									
Inflow	255,6726	208,3776	0,221865									
	−0,36548	0,189253	0,055453									
	0,466695	0,683901	0,496096									
	1,612438	0,886497	0,071036									
	−0,20794	0,516822	0,688031									
	−0,2428	0,312477	0,438442									
	0,104831	0,281763	0,710409									
	−0,35636	0,29017	0,221433									
	−2,27208	0,368419	6,83E-09									
	−0,24782	0,371569	0,505878									
	−0,62258	1,114195	0,577199									
	2,021946	0,57424	0,000578									
	0,521562	0,37435	0,165722									
Outflow	33,80005	8,680869	0,000151									
	−1,06742	0,146804	2,19E-11									
	−0,62042	0,257715	0,017352									
	−0,70689	0,227514	0,002283									
	−0,49912	0,147228	0,000905									
	−0,36479	0,107868	0,00093									
	0,000359	0,084922	0,996636									

(continued)

Table 8. *(continued)*

High regime												
Constant	1	2	3	4	5	6	7	8	9	10	11	12
	0,005836	0,091047	0,948984									
	0,054889	0,151285	0,717279									
	1,203721	0,215069	1,09E-07									
	0,252423	0,179711	0,162321									
	0,19505	0,07984	0,015792									
	0,840714	0,244213	0,000757									

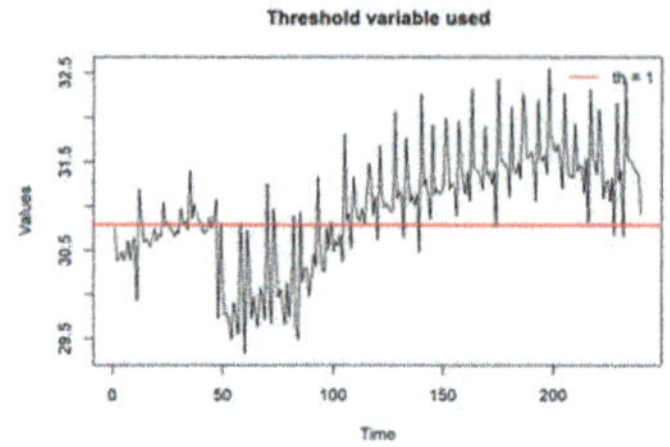

Graph 7. National Data Inflow Threshold

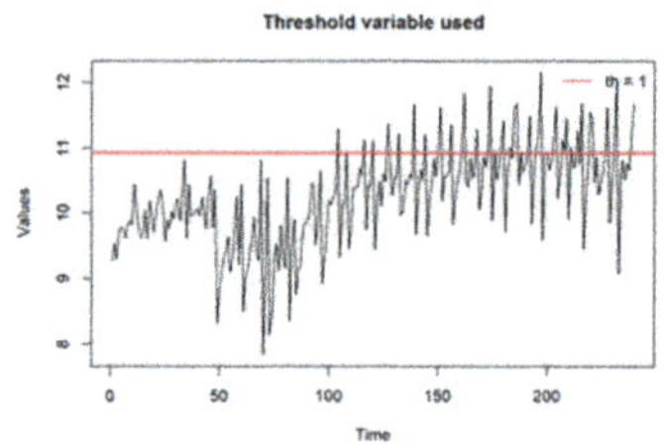

Graph 8. National Data Outflow Threshold

4 Discuss

This section will discuss the accuracy of the SETAR model in capturing linear patterns in inflow and outflow data.

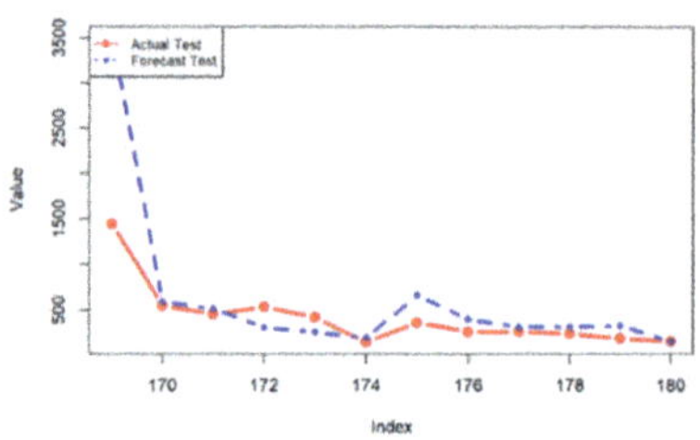

Graph 9. NTT Month Inflow Data Forecast 12Month

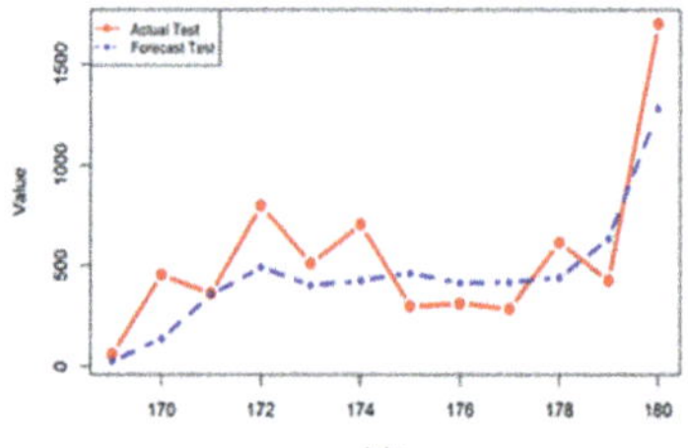

Graph 10. NTT Outflow Data Forecast 12 Months

Graphs 9 and 10 show the evaluation of the forecast results on the outsampling of Inflow and Outflow data in NTT province with the acquisition of MAPE of 1.67% and 8.9%, respectively.

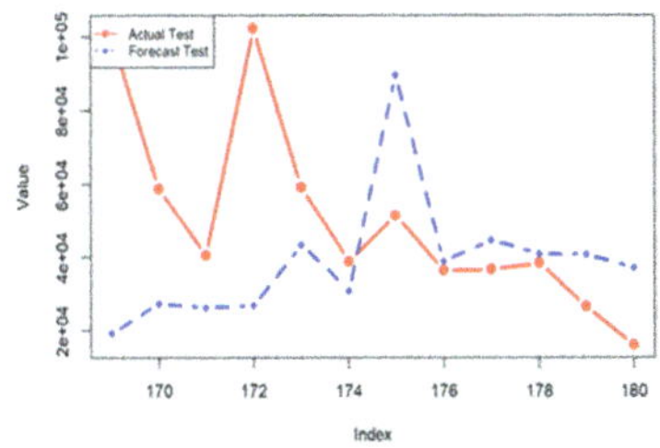

Graph 11. 12-Month National Inflow Data Forecast

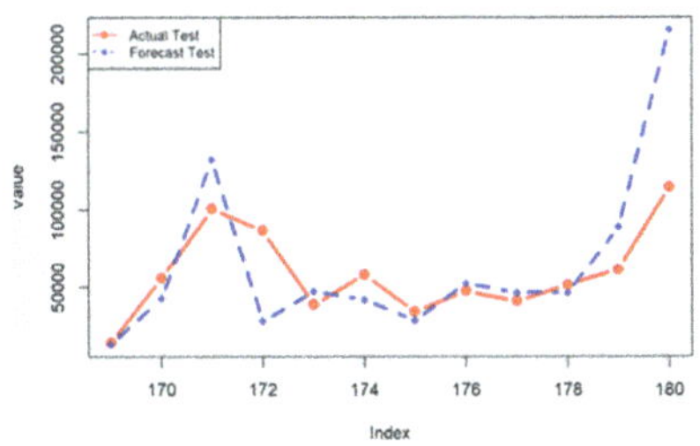

Graph 12. 12-Month National Outflow Data Forecast

Graphs 11 and 12 show the evaluation of the forecast results on the outsampling of Inflow and Outflow data in the National province with the acquisition of MAPE of 29% and 4.6%, respectively (Table 9).

Table 9. Inflow and outflow data validation

		MAPE	
		In sample (%)	Out samlpe (%)
NTT	Inflow	1.67	2.11
	Outflow	8.9	9.7
National	Inflow	29	25.9
	Outflow	4.6	3.2

Model validation is carried out to measure the validity of the forecasting model. The model shows high accuracy on national data, especially on *inflow*, with very low MAPE. The difference in MAPE between *in-sample* and *out-sample* shows the generalization ability of the model, especially seen in the NTT data which shows a decrease in MAPE in *the out-sample.*

5 Conclusions

Based on the results and discussion, several conclusions were obtained.

1. The SETAR model provides good predictions for NTT inflow–outflow data and national outflow data with low MAPE values of less than 10%
2. The results of inflow and outflow forecasts in NTT show that it is possible that data testing has more accurate results than training data.
3. In national inflow data, the MAPE value is still high, so the data pattern has not been fully captured by the SETAR model.

Acknowledgment. All authors wish to acknowledge the editors and reviewers for helping to improve this paper. Also to BIMA for helping to finance the entire international seminar process.

References

1. Ministry of Finance of the Republic of Indonesia, Directorate General of Treasury. (2023). Retrieved 4 17, 2023, from https://djpb.kemenkeu.go.id/kppn/lubuksikaping/id/data-publikasi/artikel/3145-mengenal-deflasi-dan-inflasi-serta-pengaruhnya-terhadap-perekonomian.html
2. Bank Indonesia. (2020). Bank Indonesia. Retrieved 3 24, 2024, from https://www.bi.go.id/id/fungsiutama/moneter/default.aspx#:~:text=Tujuan%20utama%20kebijakan%20moneter%20yang%20dilaksanakan%20oleh%20Bank,Tahun%202023%20tentang%20Pengembangan%20dan%20Penguatan%20Sektor%20Keuangan
3. Amalia, A., Zukhronah, E., Subanti, S.: Forecasting bank Indonesia currency inflow and outflow data in DKI Jakarta Province using the ARIMAX and SARIMAX models. Indonesian J. Appl. Stat., 4 (2021)
4. Seyyed, F.J., Abraham, A., Mohsen, A.-H.: Seasonality in stock returns and volatility: the Ramadan effect. Res. Int. Bus. Finance (RIBAF) **19**(3) (2005)
5. Karomah, A., Suhartono: Forecasting the netflow of currency with the autoregressive distributed lag (ARDL) model. Pomits J. Sci. Art **3** (2) (2014)
6. Boero, G., Lampis, F.: The forecasting performance of setar. Bull. Econ. Res. **69**(3), 216–228 (2016)
7. Fırat, E.H.: SETAR (Self-exciting threshold autoregressive). Mathemat. Stat. **5**(1), 33–55 (2017)
8. Riyansyah, H.N.G.P., Saputro, D.R.: Model 2-regime self-exciting threshold autoregressive (SETAR). In: National Seminar on Mathematics Education Ahmad Dahlan (2019)
9. Putri, T., Irhamah: Forecasting Bank Central Asia stock return using self exciting threshold autoregressive –using self exciting threshold autoregressive –genetic algorithm. ITS J. Sci. ART **5**(1) (2016)
10. Ismail, M.T., Isa, Z.: Modelling exchange rates using regime switching models. Sains Malaysiana **35**(2), 55–62 (2006)
11. Terasvirta, T., C, F. L., & C, W.G. Power of the neural networks linearity test. J. Time Series Anal., 14 (1993)

12. Wei, W.W.: Time Series Analysis: Univariate and Multivariate Methods (2nd Edition). Addison Wesley (2006)
13. Chan, W.S., Wong, A.C.S., Tong, H.: Some nonlinear threshold autoregressive time series models for actuarial use. North American Actuarial J. **8**(4), 37–61 (2004)
14. Tong, H., Lim, K.: Threshold autoregression, limit cycles and cyclical data. J. Royal Stati. Soc. Ser. B **42**(3), 245–292 (1980)

Implementation of Vasicek and Cox-Ingersoll-Ross Models in Calculating Civil Servants' Pension Using the Accrued Benefit Cost Method

Mukhlisah[1(✉)] and Novriana Sumarti[2]

[1] Master's Program in Actuarial Science, Faculty of Mathematics and Natural Sciences, Institut Teknologi Bandung, Jl Ganesha 10, Bandung, Indonesia
mukhlisah95@gmail.com

[2] Industrial and Financial Mathematics Research Group, Faculty of Mathematics and Natural Sciences, Institut Teknologi Bandung, Jl Ganesha 10, Bandung, Indonesia
bnovriana@itb.ac.id

Abstract. Pension fund programs require ongoing supervision and effective management. Key aspects of pension fund management include determining benefit sizes, calculating normal contributions, and selecting an interest rate to estimate the present value of promised benefits. Benefit sizes rely on assumptions within established benefit functions, whereas contributions reflect the actuarial calculation method used. Given that interest rates fluctuate with economic conditions, this study applies stochastic interest rate models, specifically the Vasicek and Cox-Ingersoll-Ross (CIR) models, to assess pension obligations more accurately. This study uses the Accrued Benefit Cost (ABC) method to calculate normal contributions and actuarial liabilities applied to pension data for Indonesian civil servant university lecturers. Since income growth and retirement age for civil servant lecturers are influenced by individual achievements and career classifications, which vary by person, simulations assume that a lecturer with a master's degree enters as an assistant lecturer at age 25, advancing through eight classifications, and retiring between 65 and 70. The results indicate that normal costs and actuarial liabilities rise with years of service under both the Vasicek and CIR models, underscoring the importance of interest rate fluctuations in pension fund planning. These findings provide valuable insights into managing the risks associated with civil servants' pension obligations and contribute to advancing pension planning for governmental use.

Keywords: Pension Fund · Civil Servants · Model of Income Growth · Accrued Benefit Cost Method · Vasicek Model · Cox-Ingersoll-Ross Model

1 Introduction

Pension funds play a crucial role in the global financial security system for numerous civil servants and serve as a safety net for employees during retirement. The management of these funds is of utmost importance to ensure their long-term viability and ability to

P. C. Rodrigues et al. (Eds.): ISBIS 2024, 13, pp. 254–267, 2027.
https://doi.org/10.1007/978-3-032-32458-0_18

meet future financial obligations effectively [1]. An essential challenge in overseeing pension funds is accurately estimating future pension benefits, which requires a thorough examination of various factors. Among these factors, three noteworthy aspects significantly influence pension funds' financial well-being and sustainability: determining the size of benefits, calculating regular contributions, and selecting an appropriate interest rate for present-value calculations. The pension benefits amount depends on predetermined benefit formulas that rely on a specific set of assumptions. These assumptions encompass variables such as income growth, years of service, and retirement age, all of which introduce variability and uncertainty to the estimation process.

The unpredictable nature of career progression among civil servants, notably university lecturers in Indonesia, highlights the intricate nature of accurately forecasting benefits. Regular contributions, which represent the consistent sums allocated by participants or on their behalf to the pension fund, are affected by the actuarial methodology utilized. In this investigation, the Accrued Benefit Cost method was chosen because it effectively aligns contributions with accrued benefits, thereby facilitating a fairer and more systematic funding approach [2]. The interest rate decision holds significant importance in the actuarial assessment of pension funds given its impact on the present value of future pension commitments. Because interest rates are susceptible to fluctuations in response to economic conditions, employing a stochastic interest rate model provides a more realistic and adaptable strategy [3]. Vasicek and Cox-Ingersoll-Ross (CIR) models, known for capturing the dynamics of interest rate changes, are integrated into this study to reflect the evolving economic landscape and its repercussions on pension fund valuations [4].

This study combines the Accrued Benefit Cost method with the stochastic frameworks of the Vasicek and Cox-Ingersoll-Ross models to assess the pension benefits of civil servant university lecturers in Indonesia. Through these models, this study seeks to simulate the income progression and retirement age of a typical civil servant lecturer, projecting their career path from entry at the age of 25 to retirement between 65 and 70. The primary goal of this study is to provide a comprehensive analysis of how interest rate fluctuations interact with the pension commitments of civil servants. By utilizing these advanced financial models in the actuarial computations of normal cost and actuarial liability, this study aims to generate insights that enhance the comprehension of risk management in pension funds. Ultimately, this study strives to contribute to the advancement of a sophisticated pension-planning framework, thereby assisting governmental bodies in refining their approaches to providing and maintaining pension benefits for civil servants.

Several studies have discussed the use of the Accrued Benefit Cost method and stochastic interest rates to calculate pension benefits. The estimation of pension fund size from 2024 to 2044 through the Accrued Benefit Cost approach reveals a discrepancy between benefits and regular contributions annually, ensuring that there is no deficit. This suggests that the regular contributions made to pension funds adequately cover the retirement benefits for Civil Servants who retire between 2024 and 2044 [5]. The Projected Unit Credit (PUC) method, along with Vasicek and Cox-Ingersoll-Ross (CIR) interest rate models, increases both normal cost and actuarial liabilities as the length of service increases. Conversely, the Entry Age Normal (EAN) method shows a different pattern: when paired with the Vasicek model, the normal cost initially increases before declining towards the initial contribution amount; in contrast, when using the CIR model, the EAN method starts with a high price, decreases, and then rises back to the initial contribution level. Actuarial liabilities under the EAN method for both interest rate models increase annually, suggesting that the Vasicek model yields lower normal costs for participants and that the CIR model is more profitable for pension funds [4]. The results of employing the CIR model demonstrate that its utilization yields highly favorable results, as evidenced by the relatively small MAPE value. This outcome indicates a close alignment between interest rate forecasts and actual market interest rates. The application of the CIR model typically leads to larger normal contributions compared to the fixed interest rate approach. The CIR interest rate is advantageous for pension providers because of their ability to achieve more consistent contributions while maintaining the same level of benefits. The results obtained from the computation utilizing the CIR interest rate model under the assumption that the fluctuating interest rate corresponds to the real-world scenario are intended to minimize losses for all involved parties [6]. This study compares regular contributions and actuarial obligations by employing the Accrued Benefit Cost approach alongside the Vasicek and Cox-Ingersoll-Ross (CIR) interest rate models under specific conditions.

2 Research Methods

This study utilizes a quantitative methodology employing historical data on interest rates to parameterize the Vasicek and Cox-Ingersoll-Ross (CIR) models. These models were then integrated into a simulation framework to estimate pension fund liabilities and enhance the realism and applicability of the study's findings. The empirical analysis relies on historical monthly interest rate data provided by Bank Indonesia for the period 2019–2023, forming the foundational dataset for calibrating the parameters of the stochastic interest rate models [7]. Historical interest rates played a crucial role in capturing the economic and financial dynamics experienced during this period. Both the Vasicek and CIR models, which are one-factor mean-reverting models, were parameterized using the collected interest rate data. The Vasicek model is known for its simplicity and analytical tractability, whereas the CIR model, an extension of Vasicek, includes a square root term to ensure positivity in interest rates. The calibration process involves fitting the models to historical data to extract the parameters that best replicate the observed interest rate behavior. This process commonly involves maximum likelihood estimation or other optimization techniques to minimize the difference between model predictions and actual data.

Upon completing the calibration of interest rate models, this research applies the Accrued Benefit Cost method to calculate normal costs and actuarial liabilities linked to the pension scheme. This method projects the benefits accrued by civil servant lecturers at different career stages, discounting them to present value using interest rates generated by Vasicek and CIR models. The calibrated interest rate models were then incorporated into a simulation framework to assess pension fund liabilities over time. This simulation integrates stochastic elements to model the variability in career progression, income growth, and retirement age among civil servant lecturers.

2.1 Model of Income Growth

This study utilizes simulations to implement the Accrued Benefit Cost method by incorporating stochastic interest rates derived from the Vasicek and Cox-Ingersoll-Ross models to evaluate the pension benefits of civil servant lecturers in Indonesia. The simulation process will involve a comprehensive analysis of the lecturer's income progression and retirement age. Based on PP No. 5 of 2024, there is a list of basic income for civil servants which are divided into 4 grades [8]. This simulation is carried out by tracing their professional journey from the commencement of employment at the age of 25 years to their retirement age set at 65 and 70 years. Table 1 shows some data on the growth of civil servants' income, which is considered to increase every 2 years of service in each grade.

Table 1. Income growth civil servant lecturers in Indonesia

Tenure	Grade III/b	Grade III/c	Growth by grade, r_g	Growth by tenure, r_t
0	2.903.600	3.026.400	4,23%	3,15%
2	2.995.000	3.121.700		

Based on regulations, a general formula can be formed to calculate the amount of income earned. The income received at time-n from the inception age can be expressed as follows:

$$S_n = S_0(1 + r_t)^{\frac{n}{2}} \quad (1)$$

where S_0 is the initial income, r_t is the growth by tenure, r_g is the growth by grade, g is the amount of grade promotions, and x is the floor function which returns the largest integer less than or equal to x. While based on tenure and grade, a general formula can also be formed to calculate the amount of income that will be obtained if there is an income increase and grade increase in the same year. It can be expressed as follows:

$$S_n = S_0(1 + r_t)^{\frac{n}{2}}\left(1 + r_g\right)^g \quad (2)$$

The model assumes a periodic promotion every five years, commencing from the initial rank of III/b and culminating in the final rank of IV/e upon retirement as professor, so the income is.

$$S_n = S_0(1 + r_t)^{\frac{n}{2}}\left(1 + r_g\right)^{\frac{n}{5}} \quad (3)$$

This systematic approach aims to provide a detailed and accurate assessment of the retirement benefits accrued by civil servant lecturers by considering various factors such as income growth, career advancement, and retirement planning. The results of the model of income growth are presented in Table 2. The terms 'Penata Muda', 'Penata', 'Pembina', and 'Pembina Utama' are special terms in the Indonesian civil service system.

Table 2. Model of income growth for civil servant lecturers in Indonesia

Age	Rank/grade	Functional position	Base income
25	Penata muda Tk.I/III/b	Assistant lecturer	2.903.600
30	Penata/III/c	Lecturer	3.220.000
35	Penata Tk.I/III/d	Lecturer	3.683.400
40	Pembina/IV/a	Senior lecturer	4.084.900
45	Pembina Tk. I/IV/b	Senior lecturer	4.672.800
50	Pembina utama muda/IV/c	Senior lecturer	5.182.000
55	Pembina utama madya/IV/d	Professor	5.927.800
60	Pembina utama/IV/e	Professor	6.573.900
65	Pembina utama/IV/e	Professor	7.214.700
70	Pembina utama/IV/e	Professor	7.676.300

2.2 Actuarial Fundamental Functions

To calculate pension funds accurately, it is essential to consider fundamental actuarial functions. These fundamental actuarial functions are essential for actuarial calculation. Some fundamental actuarial functions commonly used in calculating pension funding include the survival, interest rate, life annuity, and benefits functions. The survival function is used to determine the probability that an individual will continue working until a predetermined retirement age. This is expressed as follows [4]:

$$ {}_tp_x = \frac{l_{x+t}}{l_x} \tag{4} $$

where ${}_tp_x$ is the probability that an individual aged x will continue to work until the age of $(x+t)$, l_{x+t} is the total number of individuals aged $(x+t)$, and l_x is the total number of individuals aged x.

The interest rate function, also known as the present value function, is used to determine a reduction in future payments. It is expressed as follows [4]:

$$ v^n = \frac{1}{(1+i)^n} \tag{5} $$

where i is the interest rate in year t, $t = 1, 2, \ldots, n$, and v^n is the present value of unit payment in year n.

The life annuity function, denoted by $(\ddot{a}_x)$, is a series of payments made by an individual if the individual is alive. It is expressed as follows [5]:

$$ \ddot{a}_x = 1 + \mathrm{v}_1p_x + \mathrm{v}^2{}_2p_x + \cdots + v^{w-x-1}{}_{w-x-1}p_x = \frac{1}{D_x}\left(D_x + D_{x+1} + \cdots + D_{w-1}\right) = \frac{N_x}{D_x} \tag{6} $$

where N_x and D_x are the commutation symbols used to simplify the calculations in the mortality tables with ω being the highest age reached.

2.3 Interest Rate Model

The interest rate refers to the risk-free interest rate publicized by the central bank. The movement of interest rates is often rapid and is typically reported daily. Although interest rates are subject to change, fixed (deterministic) interest rate annuities are still widely used in practical applications because of their ease of calculation. However, this approach is risky because interest-rate fluctuations are inevitable. Therefore, it is essential to develop an annuity calculation method that accounts for stochastic interest rates [3]. Several stochastic models for interest rates can be utilized, such as Vasicek, Cox-Ingersoll-Ross, Hull-White, Black-Derman-Toy, Heath-Jarrow-Morton, and Ho-Lee models.

The determination of a stochastic model for pension fund calculations depends on the assumptions and level of complexity that can be handled by the entity performing the calculations. If there are historical data that show interest rate characteristics that can be accommodated by Vasicek or Cox-Ingersoll-Ross (CIR) models, these two models may prove to be suitable choices. Vasicek and Cox-Ingersoll-Ross (CIR) are stochastic models. The Vasicek model is designed to revert its equilibrium point following periods of decrease or increase, whereas the CIR model ensures a positive interest rate and reverts its mean. In Vasicek's model, the differential equation is expressed as follows [4]:

$$dr(t) = \alpha(\mu - r(t))dt + \sigma dW(t) \tag{7}$$

where α is the speed refers to how quickly the interest rate adjusts to a long-term interest rate. The long-term average interest rate is denoted by μ, volatility of the interest rate is represented by σ, interest rate at time t is $r(t)$, and $dW(t)$ is the differential Wiener process at time t. Assuming $P_1(t)$ represents the expected value of a unit payment at time t for an interest rate based on the Vasicek model, then [4]

$$P_1(t) = \exp\left((B(t) - t)\left(\mu - \frac{\sigma^2}{2\alpha^2}\right) - \frac{\sigma^2 B(t)^2}{4\alpha} - r(0)B(t)\right) \tag{8}$$

with $r(0) = r_0$ and $B(t) = \frac{1-\exp(-\alpha t)}{\alpha}$.

Cox-Ingersoll-Ross (CIR) model, the differential equation is expressed as follows [4]:

$$dr(t) = \alpha(\mu - r(t))dt + \sigma\sqrt{r(t)}\, dW(t) \tag{9}$$

Assuming $P_2(t)$ represents the expected value of a unit payment at time t for an interest rate that adheres to the CIR model, then [4]

$$P_2(t) = \left(\frac{2d\exp\left(\frac{\alpha+d}{2}t\right)}{\exp(td)(\alpha+d)+d-\alpha}\right)^{\frac{2\alpha\mu}{\sigma^2}} \exp\left(-\frac{2r(0)(\exp(td)-1)}{\exp(td)(\alpha+d)+d-\alpha}\right) \tag{10}$$

with $r(0) = r_0$ and d $= \sqrt{\alpha^2 + 2\sigma^2}$. The value of the interest rate parameter can be calculated as follows [4]:

$$\alpha = \frac{n^2 - 2n + 1 + \sum_{i=1}^{n-1} r_{t+1} \sum_{i=1}^{n-1} \frac{1}{r_t} - \sum_{i=1}^{n-1} r_t \sum_{i=1}^{n-1} \frac{1}{r_t} - (n-1) \sum_{i=1}^{n-1} \frac{r_{t+1}}{r_t}}{\left(n^2 - 2n + 1 - \sum_{i=1}^{n-1} r_t \sum_{i=1}^{n-1} \frac{1}{r_t}\right) \Delta t} \tag{11}$$

$$\mu = \frac{(n-1) \sum_{i=1}^{n-1} r_{t+1} - \sum_{i=1}^{n-1} \frac{r_{t+1}}{r_t} \sum_{i=1}^{n-1} r_t}{n^2 - 2n + 1 + \sum_{i=1}^{n-1} r_{t+1} \sum_{i=1}^{n-1} \frac{1}{r_t} - \sum_{i=1}^{n-1} r_t \sum_{i=1}^{n-1} \frac{1}{r_t} - (n-1) \sum_{i=1}^{n-1} \frac{r_{t+1}}{r_t}} \tag{12}$$

$$\sigma = \sqrt{\frac{1}{n-2} \sum_{i=1}^{n-1} \left(\frac{r_{t+1} - r_t}{\sqrt{r_t}} - \frac{\mu}{\sqrt{r_t}} + \alpha \sqrt{r_t} \right)^2} \tag{13}$$

2.4 Normal Cost and Actuarial Liability

The benefit function serves the purpose of calculates the quantity of benefits that must be disbursed to individuals upon reaching the age of retirement. It is expressed as follows [4]:

$$B_r = k(r - y)s_{r-1} \tag{14}$$

where B_r is the accumulated retirement benefit at age r, k is the percentage of income used for retirement benefits, y is the age at which the participant entered the pension fund, and $s_{r\,-\,1}$ is the previous year's income before retirement. The present value of future benefits (PVFB) for an individual aged x and reaching normal retirement age r can be represented as follows [4]:

$$^{r}(PVFB)_x = B_{r\,r-x}p_x\, P(r - x)\ddot{a}_r \tag{15}$$

Here, $_{r\,-\,x}p_x$ signifies the probability of an employee working until age r, B_r denotes the retirement benefit at age r, $P(r - x)$ represents the expected value of payment at time $(r - x)$, and $\ddot{a}_r$ denotes lifetime annuity.

The amount required to fund a portion of the current year's pension benefits, calculated according to the Accrued Benefit Cost method, is known as the Normal Cost, $^{ABC\ r}(NC)_x$. This is equal to the Benefit Accumulated at Retirement Age B_r multiplied by [5]

$$^{ABC\quad r}(NC)_x = B_{r\,r-x}p_x P(r - x)\ddot{a}_r = {}^{r}(PVFB)_x \tag{16}$$

Actuarial liability refers to the total sum of pension plan assets set aside to cover future pension payments. Based on the Accrued Benefit Cost method, it applies [4]

$$^{ABC\quad r}(AL)_x = (x - y)B_{r\,r-x}p_x\, P(r - x)\ddot{a}_r = (x - y)^{r}(PVFB)_x \tag{17}$$

where $\ddot{a}_r$ represents the lifetime annuity starting at age r, $_{r\,-\,x}p_x$ is the probability of a participant aged x living to $(r - x)$ years, $P(r - x)$ is the expected value of payments at time $(r - x)$ years, and $^{r}(PVFB)_x$ is the value of pension benefit payments at age r years. The normal retirement age is represented by r and the age of entry into the pension fund is represented by y.

3 Result and Discussion

By employing underlying assumptions, various determinations, and symbolic representations, a series of calculations are conducted to ascertain the precise sum of benefits that must be disbursed to individuals upon attaining retirement age. The results of these calculations are clearly outlined and presented in detail in Table 3. This table specifically highlights the percentage of pension benefits relative to the individual's income, drawing upon data sourced from the UU No.11 Th 1969 for accuracy and reliability [9]. The utilization of such empirical data and methodological approaches ensures a rigorous and systematic evaluation of the financial entitlements that participants are entitled to receive upon retirement, thereby promoting transparency and accountability within the pension system.

Table 3. Assigned information to calculate pension benefits

The assigned information	
Age at entry into civil service (y)	25 years
Normal retirement age (r)	65 years and 70 years
Percentage of income used for pension benefits (k)	2,5%
Accumulated income in the last year before retirement at age 65 (s_{r-1})	7.214.700 x 12 months = 86.576.400
Accumulated income in the last year before retirement at age 70 (s_{r-1})	7.676.300 x 12 months = 92.115.600

The calculation of retirement benefits relies on an estimation based on the final year's income before retirement, as detailed in Eq. (14) presented in Table 4, which serves as a pivotal factor in determining the pension amount an individual is eligible to receive upon retirement.

Table 4. Assigned information to calculate pension benefits

Retirement age	Tenure	Pension benefit
65	40 years	86.576.400
70	45 years	103.630.050

In the application of Vasicek and Cox-Ingersoll-Ross (CIR) interest rate models, it is imperative to determine the appropriate parameter values for accuracy and reliability. The process of estimating the parameters for the Vasicek and Cox-Ingersoll-Ross (CIR) interest rate models involves rigorous calculations based on monthly observations of the Bank Indonesia interest rate from 2019 to 2023, as outlined in the mathematical formulations provided in Eqs. 11, 12 and 13, the results of which can be seen in Table 5. This meticulous approach ensures that the model is calibrated effectively to reflect the dynamics of interest rates within a specified timeframe, thereby enhancing the validity of the model's predictions and analysis.

Table 5. Vasicek and cox-ingersoll-ross (cir) interest rate parameter estimation

Parameters	Estimation results
α	0,0141234
μ	0,0461864
σ	0,0218882

Given that the interest rate utilized is stochastic, it is imperative to conduct simulations for the interest rate in each respective model. The interest rate in the Vasicek model is determined by Eq. (7), whereas the interest rate in the Cox-Ingersoll-Ross (CIR) model is derived from Eq. (9). The process of simulating these interest rates involved the use of a *Python* program. The simulation extends up to 45 years into the future, enabling a comprehensive visualization of the interest rate trends through the plots depicted in Figs. 1 and 2. This approach allows for a thorough analysis and understanding of how these stochastic interest rates evolve over an extended time horizon, providing valuable insights for decision-making in various financial scenarios. Moreover, the visualization of simulated interest rates aids in interpreting the potential variability and dynamics inherent in these models, offering a nuanced perspective on the behavior of interest rates in the context of stochastic processes.

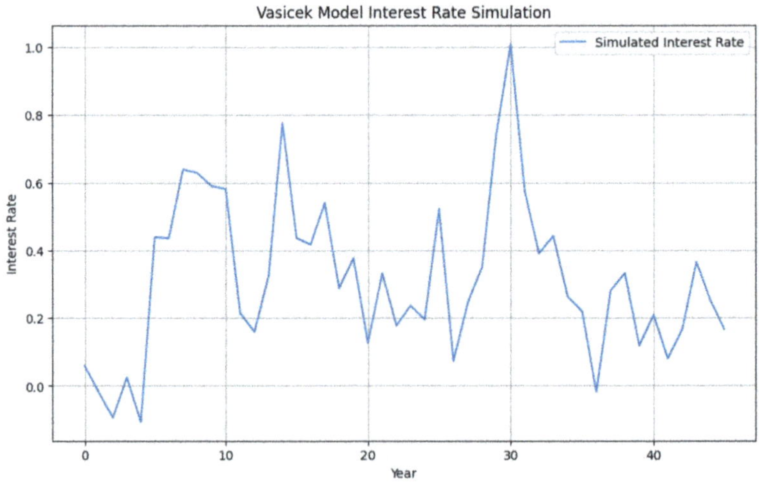

Fig. 1. Vasicek model interest rate simulation result

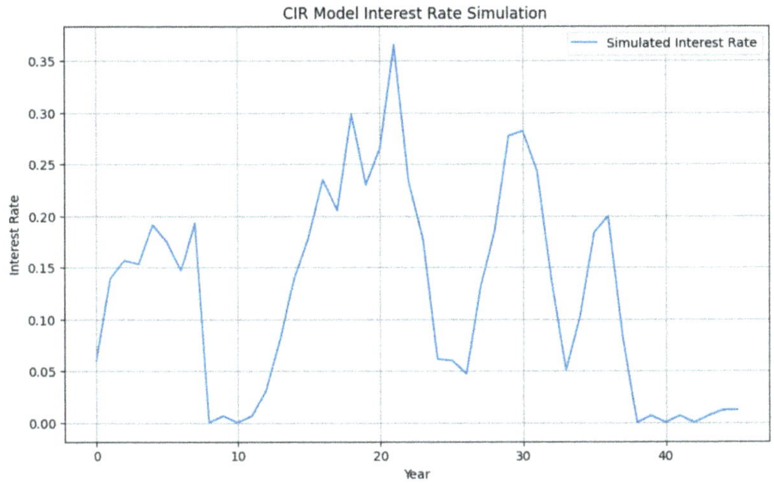

Fig. 2. Cox-ingersoll-ross (cir) model interest rate simulation result

The expected value of payment was computed using the provided data. The expected value of a unit payment according to the Vasicek interest rate model is determined through Eq. (5), while the Cox-Ingersoll Ross (CIR) interest rate is calculated using Eq. (10). For $r(0)$, short-term interest rate, we used BI rate in December 2023, the month in the last year of observation data, which is 6%. The result is shown in Fig. 3.

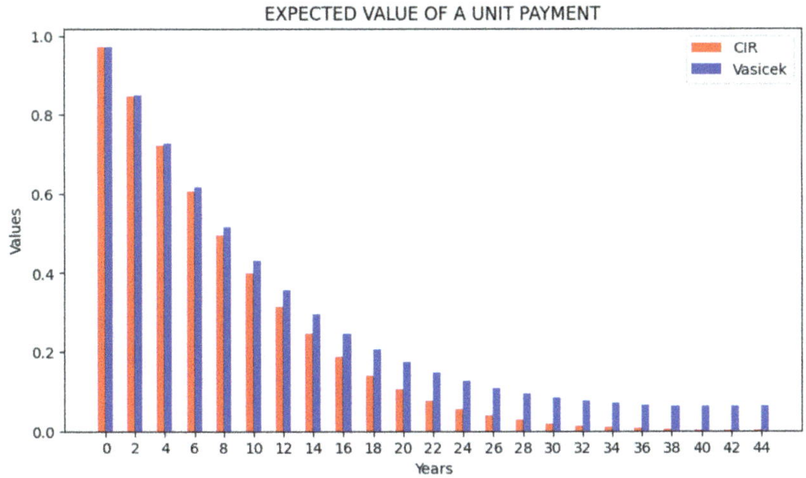

Fig. 3. Expected value of a unit payment during the working period

To determine the present value of future benefits (PVFB) in Eq. (15), it is essential to utilize the outcomes obtained from the computation of life annuities based on Eqs. (5) and (6). The derivation of the ${}_tp_{65}$ and ${}_tp_{70}$ mortality tables were initiated with the assistance of the Indonesia IV Mortality Table through the application of Eq. (4). Subsequently, the life annuity results for each respective model were meticulously compiled and are readily accessible for review in Table 6 for further calculation.

Table 6. Life annuity vasicek and cox-ingersoll-ross (cir) interest rate

	$\ddot{a}_{65}$	$\ddot{a}_{70}$
Vasicek model	6,4802	6,4792
CIR model	10,4259	10,2464

The calculation of the Present Value Future Benefits (PVFB) is greatly impacted by the projections of life expectancy obtained from a thorough analysis of the Mortality Table. This analysis offers valuable insights into the predicted lifespan of both males and females. Moreover, the computation involves the accurate assessment of retirement benefits linked to a specific retirement age denoted as r, the anticipated value of payments per unit following the Vasicek and Cox-Ingersoll-Ross models, and the overarching notion of a lifetime annuity. The computation of the PVFB is meticulously performed by applying a specific mathematical formula, denoted by Eq. (15). After this step, participants in the pension fund are mandated to fulfill their obligations in terms of Normal Cost, which represents their share of financial contributions towards the sustainability of the pension scheme. The exact amount of normal costs due to participants is determined through the utilization of the ABC methodology, coupled with the integration of two distinct interest rate models: the Vasicek model and the Cox-Ingersoll-Ross (CIR) model. The final computation of normal costs is achieved by employing a specialized Eq. (16), as shown in Fig. 4.

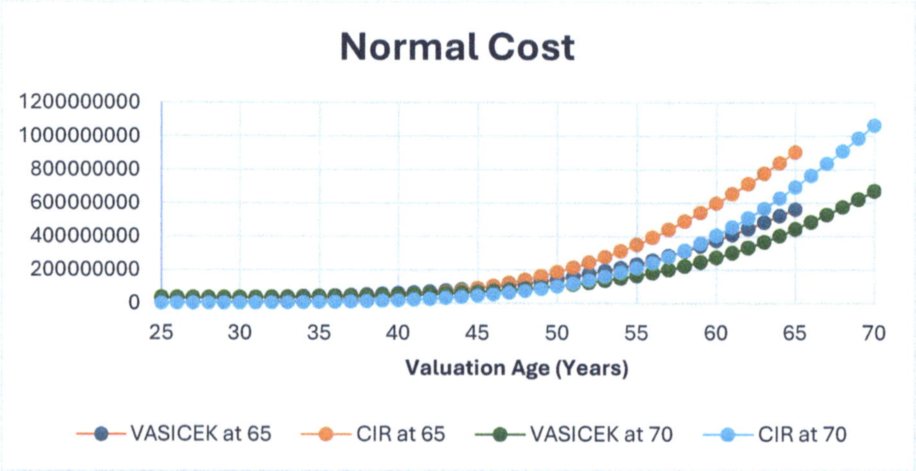

Fig. 4. Expected value of a unit payment during the working period

Normal Cost using the Accrued Benefit Cost Method under two different interest rate models (Vasicek and CIR) at two different ages (65 and 70). Throughout the period from age 25 to approximately 60 years, the costs in all scenarios exhibit a pattern of stability and remain at relatively low levels. This pattern implies that, during these years, the expenses related to accrued benefits under the specified models and age brackets do not undergo significant increments. However, once individuals reach the age of 60, there is a noticeable surge in costs across all the scenarios. The escalation in expenses is particularly striking for the models that factor in retirement at age 70 (both Vasicek and CIR), displaying curves that are steeper than those associated with retirement at 65. Such observations signify that opting for a delayed retirement age of 70 results in a more substantial rise in normal costs, as the age of valuation approaches the retirement phase. Furthermore, the costs linked to the Vasicek model at both retirement ages seem marginally less than those corresponding to the CIR model at equivalent ages, indicating that the Vasicek model potentially generates an estimate of normal costs that is lower than that of the CIR model under similar circumstances.

The actuarial liability using the Accrued Benefit Cost (ABC) method is calculated using Eq. (17), the result shown in Fig. 5.

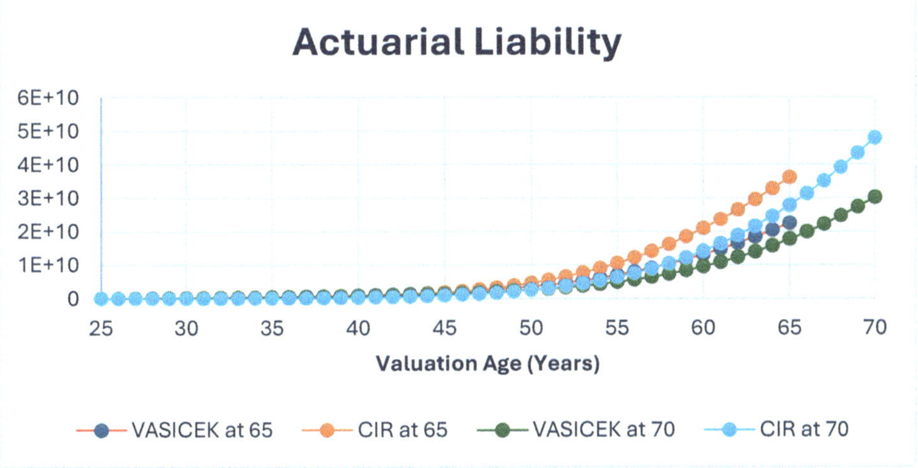

Fig. 5. Expected value of a unit payment during the working period

The Actuarial Liability illustrates the forecast of actuarial obligations across the valuation age range of 25 to 70 years. It employs the ABC Method and integrates two distinct interest rate frameworks: the Vasicek and CIR models. The computation of liabilities was conducted for two scenarios, predicated on retirement ages set at 65 and 70 years. Throughout the period from 25 to approximately 50 years of age, actuarial liabilities exhibit a relatively stable trend across all scenarios. This stability implies that the rise in liabilities attributable to employees nearing retirement is counteracted by the discounting impact of the forthcoming payments. After the age of 50, there is a noticeable escalation in liabilities across all scenarios. The pace of this escalation intensifies as the valuation age approaches retirement thresholds of 65 and 70 years. In the Vasicek model, at the age of 65 years, there is a gradual upsurge observed from the age of 50, extending up to 65 years. On the other hand, in the CIR model at 65, the rise is initiated around the age of 50 but at a marginally steeper rate compared to the Vasicek model, surpassing the liabilities projected by the Vasicek model as the age approaches 65. Moving on to the Vasicek model at 70, the trajectory of this curve remains below the curves corresponding to age 65 until approximately 60 years, after which it embarks on a sharp upward trajectory, exceeding the liabilities computed using the Vasicek model at 65 by the time 70 years of age. In contrast, within the CIR model at 70, akin to the Vasicek at 70 curves, there is a significant escalation commencing at around 60 years, demonstrating a steeper incline when compared to its Vasicek equivalent, thereby indicating higher liability estimations at the age of 70. At 70 years of age, liabilities peak under the CIR model, followed by the Vasicek model, both determined at the retirement age of 70. This outcome mirrors the trend of elevated projected obligations with increasing retirement age, further implying that the CIR model is inclined to anticipate higher liabilities than the Vasicek model under similar circumstances.

4 Conclusions

This study illustrates that the selection of an interest rate model and the designated retirement age have a substantial impact on the estimated normal cost and actuarial liabilities within pension schemes. A notable observation is that postponing the retirement age leads to an increase in the normal cost, particularly after the age of 60. It is worth noting that the CIR model generally forecasts slightly elevated normal costs compared to the Vasicek model. Regarding actuarial liabilities, it is observed that the liabilities exhibit stability until approximately the age of 50, after which they start to rise significantly as retirement approaches. This upward trend is more pronounced for later retirement ages, such as 70, as opposed to 65, especially when applying the CIR model instead of the Vasicek model. Overall, the CIR model shows a tendency to anticipate higher liabilities and, to a lesser degree, increased normal costs when compared to the Vasicek model under similar circumstances. These outcomes emphasize the critical nature of meticulously choosing interest rate models and considering assumptions regarding retirement age in the administration of pension plans. The decision concerning the model used can have a momentous effect on anticipated financial commitments, subsequently influencing the contribution rates and funding tactics. Opting for a more cautious model, such as the CIR, might result in higher envisaged expenses, thereby necessitating elevated contributions or enhanced investment yields to preserve the financial stability of the pension scheme.

References

1. Ananta, A., Ahmad, I.A., Moeis, H.T., Widianto, H.Y., Arifin, E.N.: Pension and active ageing: lessons learned from civil servants in Indonesia. Soc. Sci. **10**, 436 (2021). https://doi.org/10.3390/socsci10110436

2. Putri, S.N.S.: Perhitungan Dana Pensiun Pegawai Negeri Sipil (PNS) Di Suatu Perguruan Tinggi Negeri Di Indonesia Dengan Menggunakan Metode Accrued Benefit Cost. Tesis Program Magister, Institut Teknologi Bandung (2020)
3. Erlangga, C.N., dan Kusumawati, R.: Aplikasi Model Suku Bunga Stokastik Black-Derman-Toy dengan Forward Induction dalam Penghitungan Anuitas. Jurnal Kajian dan Terapan. Matematika. **5, 5** (2016)
4. Sulma, I.N., Widana, S.T., Fitria, I.: Comparison of projected unit credit and entry age Normal methods in pension fund Vasicek and cox-Ingersoll-Ross models. BAREKENG: J. Math.App. **17, iss. 4**, 2421–2432 (2023)
5. Yasyfa, H.K.: Prediksi Manfaat Pensiun Pegawai Negeri Sipil pada Suatu Perguruan Tinggi Negeri Berdasarkan Perhitungan Dana Pensiun dengan Metode Accrued Benefit Cost. Tesis Program Magister, Institut Teknologi Bandung (2023)
6. Limbong, M.M.Y., Rachmatin, D., Priatna, B.A.: Penerapan Model Tingkat Suku Bunga Cox Ingersoll Ross (CIR) Dalam Menentukan Iuran Normal Pensiun. J. EurekaMatika. **10**(2), 111–120 (2022)
7. BI-rate 2019–2023. https://www.bi.go.id/id/statistik/indikator/BI-Rate.aspx
8. Pemerintah Indonesia. Peraturan Pemerintah Republik Indonesia Nomor 5 Tahun 2024 Tentang Perubahan Kesembilan Belas atas Peraturan Pemerintah Nomor 7 Tahun 1977 Tentang Peraturan Gaji Pegawai Negeri Sipil.
9. Pemerintah Indonesia. Undang-Undang Nomor 11 Tahun 1969 Tentang Pensiun Pegawai dan Pensiun Janda/Duda.
10. Ahmad, I.A., Moeis, N.D., Nachrowi, A.A., Adrison, V.: A trade-off between old-age financial adequacy and state budget sustainability: searching a government optimum solution to the pension system in Indonesia. Cogent Econ. Financ. **10**(1), 2079176 (2022). https://doi.org/10.1080/23322039.2022.2079176
11. Fatichadiasty, Fiqi Reformasi Sistem pensiun Pasca Undang-Undang Nomor 5 Tahun 2014 Tentang Aparatur Sipil Negara Guna Mewujudkan Kesejahteraan Bagi Pegawai Negeri Sipil. SASI 26 Nomor 2, April-Juni 2020: h. 162–175 (2020)
12. Pemerintah Indonesia. Undang-Undang Republik Indonesia Nomor 20 Tahun 2023 Tentang Aparatur Sipil Negara.
13. Pemerintah Indonesia. Peraturan Kepala Badan Kepegawaian Negara Nomor 25 Tahun 2014 Tentang Petunjuk Teknis Penetapan Pensiun Pokok, Pensiun Pegawai Negeri Sipil dan Janda/Dudanya.

Author Index

A
Abdurakhman, 17
Afwan, Yaumil 117
Agustin, Ma. Zenia N. 28
Agustin, Marcus A. 28
Ahsan, Muhammad 70
Akbar, Muhammad Sjahid 232
Amri, Ihsan Fathoni 219
Anggraini, Bianda Shafira Kartika 134
Ariady, Fandy A. 175

C
Chamidah, Nur 219
Choiruddin, Achmad 55, 205

E
Effendie, Adhitya Ronnie 17, 39

F
Fajriyah, Rohmatul 175
Fitriyanah, Vanda 55

H
Hakim, R. B. Fajriya 134
Handajani, Sri S. 152
Handajani, Sri Sulistijowati 86
Huff, Atwood J. 28

K
Kesumawati, Ayundyah 100
Khusna, Hidayatul 205
Kolo, Veronika 232
Kumar, Ansh 163
Kusumastuti, Ari 163
Kuswanto, Heri 70

M
Mondal, Kartick Chandra 163
Mostert, Paul J. 1
Mukhlisah, 254
Mulyana, Sri 117

N
Nirwana, Muhammad Bayu 86
Nurazizah, Nabila Isna 55
Nurtiyasari, Devi 17

P
Pal, Ananya 163
Pardede, Hilman F. 152
Pramesti, Regita Diah 152
Pratama, Alfito Putra Fajar 191
Pratiwi, Hasih 86, 152, 191
Primandari, Arum Handini 100

R
Rahman, Annisa Auliya 205
Respatiwulan, 86
Riadi, Rini Aprilianty 100
Rosadi, Dedi 17, 100

S
Safira, Dinda Ayu 70
Saifudin, Toha 219
Samanta, Isika 163
Setiawan, 232
Slamet, Isnandar 191
Sulandari, Winita 152
Sumarna, Zahra Maharani Putri 175
Sumarti, Novriana 254
Susanti, Yuliana 86
Susyanto, Nanang 39
Sutikno, 55

T
Tjen, Yoel Christopher 175

P. C. Rodrigues et al. (Eds.): ISBIS 2024, 13, pp. 269–270, 2027.
https://doi.org/10.1007/978-3-032-32458-0

U
Utari, Dina Tri 134

W
Wijaya, Andreas Rony 86

Y
Yulianti, Silvina Rosita 39

Z
Zilvan, Vicky 152